AI, Literacy, and Human Agency in Education

Jason D. DeHart
https://orcid.org/0009-0005-5210-4738
The University of Tennessee, USA

IGI Global
Scientific Publishing
Publishing Tomorrow's Research Today

Vice President of Editorial	Melissa Wagner
Director of Acquisitions	Mikaela Felty
Director of Book Development	Jocelynn Hessler
Production Manager	Mike Brehm
Cover Design	Jose Rosado

Published in the United States of America by
IGI Global Scientific Publishing
701 East Chocolate Avenue
Hershey, PA, 17033, USA
Tel: 717-533-8845 | Fax: 717-533-7115
Website: https://www.igi-global.com E-mail: cust@igi-global.com

Library of Congress Cataloging-in-Publication Data

LCCN: 2026025848 (CIP Data Pending)
ISBN13: 9798260021637
Isbn13Softcover: 9798260021644
EISBN13: 9798260021651
British Cataloguing in Publication Data
A Cataloguing in Publication record for this book is available from the British Library.

Table of Contents

Detailed Table of Contents

classrooms, the importance of digital literacy, problem-solving, and critical thinking skills, as well as the ethical considerations of AI education. Additionally, the research investigates the role of educators in adapting to AI advancements and the challenges of balancing technology with traditional learning methods. By analyzing current trends and best practices, this study provides insights into how elementary education can be restructured to ensure students are not only consumers of AI but also capable contributors to future technological advancements. The findings emphasize the need for curriculum reforms, teacher training, and collaborative efforts.

Higher education as well as K–12 education are rapidly being impacted by AI & ML. They offer fresh resources and approaches to education. One crucial international strategic endeavor to prepare the next generation is incorporating AIML courses into K–12 curricula. Since AI education is still relatively new in both higher education and schools, there is a dearth of research to help teachers create AI curricula. Main goal of school systems' emphasis on diversity & inclusion is to increase the participation of underrepresented groups in the classroom. All activities that are purposefully designed & guided by teachers are included in the curriculum. Freedom of teachers influences their desire & commitment to deliver effective learning experiences for their students. It aids in administrative tasks and offers personalized learning experiences. Taking everything into account, they offer considerable opportunities to improve education overall. However, it is essential to consider ethical factors, ensure fair access, and cultivate suitable AI literacy for everyone involved.

Modern digital learning environments struggle to deliver personalized, engaging, and scalable instruction. To address the gaps, the work presents a layered Multi-agent System (MAS) based framework for intelligent knowledge dissemination. The proposed MAS employs various autonomous software agents, such as the domain agent, the text-to-speech (TTS) agent, etc., with different functional roles. These software agents coordinate using standardized communication protocols to generate the multimodal instructional content in real time. A central coordination mechanism is used to handle task allocation, workflow sequencing, and multimodal

chapter analyzes current challenges in technology adoption, including digital divides, misinformation, and the need for adaptive pedagogical approaches. It presents comprehensive frameworks for developing AI literacy among students and educators, emphasizing the importance of ethical considerations, human rights implications, and sustainable practices.

Preface

Human at Center: A Pedagogy of Agency Across Ages

INTRODUCTION

In the context of more attention to screens and the increase of Artificial Intelligence (AI) dispersed in accessible spaces, conversations about competency versus ethics are at the forefront. Contributors in this volume examine questions of practical and theoretical value related to the concept of keeping the human at center in terms of agency relative to amorphous notions of literacy and technology.

Reflecting on the ideas shared in this collection, I note the importance of agency as a linking of both competencies, or thought applied with action and intention, and/or ethical grounding. This grounding provides a reflective space, including considerations of the wider environment and interactions, to sufficiently empower a competent choice. This know-how combined with philosophical and personal ramifications links with a conceptualization of literacy that involves the complex ontology of what it means to be human.

These questions have been taken up for some time as challenges have arisen, including considering ideas about social justice (Hempel-Jorgensen, 2015). Additionally, the relationship between AI agency and morality has been examined from a philosophical stance (Dung, 2025) including a definitional approach to agency that includes goal-oriented behaviors and self-sustaining autonomy. Dung (2025) notes that this raises concerns of power dynamics with implications for wider impact on humanity.

In the field of literacy, readership and literate behaviors are connected with developing empathetic stances and behaviors (Denham, 2024); indeed, my work on the functionality for multimodal texts (i.e., graphic novels) in pedagogy links directly with concepts of criticality as well as empathy. The emotive self is not divorced from the intellectual self in an embodied conceptualization of what it means to be literate, and notions of power are gained through access to literacy. What individuals do with this power is as important to consider for the reader as it is for the generative text that reads and produces content based on existing stimuli.

The use of the phrase "across ages" in the title of this preface links with the idea that human beings are in a state of change as they grow from early levels of development to adulthood; at the same time, this notion of an age of change links with the movements that ebb and flow in technology as access increases.

Contributors address questions of governance, policy, preparation, creativity, aesthetic democracy, perceptions, and more as concepts like competency and ethics act as a background for framework development and further discussion.

IN THIS VOLUME

In Chapter 1, entitled, "Impact of AI on Educational Policy and Governance," the author team of Krutika Patre, Kritikka Kunte, Sunil Sankathala, Aryan Vasa, and Susanta Das lead the conversation in this volume with an examination of concepts of technology and responsibility relative to the titular concerns of policy and governance. The authors focus on those who hold or arguably should hold responsibilities for the implications of AI in educational spaces, linking to the positives of inclusivity, efficiency, and equity, among other potential benefits, with a balanced conversation around lingering concerns about AI. In particular, the authors delve into a rich discussion of algorithm bias and privacy concerns. These authors provide commentary on the necessary function of policy relative to multimodality and AI.

Shuchita Mudgil, Rohan Rajoriya, and Shaheen Tazir seek to critique and reimagine academic processes and literacy practices in Chapter 2, "Redefining Success Using AI to Help You Learn." The authors move the conversation from the general and theoretical to a focus on criticality in spaces of learning with attention to the individual learner's needs. Mudgil and co-authors explore three domains of transformation – platforms, systems, and tools – in a balanced conversation that considers affordances as well as limitations. Both this and the subsequent chapter explore implications of multimodality and AI for learning growth and development.

In Chapter 3, "Artificial Intelligence in Education: Creativity, Literacy, and Human Agency in AI-Enhanced Learning Environments," Renalyn Joy Ruiz Alonsabe, Amera C. Malaco, Leslie C. Elevado, and Fahad A. Salendab base their conversation around creativity and literacy with a clear pedagogical focus. The chapter includes attention to both rewards and risks. The authors consider the ways in which reading, writing, and other dimensions are literacy are influenced by AI in learning environments, speaking to the possibilities of enhancements relative to engagement and creative ideation, among other findings. From the notions of early human development in school to more lifelong perspective, these authors help center concepts of the individual person and community.

Chapter 4, "Education for the Future: Preparing Elementary Students for an AI-Driven World," explores elementary education spaces with attention to the topics explored in this book. Authors Ramesh Kumar, Raj Kumar Verma, Rohit Kumar Verma, Anand Pawar, Anand Pawar, and Tariq Abubakar Ally focus on the competencies that young children should explore relative to AI and multimodal literacy concepts, positioning these as crucial topics for students to develop from early years onward. The authors present an analysis of trends and practices and suggest steps for reconceptualizing instruction to support the agency of learners. Thus begins a future focus that culminates in the final chapters of this volume.

Pooja Dehankar and Susanta Das contribute Chapter 5, "Revolutionizing Education with AI and ML in K-12 and Higher Education" and focus on the construction of curricula that engages with concepts of AI and multimodality. The authors consider academic freedom and the implications for a lack of freedom, as well as the affordances of AI and multimodal literacy with attention to notions of fair access. This chapter helpfully includes conversation around matters of curriculum. The role of the teacher and institution is voiced to some degree in this chapter.

Janisha Sharma, Vibha Gaur, and Shiva Saini author Chapter 6, "A Framework for an Educational Multi-Agent System." As this volume draws to a close, this discussion around a framework feels like an appropriate penultimate offering. The authors note the potential for digital learning environments to be welcoming community. This culminates in a proposed Multi-agent System (MAS) with the purpose of dissemination of knowledge, stemming from ideas in large language models (LLM), media product, and more. The technical considerations of this author team incorporate notions of workflow, allocation, adaptation, and multimodal content generation for a detailed model that can serve as a springboard for further modeling and modifying.

In Chapter 7, Hamna K and Ayyoob A share an exploration of "Exploring Reader Perceptions of Literary Narratives: A Quantitative Study on Identity Construction, Social Impact, and Ecological Awareness" expand on the Identity Reflection through Literature (IRL), Narrative Impact on Social Awareness (NISA), and Ecological Consciousness through Literary Engagement (ECLE) processes to probe the links between identity reflection and ecological awareness. This chapter stems from a quantitative analysis of 246 readers, and the authors employ descriptive statistics, t-tests, and ANOVA to delineate the results of the survey instrument. The authors speak to the ways that the dimensions of critical awareness and links to literacy hold salient implications for the perceptions and ethical debates that surround the use of

AI. From a theoretical perspective, the authors share work that offers a number of considerations for scholars relative to both multimodality and concerns around technological innovation.

Siri Mohammed-Roe offers Chapter 8, "Aesthetic Democracy in Practice: Student Agency Through Blackout Poetry," locating the discussion in a particular avenue of literacy practice relative to the concept of student agency. Mohammed-Roe locates this chapter in contemporary conversations, including concerns of the creative and agentical, while also noting the possibilities for poetic work not simply as an artistic or literary end to itself, but as a means of sharing voice and choice. These notions of voice and choice correspond with the author's focus on democratic practices and civic positioning. As the individual continues to explore and gain agency, notions of civic role and responsibility form a necessary next thread.

In Chapter 9, Pooja Dehankar and Susanta Das present "EMI in STEM: A Pathway to Global Competence." This author team explores English Medium Instruction (EMI), including changing standards and the ways that changes in laws effect teachers and students. The implementation of EMI in STEM, from these authors' positioning, has implications for both technological innovations and changes in meaning-making practices as afforded by multimodal developments. The authors include a focus on teacher perspectives and practices with implications that include both linguistic and technological/digital concepts. The problematizing of competence focus to more intrinsic questions of ethics and intentionality serve as a thematic element continuing in subsequent chapters.

Deepak Gupta, Karimov Abror, Temur Eshchanov, Dilnoza Butanova, Khudaybergen Kochkarov, Melikov Otabek Maxmadaminovich, Divyang Raval, and Deepak Dharrao then share Chapter 10, "Media and Technology Literacy in the Age of AI." This chapter consists of an overview of empirical research and theoretical framing from 2021 to 2025 from which the authors share proposed interventions and recommendations for assessment. The authors explore the ways this body of research includes links between and among technical competencies, ethics, and pedagogy relative to AI literacy, including both challenges and affordances. This chapter continues the conversation around competency to link with pedagogy.

At some points, analysis can be most helpfully located in discrete areas of the globe. In Chapter 11, Bogdan Petrov, Ainur Abiltayeva, and Amangeldy Shurentayev explore "AI-Driven Media Literacy in National Identity Coverage: Ethics, Manipulations, and Challenges in Kazakhstan," lending this conversation to a specific context. The authors engage in robust theoretical groundwork focused on mediatization and community, among other concepts, to explore this social space. They give attention to a range of barriers, including hate speech, manipulation, and distortion in light of the role of generative AI and algorithms. The authors give shape and detail to philosophical questions, anchored in a particular geography.

Chapter 12 entitled "Media and Technology Literacy in the Age of AI: Frameworks, Competencies, and Educational Imperatives" is authored by Deepak Gupta, Anbarjon Kurbanboeva, Nurullaeva Shakhlo, Yusubov Jaloliddin, Guljahon Ozodova, Nilufar Samandarova, and Farkhod Egamberdiyev. These authors explore and describe the media and technological literacy corpus utilizing an interdisciplinary lens and presenting extant empirical research through an analysis of challenges. The chapter includes frameworks focused on developing AI literacy skills, with emphasis on ethics and sustainable practices, furthering conversation and threads from the previous chapter.

FORWARD MOVEMENT AND FINAL POINTS

From this conversation, it is my hope that continued attention is placed on the widespread implications of what changes in technology, including AI, mean for learners and for social connections. Literacy is a permeable set of practices that can allow for flexible responses and adaptive communication; on the other, institutions of learning sometimes struggle with how best to take up literacy practices in terms of instructional practices or even in terms of what is seen as valid.

AI has been increasingly accessible the past few years, regardless of whether or not AI literacies and practices are validated by institutions of learning. The mechanism has not waited on widespread approval. While academic spaces are often useful sites for developing position statements, I hope that the chapters in this volume and subsequent conversation in literature and across learning spaces lead to a thoughtful and robust approach that continues to consider the human being and human agency as the central axis of any communication – be it analog or digital.

As with Book 1, I now conclude this preface with some questions for further consideration:

1. What is the role of the self in an AI-driven world?
2. How does the identity of the reader/learner interact with increasingly autonomous tools?
3. What are the situational implications for these relationships in institutions of higher learning, as well as in early stages of literacy development?
4. How might we continue to critically and ludically, as well as empathetically, utilize technology as competent readers/thinkers who recognize agency as essentially human?

Jason D. DeHart

The University of Tennessee, USA

REFERENCES

DeHart, J. D. (2024). *Building critical literacy and empathy with graphic novels*. NCTE.

Denham, A. E. (2024). Empathy & literature. *Emotion Review*, *16*(2), 84–95. DOI: 10.1177/17540739241233601

Dung, L. (2025). Understanding artificial agency. *The Philosophical Quarterly*, *75*(2), 450–472. DOI: 10.1093/pq/pqae010

Hempel-Jorgensen, A. (2015). Learner agency and social justice: What can creative pedagogy contribute to socially just pedagogies? *Pedagogy, Culture & Society*, *23*(4), 531–554. DOI: 10.1080/14681366.2015.1082497

Chapter 1
Impact of AI on Educational Policy and Governance

Krutika Patre
http://orcid.org/0009-0001-7969-4409
Ajeenkya D.Y. Patil University, India

Kritikka Kunte
Ajeenkya D.Y. Patil University, India

Sunil Sankathala
http://orcid.org/0009-0004-7809-7647
Ajeenkya D.Y. Patil University, India

Aryan Vasa
http://orcid.org/0009-0000-1837-8587
Ajeenkya D.Y. Patil University, India

Susanta Das
http://orcid.org/0000-0002-9314-3988
Ajeenkya D.Y. Patil University, India

ABSTRACT

AI is dramatically transforming the educational policy & governance arena of the world. Its ability to handle elaborate data, tailor the learning process, & evidence-based decision-making has made it an essential tool towards innovation and inclusiveness in learning. Nevertheless, although AI has the potential of increased efficiency and equity, there are also major ethical, regulatory, and philosophical concerns. In this chapters, the authors are going to discuss the impact of AI on educational

DOI: 10.4018/979-8-2600-2163-7.ch001

policy, governance, & institutional leadership. It explores the increasing conflict between technology & moral responsibility, emphasizing the issues of the broken regulatory framework, algorithm bias, & privacy of data. Besides, it evaluates how policymakers, educators, and institutions are gradually becoming more responsible in adopting AI. Finally, it contends that the future of the AI in education lies in the development of adaptive, ethical, and inclusive forms of governance that would put human judgment as the priority and protect against the loss of integrity in education.

INTRODUCTION

The idea of AI has become a disruptive force which influenced the world education and state. The ability to process large volumes of data, tailor the learning process, and enhance evidence-based decision-making has opened new opportunities and challenges that have never been experienced before by both teaching and learning sets and administrative and policy-makers (Ignjatović, 2024). Incorporation of AI in learning is not technology change, but change in structures and philosophies, which transform the conceptual framework of knowledge, equity, and governance in societies. In this sense, countries and agencies across the globe are interested in how AI can result in innovation, efficiency, and inclusiveness in this respect, as part of the general goals of the digital transformation and sustainable development (Mahrishi et al., 2024). However, this rapid evolution is accompanied by the disorganized mode of regulation, often driven by competition, and not coordination, and this approach will only further polarize the world and make it impossible to evolve AI ethically and fairly (Neuwirth, 2024).

AI can influence the sphere of education, which is much more significant. It encompasses broader scopes of educational governance like data-based policymaking, automated administration, and decision-making processes in an institution (Hilb, 2020). The AI technologies will assist the policy makers in analysing some complex educational data, anticipating learners and making adjusting policies that may improve access and learning outcomes. Most countries have however, published their national AI strategies and the education is usually in an economic context that is in preparing workforce and technological competitiveness and not a humanistic or ethical approach. Tunnel vision disregards such crucial issues as fairness, prejudice, privacy, and responsibility to a large degree (Schiff, 2022).

Global agencies such as UNESCO, OECD and the European Union have developed ethical standards by which AI is applied in an ethical manner in the education sector. Such models embrace the notions of transparency, accountability, equity and human-driven innovation since technology must assist learning and not dictate a learning process. However, despite the fact that the principles of these ethical principles are quite well-founded in theory, the practical implementation of these principles is quite imbalanced depending on the country and organization-specific circumstances (Nguyen et al., 2022).

In the case of higher education, AI is revolutionizing the traditional leadership, management and governance paradigms. The implementation of AI within the administrative optimization procedure, strategic planning, and quality assurance of universities is creating opportunities and straining universities. On the one hand, these technologies can enhance the effectiveness and transparency of the institution, on the other hand, they also shed a dark cloud over the concept of academic integrity, autonomy, and redistribution of the power of the decision (Mariam et al., 2024). The advent of generative AI as represented by ChatGPT has also raised the conventional concept of authorship, assessment, and intellectual integrity. As a result, higher education institutions are also coming with governance policies that are more of innovation, accountability, and inclusiveness and will ensure that AI will be supplementary rather than replace human judgment (Chan, 2023; Dabis & Csakis, 2024; Spivakovsky et al., 2023).

However, the fast pace of the AI development is typically out of the scope of the available policy instruments. The machine learning and algorithmic governance are volatile and hard to follow by older regulatory tools, such as law, institutional standards and moral codes. This adds loopholes and inconsistencies in AI systems monitoring and evaluation (Taeihagh et al., 2021). Since the application of AI in educational institutions has become more significant to make decisions about the performance of students, the evaluation of teachers, and resource distribution, the issue of algorithmic bias, data misuse, and the loss of the human factor has become of significant concern. So that such issues are addressed, the flexible, anticipatory governance must be established, which may be tracked after the technological process.

The dualistic character of AI as the cause of educational change and the source of moral confusion justifies why policy reactions should be approached with holistic and contextualized reactions. The quality governance systems should be able to integrate the technological innovations, democracies, human rights, and social justice (Hagendorff, 2020; Jacques et al., 2024; Walter, 2024). These models will need to be aimed at ethical AI creation, improve transparency in algorithm decision making, human agency should be the key component of the educational process.

In addition, the emergence of AI in the field of governance offers an opportunity to re-establish the notion of participation and inclusivity in education. A more responsive and fair policymaking can be facilitated by AI through ensuring that real-time analysis of educational patterns and needs of learners occurs. However, all this is possible when the data which is used to operate these systems are representative, unbiased and the data are ethically managed. The data privacy and integrity of the learners then have to be set as the initial points of AI policy development. The policymakers are encouraged to introduce effective accountability and stakeholder involvement mechanisms that will facilitate the use of AI in the learning processes by the educators, learners, and communities (Paschal & Melly, 2023).

After all, any introduction of AI into the educational policy and the governance is a matter of moral and strategic perspective and not technological competence. As the concept of AI-driven change is implemented in the educational system in all parts of the globe, the most important issue is how to establish the balance between innovation and responsibility. The human dignity, independence, and justice are not to be violated, but the AI should be employed as the empowerment tool that will enhance the learning process, enhance the efficiency of the governing system, and include the inclusiveness of the decision-making mechanism (OECD et al., 2024).

LITERATURE REVIEW

The discussion of AI in education reports the potential of AI to interest and provoke innovation on the one hand and troubling regulatory consequences on the other. The initial international policy principles by UNESCO that put emphasis on equity, ethical use, and AI literacy necessity. Its later Recommendation on the Ethics of AI (2021) and Guidance on Generative AI in Education (2023) further cemented the approaches which were founded on human-centred and pedagogical approaches. Besides this, the OECD elaborated the guidelines of credible AI, which were related to sustainability, transparency and accountability. At the regional scale, the European Union has introduced the Ethics Guidelines on Trustworthy AI (2019) and EU AI Act (2024), in which education is one of the most dangerous fields due to the possible consequences of human rights and fairness. The surveys that the Council of Europe (2022) developed demonstrate that the majority of the states possess AI plans, though not every one of them has education-based systems or training courses. At the national level, AI Development Strategy of Serbia (2019-2025) provided the basis of infrastructure and competencies of teachers, however, it lacks any legislative frameworks related to education (Ignjatović, 2024).

The literature on AI governance demonstrates that the consensus is growing that it is no longer possible to confine regulation only to the national borders. The first arguments were competition among the world superpowers in which AI was regarded as a race between the United States and China. The international institutions have responded with moral theories such as different systems in the UNESCO report or the OECD which have highlighted transparency, fairness, and international cooperation. This is however, criticized by critics who hold the view that principles are not sufficient and that there should be legal mechanisms in place that are enforced. Overall, the literature demonstrates the fact that the multilateral form of governance should be unified to enable AI to promote human rights, morals, and sustainable development (Neuwirth, 2024).

The articles of the AI policy refer to the rising worldwide interest in the field of ethics, innovation, and competitiveness. The governments have been investing now in billions of dollars in the development of AI that has been credited to economic growth and global competitiveness. However, education has a very minor and functional role in this argument. As per studies made there are not numerous policies concerning the ethical questions of AI in Education (AIED). Most of the national policies are aimed at creating AI professionals, enabling employees to become automated, and educating the population. On the other hand, the list of countries, in which AIED applications are concentrated, including personalized learning, intelligent tutoring or predictive tools, is very short namely Spain, India, Kenya and Malta. This gap means that researchers and policy makers must give maximum efforts to the ethical framework and educational practices to ensure that AIED can be in a position to engage in the inclusion, equity, and human rights as well as innovation (Schiff, 2022).

AIED has expanded to the classroom tools, and now it also encompasses the intelligent systems, which are capable of adapting to the learning process, delivering real-time feedback and personalised experience. It is an in-the-open fact among scholars that AI is disruptive in the field of higher education, and it can enable collaboration and enhance virtual learning, in addition to distance learning or a healthcare curriculum. However, the development of artificial intelligence has been gaining momentum too rapidly and this has raised significant concerns related to ethics and governance. The importance of structures, which would put into consideration fairness, transparency, accountability as well as privacy, is not understated by scholars. Another factor leading to the popularity of the ethical standards and academic integrity issue today is the growing popularity of generative AI applications and their use in the educational sector, including ChatGPT (Mahrishi et al., 2024).

AI application in the government and policymaking is a newly researched field that has created opportunities and challenges. Among the key areas of concern, one can identify how it is possible to create AI that is fair, transparent, and accountable without being harmful (bias, misinformation, or violation of privacy). Another theme is discussed by researchers when they speak about the possibility to apply AI to the sphere of sustainable development, predict the demands of the society in real-time and improve cooperation on the international level. The literature emphasizes that AI can process large amounts of data and detect trends and provide forecasting information, which may allow policymakers to become more engaged and participatory in their decisions. Overall, the literature determines the need to establish the multi-stakeholder collaboration, constant control, and vibrant managing to ensure the responsible engagement of AI in the development of the sphere of the agencies (Saxena, 2024).

However, AI is increasingly being used and this raises ethical and safety issues. Among the most important arguments of debate are the issues of algorithmic bias, transparency, liability of accidents, privacy and autonomy risks. It is even harder to fit in because of the fear of unemployment, and the increasing inequality. The current form of governance is barely able to strike the balance between innovation and accountability, which means that adaptive, inclusive, and ethical governance is required that would ensure that the AI is beneficial to the society without endangering the safety, fairness, and human dignity (Taeihagh et al., 2021).

Since it was founded in 1956, AI has been linked with systems, which think, behave or even think as human beings, and it is recognized by the names of robots, intelligent agents, and autonomous systems. To avoid this confusion, the High-Level Expert Group of the European Commission sees AI as systems developed by people and that, when they are faced with complex goals, perceive their environment, process information, and make a decision and alter their behaviour over time. AI is associated with both ethical and social risks, both regarding biases and privacy violations, and intentional abuse, including deepfakes and online attacks. The stakeholders have to overcome these threats with the help of ethical frameworks, risk analysis theories, and awareness of human rights (Smuha, 2020; Taddeo & Floridi, 2018).

The AI regulation aims at balancing innovation and protection in ways such as transparency, explainable AI and incremental regulation approach. Governments, international organizations and other initiatives by individuals have developed guidelines that address privacy, accountability, fairness, safety, and human values. Despite the development, there are loopholes between the ethics, laws and ethics practice. The study located and examined 109 peer-reviewed articles on AI regulation, governance, and ethical practices in the global arena published in 2010-2020 (Almeida et al., 2021).

The term AI can be described as the capacity to utilize machines to process tasks that previously might have been performed by human intellect, i.e. learning, problem-solving, pattern recognition, and natural language understanding. The applicability of the fields like mathematics, computer science, linguistics, and cognitive psychology has further brought AI to the development of elaborate algorithms that enable machines to act on their own, adapt to new situations, and develop over time. AI also simplifies the administrative procedure like schedule, resource schedule and performance evaluation to allow educators focus on teaching. Besides, AI can support students with special needs through personal learning support, and the interactive and engaging environment is offered with the assistance of simulations and virtual experience. The policies must be clear, the infrastructure must be robust and persistent assessment to make the best out of it and to ensure learning opportunities are not different among the students (Mariam et al., 2024).

The big ethics principles that should be utilized in the process of implementing AI in education include transparency, accountability, privacy and equity. The intent, operation, and decision-making processes of the AI systems can be made transparent via transparency and trust is built between the students, the educators and the parents and the biases in the algorithms can be defined and addressed. Responsibility requires that the institutions, developers and stakeholders of the learning process are responsible to the design, implementation and impacts of the AI systems and remain human in the sense of facilitating regular auditing that may be conducted to aid ethical principles. Ethical implementation of AI also includes data governance, AI systems validation and stakeholder participation to make sure that technology is properly balanced with society values. The combination of these principles will help to apply AI responsibly and develop a trustful, non-discriminatory, and safe learning experience and address the potential social, cultural, and ethical challenges (Paschal & Melly, 2023).

The recent scholarly works are dedicated to the opportunities and threats of AI in higher education. Most companies will be looking at AI because there is a high probability of AI to be incorporated in business and therefore the necessity of being AI literate throughout. The researchers state that the use of generative tools is assistive because of their virtual assistant or co-writer feature, which is effective in their jobs, e.g., coding, content creation, and research. However, they are skewed in their assimilation in education. Some universities have published guidelines and UNESCO has constructed global recommendations to allow the responsible use of AI. Despite all the benefits, there remains a problem that should be of concern like misinformation, moral concern, school cheating, and absence of critical thinking. According to the researchers, the successful institutional policies are to be addressed both to the technical applications, but to the socio-emotional and ethical ones as well and create an inclusive digital environment that will facilitate collaboration and integrity (Spivakovsky et al., 2023).

The education practice is replaced with AI that offers opportunities to personalise education, simplify the administrative work and allows creative teaching. The areas where AI may be used in education can be split into intelligent tutoring systems and adaptive learning systems, policy-making/student-tracking support that enables providing personalized feedback, predictive analytics, and collaborative learning experiences. These technologies can lead to new pedagogies and learning practices that were not previously available such as computer assisted language learning, automated assessment and learning analytics inspired insights. Moreover, too much reliance on AI could also disrupt the learner autonomy, critical thinking and interaction. It is possible to apply such ethical theories to create trustworthy AI that will help to make education fair, efficient, and responsible (Nguyen et al., 2022).

The existing literature highlights that AI is becoming an important tool in revolutionizing the educational governance and policymaking. Scholars claim that AI can have a beneficial effect on the data-driven decision-making process by offering forecasting models to forecast the result of students, establish areas of learning and increase the accountability of the institution. The studies suggest that AI is introducing a novel form of algorithmic governance within education whereby, policies are being developed on the basis of automated data systems rather than using human considerations. This is an efficient and personalized change but it is ethically challenging in the sense that it puts privacy of data, surveillance, and exclusion of human educators in policy making into consideration. Overall, the literature agrees on the idea that, although AI would maximize governance, it has to be approached with a critical attitude keeping in mind the prospects of preserving the democratic and equal principles of education (Hilb, 2020).

The most recent sources reveal that there is an emerging concern that even with the efficiency and data-based governance policies floated by AI, the policies outshine ethical and regulatory preparedness. The fact that AI ethics standards are not practical but symbolic in their nature, it is required to make them enforceable. Research has shown that AI systems in education are expected to be open and answerable and socially answerable to prevent the abuse and discrimination of the algorithms. Moreover, note that AI applications in relation to education need to be more vigorously overseen by institutions to prevent degradation of policies on the ethical front. Overall, the legal governance of AI in education should change to mandatory policies which are practical and must be supported by voluntary codes of ethics (Hagendorff, 2020).

The available literature on the AI in educational policy and governance demonstrates that the creation of a framework of ethical principles should be developed to promote responsible AI usage. Despite the greater application of AI, there are no standards and rules which can manage the factors of fairness, transparency and accountability in education. Raise concerns on the matter of the privacy of data, the problem of informed consent, and the outcomes of the application of algorithms to arrive at a decision concerning the teachers and students. The findings demonstrate that AI can allow the policies to be more efficient, yet will be harmful to the inequality and humanity as a whole, without controlling. The ethical issues include some of ownership of educational data, or bias in algorithms, or the displacement or replacement of the role of teachers. To achieve a more just social governance researchers, propose the multidisciplinary approach to social governance, where ethical reflection, human centred design and regulatory oversight are combined in such a manner that AI does not undermine, but rather strengthens educational principles and democratic accountability.

The existing literature indicates that implementation of AI in the educational sector needs a well-grounded policy framework that will bring the technology in line with both ethical and pedagogical goals. AI can enhance the personalized learning experience, administration, and equity, yet it introduces the problem of privacy, bias, and academic misbehaviours. Most national and institutional AI policies most frequently take into account ethical principles such as accountability, transparency, and fairness. However, the works stress that the current education policies are universal and can be defined by considering the attention to the workforce preparation rather than the transformative effect of AI in education (Schiff, 2022). UNESCO proposes the human-centric approach to AI, which implies interdisciplinary planning, inclusivity, and responsible use. The policy framework of developed AI Ecological Education is built on these ideas and concerns pedagogical, governance, and operational issues of AI in the higher education field. Together, these writings focus on the notion that how to approach AI policy include continuous oversight, equal access, and ethical literacy to generate responsible and sustainable insatiable change in education (Chan, 2023).

The academic literature about AI impact on the policy and governance of education abounds with both the promise of transformation and the problem of ethics. As it has been claimed by researchers, despite such positive aspects of AI as personalized learning or automatization of assessment or better decision-making, the risks include bias, data privacy loss, or even plagiarism. UNESCO (2022) Ethics Guidelines of Trustworthy AI and the EU dwell on the Transparency, accountability, and inclusiveness as educational AI policies. Studies show that the initial responses of universities to generative AI were conditioned by these international systems as it presupposed the need to reconcile between the elements of innovation and integrity. The use of AI has had old restrictions being adjustable to accommodate regulations that support moral consciousness, human control, and the implementation of AI in the teaching and learning process. The researchers have fronted participatory versions of governance whereby educators, students, and policymakers collaborate to ensure that the implementation of AI can enhance and not reduce values of fairness, critical thinking, and inclusivity in education (Dabis & Csaki, 2024).

The researches of the impacts of AI on the educational policy and governance reveal that the dilemma between innovation and regulation is an issue. The rapid level of AI innovation has outpaced the usual policy/government reaction, which has caused international imbalances in the governance approaches. An example of such an attempt to define the risks of AI by their severity and regulate it, which ensures the establishment of ethical norms and responsibility, is the AI Act of the European Union. The similarity of this worldwide initiative is related to the quest to reconcile AI and democratic and social ideals. However, the issues that may be commonly present in literature are the absence of consistency in cultural standards, regulatory delays, and business monopoly in the development of AI. In turn, good governance requires agencies, education, and industry to collaborate in the creation of flexible, inclusive, and morally-based policies (Walter, 2024).

The new body of literature on the governance of AI and education has emphasised the duality of AI as an opportunity and a challenge. The AI can come in handy to maximize productivity and innovation but threaten the existence of inequality, surveillance, and data monopolization. In a study conducted by Research Policy (2024), the success of AI governance is based on the fact that innovation and ethical issues must hold each other in balance, which contributes to the availability of human control and involvement. The studies indicate that the effectiveness of AI in education industry depends on the openness of information, equal access, and adjustable policy constructions. An example of AI governance model offered under the European Union in the shape of the Data Governance Act creates a reference point as far as accountability, fairness, and sharing data in the common good are concerned. Overall, the literature states that there is a necessity to possess interdisciplinary and participatory policy approach that will ensure that AI in education can represent sustainable development, privacy assurance, and democracy in governance (OECD, 2024).

The general consensus is that the role of AI in the educational governance and policy is intricate as it involves an element of innovation along with ethical and regulatory issues, which are interconnected. The new system of analytics and data that is driven by AI is influencing the process of decision-making, the manner in which education is responsible, and the manner in which the policy-making is being redefined by the new system. Similar to UNESCO (2021), the OECD (2022) advances human-centred AI models that are grounded on transparency, inclusiveness and ethical responsibility. Overall, one can see that the effective AI policy related to education requires interdisciplinary collaboration, continuous oversight, and alignment with the social and ethical values to ensure that technology is truly useful in education and policymaking (Jacques et al., 2024).

BIBLIOMETRIC ANALYSIS

Figure 1 demonstrates the network visualization of the co-occurring keywords in PubMed database that provides a detailed view of the thematic relationship and collaborative structure that characterizes the area of AI influence on educational policy and governance. VOSviewer software was used to visualize the data. The colour of each network denotes the thematic group of a word, and the linking lines indicate how frequently and how strong the co-occurrence of words. It is through the visualization that we can identify the connections between various research themes in the larger intellectual framework.

The human being is the central aspect of the network that forms the major node between different thematic groups. This centrism is manifested by the fact that the vast majority of research in the sphere of AI-based educational policymaking remains focused on human interaction, morals, and decision-making. It is an embodiment of technology and human's interaction as the manner in which governance systems evolve and align themselves to AI tools and vice versa preserving equity, transparency, and accountability.

Figure 1. Bibliometric analysis of "Impact of AI on educational policy and governance" using VOSviewer with data from PubMed. (Data may vary slightly).

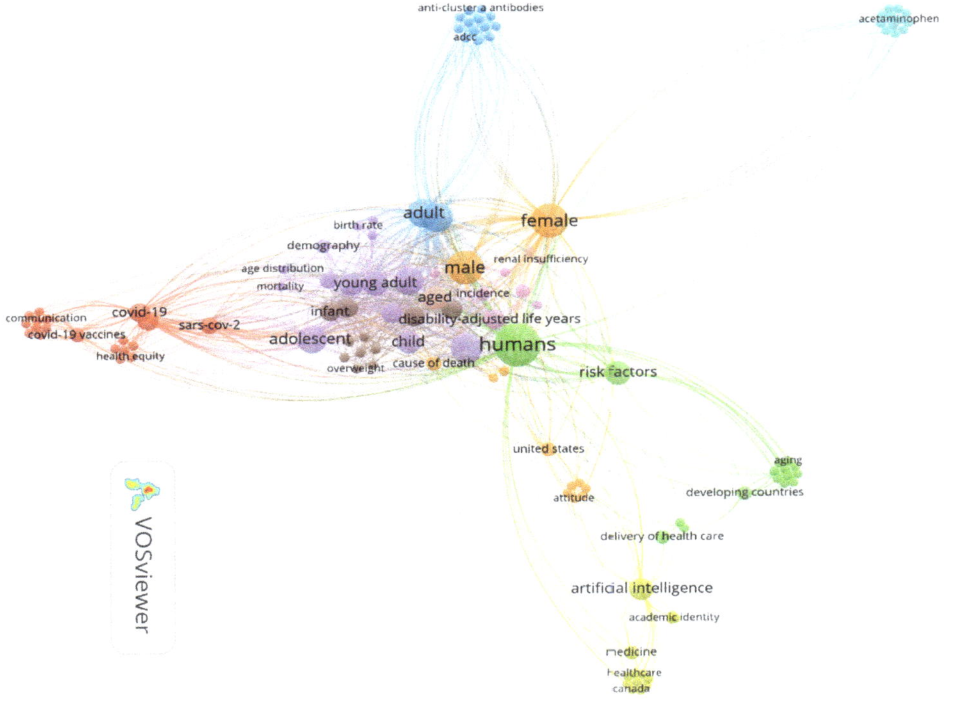

The green cluster that is located in the lower-right part of the map deals with the artificial intelligence of the term, academic identity, provision of health care and medicine. The intersection point between AI, governance, and institutional management is such a combination. The inclusion of health-related words and learning ideas proves the cross-sectoral learning of the healthcare governing system and the educational system that are grounded in AI to make informed choices and allocate resources.

The group of red nodes on the left of the network, in its turn, consists of COVID-19, SARS-CoV-2, communication and health equity. It is a sign of research resurrection due to the world pandemic, when AI played a key role in crisis communications, distance learning, and access to education. The association of the COVID-related keywords with the word communication and health equity suggests that the policy is well-focused on the application of AI in helping with the resolutions of the differences in the case of an emergency to guarantee the continuity of the administration and education services.

The groups which are blue and orange (adult, female, male, child and aged) are preoccupied with the behavioural and demographic aspects. Such groups show that gender, age, and social heterogeneity are significant concerns in developing inclusive AI based systems of governance in education. Scholars appear to be studying how demographic characteristics influence the implementation of policies, learning and access to digital systems.

It is important to note that the interconnections between the clusters are thick, which demonstrates the interdisciplinarity of the research area. The AI education and governance studies tend to follow the frameworks of health policy, sociology, data science, and psychology. The complication of the network shows how the field of study is no longer on the niche issue and is now a multidimensional policy debate.

The overlay view generated with the assistance of VOSviewer and adding time dimension into the bibliometric mapping is displayed in Figure 2. It represents the time-varying research topics, as colours signify different times, i.e. blue (Older studies, about 2022) to yellow (Newer studies, about 2025). This gradient is practically expressed to show the chronical sequence of the research priorities in the field of the influence of AI on the educational policy and government.

Figure 2. Time analysis of "Impact of AI on educational policy and governance" using VOSviewer with data from PubMed. (Data may vary slightly)

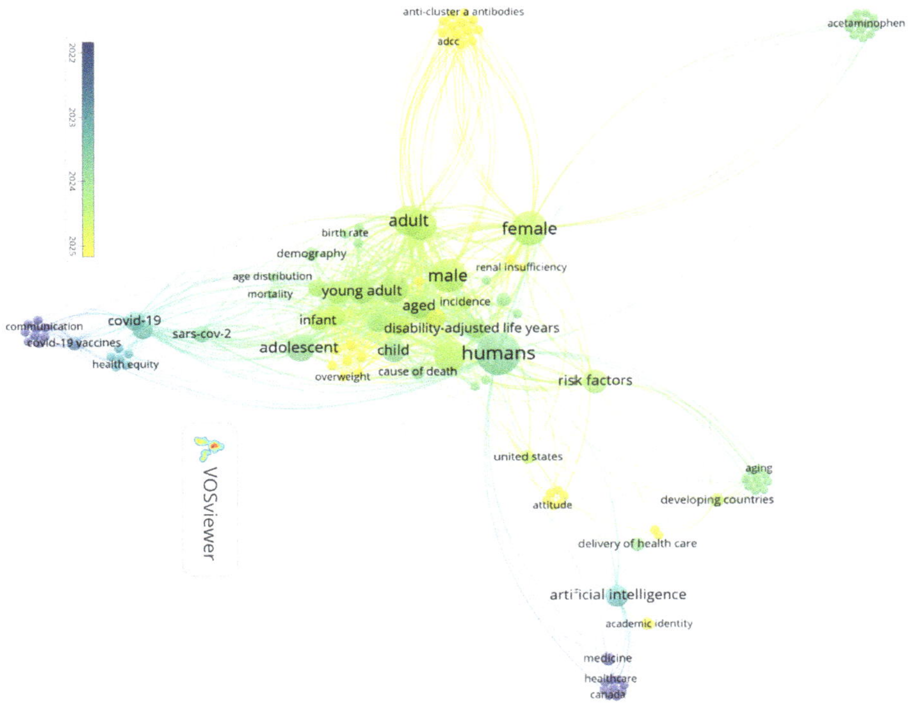

The enormous focus on COVID-19, SARS-CoV-2, health equity, and communication was placed in the researches in the previous years (illustrated with blue and green colour). This is when the direct response to the pandemic came into place when scholars and policymakers started asking themselves how AI can be used to organize remote learning systems, digital governance, and communication options. The key information covered by these studies was the adaptation to the crisis and short-term policy reactions on the criterion of the need to maintain the educational process.

Tilting the colour gradient towards the yellow hue introduces more recent issues, like the ones on artificial intelligence, academic identity, medicine, the provision of health care, and developing nations. The yellow highlights on these nodes refer to a current wave of discussion on the spheres of AI regulation, morals and global policy models. The research at this phase is not reactive anymore but proactive formulation of policies and how AI may be institutionalized in a responsible manner within the education systems.

The emergence of the recent keyword of academic identity can be viewed as a sign of a growing interest in the research of how AI is changing the roles of educators, students, and administrators. The problems of academic independence, the data ownership, the algorithm-based evaluation become the centre of focus in the debate on the education governance. Similarly, the increased prominence of the so-called developing countries in more recent studies suggests the extension of interest in equity in the world in the realms of implementing AI to the education policy systems of various social and economic contexts.

Meanwhile, the employment of constant central terms like humans, risk factors, and child points to the fact that the anthropocentric approach to ethics and developmental issues will be similar in the time span. This shows that despite the evolution of technology; the research has established its presence based on the principles of social justice and equity as a basis of governance.

Using its overlay visualization, one can thus observe that there is a presence of an apparent temporal trend: health-conscious AI applications in the pandemic (2022-2023) and then education governance, identity, and inclusivity (2024-2025). It demonstrates how the field has already evolved to become mature no longer digital transformation at the short-term scale, but systemic integration at the long-term scale.

Figure 3 is the density visualization map developed with the assistance of VOSviewer and depicts the concentration and intensity of the research topics according to the impact of AI on the educational policy and governance. The warmer (yellow and orange) and the cooler (green and blue) colours of this visualization are the localities of more and less frequently investigated themes respectively. Density map is also a useful tool of the hotspots of research, trends and patterns of this interdisciplinary research.

Figure 3. Density visualization of "Impact of AI on educational policy and governance" using VOSViewer with data from PubMed. (Data may vary slightly).

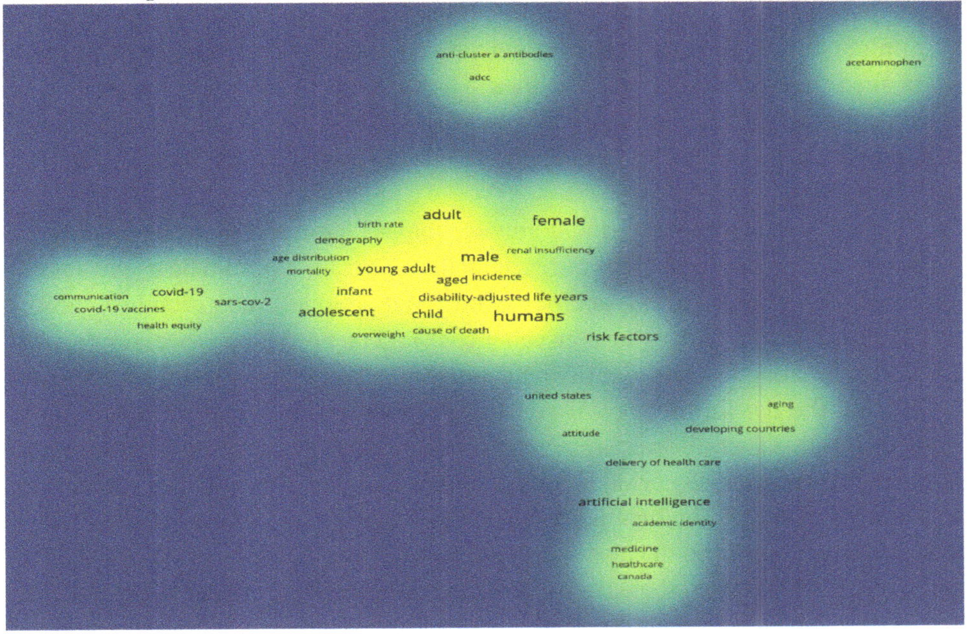

The humans are depicted in the middle of the map, and terms that occur most frequently are given next to it, among them such concepts as adult, male, female, child, and young adult. It means that the majority of the research works consider human and demographic factors as key elements of educational and governance studies based on AI. The general emphasis on the ethical, social, and developmental components of the introduction of AI in education systems and policy frameworks is suggested by the fact that the central figure was a human being. It is an effort to contemplate the impact of AI on the learning process, inclusiveness and the human dimension of governance.

Surrounding this main node are clusters that are related to artificial intelligence, risk factors, healthcare and delivery of health care, which shows the increasing scope of the study to explore AI as a governance mechanism not only in the field of education but also in the general spheres of the population. The repetition of having used the term risk factors implies the policy aspects of bias, privacy, and accountability of the AI-driven educational systems. It also presupposes that policymakers are addressing not only ethical but also systemic risks that are related to algorithmic decision-making and automation in the sphere of educational management.

One may also find a considerable level of concentration related to COVID-19, SARS-CoV-2, communication, and health equity. These words represent the reality that the pandemic has altered the priorities of the world in education and governance. AI in online studies, AI in data analysis and the governance of communication became established during the COVID-19 times. The high position of these keywords is based on the fact that researchers have investigated the use of AI-based educational technologies to proceed with learning and make informed policy decisions during crisis situations.

The term peripheral node (including academic identity, developing countries, and medicine) reveals new areas of research that cover how AI can be used to assist educational politics in various socioeconomic and national backgrounds. Scholars are also beginning to look at the consequences of AI on academic processes, institutional change and growth of identity in technologically-advanced learning contexts.

Overall, the density display of AI studies in education serves to reveal three important truths: first, the research continues to be deeply rooted in the human and demographic analysis framework, second, an expanding interdisciplinary uptake with the research of the public health and social governance, and third, the COVID-19 pandemic has intensified the discourse on the policy implications of AI to a significant degree. The fact that the terms of artificial intelligence, human beings, and risk factors have the yellow areas proves that it is a vivid study area that is concentrated on ethical governance, data control, and equity.

Figure 4, with the theme of impact of AI on educational policy and governance, presents the annual distribution of documents in Figure 4 in terms of the number of documents Granted Patents, Patent Application and Search Report. The data that is found in the Lens database tells us the timeframe of 1994-2025 and at least provides a fair notion as to how the development of intellectual property in this interdisciplinary area has evolved over the years.

Figure 4. Yearly publication of documents using data from Lens. (data may vary slightly).

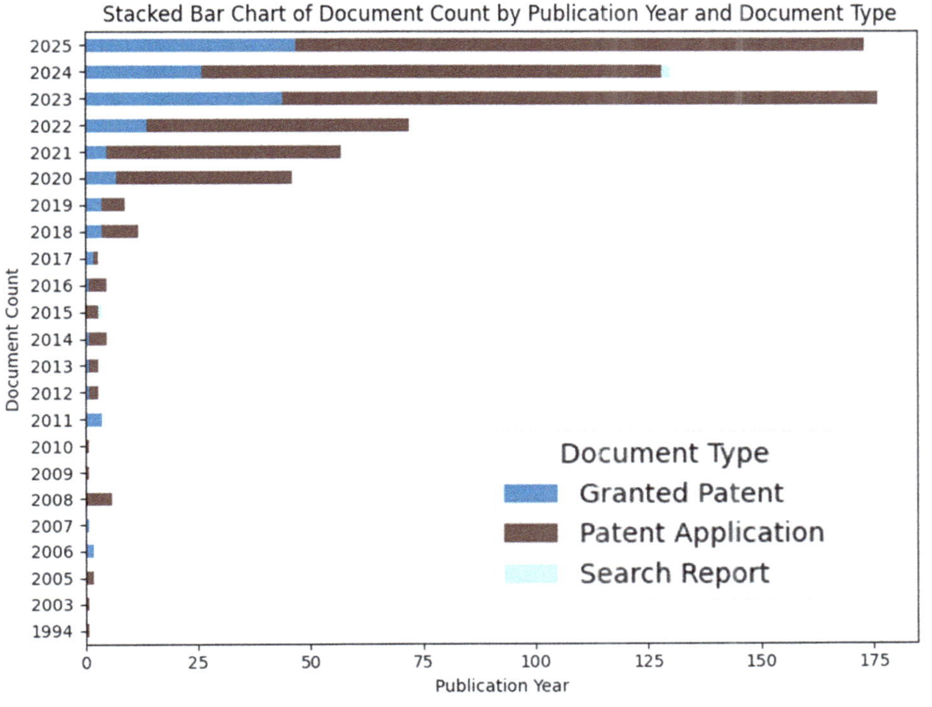

According to the chart, one can observe that the research and innovation activities between the AI and educational policy and governance were virtually unimportant before the year 2015. The rate of publications in such period was extremely low, which provides the evidence that the use and debate of AI as the instrument of education policy-making was not becoming popular yet. The period of 2015-2019 is marked by a minor increase in the quantity of patents that illustrates a positive sign of the premature implementation of AI technologies in the system of educational management, data-driven governance, and learning analytics. Such gradual growth can be considered a sign of the growing value of AI application in streamlining the administrative decision-making and educational policy evaluation processes.

It is possible to notice a significant turn starting in 2020, which is connected with the COVID-19 pandemic in the world. The pandemic accelerated the process of introducing AI into digital learning systems and remote learning systems, and institutional decision systems. Thus, the numbers of Granted Patents and Patent Applications have sharply increased in 2021 and 2022. The rise in the number of patent applications is an indicator of more attempts at innovation since institutions of education, technology developers, and policymakers tried to locate AI-solutions to the change management of scale-based changes in the education systems.

This trend is continuing to increase steeply until 2023-2025 at which point the Patent applications would be several times higher than the Granted Patents and the Search Reports. This kind of domination in the number of patent applications compared to the granted rights point out to the fact that research and technological experimentation is still under exploration and developmental stages. It is likely that there are a lot of innovations on the table, and it means that there are a constant interest and investment in the same field of emergence. This filing intensity also shows that competition exists between the ed-tech companies, AI developers and government related organizations, which seek to obtain intellectual property rights on the new AI-based educational governance models.

Amazingly, the relatively few numbers of Search Reports is a sign of limited information disclosed to the public or pre-grant analysis than the relatively large growth of filings patents. It is an indication of this trend that much of the innovation that is already present is either under scrutiny by the patent office or at a relatively immature phase of development, which is being quickly advanced into a rapidly growing but still developing industry.

The data distribution shows a smooth steady ness of the AI technologies such as predictive analytics, automated assessment tools, and policy simulation tools to the governing structure of the education system. The 2020 boom and its aftermath highlight the growing policy interest in AI regarding such areas as the equal allocation of resources, the individual control of learning, as well as the national educational data management.

Figure 5 illustrates the pie chart, demonstrates the number of types of documents (Patent Applications, Granted Patents, and Search Reports) by the data that were gathered in The Lens database on the subject of Impact of Artificial Intelligence on Educational Policy and Governance. This kind of visualization provides a notion of the intellectual property climate at the border of AI and education governance, as well as the level of innovativeness, patenting, and research work in the sphere of active development.

Figure 5. Pie chart of number of types of documents (Patent Applications, Granted Patents, and Search Reports). (Data may vary slightly).

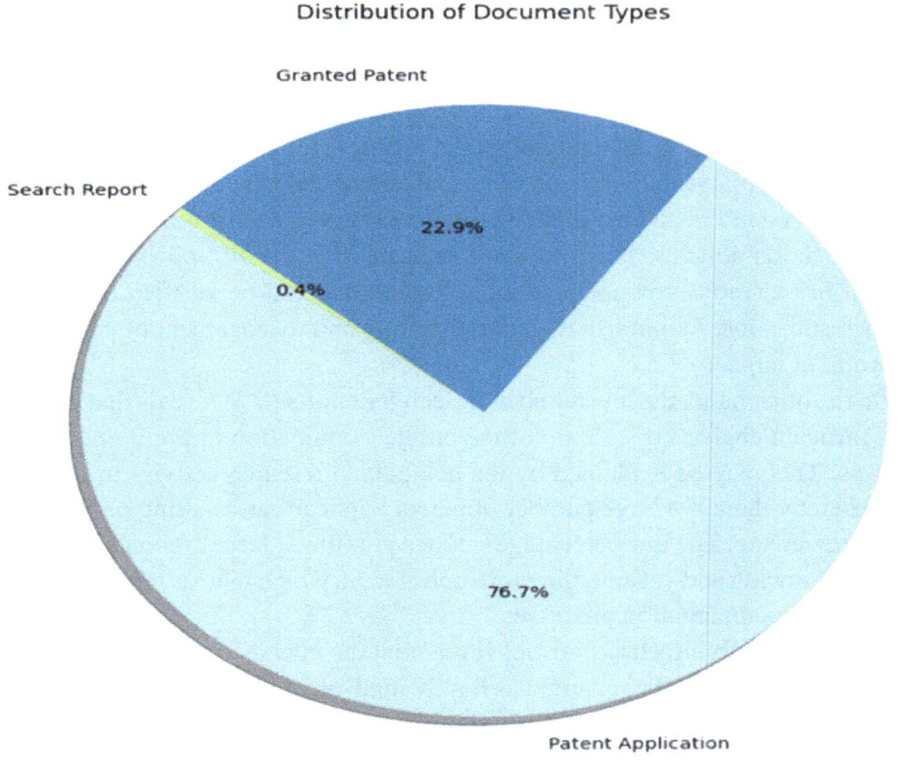

According to the figure, most of the total documents are occupied by the excess majority of Patent Applications that comprised the 76.7 percent of the total number. Granted Patents have 22.9 with the remaining percent being Search Reports which is 0.4. This allocation can give useful clues on maturity, the innovations, and the evolving nature of AI application in education policy and management.

It is a sign of an active and discovery stage of this field that is represented by the preponderance of the patent applications. A high rate of patenting applications demonstrates that there is a high number of innovators, educational technology firms and policy bodies that are seeking to discover AI based technology to improve governance and administrative decision making in education. The examples of such applications include smart educational data analytics systems, policy outcome predictive modelling systems, artificial intelligence assessment system and algorithmic governance ethical system. However, considering the fact that a lot of such ideas are still under review, it is a clue that the field of AI application to the education governance is a field of research to be turned to more grown-up technologies or proven patents.

The 22.9 percent market share of the patents awarded is attributed to that of such innovations that have undergone the process of examination and verification. These are technologies that have proved unique, practically applicable and technically sound in nature. The most likely obtained patents include AI-powered education management, policy analytical software, and automated governance systems which can be utilized in the context of facilitating data-driven decision-making and equitable education policies. Their presence indicates that the discipline is an infantile one but has already provided a set of solutions that can be verified and put into practice and can revolutionize the administration and management of education in the world at large.

On the other hand, the low number of Search Reports (0.4) reveals that there was no significant analysis disclosure of the public examination or preliminary patent analysis. This may be explained by the heightened research activity in the recent past whereby there are large number of patent applications awaiting processing or formal reviewing. The low percentage is also a plus towards the argument that this is a rapidly growing and yet emerging research area, in which innovation is overtaking the official documentation processes.

Overall, the bibliometric statistics reveal that the intersection of AI-educational policy/governance can be regarded as highly innovative in terms of the level of innovation and low-in terms of maturity. The mere fact that there are now, as a matter of fact, applications to patents that have never been granted, makes the argument that there is still an innovation pipeline that is under development, and that there is much more potential breakthroughs that have never been made. Moreover, this tendency means the heightened understanding of the revolutionary character of AI in the further evolution of the education system, whether it is connected with the individualization of policy implementation, data-driven governance, or the monitoring of fair access.

CONCLUSION

One of the most significant shifts in the modern education, in terms of paradigm change, is the influence of Artificial Intelligence on the educational policy and governance. The introduction of AI introduces the possibility to revolutionize how the educational systems work which is, make the policymaking process more evidence-based, administration more efficient, and learning more personalized. There are however complex ethical and governance challenges that are linked to such developments. The speed of the AI evolution is still to be quicker than with more traditional regulatory models, and the policy-makers have a tough time to attempt to ensure transparency, fairness, and accountability in its application. As the analysis demonstrates, AI-driven governance can enhance the decision-making process, as well as institutional performance, yet it also can pose a threat to human agency unless it is controlled by setting specific ethical standards. Algorithms bias and the delivery of unequal access as well as privacy of data must be addressed using context-based policies that would point at both local and global educational priorities. UNESCO, OECD and other global systems do point to a good direction to be followed, but need institutional ability and cooperation of players. Lastly, the question of the educational policymakers is how to be creative but in a responsible fashion. AI should not replace human judgment, but rather complement it in helping teachers and administrators to create inclusive, open and responsible learning provisions. The principle of governance, which should be rooted in democratic ideas, human dignity, and social justice, should be used since the concept of education systems is going to evolve with the creation of AI. Only under these conditions of ethical and flexible policymaking, AI will become a source of equitable and sustainable educational transformation.

REFERENCES

Almeida, P. (2021, September). Chamber of Deputies, Santos, C., University of Brasília, Farias, J., & University of Brasília. (2021). Artificial Intelligence Regulation: A framework for governance. *Ethics and Information Technology*, *23*(3), 505–525. Advance online publication. DOI: 10.1007/s10676-021-09593-z

Chan, C. K. Y. (2023). A comprehensive AI policy education framework for university teaching and learning. *International Journal of Educational Technology in Higher Education*, *20*(1), 38. DOI: 10.1186/s41239-023-00408-3

Dabis, A., & Csáki, C. (2024). AI and ethics: Investigating the first policy responses of higher education institutions to the challenge of generative AI. *Humanities & Social Sciences Communications*, *11*(1), 1006. Advance online publication. DOI: 10.1057/s41599-024-03526-z

Hagendorff, T. (2020). The Ethics of AI Ethics: An Evaluation of Guidelines. *Minds and Machines*, *30*(1), 99–120. DOI: 10.1007/s11023-020-09517-8

Hilb, M. (2020). Toward artificial governance? The role of artificial intelligence in shaping the future of corporate governance. *The Journal of Management and Governance*, *24*(4), 851–870. DOI: 10.1007/s10997-020-09519-9

Ignjatović, G. (2024). AI technologies in education: Regulatory frameworks at the international, regional and national level. *Zbornik Radova Pravnog Fakulteta Nis*, *63*(103), 235–260. DOI: 10.5937/zrpfn1-55374

Jacques, P. H., Moss, H. K., & Garger, J. (2024). A synthesis of AI in Higher Education: Shaping the future. *Journal of Behavioral and Applied Management*, *24*(2). Advance online publication. DOI: 10.21818/001c.122146

Lens. (2025). Retrieved, 2025, from https://www.lens.org/

Mahrishi, M., Abbas, A., & Siddiqui, M. K. (2024). *Global Initiatives towards Regulatory Frameworks for Artificial intelligence (AI) in Higher Education*. Digital Government Research and Practice. DOI: 10.1145/3672462

Mariam, G., Adil, L., & Zakaria, B. (2024). The integration of artificial intelligence (AI) into education systems and its impact on the governance of higher education institutions. *International Journal of Professional Business Review*, *9*(12), e05176. DOI: 10.26668/businessreview/2024.v9i12.5176

Neuwirth, R. J. (2024). The global institutional governance of AI: A four-dimensional perspective. In *Int. J. Digit. Law Gov*, *1*(1), 13–153. DOI: 10.1515/ijdlg-2024-0004

Nguyen, A., Ngo, H. N., Hong, Y., Dang, B., & Nguyen, B.-P. T. (2022). Ethical principles for artificial intelligence in education. *Education and Information Technologies, 28*(4), 4221–4241. DOI: 10.1007/s10639-022-11316-w PMID: 36254344

OECD. (2024). The governance of artificial intelligence: Harnessing opportunities and mitigating challenges. In *Research Policy* 53, 104928. DOI: 10.1016/j.respol.2023.104928

Paschal, M. J., & Melly, I. K. (2023). Ethical guidelines on the use of AI in education. In *Advances in educational technologies and instructional design book series*, 230–245. DOI: 10.4018/979-8-3693-0205-7.ch013

Saxena, A. K. (2024). AI in Governance and Policy Making. *International Journal of Science and Research (Raipur, India), 13*(5), 1218–1223. Advance online publication. DOI: 10.21275/SR24519015426

Schiff, D. (2022). Education for AI, not AI for education: The role of education and ethics in national AI policy strategies. *International Journal of Artificial Intelligence in Education, 32*(3), 527–563. DOI: 10.1007/s40593-021-00270-2

Spivakovsky, O. V., Omelchuk, S. A., Kobets, V. V., Valko, N. V., & Malchykova, D. S. (2023). Institutional policies on artificial intelligence in university learning, teaching and research. *Information Technologies and Learning Tools, 97*(5), 181–202. DOI: 10.33407/itlt.v97i5.5395

Taeihagh, A., & the Policy Systems Group. Lee Kuan Yew School of Public Policy, & National University of Singapore. (2021). Governance of artificial intelligence. In *Policy and Society, 40*(2), 137–157. DOI: 10.1080/14494035.2021.1928377

UNESCO. (2026). (https://www.unesco.org/en)

VOSviewer. (2026). https://www.vosviewer.com/

Walter, Y. (2024). Managing the race to the moon: Global policy and governance in Artificial Intelligence regulation—A contemporary overview and an analysis of socioeconomic consequences. *Discover Artificial Intelligence, 4*(1), 14. Advance online publication. DOI: 10.1007/s44163-024-00109-4

KEY TERMS AND DEFINITIONS

AI Literacy: The skills, knowledge, and understanding that allow people to make knowledgeable decisions about AI systems by understanding their opportunities, hazards, and potential harms.

Artificial Intelligence: Machines that have been taught to think and learn like people are capable of simulating human intelligence by seeing, reasoning, solving problems, and acting in ways that accomplish particular objectives.

Education: A structured system of rules, laws, and principles designed to develop human potential, promote social movement, and foster national progress.

Ethics: The application of moral principles to guide the actions and decisions of public administrators, certifying they are fair, just, and responsible.

Global Governance: The complex system of rules, organizations, and devices that manage global issues across national borders without a single world government.

Governance: The process of making and applying decisions to manage a nation, organization, or country.

Human Centred Design: A problem-solving method that places the needs and experiences of people at the centre of the policymaking process to create more effective and applicable public services.

Policy Framework: A structured set of policies, events, and principles that guide an society or government in achieving its goals.

Chapter 2
Redefining Success Using AI to Help You Learn

Shuchita Mudgil
http://orcid.org/0000-0002-6707-865X
Government Kalaniketan Polytechnic College, Jabalpur, India

Rohan Rajoriya
Government Kalaniketan Polytechnic College, Jabalpur, India

Shaheen Tazir
Government Kalaniketan Polytechnic College, Jabalpur, India

ABSTRACT

The integration of Artificial Intelligence (AI) into learning ecosystem is not just a scientific change but a basic reimagining of academic process, literacy practice, and the very description of educational achievement. This chapter move further than a evocative general idea of AI tools to offer a critical blend of how AI is reshape multimodal literacy—the aptitude to create and understand meaning across a variety of digital, linguistic, and visual modes—within learning environments. We dispute that AI's core promise lies in personalization, transform the monumental classroom into an adaptive room approachable to individual learner needs, styles, and pace. The chapter scientifically examine this transformation across three key domains: AI-driven adaptive learning platforms, automated assessment and response systems, and AI-augmented investigate and inscription tools. However, this analysis is temper by a critical lens focused on the assistant ethical, social, and academic challenges.

DOI: 10.4018/979-8-2600-2163-7.ch002

INTRODUCTION

Education stands at a cliff, shaped by the twin services of digital alteration and a rising acknowledgment of beginner variety. The conventional, manufacturing model of teaching, characterized by consistent curriculum, homogeneous pace, and collective assessment, has been critiqued for its breakdown to get together varied beginner requirements (Robinson, 2010). In this circumstance, Artificial Intelligence (AI) emerge not as a meager incremental improvement, but as a potentially paradigm-shifting power able of catalyzing a shift towards truthfully modified, receptive, and multimodal knowledge environment.

This chapter, positioned surrounded by the dialogue of *Multimodal Literacy Studies in the Age of AI*, posits that AI is basically varying the semiotic scenery of teaching. Multimodal literacy, defined as the capability to understand, analysis, and generate meaning transversely included mode such as text, image, sound, and gesticulation (Kress, 2010; Cope & Kalantzis, 2015), is both prolonged and complex by AI. AI systems curate multimodal happy pathways, produce textual and visual criticism, and examine patterns in student communication data, thereby mediate the literacy practice of learners in unparalleled habits. The essential query we discover is: How is AI redefining the pathway to and meaning of enlightening success, and what are the significant literacy's mandatory to steer this innovative site sensibly?

Our purpose is to move from a list of applications to a significant assessment. We begin by establishing a hypothetical base that links AI in education to multimodal literacy and significant pedagogy. Consequently, we examine AI's role in three nucleus areas: (1) personalizing knowledge journey, (2) transform evaluation and opinion, and (3) augment academic examination and inscription. Each section integrates psychoanalysis of reimbursement with a bottomless conversation of moral and educational tension. We wrap up by framing "success" in this AI-mediated era as dependent upon the growth of *critical AI literacy*—the ability to use, appreciate, query, and morally preside over AI systems. This chapter aims to supply educators, researchers, and policymakers with a synthesized, critical agenda for engaging with AI's transformative prospective while watchfully defense humanistic learning principles.

LITERATURE REVIEW & HYPOTHETICAL FUNDAMENTALS

To significantly examine AI's role in learning, we must ground our conversation in healthy hypothetical soil. These base bridge theories of how significance is completed with theory of how authority operates in education.

Multimodal Literacy in the Digital Age

Gunther Kress's (2010) employment on multimodality argue to communiqué is never monomial; significance is made from side to side the orchestration of dissimilar semiotic assets (writing, speech, image, layout). The digital environment, and now AI, exponentially increases the ease of use and combinability of these modes. AI-powered platforms do not simply convey text; they energetically accumulate modified learning sequences comprise videos, interactive simulation, podcasts, and info graphics. This stresses a form of literacy that is intrinsically *design-oriented* (Cope & Kalantzis, 2015), wherever learners are not just consumers but potential designers of multimodal sense, although within AI-curate limitations. AI thus become a co-participant in the semiotic procedure, signifying which mode might be most effectual for a known beginner—a influential, yet potentially narrow, authority.

Critical Pedagogy and the Ethics of Expertise

Paulo Freire's (2000) analysis of the "banking model" of teaching, where information is deposited into inert students, finds a novel circumstance in AI. While AI can personalize the "set down," it risks automate and obscure the power dynamics intrinsic in education. Critical pedagogy urges us to inquire: Who designs the algorithms? Whose facts and values are programmed? Who profit? This lens is necessary for exploratory AI in education, pushing us beyond competence gains to questions of impartiality, society, and liberation. It frames the principled concern—preconceived notion, observation, the digital split—not as technological glitches but as complete issue of authority (Benjamin, 2019).

Synthesis of AI in Education Research

Recent scholarship (2020-2025) on AI in learning cluster around numerous themes. A leading thread celebrates AI's potential for *personalization* (Hooda et al., 2022; Walter, 2024), significance adaptive education systems that regulate content complexity and modality. One more significant core of awareness is on *automated assessment*, discover natural language dispensation for article grade and proctoring system (Yakkala, 2024; Zhang & Aslan, 2021). A rising mass examines *AI as a research tool*, aiding literature review, data examination, and writing (Huang & Tan, 2023; Khalifa & Albadawy, 2024). At the same time as a decisive literature highlights *ethical challenges*: algorithmic prejudice perpetuates chronological inequality

(Noble, 2018), the privacy inconsistency in knowledge analytics (Tsai et al., 2020), and impact on learner-instructor communication (Seo et al., 2021).

A key gap in this section deals with the relative absence of discussion trapped among this realistic AI observe and the gap hypothesis of multimodal literacy and important pedagogy. Furthermore, much journalism scraps also utopian or dystopian; we seek announce, critical-pragmatic combination that acknowledges both transformative latent and grave risk.

Customized Learning and Adaptive Platforms

The visualization of teaching modified to the individual learner is an antique ideal, now verdict a strong guide in AI. Adaptive learning platform influence machine learning algorithms to analyze a student's presentation, meeting patterns, and sometimes even emotional state, to dynamically adjust the education pathway.

Mechanisms of Personalization

At the scientific foundation, these systems rely on incessant information compilation: answer period, quiz score, incidence of video replay, discussion contribution, etc. Algorithms recognize acquaintance gap misconception, and best education modalities (e.g., visual vs. textual explanation). For instance, if a learner struggles with an idea in arithmetical word troubles, the stage strength in attendance a following dilemma with a visual illustration or an interactive imitation, contravention downward the stepladder further. This aligns with multimodal literacy hypothesis by deliberately selecting and sequencing modes to gallows concerned. The classification, during outcome, performs an immediate *multimodal discourse analysis* of the learner's communication to notify its after that academic shift.

Case in Focus: Squirrel AI

Consider Squirrel AI, an extensively cited adaptive teaching arrangement used in China. This AI employs coarse information graph, decaying subject like arithmetic into tens of thousands of micro-concepts. By identify a student's mastery at this micro-level, it generates an exclusive knowledge pathway, bypass identified concept and focus persistently on weakness (Beard, 2020). Success currently is redefined as the well-organized mastery of a predefined facts chart. At the same time as this can noticeably get better consistent examination score, critic disagree it represent a hyper-efficient shape of "drill and kill," potentially reducing originality, investigative education, and the capability to make unexpected associations crosswise domain—capacity fundamental to bottomless literacy.

Benefits and Critical Limitations

The benefit is convincing: augmented rendezvous from related content, condensed irritation through suitable confrontation, and sustained for miscellaneous learner, together with individual disabilities. On the other hand, the significant pedagogue asks: What is being modified, and what is being uniform? The *content and pace* are modified, but the *learning objectives and the significance of information* are often strictly programmed by the organization designer. This can guide to a "filter bubble" of education, where student are infrequently bare to perspective or mode of opinion outside their diagnose sketch. In addition, personalization is based on noticeable performance statistics, which may misconstrue nervousness as lack of acceptance or rapid, guess-based answer more than profound, thoughtful effort. Factual personalized learning has to give freedom for beginner organization to set goal, decide topic of obsession, and hold in unrestricted, multimodal work of art—not just utilization. More and more, AI is being used in schools to make learning more individualized for each student.

It gives them personalized lessons depending on their talents, interests, and ways of learning. AI looks at student performance data and finds trends in where they are having trouble learning or where they don't comprehend something.AI and ML (machine learning) algorithms are used by adaptive platforms to look at a lot of data on how well students are doing. The information helps figure out what they are good at and what they need to work on. AI takes into account each person's needs, wants, and learning style to build personalized learning routes (Hooda et al., 2022; Walter, 2024).

For example, if a student is good in a certain subject, the platform can skip past the basics and go straight to the more advanced material. In the same way, if a student has trouble with a concept, the platform can give them more resources and change speed to fit their learning needs.

Adaptive platforms also take into account how pupils learn, like whether they learn better by seeing or hearing. It gives learners information in the way that works best for them. A personalized way of learning helps pupils learn more and stay engaged. E-learning platforms have altered the way students learn by making it easier and more flexible for them to receive the education they need from anywhere in the world. But this evolution has also caused problems, mostly with testing and feedback, which will be spoken about below. Most traditional grading methods require the teacher to do a lot of boring math. Teachers can't use them to grade big classes; they're subjective, and they could provide different scores for the same work in various classes (Zhang & Aslan, 2021).

AI IN ASSESSMENT AND FEEDBACK

Assessment is a foundation stone of learning, signal what counts as information and achievement. AI promises to transform this area by making appraisal incessant, immediate, and, evidently, extra point.

Automated Grading and Formative Feedback

AI-driven tackle can now attain not only multiple-choice questions but also prearranged response, short essays, and even training coursework. Natural Language Processing (NLP) models evaluate student writing against score rubrics, model answers, and big corpora of grade text. For determining evaluation, AI can provide real-time response on draft, importance grammatical error, signifying better clearness, or asking questions. This immediate response ring aligns with Vygotskian concepts of being well-informed now instantiated in system, providing scaffolding surrounded by the neighborhood of proximal expansion.

The Case of Automated Proctoring: Proctorio

The shift to online learning, accelerated by COVID-19, spur the acceptance of AI proctoring tools like Proctor. This system supervises students via webcam and microphone, by means of computer vision and audio examination to ensign "distrustful behaviors" such as eye actions away from the screen, the existence of one more person, or abnormal sounds. Proponents dispute it ensure educational reliability in scattered environment. However, experiential study and student testimonials disclose a dark side (Students effort with Online Test Proctoring Systems, 2020). This practice is often one of invasive concern and professed observation, transforming an educational evaluation into a stress-inducing concert for the machine. Furthermore, this system has been shown to reveal cultural prejudice, wrongly deteriorating darker-skinned students more normally due to boundaries in facial identification algorithms (Buolamwini & Gebru, 2018). This is a bare case of how AI evaluation can implement unfairness and challenge belief.

Critical Analysis: Efficiency vs. Epistemology

The computerization of grade saves educator vast creativity, potentially releasing them for higher-order communications. Though, it risks plummeting multifaceted, multimodal scholar job to what is computationally understandable. An AI can evaluate sentence structure, and observance to a rubric, but can it distinguish within a narrative dispute, an influential figure of speech, or an imaginative blend of ideas obtainable in a record article? The over-reliance on AI evaluation may unintentionally slim the set of courses to what AI can score, sideline the untidy, artistic, and serious form of literacy that are fundamental for the prospect. Assessments have to remain not just as computerized scores, but as a *multimodal conversation* among student, teacher, and AI, where the AI's logical supremacy is used to notify, not put back, human being academic decision.

Therefore, employing artificial intelligence (AI) to grade tests and quizzes could be beneficial as it seeks to simplify and enhance the grading process AI in education isn't only about automating tasks; it's also about making learning better. AI apps can give students fast feedback, change the test based on how well they do, and check on their progress in real time during formative assessment. It can also assist in automating the grading of several types of tasks, such as multiple-choice questions, open-ended questions, and even programming assignments. AI also reduces things like grading prejudice and makes sure that all students get the same outcomes, no matter what their background is.

This chapter looks at new technologies, especially AI tools, that can be used to give feedback and assessments in e-learning. This article explores the various applications of AI in adaptive grading, feedback provision, and even proctoring. The article also talks about the benefits of using AI, such as its ability to scale, its ability to reduce bias, and its ability to help teachers. It also talks about the pros and downsides of using AI in learning. As e-learning assessments continue to develop, embedded AI is likely to play a big role in their future (Yakkala, 2024; Zhang & Aslan, 2021).

Assessment started a never-ending cycle of improvement and shows that learning has taken place. In higher education, assessment and feedback are considered very important because they affect everyone involved, including students, teachers, and administrators. Teachers spend a lot of time giving feedback and grading, but there hasn't been much progress in figuring out how to plan assessments, supply reliable feedback, and study the effects of both in college (Lynam & Cachia, 2018). The importance of evaluation in higher education enhances their ability to grade, their motivation, their performance, and their ability to learn (Umar, 2018) .

As electronic technologies and information science improve, we are moving toward a world where computers are being made and programmed to satisfy human needs while being smarter (Sujith et al., 2022; Y. Zhang et al., 2021). A lot of scholars have talked about how important and powerful assessments are for students' learning in college. The function of evaluation and feedback has grown in recent years. It now includes not only students but also curriculum design, teachers' directions, and administrators' settings. Assessment helps kids learn better and is a big part of their future success (Pereira et al., 2016). Many people feel that AI will be one of the most beneficial technologies in the next few years, along with robots, virtual worlds, 3D printing, and the Internet (Holmes, 2018). There are also many suggested frameworks for evaluation that can help pupils learn better.

AI AS A RESEARCH AND WRITING TOOL

AI's invasion into the conservatory extends to the very core of academic practice: do research and work. These tools reshape the literacy practice of students and academics, contribution to both authoritative support and airs basic question concerning authorship and academic work.

The AI-Augmented Research Workflow

AI now assists crossways in the study lifecycle. Tools like Semantic Scholar and Elicit use AI to examine millions of documents, summarizing conclusions, identify key papers, and even signifying research gaps. For data examination, AI-powered features in tools like NVivo can carry out automatic code of qualitative statistics, sentiment analysis, and idea finding. In the writing stage, Large Language Models (LLMs) like ChatGPT can help suggest thoughts, sketch papers, outline section, improve verbal communication, and make abstract (Huang & Tan, 2023; Khalifa & Albadawy, 2024). Citation managers like Zotero and Mendeley have improved with AI and can advise the related literature base on one's documentation.

Scenario: A Graduate Student's Dilemma

Consider XYZ, a graduate scholar scripting her thesis. She uses an AI tool to demeanor a preface literature evaluation, which professionally cluster related papers. She uses ChatGPT to conquer writer's wedge for a hard preliminary section, then uses Grammarly to spark her style. Her workflow is exponentially quicker. However, innovative literacy challenges occur. Does she truly recognize the synthesized literature, or has she outsourced the fusion? Is the voice in the preface hers or the AI's? When her AI-augmented citation manager misses a decisive but less-cited paper from the worldwide South, is her literature review perpetuate an algorithmic unfairness in academic interest? Her achievement is no longer now about the concluding result, but about her met cognitive capability to coordinate these AI tools evidently, significantly, and morally.

Ethical Considerations: Plagiarism, Originality, and Academic Integrity

The availability of AI-generated text raises a challenge in determining between genuine assistance and academic illicit use. Therefore, educational institutions are now updating their plagiarism policies to embrace the consequences of AI co-authorship. Additionally, AI technological innovation radically challenges the literary values of the individual's original author. It calls for a reconsideration of writing, often perceived as a process of curation, reorganization, and intelligent editing. The critical literacy required in this scenario demands an understanding of the probabilistic nature of large language models (LLMs), which generate possible text rather than legitimate claims, in addition to the validation of all information sourced from AI and the accessible release of its Use The ultimately goal is to prevent AI from assisting as a shortcut that overcomes the profound, critical engagement that research and writing are meant to cultivate.

AI is changing education by making learning more personal and tutoring more intelligent. But there are ethical issues that need to be dealt with, such as algorithmic bias, data privacy, and the digital divide. The study's goal is to look into different AI technologies, how often they are used, and how students feel about them as learning tools. This will help address these issues in education (Vieriu & Petrea, 2025).

The article talks about six main ways that AI makes research easier. It shows how it helps in coming up with ideas, writing material, reviewing literature, managing data, editing, reviewing, and publishing. It also shows how it may help students write better by proofreading, editing, and composing abstracts. Lastly, it talks about how it helps with communication, outreach, and following the rules (Huang & Tan, 2023; Khalifa & Albadawy, 2024).

AI can help with six parts of research: coming up with ideas, designing research, making and organizing material, reviewing and analyzing literature, managing and analyzing data, editing and publishing, communicating, reaching out, and making sure that research is done ethically and with integrity. Some of these areas are coming up with ideas, planning research, writing material, reviewing and analyzing literature, managing data, editing and publishing, communicating, reaching out, and making sure that ethics and integrity are upheld (Alshater, 2022; Khalifa & Albadawy, 2024; Kocak et al., 2023).

Discussion and In-Depth Study

AI systems that help with writing, managing literature, spotting plagiarism, and analyzing data all make academic writing and research better. To manage citations, organize your work, and use a word processor, you need Zotero, Mendeley, and End-

Note. It's not possible to write or make text. ChatGPT from OpenAI and Grammarly both check for plagiarism and help you write better. Turnitin and Copyscape are good at finding plagiarism, but they can't process text or analyze data. Tableau makes hard-to-understand data easier to understand, but it doesn't have any AI-generated content. AI systems tailored for specific tasks, like ArXiv and Semantic Scholar, make it easier to find scholarly papers. Tools for analyzing qualitative data, such as NVivo, MAXQDA, Leximancer, Quirkos, ATLAS.ti, and Dedoose, can automatically code, find patterns, and analyze feelings (Khalifa & Albadawy, 2024).

AI is changing science and education by gathering information from a lot of different places to make new research plans and ideas. It helps you find gaps in the literature, make guesses about relationships and causes, and come up with new ideas. AI can also help make and organize research materials, but caution should be applied because AI can also make fake scientific papers. AI also helps with organizing and planning research, which makes it easier to read.AI helps put together and check books, making sure that they are honest. AI enhances data analysis, research, and academic paper comprehension. AI Publishing Help ensures fairness, while maintaining open, honest, and human communication in scientific communication (Májovský et al., 2023; Semrl et al., 2023).

Using Artificial Intelligence in Online Learning

More AI technologies are making online learning better for both teachers and students. Some of these answers are adaptive tests, Jill Watson, an AI teaching assistant, and an AI grading system. It's not clear yet how new shoulder pads will change the ways students and teachers interact.(Goel & Polepeddi, 2018). They claim Proctorio, which keeps an eye on students and their computers to stop cheating, makes them feel uneasy and anxious when they take tests.(*Students Struggle with Online Test Proctoring Systems*, 2020) Researchers say that Squirrel AI, which helps kids learn in different ways, stops them from being creative. These systems are able to select teaching strategies, evaluate student learning, and self-read data. Speed Dating with Storyboards looks at how AI technology affects the way students and teachers interact. Learn when teachers and kids think AI systems are "intrusive" (Beard, 2020; Seo et al., 2021).

This study asks teachers and students how AI technologies affect online class interactions. The study examined sites that needed greater care and where AI systems kept people interested throughout the COVID-19 pandemic. The project created eleven four-cut storyboards using "Speed Dating with Storyboards" to demonstrate how AI may be utilized in online learning. The study examines how teachers and students view AI systems' impact on student-teacher relationships (Zimmerman & Forlizzi, 2017).

The study found that AI systems can boost online learner-instructor engagement by improving communication and providing tailored support. Teachers and students believe that AI may foster connection and support, but they worry about misconceptions, accountability, and social boundary violations. To successfully integrate AI in education, these benefits and challenges must be balanced (Seo et al., 2021; Tsai et al., 2020).

AI technologies affect how students and teachers interact based on their perspectives. Teachers assume AI can answer repeated questions, while students think its anonymity and quality will make them less self-conscious. Unreliability and disputes are concerns. AI can help personalize learning, but too much can hinder exploration. Students think AI will improve privacy and connections, but teachers worry about surveillance. Both groups disagree on AI in education's pros and disadvantages (Tsai et al., 2020).

ETHICAL, SOCIAL, AND PEDAGOGICAL CONSIDERATION

The application discusses previous require assessment within a multifaceted principled structure.

This section aims to incorporate and complicated on the significant concern that have been addressed all through the section.

Algorithmic Bias and Equity

AI systems, which was discovered from sequential statistics, frequently amalgamate society bias. For example, an AI grade put into practice capable on essay from privileged cluster might undervalue figurative style extensive in other imaginative or socio monetary circumstance (Noble, 2018). In addition, adaptive association could directly scholar from under-resourced discipline towards remedial way bottom on innovative arrangement, thereby expansion a self-fulfilling forecast of reduce achievement. As a result, focus on this matter damages the arrangement of a diverse planning team, the execution of algorithmic audit, and an academic pledge to utilize AI to recognize and correct unfairness, rather than strengthening it.

Data Privacy, Surveillance, and the Loss of Autonomy

The "personalization engine" functions at the same time as an "observation engine." The careful data gathering surrounding each communication, interruption, and fault, facilitates the building of complicated behavioral profile. Possession of this information, its application, and the possible for predict prospect presentation to limit opportunity are all relevant questions. The enveloping observation surroundings, as established by proctor software, undermine the belief and academic investigation that are primary to the knowledge process. Consequently, policies such as the General Data Protection Regulation (GDPR) within instructive context, beside clear information authority agreement, are of principal significance. In addition, from a pedagogical viewpoint, students must be given training on digital nationality, especially concerning their information privileges.

The Digital Divide and Access

The assure of AI-enriched learning risk creating a new tiered scheme: the AI-haves and have-nots. More affluent schools and students will have right of entry to stylish, human-supported AI tools, while beneath fund school may get uncovered downward, automatic system that reinstate individual teachers. This "enlightening AI divide" could make worse obtainable inequality on a worldwide level. Ensuring evenhanded right of entry is a basic rule confront.

Teacher and Student Agency

A constant alarm is the decrease professionalism of education, plummeting educator to "AI overseer." equally, well-made AI be supposed to expand teacher, automate managerial everyday jobs (grade, presence) and as long as wealthy analytic insight, so teacher can spotlight on mentorship, facilitate debate, and sustaining social-emotional knowledge. Similarly, scholar organization must be preserved. Education platform must comprise "take priority over" option, allow student to decide their individual course, query the AI's recommendation, and connect in autonomous, multimodal project.

AI IN ONLINE LEARNING: COMMUNICATION AND RENDEZVOUS

Online knowledge environments are the principal tested for numerous AI applications. Here, AI in a straight line mediate the critical association involving beginner and lecturer.

AI Teaching Assistants and Communication

Systems similar to Watson, an AI training assistant urbanized at Georgia Tech, can respond schedule scholar question in chat forums 24/7, let go human being instructor for more multifaceted intervention (Goel & Polepeddi, 2018). This can give instant assistance. Research via Seo et al. (2021), though, reveals subtle perception. Student appreciates the steady accessibility and ambiguity for "straightforward" question, which can decrease concern. Instructor worth the condensed managerial load. But equally cluster state concerning inaccurate communication if the AI misunderstand a subtle inquiry, in addition to a fret that over-reliance on AI might make the educational process less personal.

Designing for Human-AI Collaboration

The input verdict from communication study is so as to AI be supposed to be intended as a *complement*, not a substitute, for individual association. AI must make easy, not dominate, announcement. For example, an AI could ensign a scholar who is frequently stressed with a perception and confidentially alerts the human being trainer to arrive at out. It might sum up discussion for the trainer, highlighting point of uncertainty or dispute. The objective is to make use of AI to *augment individual thoughtfulness*, not to replicate a person association. The most effectual online environment will be those that considerately compose the role of the individual trainer, the AI system, and the examiner culture.

FUTURE DIRECTIONS AND RECOMMENDATIONS

As AIs evolve, so must our educational and strategy frameworks. The opportunity lies in focused integration, not inactive acceptance.

Developing Significant AI Literacy

The supreme advice is to implant significant AI Literacy across the prospectus. This involves:

- Functional Literacy: Accepting how AI tools operate and how to utilize them efficiently.
- Critical Literacy: Inquiring about the principles, bias, and profit-making welfare entrenched in AI system. Analyze who recompenses and who might be debilitated.
- Ethical and Democratic Literacy: Attractive in deliberations about information human rights, algorithmic justice, and the kind of prospect we want to construct with AI.

This literacy should be refined for both students *and* teachers through specialized growth.

Policy and Governance

Enlightening institutions need obvious, moral rules for AI procurement and utilization. These must authorize algorithmic lucidity, require evenhandedness crash assessment, implement authoritarian information privacy standards, and set up clear policies on AI-assisted authorship. Government has a role in financial support for research on fair AI in teaching and adaptable the Educational Technology market to save from harm to learner.

Research Plan

Upcoming research should go further than tool-center study to longitudinal investigation of AI's impact on education disposition, imagination, and integrity. It should discover pedagogical models for human-AI teamwork and expand healthy frameworks for assessing the versatile outcome of AI-integrated teaching.

CONCLUSION

AI is irreversibly altering the topography of teaching and literacy. Its authority to personalize knowledge, offer immediate response, and expand logical job is indisputable. In this section, we have argued that this authority does not mechanically lead to improved teaching or in additional significant description of success. Throughout the lenses of multimodal literacy and significant pedagogy, we have examined how AI can both enlarge and restrain learners' meaning-making capacity, often in the same illustration.

The redefinition of success in the age of AI, consequently, cannot be calculated by effectiveness or test score only. Accurate success will be characterized by:

1. Agency: Learner who can competently use AI tools while maintaining academic sovereignty and the ability for significant decision.
2. Critical Literacy: Educator in addition to student who can cross-examine the biased, moral, and social scope of the AI system that act as a go-between their knowledge.
3. Equity: An educational ecology that uses AI to recognize and association gaps, not expand them.

4. Human-Centricity: Knowledge environments where AI handle the transactional, releasing human involvement for the transformation in the mentorship, motivation, and multifaceted conversation that stay in the spirit of teaching.

The pathway ahead is not to refuse AI, but to connect with it seriously, imaginatively, and morally. By doing so, we can reach the potential not to return individual teacher or homogenize individual mind, but to develop more varied, empower, and intensely knowledgeable learner, ready to appearance their possess futures and a just world. The achievement of the AI age in teaching will be strong-minded not by the complexity of our algorithms, but by the knowledge of our pedagogy and the power of our moral commitment.

REFERENCES

Alshater, M. M. (2022). Exploring the role of artificial intelligence in enhancing academic performance: A case study of ChatGPT. *Available at SSRN* 4312358. DOI: 10.2139/ssrn.4312358

Beard, A. (2020, March 19). Can computers ever replace the classroom? *The Guardian.* https://www.theguardian.com/technology/2020/mar/19/can-computers-ever-replace-the-classroom

Buolamwini, J., & Gebru, T. (2018). Gender shades: Intersectional accuracy disparities in commercial gender classification. *Proceedings of the 1st Conference on Fairness, Accountability and Transparency*, 77–91.

Cope, B., & Kalantzis, M. (2015). The things you do to know: An introduction to the pedagogy of multiliteracies. In Cope, B., & Kalantzis, M. (Eds.), *A Pedagogy of Multiliteracies: Learning by Design* (pp. 1–36). Palgrave Macmillan. DOI: 10.1057/9781137539724_1

Freire, P. (2000). *Pedagogy of the oppressed* (30th anniversary ed.). Continuum.

Goel, A. K., & Polepeddi, L. (2018). Jill Watson: A virtual teaching assistant for online education. In Dede, C., Richards, J., & Saxberg, B. (Eds.), *Learning Engineering for Online Education* (pp. 120–143). Routledge. DOI: 10.4324/9781351186193-7

Holmes, N. (2018). Engaging with assessment: Increasing student engagement through continuous assessment. *Active Learning in Higher Education, 19*(1), 23–34. DOI: 10.1177/1469787417723230

Hooda, M., Rana, C., Dahiya, O., Rizwan, A., & Hossain, M. S. (2022). Artificial Intelligence for assessment and feedback to enhance student success in higher education. *Mathematical Problems in Engineering, 2022*, 1–19. DOI: 10.1155/2022/5215722

Huang, J., & Tan, M. (2023). The role of ChatGPT in scientific communication: Writing better scientific review articles. *American Journal of Cancer Research, 13*(4), 1148. PMID: 37168339

Khalifa, M., & Albadawy, M. (2024). Using artificial intelligence in academic writing and research: An essential productivity tool. *Computer Methods and Programs in Biomedicine Update, 5*, 100145. DOI: 10.1016/j.cmpbup.2024.100145

Kocak, B., Baessler, B., Bakas, S., Cuocolo, R., Fedorov, A., Maier-Hein, L., Mercaldo, N., Müller, H., Orlhac, F., Pinto dos Santos, D., Stanzione, A., Ugga, L., & Zwanenburg, A. (2023). CheckList for EvaluAtion of Radiomics research (CLEAR): A step-by-step reporting guideline for authors and reviewers endorsed by ESR and EuSoMII. *Insights Into Imaging*, *14*(1), 75. DOI: 10.1186/s13244-023-01415-8 PMID: 37142815

Kress, G. (2010). *Multimodality: A social semiotic approach to contemporary communication*. Routledge.

Lynam, S., & Cachia, M. (2018). Students' perceptions of the role of assessments at higher education. *Assessment & Evaluation in Higher Education*, *43*(2), 223–234. DOI: 10.1080/02602938.2017.1329928

Májovský, M., Černý, M., Kasal, M., Komarc, M., & Netuka, D. (2023). Artificial intelligence can generate fraudulent but authentic-looking scientific medical articles: Pandora's box has been opened. *Journal of Medical Internet Research*, *25*(1), e46924. DOI: 10.2196/46924 PMID: 37256685

Noble, S. U. (2018). *Algorithms of oppression: How search engines reinforce racism*. NYU Press. DOI: 10.18574/nyu/9781479833641.001.0001

Pereira, D., Flores, M. A., & Niklasson, L. (2016). Assessment revisited: A review of research in *Assessment and Evaluation in Higher Education*. *Assessment & Evaluation in Higher Education*, *41*(7), 1008–1032. DOI: 10.1080/02602938.2015.1055233

Semrl, N., Feigl, S., Taumberger, N., Bracic, T., Fluhr, H., Blockeel, C., & Kollmann, M. (2023). AI language models in human reproduction research: Exploring ChatGPT's potential to assist academic writing. *Human Reproduction (Oxford, England)*, *38*(12), 2281–2288. DOI: 10.1093/humrep/dead207 PMID: 37833847

Seo, K., Tang, J., Roll, I., Fels, S., & Yoon, D. (2021). The impact of artificial intelligence on learner–instructor interaction in online learning. *International Journal of Educational Technology in Higher Education*, *18*(1), 54. DOI: 10.1186/s41239-021-00292-9 PMID: 34778540

Students struggle with online test proctoring systems. (2020, December 17). BYU Daily Universe. https://universe.byu.edu/2020/12/17/students-struggle-with-online-test-proctoring-systems/

Sujith, A. V. L. N., Sajja, G. S., Mahalakshmi, V., Nuhmani, S., & Prasanalakshmi, B. (2022). Systematic review of smart health monitoring using deep learning and Artificial intelligence. *Neuroscience Informatics (Online)*, *2*(3), 100028. DOI: 10.1016/j.neuri.2021.100028

Tsai, Y.-S., Whitelock-Wainwright, A., & Gašević, D. (2020). The privacy paradox and its implications for learning analytics. *Proceedings of the Tenth International Conference on Learning Analytics & Knowledge*, 230–239. DOI: 10.1145/3375462.3375536

Umar, A. M. A.-T. (2018). The impact of assessment for learning on students' achievement in English for specific purposes: A case study of pre-medical students at Khartoum University: Sudan. *English Language Teaching*, *11*(2), 15–26. DOI: 10.5539/elt.v11n2p15

Vieriu, A. M., & Petrea, G. (2025). The Impact of Artificial Intelligence (AI) on students' academic development. *Education Sciences*, *15*(3), 343. DOI: 10.3390/educsci15030343

Walter, Y. (2024). Embracing the future of Artificial Intelligence in the classroom: The relevance of AI literacy, prompt engineering, and critical thinking in modern education. *International Journal of Educational Technology in Higher Education*, *21*(1), 15. DOI: 10.1186/s41239-024-00448-3

Yakkala, K. K.Krishna Kashyap Yakkala. (2024). AI-powered assessment tools for E-learning: Enhancing feedback and grading systems. *World Journal of Advanced Engineering Technology and Sciences*, *13*(1), 792–802. DOI: 10.30574/wjaets.2024.13.1.0497

Zhang, K., & Aslan, A. B. (2021). AI technologies for education: Recent research & future directions. *Computers and Education: Artificial Intelligence*, *2*, 100025. DOI: 10.1016/j.caeai.2021.100025

Zhang, Y., Kou, X., Song, Z., Fan, Y., Usman, M., & Jagota, V. (2021). Research on logistics management layout optimization and real-time application based on nonlinear programming. *Nonlinear Engineering*, *10*(1), 526–534. https://doi.org/doi:10.1515/nleng-2021-0043. DOI: 10.1515/nleng-2021-0043

Zimmerman, J., & Forlizzi, J. (2017). Speed dating: Providing a menu of possible futures. *She Ji: The Journal of Design, Economics, and Innovation*, *3*(1), 30–50. DOI: 10.1016/j.sheji.2017.08.003

Chapter 3

Artificial Intelligence in Education: Creativity, Literacy, and Human Agency in AI-Enhanced Learning Environments

Renalyn Joy Ruiz Alonsabe
http://orcid.org/0009-0005-2322-4001
Artemio L. Martin Integrated School, Philippines

Amera C. Malaco
http://orcid.org/0000-0002-3813-5889
Sultan Kudarat State University, Philippines

Leslie C. Elevado
http://orcid.org/0009-0005-5612-2511
Davao del Sur State College, Philippines

Fahad A. Salendab
http://orcid.org/0000-0003-4459-443X
Sultan Kudarat State University, Philippines

ABSTRACT

This chapter examines the transformative role of artificial intelligence (AI) in reshaping creativity and literacy within educational contexts. Drawing on recent empirical studies, conceptual frameworks, and illustrative case examples, it explores how AI-enhanced learning environments influence reading, writing, creative thinking, and meaning-making. Creativity and literacy are conceptualized as multidimensional constructs encompassing multimodal, digital, computational, and AI literacies. The

DOI: 10.4018/979-8-2600-2163-7.ch003

chapter highlights evidence that AI can enhance learner engagement, personalization, and creative ideation when integrated through pedagogically sound and ethically informed practices. It also addresses risks such as overreliance, reduced cognitive autonomy, homogenization of creative outputs, and persistent inequities, concluding with recommendations for ethical, human-centered AI integration.

INTRODUCTION

Creativity and literacy in the 21st century have moved beyond traditional literacy practices such as reading and writing to include multimodal literacy, digital literacy, and AI literacy. In the education domain, the rapid development of AI technologies has changed the dynamics of how learners learn and how they make meaning and generate new ideas (Bećirović et al., 2025).

In the education domain, AI has emerged as a critical component of facilitating personalized learning, giving immediate feedback, and assisting in creative activities. Research has indicated that the integration of AI in the classroom has a positive impact on enhancing the creative performance of students; however, it is critical that the engagement level of the students is high and that both the students and teachers have high AI literacy skills (Zhou & Peng, 2025). AI has emerged as a critical component of the classroom; however, it has also emerged as a partner for co-creative activities with human beings, prompting a critical analysis of the concept of collaboration in the classroom (Romero, 2025).

As AI becomes a critical component of literacy education, it has also changed the dynamics of how students make meaning of texts and how they produce texts for both creative and non-creative purposes. For instance, AI story writing has shown promising results for enhancing digital literacy and 21st-century competencies for preservice teachers; however, it is critical that AI integration in literacy education is done in a manner that is pedagogically sound (Bircan et al., 2025).

In spite of these opportunities, the increasing trend of AI also poses critical challenges of over-reliance on AI results, decreased cognitive engagement, and decreased diversity of creative expression. Some emerging research findings show that AI may result in decreased diversity of ideas compared to human-only processes. This underlines the importance of pedagogical approaches that ensure creativity and originality of thought (Romero, 2025). In addition, there are also ethical issues related to authorship, equity of access, and teacher preparedness that point to systemic challenges related to the integration of AI in education.

In light of these considerations, this chapter explores the impact of artificial intelligence on human creativity and literacy in various contexts. This chapter draws upon emerging research findings, conceptual perspectives, and pedagogical approaches.

Through an examination of the emerging trends in AI-mediated learning through evidence-based perspectives, this chapter argues that the value of AI in education lies in enhancing human potential rather than replacing it.

THE EVOLUTION OF LITERACY IN AI-ENRICHED CONTEXTS

Redefining Literacy

The construct of literacy in the context of contemporary education has undergone a tremendous shift in its scope, moving beyond the confines of print literacy to include various forms of digital, computational, artificial intelligence-related, and multimodal literacy. This shift is a reflection of the changing nature of the learning environment in which the construction of knowledge is increasingly influenced by the integration of various forms of text, images, audio, and even artificial intelligence. In the context of multimodal literacy, for instance, there is an increased focus on the role of the learner in the construction of knowledge through various forms of semiotics. In fact, Carcamo and Pino (2025) have pointed out the positive impact of the inclusion of infographics in the context of the classroom, as reflected in the enhanced reading comprehension of the students. An analysis of the perception of the instructor, as reflected in the logs of the teachers, reveals the effectiveness of the content in the context of print literacy and the need for additional support in the context of the first language.

Multimodal literacy is also linked to the notion of digital literacy, which refers to the various competencies required to effectively engage in the process of accessing, evaluating, and communicating information through digital technologies. In fact, the impact of artificial intelligence has been found to be tremendous in the context of the development of creative thinking, as reflected in the findings of Agaoglu et al. (2025). In the context of the present framework, digital literacy is proposed to act as a mediator in the context of the impact of artificial intelligence on the development of creative thinking. This is a reflection of the proposed notion of digital literacy as a prerequisite for the development of higher-order thinking skills in the context of the changing nature of technology.

Apart from this, the concept of computational literacy has emerged as another essential aspect of the broader concept of literacy in the context of the AI era. The concept of computational literacy refers to the knowledge of the ways in which algorithms, data, and models function and impact decision-making processes. The current study undertaken by Guan et al. (2025) focuses on the interactive mechanisms and factors that shape the relationship between the levels of high school students' computational thinking and their AI literacy, along with the ways in which the background of the students contributes to the development of AI literacy and computational thinking. The results of the study indicate that the background of the students, such as gender and the location of the families, influences the levels of creativity, algorithmic thinking, and critical thinking positively and negatively. However, there is a significant impact of the educational level of the parents and the use of AI tools on the AI knowledge and skills of the students. Additionally, there is a positive correlation between the dimensions of computational thinking and artificial intelligence literacy. The data indicate that the concept of computational literacy acts as a cognitive bridge between AI-enabled activities and the broader concept of traditional literacy.

Within this framework, the concept of AI literacy has become a crucial and distinct aspect of the broad notion of literacy. The concept of AI literacy refers to the ability of the learner to comprehend the concepts of AI, interact with AI, and critically evaluate the results produced by AI. According to the findings of Almatrafi et al. (2024), the importance of AI literacy has become increasingly significant in the current technological environment, emphasizing the need for learners to acquire the knowledge and skills they need to interact with AI. The importance of this concept is reinforced by the findings of Kaplan & Meylani (2025), which examine the aspects of AI literacy, its application in the professional and educational sectors, and the challenges related to its implementation.

Studies related to the empirical investigation of the effects of AI on the academic literacy of university students provide a clear understanding of the impact of AI on the academic literacy of learners. Baldrich et al. (2025) argue that academic writing and reading are crucial aspects of academic literacy in the university context, which allow the learner to become part of the academic community and gain access to knowledge. The five critical aspects identified by the researchers include the effect of AI on the acquisition of academic literacy, the ethical aspects related to authorship, the need for critical digital literacy, the level of preparedness and attitudes, and the need for redefining the assessment criteria. The importance of this study lies in the fact that the critical aspect of the academic literacy of the learner is intrinsically linked with the concept of AI literacy.

In addition, the importance of AI literacy is increasingly recognized as a global educational priority. Mansoor et al. (2024) pointed out the presence of regional variations in the levels of AI literacy. This again emphasizes the importance of the integration of AI literacy in the curriculum. In the earlier stages of education, Yim & Su (2025) defined AI literacy as having a fluid concept of digital literacy, such as interacting and co-working with AI, computational thinking, critical data literacy, and AI ethics.

Further, the connection between multimodal literacy and AI literacy is becoming more obvious in the context of language and literacy education. Nguyen & Nguyen

(2025) pointed out the importance of the integration of AI literacy in the curriculum, as it increases creativity through the process of iterative revision and co-creation, while non-AI literacy frameworks focus more on structural coherence.

AI's Role in Literacy Development

Artificial intelligence is gradually reshaping the literacy learning process by changing how students learn to read, write, and think critically across different educational levels. AI-based writing tools include automated feedback tools, grammar and coherence checkers, and idea generators that help students learn how to write more fluently and accurately in a scholarly manner. According to Chen and Gong (2025), AI-based learning tools have the potential to improve students' performance by helping them learn more efficiently, creating a favorable learning environment for students, and enhancing their motivation levels. Baldrich et al. (2025) also argued that AI-based tools have the potential to change the way students improve their reading and writing skills in a scholarly manner by allowing students to engage with academic communities and access knowledge within those communities.

In terms of reading education, AI-based tools have the potential to improve students' abilities to read and comprehend texts more accurately by using adaptive questioning strategies, vocabulary tools, and metacognitive strategies to improve students' higher-order literacy abilities, such as synthesis and evaluation of texts. Shafiee Rad (2025) argued that AI-based intervention has a positive effect on students' engagement with texts since it improves their motivation levels, participation rates, and attentiveness while interacting with AI-based tools. According to Shafiee Rad's qualitative research findings, a majority of students who were exposed to AI-based tools argued that they were effective in enhancing self-regulation and participation while interacting with AI-based tools; however, they also emphasized how AI-based tools enhanced their motivation levels and attentiveness while interacting with AI-based tools. According to Silor & Silor's research findings, students who were exposed to AI-based adaptive tools showed marked improvement in terms of reading comprehension abilities across different proficiency levels.

Adaptive learning systems take literacy instruction a step further by matching learning with the changing needs of the learner. In this regard, there is a tremendous potential for AI systems to improve learning outcomes and critical thinking capabilities of the learner, as emphasized by Ismaili (2024). In addition, Alazemi (2024) has demonstrated the potential of AI-based formative assessment tools to improve academic and psychological outcomes of the learner. In this context, AI systems are positioned as a vital tool for a shift from universal literacy training to learner-centered training through data-driven instruction facilitated by a personalized approach.

Another significant contribution of AI systems is their potential to promote multilingualism and inclusivity in literacy training. AI-based translation tools, text-to-speech tools, and language learning tools assist learners in gaining access to texts in their first language or preferred language. In this regard, AI systems play a vital role in promoting inclusivity by reducing linguistic barriers to understanding and learning. AI systems assist learners in becoming fluent and understanding texts better by providing real-time language support and contextual translations. In this context, AI systems are positioned to improve reading fluency and comprehension at a large scale, as emphasized by Seerat (2025), who has highlighted the potential of AI-based tools to improve reading comprehension and engagement of multilingual learners. Olszak (2025) has also demonstrated a rich understanding of the potential of AI systems by indicating that AI tools improved the overall metacognitive awareness of the learner while reading difficult texts and also increased the autonomy of the learner while drafting, revising, and analyzing texts.

In addition, AI-based assistive technologies provide a wide range of opportunities for the development of literacy among people with disabilities. In this regard, Yang & Taele (2025) show that AI-based assistive technologies provide improved reading comprehension and writing organization among people with visual impairments and autism spectrum disorder. This further indicates the importance of AI in the development of literacy.

Table 1. AI's Role in Literacy Development: A Synthesis of Functions and Key Insights

AI Application Area	Description	Key Contributions to Literacy Development
AI-Assisted Writing Tools	Includes automated feedback systems, grammar and coherence checkers, and idea-generation platforms	Enhances writing fluency, organization, accuracy, and revision skills; supports academic writing and disciplinary literacy
Automated Feedback and Assessment	Provides immediate, personalized responses to learners' writing and reading tasks	Promotes self-regulation, formative learning, and metacognitive awareness
AI-Supported Reading Comprehension Tools	Uses adaptive questioning, vocabulary scaffolding, and metacognitive prompts	Improves comprehension, engagement, motivation, synthesis, and evaluative reading skills
Adaptive Learning Platforms	Adjust text difficulty, pacing, and instructional strategies using learning analytics	Enables individualized literacy development and supports learner-centered instruction
Critical Thinking Enhancement	Encourages analysis, reflection, and evaluation of AI-generated and human-authored texts	Strengthens higher-order literacy skills and critical digital literacy

continued on following page

Table 1. Continued

AI Application Area	Description	Key Contributions to Literacy Development
Multilingual Literacy Support	AI-powered translation, language modeling, and first-language scaffolds	Reduces linguistic barriers and supports comprehension for multilingual learners
Accessibility and Assistive Technologies	Includes text-to-speech, speech-to-text, screen readers, and adaptive writing tools	Expands literacy access for learners with disabilities and diverse learning needs
Metacognitive Literacy Development	Supports planning, monitoring, and evaluating reading and writing processes	Enhances learner autonomy and reflective literacy practices

Challenges and Risks

While AI holds considerable promise for enhancing learning and literacy, its adoption in the academic sphere also raises considerable challenges and threats. One major concern, for instance, is the possibility of over-reliance on AI-generated content, which might compromise fundamental literacy, critical thinking, and independent problem-solving competencies. To mitigate this threat to academic integrity, Ncube et al. (2026) highlight the importance of AI-resistant, process-based assessments such as oral examinations and multi-stage evaluations. In addition, the authors also stress the importance of AI policies in the academic sphere, as well as the implementation of digital literacy programs to ensure responsible AI use and curb academic dishonesty. In another related study, Prambudi et al. (2024) found that the majority of students perceive AI as invaluable for enriching their understanding, productivity, and creativity in academic tasks. The students argue that AI tools help them stimulate their idea generation, thus encouraging them to look at issues from different perspectives. However, the students also perceive the possibility of over-reliance on AI tools, which might compromise their critical thinking and independent competencies.

Tied to overreliance are information misrepresentation, bias, and ethics. AI produces information based on the information it was trained on, which could include misinformed or biased information. Such information could lead to a perpetuation of inequality if the learner adopts it without a critical examination of the information produced by the AI. According to Lim et al. (2025), AI has greatly enhanced the accuracy and efficiency of educational assessments. However, such a move has also created salient ethical concerns that include bias in grading, threats to data privacy, and a lack of accountability. The formulation of a framework for ethics is therefore important since it could undermine the use of AI in assessments and education in general. According to Llerena-Izquierdo and Ayala-Carabajo (2025), AI incorporation in education poses both human and ethical risks and opportunities of great significance. The risks include the erosion of critical thinking, overdependence on technology, and the homogenization of thought. The opportunities include the optimization of research and the promotion of personalized learning. To ensure that AI becomes an augmenting tool rather than a replacement for human intellectual performance and that it becomes a tool for human action and discernment in information generation, it is important to adopt a strategy with set standards that prioritize human agency. Other ethical concerns include those related to data privacy, which pose a significant concern for the need for institutional frameworks and educators' awareness of AI use ethics.

Another major risk factor involves the challenges to critical thinking and authorship. The polished language produced by generative AI tools makes it easy for learners to fall into the trap of using the tool for tasks that require original analysis and synthesis. Leaton Gray et al. (2025) showed that overuse of AI tools for generating content can lead to learners becoming less engaged in critical thinking, thus affecting their academic integrity (Najjar et al., 2025). In addition, it has been observed that AI content detection tools, although helpful, have some limitations, such as failing to detect cleverly created AI content or mistakenly identifying content created by non-native speakers, thus creating equity issues (Perkins et al., 2024). The other major risk factor for learners using generative AI tools involves challenges to cognitive autonomy and critical thinking. It has been reported by Izquierdo-Condoy et al. (2025) that the use of Gen AI tools increased efficiency and improved the linguistic output. However, some concerns have been expressed, such as the overuse of cognitive functions, thus becoming overdependent on AI, and the lack of opportunities for learners to analyze, synthesize, and evaluate the content on their own. To overcome the challenges, teachers need to ensure the ethical use of AI tools, thus becoming an essential part of the learning process.

Table 2. Key Challenges and Risks of Artificial Intelligence Integration in Literacy and Learning

Challenge / Risk Area	Description	Implications for Literacy and Learning
Overreliance on AI Tools	Excessive dependence on AI-generated content for reading, writing, and problem-solving	Weakens foundational literacy skills, autonomy, and independent critical thinking
Erosion of Critical Thinking	Learners may accept AI outputs without questioning accuracy, logic, or relevance	Reduces opportunities for analysis, synthesis, and reflective reasoning
Threats to Academic Integrity and Authorship	AI-generated texts may replace original student work	Undermines authentic authorship, originality, and ethical scholarship
Misinformation and Algorithmic Bias	AI systems may generate inaccurate, biased, or culturally skewed content	Risks perpetuating inequities and misleading learners if outputs are uncritically accepted
Ethical and Data Privacy Concerns	AI-driven systems rely on large datasets with limited transparency	Raises issues related to data security, accountability, and trust in educational systems
Assessment Validity Challenges	Difficulty distinguishing AI-assisted work from independent student performance	Complicates fair evaluation and measurement of genuine learning outcomes
Equity and Detection Bias	AI detection tools may misclassify non-native speakers' work	Creates fairness concerns and potential discrimination in assessment
Loss of Cognitive Autonomy	Continuous AI support may replace effortful thinking	Limits learners' capacity to independently analyze, evaluate, and create knowledge
Homogenization of Ideas	AI-generated content may encourage standardized responses	Reduces originality, diversity of perspectives, and creative expression

CREATIVITY IN AI ENVIRONMENTS

Understanding AI-Augmented Creativity

Creativity in AI-based environments is now more often described as a co-creative process in which AI plays a collaborative rather than a substituting role for human creativity. Current empirical research findings on human-AI collaboration suggest that it has a positive impact on enhancing creative performance, especially in terms of ideation and exploration activities. According to Holzner et al. (2025), there is no discernible difference in terms of creative performance between humans and GenAI; however, humans who work in collaboration with GenAI are found to have a substantial performance advantage over those who do not collaborate with GenAI models. Nevertheless, the scope of idea generation in human collaboration with GenAI is considerably limited. In addition, Wang et al. (2025) found that the application of the Human-AI Co-Creative Design Process (HAI-CDP) model has a substantial impact on enhancing creative performance compared to the traditional design process. The most important advantage of the HAI-CDP for inexperienced designers is related to idea generation, while for experienced designers, it is related to the quality of creative outcomes.

The presence of AI-augmented creativity can be observed in various fields, such as design, visual arts, music, writing, and problem-solving, where the tools based on generative AI extend the range of the possible. In the field of graphic design, AI-based co-creative tools allow designers to explore various design options while maintaining control over the aesthetic judgments involved. Martins et al. (2025) argue that the importance of artificial intelligence (AI) in the field of creativity has increased, leading to the development of tools that allow individuals to co-create during the design process. The inclusion of computational tools in the co-creative design process in the field of graphic design faces unique challenges, such as the need to strike a balance between the subjective and visual nature of the design process and the scientific nature of the tools involved. This argument is supported by the claims of Salma et al. (2025), who argue that the design field has started to transform into a co-creative process involving humans and AI tools due to the rapid development of generative AI tools in the field. The tools currently in use, however, operate in the linear "executor" mode, which is in direct conflict with the nature of human creativity.

In the context of creative education and culture production, AI tools have become increasingly important as inspiration generators, which facilitate divergent thinking. Chang (2025) reveals the evolution of AI-assisted design, which no longer remains a utility tool but a collaborative partner in the creative process, enhancing the effectiveness of the design, expanding the scope of culture, and even changing the paradigm of the design. To achieve the objective of converting cultural values into tangible forms, the concept of cultural creativity, as a method of design, combines the elements of creative thinking, culture, and technological innovation. Although the element of culture is incorporated into the design through the medium of storytelling and humor, which helps in the understanding of the historical and geographical identity of the culture, the entire process of interpreting and valuing the culture depends significantly on the expertise of the designers (Chang, 2025). Although some of the students were apprehensive about the limitations and negative aspects of using the technology, Hwang & Lee (2025) found that the students, in the context of the higher education scenario, perceived the use of generative AI technology as a constructive element for the development of ideas, efficiency, and dynamic exploration of the creative potential. Wei et al. (2025) found that the collaborative problem-solving potential of the students improved significantly by using the GenAI tools for the production of DST. The experimental group outperformed the control group in the context of team innovation, especially in the context of novelty and user experience. In addition, the research revealed that the overall attitudes of the students, although positive, were related to the use of GenAI technology for the production of DST. There were some apprehensions related to the potential of cognitive offloading, overdependence on the technology, and the lack of emotional support.

Despite these advantages, the literature has always made a clear distinction between AI's generative innovation and human originality. Heymann & Briedis (2025) argue that while artificial intelligence can offer useful information, human subjects may always prefer human-generated narratives. There are also concerns about how AI can improve the creative process by speeding up brainstorming and reducing cognitive overload. However, there are concerns about the uniqueness and variety of content created by AI. Huang et al. (2026) argue that human-GenAI collaboration at the idea generation stage has a significant effect on creative novelty by enhancing cognitive flexibility. On the other hand, human-GenAI collaboration at the concept elaboration stage has a significant effect on creative usefulness by reducing cognitive overload.

Opportunities for Human Creativity

There are many opportunities for human creativity to be enhanced in AI-augmented environments for rapid prototyping and idea generation. In a research paper by Chen et al. (2025), it was shown that while concept selection and evaluation are largely human-centric, generative AI was found to aid humans mainly in the problem characterization and idea generation phases of the creative process, with significant improvements in the idea selection and evaluation phases attributed to Generative AI. Another research paper by Holzner et al. (2025) showed that human subjects who used generative AI were found to outperform those who did not use it for creative activities, thereby proving that AI is an augmentative tool for humans for creative problem-solving and ideation.

The potential of AI for rapid prototyping and iteration is also shown in many different creative processes. For example, in a research paper by Hulekal & As (2025) on the effect of generative AI on human creativity for event theme creation and design conceptualization, it was shown that generative AI accelerates ideation, visualization, and rapid prototyping to enable human designers to explore more creative options within a much shorter period of time. Thus, while human-AI collaboration is shown to enhance human creativity and innovation, a lack of richness in prompts or datasets could potentially limit the scope of artistic diversity.

In addition, AI has been seen to impact cross-disciplinary and collaborative creative processes positively. For instance, according to Wei et al. (2025), the incorporation of GenAI tools was seen to have a significant positive effect on students' collaborative problem-solving skills during the creation of digital stories. In addition, the students were able to showcase improved performance in team creativity, specifically concerning user experience and novelty dimensions. Similar findings by Wang et al. (2025) indicate that structured human-AI collaboration has a significant positive effect on creative expression, regardless of levels of experience, implying that interdisciplinary creative work stands to gain significantly from the use of AI, specifically concerning ideation and execution.

The integration of AI within creative learning and production has been seen to have a positive effect on the democratization of creative production, specifically concerning entry barriers. For instance, according to Hwang & Lee (2025), even though some students were worried about its limitations and ethical concerns, it was observed that students were able to showcase significant improvements in their creative problem-solving skills. They were able to see the importance of AI as a tool for creative production, specifically concerning ideation, efficiency, and dynamic creative exploration. This is consistent with further findings on how AI has been effective in lowering entry barriers for creative participation, specifically concerning how people without technical skills are able to actively participate in creative processes, from digital design to storytelling (Tsao et al., 2025). According to Huang et al. (2026), through its ability to provide a range of prompts and recommendations, specifically concerning how it broadens the ideational space, AI has been able to positively impact cognitive processes concerning human creativity, specifically concerning flexibility and novelty, allowing for a positive interplay between human and AI inputs concerning creative work.

Table 3. Opportunities for Human Creativity in AI-Augmented Environments

Opportunity Area	Description	Implications for Human Creativity
AI-Supported Idea Generation	Generative AI assists during problem definition and early ideation stages	Expands ideational space, stimulates divergent thinking, and accelerates creative starts
Rapid Prototyping and Iteration	AI enables fast visualization, modeling, and refinement of creative outputs	Enhances creative agility, experimentation, and iterative improvement
Human–AI Co-Creation	Collaborative interaction between human judgment and AI-generated suggestions	Augments human creativity while preserving human-led evaluation and decision-making
Cross-Disciplinary Collaboration	AI facilitates collaboration across disciplines and expertise levels	Strengthens team creativity, shared problem-solving, and innovation outcomes

continued on following page

Table 3. Continued

Opportunity Area	Description	Implications for Human Creativity
Democratization of Creative Production	AI lowers technical and skill barriers to creative participation	Broadens access to creative expression for non-experts and novice creators
Enhanced Cognitive Flexibility	AI provides diverse prompts, perspectives, and alternatives	Improves novelty, flexibility, and creative problem-solving capacity
Educational Creativity Support	AI functions as a creative partner in learning environments	Promotes creative confidence, efficiency, and exploratory learning among students

Limitations and Ethical Considerations

Despite the rise of artificial intelligence in creative settings, various ethical and structural barriers exist to hinder its effective and ethical application. One of the contested issues is related to intellectual property and authorship rights. It is essential to understand that Generative AI is trained on vast amounts of material created by humans and thus raises concerns regarding originality and rightful ownership of such material. As Islam and Greenwood (2024) explain, Generative Artificial Intelligence (GenAI) is embedded in a framework called the "hyper commons," which is related to shared labor and input that is largely invisible and/or untraceable. Furthermore, Islam and Greenwood (2024) explain how the automation of exploiting standard input through remix and re-configuration can create an academic authorship dilemma in which moral authority for academic output is gradually erased. Bozkurt (2024) explores the ethical and legal issues related to authorship and ownership, focusing on copyright regulations and artificial intelligence, and examines the role of various GenAI functionalities and their support for transparency in maintaining academic integrity.

The other notable limitation is the issue of AI bias in creative products. As discussed in the previous paragraph, the nature of the data used to train these generative AI models is such that these products usually end up reflecting the cultural biases and norms embedded in these data sets. Barve et al. (2025) show how these products end up reflecting racial, gender, and cultural biases and stereotypes, and how these biases are not challenged by these products. Tsao et al. (2025) show how creative workers view and use GenAI in the areas of visual art and design, creative writing and literature, performing arts, and environmental and spatial design. Al-kfairy et al. (2024) highlight the ethical implications of these biases and how these biases pose a threat to society at large due to the cultural and societal impact of these creative products.

In this regard, various authors have highlighted the possible homogenization and over-standardization of creativity due to the overdependence on artificial intelligence tools for the facilitation of creative thinking and practices. For instance, Zafar et al. (2025) highlighted the various concerns and issues related to the overdependence on artificial intelligence for the facilitation of creative thinking and practices. Moreover, Karagoz (2024) showed various aspects of artificial intelligence and its possible contribution to the facilitation of creative thinking and practices; however, these tools also have certain ethical drawbacks and biases due to their possible over-standardization of creativity and thinking. In this regard, various authors have highlighted the need for an ethical framework to understand artificial intelligence as a creative partner rather than a creative authority to facilitate and promote creative thinking and practices without confining or over-standardizing these aspects of thinking and practices (Hofman, 2024; Hemraj, 2025).

AI, EQUITY, AND ACCESS

The potential of artificial intelligence lies in its transformative power in ensuring the expansion of equal opportunities for the use of creative, literacy, and learning tools. The empirical evidence suggests the potential of artificial intelligence in improving the learning outcomes and engagement of socially disadvantaged students. For example, Katona & Gyonyoru (2025) conducted a study aimed at investigating the effect of artificial intelligence-based adaptive programming education on the learning outcomes and engagement of socially disadvantaged students. The empirical evidence suggests that the use of artificial intelligence-based adaptive programming education improved the level of knowledge and comprehensive engagement of the students.

Nevertheless, not all learners immediately enjoy the advantages of artificial intelligence (AI). In addition, the digital divide is a major hindrance to the effective use of AI-based learning tools. Ahmed (2024) observes that the digital divide has continued to be a major issue that has exacerbated disparities in the use of AI-based learning tools. Socioeconomic disparities, geographical limitations, and infrastructural barriers hinder equal opportunities for all students. Such a situation has been largely experienced in developing countries. Studies conducted on disadvantaged communities show similar trends. In this case, Hongli & Leong (2024) highlight how cloud-based AI tools and mobile-based learning tools can be effective tools for bridging the digital divide and improving learning efficiency and engagement in remote areas.

Recent studies suggest that AI has the potential to contribute to the promotion of inclusive learning for diverse student populations, including those with disabilities. In this regard, Li et al. (2025) assert that despite the existing barriers to AI adoption, such as a lack of digital literacy and infrastructural barriers, AI has the potential to promote inclusivity and engagement, particularly for students with disabilities. In addition, Melo-López et al. (2025) agree with the assertion that AI has the potential to promote inclusivity by providing alternative learning materials, such as audio texts for the hearing-impaired and descriptions of images for the visually impaired. In addition, the use of AI reduces the burden of work for teachers, who can focus more on guiding their students during classroom learning.

Other scholars also highlight the need for the development of equity-based AI design and implementation models. In this case, Okonkwo & Schmid-Meier (2025) assert that AI tools should be co-designed with input from diverse populations, particularly from underrepresented groups and persons with disabilities. In the absence of such a framework, AI tools are likely to contribute to the promotion of existing inequalities.

Case Examples of Creativity and Literacy in AI-Enhanced Environments

Zhou & Peng (2025) conducted a study to examine the impact of the integration of AI in instructional settings on student creativity, considering learning engagement as a mediator and AI literacy as a moderator of the relationship between the integration of AI and student engagement in the classroom setting. The researchers used a sample of 432 university students from Sichuan Province in China. The results of the study revealed that the integration of AI in the classroom setting is highly beneficial for increasing the creativity of students; however, the role of learning engagement is also evident as a mediator between the integration of AI and student creativity. Furthermore, the role of AI literacy is also highlighted as a moderator of the relationship between the integration of AI and student engagement in the classroom setting. Moreover, the moderating role of teachers' perceived AI literacy is also highlighted in the study; the impact of the integration of AI in the classroom setting on learner engagement and, as a result, on learner creativity is more pronounced when teachers are perceived to be highly literate in terms of AI literacy; otherwise, the impact of the integration of AI is low when teachers are perceived to be low in terms of their AI literacy.

The second case study is a comprehensive synthesis of contemporary empirical research on the role of artificial intelligence in promoting creativity in various educational settings. In the case study, Urmeneta & Romero (2025) conducted a comprehensive PRISMA-based evaluation of the literature and selected 20 articles from the ScienceDirect database after carrying out a systematic review of 111 research papers on the various contexts and use cases of artificial intelligence in supporting creativity. The 20 articles present five major use cases of artificial intelligence in promoting creativity in educational settings. These include academic achievement, chatbots, diagnostics and assessment, and literature reviews and frameworks. The case study concludes that the role of artificial intelligence in promoting creativity is highly context-dependent and is linked to learner agency. While artificial intelligence is highly effective in promoting limited or incremental creativity and enhancing divergent thinking in generic contexts, high levels of automation undermine human autonomy and freedom when artificial intelligence is the primary agent of creativity. However, there is a clear trade-off in the effectiveness of artificial intelligence in promoting creativity, and the case study concludes that artificial intelligence is most effective in promoting creativity when it is combined with human creativity. In the case study, there is also a concern for the ethical and pedagogical implications of the role of artificial intelligence in promoting creativity in educational settings.

In their study, Hwang & Lee (2025) investigated university students' attitudes toward working with generative AI in the production of digital content. Students were asked to use generative AI to participate in a digital competition focused on addressing sociocultural concerns, with emphasis on improving and perfecting the output of generative AI rather than directly using its output as content for the competition. The study had two cohorts: one was a control group using digital tools only (Digital Literacy; DL), and the other was an experimental group using generative AI (Prompt Literacy; PL). The study compared the ability of each group to come up with creative problems and their level of curiosity. The findings revealed significant differences between the PL and DL groups, with the PL group showing significantly better creative problem-solving skills compared to the DL group. Although some members of the PL group expressed their concerns about the capabilities and implications of generative AI, they perceived it as a helpful tool for generating ideas, improving productivity, and providing dynamic routes for creative exploration. This study emphasizes the role of human agency with technology, and it is imperative for humans to develop digital literacy quickly, not only for understanding human-AI interaction but also for understanding human-AI collaboration. The study findings are used by the authors to explain how AI may be used to develop emergent creativity, as well as its implications for pedagogy.

FUTURE TRENDS AND RESEARCH DIRECTIONS

With the development of AI, the projected pathways for research on creativity and literacy studies reveal the possibility for the development of more integrated human-centric, ethical, and context-aware AI systems in the field of education. One major trend in this regard is the shift from the conventional use of AI tools to the development of human-AI co-creative systems, where AI not only creates but also enhances thinking, reflection, and awareness. Future research on this topic will likely focus on the impact of different types of human-AI interactions on the development of creativity, originality, and the long-term development of literacy.

Another emerging trend in this regard is the development of AI, creativity, and critical literacies as integrated constructs, not as distinct constructs. Although previous research has proven the importance of AI literacy and prompt literacy, it is necessary to carry out further research to determine the long-term development of these literacies, their interrelationship with conventional academic literacies such as reading comprehension, writing proficiency, and disciplinary thinking, and the development of AI literacy constructs for different ages, especially for K-12 students and teachers, to ensure the development of critical AI literacy for the next generation.

Equity-related issues will continue to be a primary concern. Although AI research has shown promise in democratizing access to creativity and literacy tools, the persistent digital divide suggests that future research must continue to examine the underlying determinants of AI adoption at the infrastructural and policy levels. In particular, future research should seek to build upon existing work by investigating the impact of differences in connectivity, language, disability, and socio-economic background on the ability of students to benefit maximally from AI-supported creativity and literacy development. Co-design approaches will be essential in ensuring that AI does not exacerbate existing inequalities among marginalized and underserved groups. In terms of creativity research, it is likely that future research will continue to scrutinize the trade-offs between efficiency and creativity in AI-supported creative environments. Although AI-supported creativity tools have been shown to have considerable potential in enhancing ideation and prototyping speed, future research must seek to build upon existing work by investigating the underlying determinants of AI-supported creativity. In particular, future research should seek to build upon existing work by investigating the underlying determinants of AI-supported creativity. Experimental research will be essential in establishing more definitive evidence of the impact of AI-supported creativity on human cognition.

Future studies must focus on ethical governance and assessment as a significant research area. With the integration of generative AI into academic writing, designing, and problem-solving, future studies must focus on how assessment strategies can effectively measure human learning, creativity, and critical thinking within AI-rich contexts. This means that future studies must develop process-based assessment models that are reflective and AI-transparent while recognizing the ethical use of AI without promoting uncritical dependency. Furthermore, future studies must also focus on interdisciplinary studies that bring together education, ethics, law, and computer science to address the issue of authorship and data management in AI-based learning systems.

Future studies are also expected to use longitudinal, mixed-methods, and cross-cultural designs. Since existing literature is based on short-term studies and perceptions of AI-based learning systems, there is a need for long-term studies to examine how long-term exposure to AI can impact learners' cognitive autonomy, creative identity, and literacy practices. In addition, future studies must also use comparative studies from different cultural and national contexts to develop a universal framework for AI-based creativity and literacy.

DISCUSSION

This chapter explores the effects of artificial intelligence on creativity and literacy within modern learning environments, with specific emphasis on human agency, equity, and ethical considerations. Through a synthesis of recent empirical studies, theoretical underpinnings, and case studies, the discussion underscores the point that the potential of artificial intelligence for learning within the modern classroom is not about substitution but about enhancement of human cognition, creative inquiry, and literacy potential.

One of the significant points of convergence within the existing body of literature on artificial intelligence and its effects on creativity and literacy potential is the notion that the potential of artificial intelligence for creative and literacy potential is largely dependent on learner engagement, AI literacy, and pedagogy. Indeed, the Zhou & Peng (2025) study also underscores this point by revealing that while AI by itself does not seem to contribute to creative potential, the combination of learning engagement and teacher/student AI literacy determines the potential of AI to act as a scaffolding tool or a superficial substitute. This point is also supported by the existing literature on the potential of AI for learning, as revealed by the existing literature within this chapter.

The discussion, therefore, reveals the development of literacy in AI-supported contexts as a multidimensional construct. In the current era, literacy has been viewed as comprising various forms, including multimodal, digital, computational, and AI literacies, which collectively allow learners to read, create, and evaluate both human- and AI-produced texts. In all the studies, the research findings reveal the potential for AI-supported writing, reading, and learning to enhance learners' higher-order literacy competencies, such as synthesis, evaluation, and metacognitive literacy, if learners are encouraged to engage with AI-produced outputs critically. This, therefore, reveals the inseparable nature of critical literacy and AI literacy in the current era.

With regard to creativity, the research findings reveal the potential for the co-creative model of human-AI interaction, where the AI plays the primary role in ideation, exploration, or prototyping, but the human plays the dominant role in the evaluation, interpretation, and ethical decision-making. The research studies reviewed reveal the potential for AI-supported creativity to be most beneficial if the AI plays the primary role in facilitating divergent thinking and cognitive flexibility, but the human plays the dominant role in the evaluation, interpretation, and ethical decision-making. The literature, however, reveals the potential for AI-supported creativity to be detrimental to the homogenization of ideas, originality, and creative ownership.

Equity and access represent overarching themes in the discourse. Despite the fact that artificial intelligence provides opportunities for personalization, multilingualism, and accessibility for learners with disabilities, the advantages offered by AI are not equitable. The study reveals the fact that equity in AI requires not only access but also capacity building, inclusive design, and institutional support, especially for underserved and resource-poor contexts.

Ethical considerations also present complexities in the integration of AI in creativity and literacy education. The complexities include authorship, bias, data privacy, and the validity of AI assessments, all of which represent challenges to the conventional academic paradigm. The discourse reveals the fact that ethical literacy requires the development of new governance structures, where the educator or the learner is positioned as an agent who can critically evaluate the affordances and limitations of AI. In the absence of such structures, AI has the potential to undermine cognitive autonomy, academic integrity, and trust in the education system.

CONCLUSION

In this chapter, the dynamic relationship between AI, creativity, and literacy within the context of current educational environments will be explored, highlighting the potential for transformation and the challenges facing the integration of AI within these environments. Through the use of current empirical research and theory, along with case studies of AI integration within education, it has been made clear that AI is most effective when it is used in a collaborative role with human thought processes rather than replacing human creativity and literacy.

Through the research and evidence provided within this chapter, it has been made clear that creativity and literacy within the AI age are no longer simply about traditional forms of reading and writing but also involve new forms of multimodal literacy, digital literacy, computational literacy, and AI literacy. These forms of literacy are linked and work together to ensure that learners are able to make sense of a world that is becoming increasingly influenced by AI and intelligent technologies.

At the same time, the chapter also identifies several critical risks, such as over-reliance on artificial intelligence, cognitive autonomy, homogenization of creative works, ethical complexities in authorship, and inequities in access. This also serves to support the view that the educational potential of AI is not inherent in the technology itself but is rather dependent upon the quality of implementation. The case examples also highlight the importance of learner engagement, prompt literacy, and teacher expertise in the integration of AI in determining the impact of AI on creativity and literacy development.

REFERENCES

Agaoglu, F. O., Bas, M., Tarsuslu, S., Ekinci, L. O., & Agaoglu, N. B. (2025). The mediating digital literacy and the moderating role of academic support in the relationship between artificial intelligence usage and creative thinking in nursing students. *BMC Nursing*, *24*(1), 484. DOI: 10.1186/s12912-025-03128-3

Ahmed, F. (2024). The digital divide and AI in education: Addressing equity and accessibility. *AI EDIFY Journal*, *1*(2), 12–23.

Al-kfairy, M., Mustafa, D., Kshetri, N., Insiew, M., & Alfandi, O. (2024). Ethical challenges and solutions of generative AI: An interdisciplinary perspective. *Informatics (MDPI)*, *11*(3), 58. DOI: 10.3390/informatics11030058

Alazemi, A. F. T. (2024). Formative assessment in artificial integrated instruction: Delving into the effects on reading comprehension progress, online academic enjoyment, personal best goals, and academic mindfulness. *Language Testing in Asia*, *14*(1), 44. DOI: 10.1186/s40468-024-00319-8

Almatrafi, O., Johri, A., & Lee, H. (2024). A systematic review of AI literacy conceptualization, constructs, and implementation and assessment efforts (2019–2023). *Computers and Education Open*, *6*, 100173. DOI: 10.1016/j.caeo.2024.100173

Baldrich, K., Pérez-García, C., & Santamarina Sancho, M. (2025). Artificial intelligence in academic literacy: Empirical evidence on reading and writing practices in higher education. In *Frontiers in Education* (Vol. 10, p. 1701238). Frontiers., DOI: 10.3389/feduc.2025.1701238

Barve, S., Mao, A., Shi, J. M., Juneja, P., & Saha, K. (2025). Can we debias social stereotypes in AI-generated images? Examining text-to-image outputs and user perceptions. *arXiv preprint arXiv:2505.20692*. https://doi.org//arXiv.2505.20692DOI: 10.48550

Bećirović, S., Polz, E., & Tinkel, I. (2025). Exploring students' AI literacy and its effects on their AI output quality, self-efficacy, and academic performance. *Smart Learning Environments*, *12*(1), 29. DOI: 10.1186/s40561-025-00384-3

Bircan, M. A., Şeref, İ., & Nacaroğlu, O. (2025). The effect of STEM themed story writing training with artificial intelligence tools on the digital literacy and 21st century skills of preservice teachers. *Education and Information Technologies*, *30*(15), 1–20. DOI: 10.1007/s10639-025-13625-2

Bozkurt, A. (2024). GenAI co-creation, authorship, ownership, academic ethics and integrity in a time of generative AI. *Open Praxis*, *16*(1), 1–10. DOI: 10.55982/openpraxis.16.1.654

Carcamo, B., & Pino, B. (2025). Developing EFL students' multimodal literacy with the use of infographics. *Asian-Pacific Journal of Second and Foreign Language Education*, *10*(1), 16. DOI: 10.1186/s40862-025-00322-3

Chang, S. H. (2025). Research on the construction of a collaborative AI-assisted design model for cultural creativity. *International Journal of Education. Cultura e Scuola*, *10*(6), 321–335. DOI: 10.11648/j.ijecs.20251006.12

Chen, C., & Gong, Y. (2025). The role of AI-assisted learning in academic writing: A mixed-methods study on Chinese as a second language students. *Education Sciences*, *15*(2), 141. DOI: 10.3390/educsci15020141

Chen, L., Song, Y., Guo, J., Sun, L., Childs, P., & Yin, Y. (2025). How generative AI supports human in conceptual design. *Design Science*, *11*, e9. DOI: 10.1017/dsj.2025.2

Guan, Y., Zhang, C., He, H., Zhang, W., Hu, Z., Bi, T., & Jin, X. (2025). AI literacy predicts computational thinking through multidimensional interactions among Chinese high school students. *Scientific Reports*, *15*(1), 33092. DOI: 10.1038/s41598-025-16712-z

Hemraj, S. (2025). AI and the future of creative development: Redefining digital media production. *AI and Ethics*, *5*(5), 1–15. DOI: 10.1007/s43681-025-00765-x

Heymann, B. F., & Briedis, M. (2025). Challenging human creativity: An exercise of co-creation with generative artificial intelligence. *Creativity Studies, 18*(2), 570-583.4

Hofman, G. (2024). Towards a practical ethics of generative AI in creative production processes. *arXiv preprint arXiv:2412.03579.* https://doi.org//arXiv.2412.03579DOI: 10.48550

Holzner, N., Maier, S., & Feuerriegel, S. (2025). Generative AI and creativity: A systematic literature review and meta-analysis. *arXiv preprint arXiv:2505.17241.* https://doi.org//arXiv.2505.17241DOI: 10.48550

Hongli, Z., & Leong, W. Y. (2024). AI solutions for accessible education in underserved communities. *Journal of Innovation and Technology*, 2024. Retrieved from https://iuojs.intimal.edu.my/index.php/joit/article/view/528

Huang, S., Long, L., Zhu, Y., & Zhu, J. N. (2026). Human–GenAI collaboration across creative phases: Cognitive mechanisms shaping novelty and usefulness. *International Journal of Information Management*, *86*, 102986. DOI: 10.1016/j.ijinfomgt.2025.102986

Hulekal, R., & As, S. (2025). AI-driven creativity: The role of generative models in event theme and design conceptualization. *Journal of Environmental Management and Tourism*, *16*(4), 435–444. DOI: 10.14505/jemt.v16.4(80).07

Hwang, Y., & Lee, J. H. (2025). Exploring students' experiences and perceptions of human-AI collaboration in digital content making. *International Journal of Educational Technology in Higher Education*, *22*(1), 44. DOI: 10.1186/s41239-025-00542-0

Islam, G., & Greenwood, M. (2024). Generative artificial intelligence as hyper commons: Ethics of authorship and ownership. *Journal of Business Ethics*, *192*(4), 659–663. DOI: 10.1007/s10551-024-05741-9

Ismaili, Y. (2024). AI literacy and adaptive learning in Moroccan education: Advancing critical thinking and personalized learning. *Research on Education and Media*, *16*(2), 20240017. Advance online publication. DOI: 10.2478/rem-2024-0017

Izquierdo-Condoy, J. S., Arias-Intriago, M., Tello-De-la-Torre, A., Busch, F., & Ortiz-Prado, E. (2025). Generative artificial intelligence in medical education: Enhancing critical thinking or undermining cognitive autonomy? *Journal of Medical Internet Research*, *27*, e76340. DOI: 10.2196/76340

Kaplan, R., & Meylani, R. (2025). Dimensions of artificial intelligence literacy: A qualitative synthesis of contemporary research literature. *Journal of Computer and Education Research*, *13*(26), 790–825. DOI: 10.18009/jcer.1648380

Karagoz, A. (2024). Ethics and technical aspects of generative AI models in digital content creation. *arXiv preprint arXiv:2412.16389*. https://doi.org//arXiv.2412.16389DOI: 10.48550

Katona, J., & Gyonyoru, K. I. K. (2025). AI-based adaptive programming education for socially disadvantaged students: Bridging the digital divide. *TechTrends*, *69*(5), 1–18. DOI: 10.1007/s11528-025-01088-8

Leaton Gray, S., Edsall, D., & Parapadakis, D. (2025). AI-based digital cheating at university, and the case for new ethical pedagogies. *Journal of Academic Ethics*, *23*(4), 1–18. DOI: 10.1007/s10805-025-09642-y

Li, J., Yan, Y., & Zeng, X. (2025). Exploring artificial intelligence in inclusive education: A systematic review of empirical studies. *Applied Sciences (Basel, Switzerland)*, *15*(23), 12624. DOI: 10.3390/app152312624

Lim, T., Gottipati, S., & Cheong, M. (2025). What students really think: Unpacking AI ethics in educational assessments through a triadic framework. *International Journal of Educational Technology in Higher Education*, *22*(1), 56. DOI: 10.1186/s41239-025-00556-8

Llerena-Izquierdo, J., & Ayala-Carabajo, R. (2025). Ethics of the use of artificial intelligence in academia and research: The most relevant approaches, challenges and topics. *Informatics (MDPI)*, *12*(4), 111. DOI: 10.3390/informatics12040111

Mansoor, H. M., Bawazir, A., Alsabri, M. A., Alharbi, A., & Okela, A. H. (2024). Artificial intelligence literacy among university students: A comparative transnational survey. *Frontiers in Communication*, *9*, 1478476. DOI: 10.3389/fcomm.2024.1478476

Martins, J. R., Martins, P., & Boavida, A. (2025). GRAPHIC—guidelines for reviewing algorithmic practices in human-centered design and interaction for creativity. *arXiv preprint arXiv:2511.17443*. https://doi.org//arXiv.2511.17443DOI: 10.48550

Melo-López, V.-A., Basantes-Andrade, A., Gudiño-Mejía, C.-B., & Hernández-Martínez, E. (2025). The impact of artificial intelligence on inclusive education: A systematic review. *Education Sciences*, *15*(5), 539. DOI: 10.3390/educsci15050539

Najjar, A. A., Ashqar, H. I., Darwish, O. A., & Hammad, E. (2025). Detecting AI-generated text in educational content: Leveraging machine learning and explainable AI for academic integrity. *arXiv preprint arXiv:2501.03203*. https://doi.org//arXiv.2501.03203DOI: 10.48550

Ncube, P. D., Dzvapatsva, G. P., Matobobo, C., & Ranga, M. M. (2026). Redefining student assessment in AI-infused learning environments: A systematic review of challenges and strategies for academic integrity. *AI and Ethics*, *6*(1), 68. DOI: 10.1007/s43681-025-00871-w

Nguyen, T. N. Q., & Nguyen, T. T. (2025). AI literacy in language learning through digital multimodal composing: A systematic review. *VNU Journal of Foreign Studies*, *41*(3), 142–156. DOI: 10.63023/2525-2445/jfs.ulis.5517

Okonkwo, S., & Schmid-Meier, C. (2025, September 17). AI for inclusion?! Challenging the design of educational AI through equity & disability perspectives. AIEOU Inaugural Conference, University of Oxford. *Zenodo*. https://doi.org/DOI: 10.5281/zenodo.17226470

Olszak, I. (2025). Artificial intelligence and the transformation of literacy: Trilingual students' perspectives on AI-supported writing development. *European Journal of Applied Linguistics Studies*, *8*(4). Advance online publication. DOI: 10.46827/ejals.v8i4.664

Perkins, M., Roe, J., Vu, B. H., Postma, D., Hickerson, D., McGaughran, J., & Khuat, H. Q. (2024). Genai detection tools, adversarial techniques and implications for inclusivity in higher education. *arXiv preprint arXiv:2403.19148*. https://doi.org//arXiv.2403.19148DOI: 10.48550

Prambudi, N. L., Putawa, R. A., & Izumi, C. (2024). A quantitative analysis of artificial intelligence's impact on students' mindset and critical thinking in higher education. *International Journal of Informatics and Information Systems*, *7*(4), 168–178. DOI: 10.47738/ijiis.v7i4.222

Romero, M. (2025). From consumption to co-creation: A systematic review of six levels of AI-enhanced creative engagement in education. *Multimodal Technologies and Interaction*, *9*(10), 110. DOI: 10.3390/mti9100110

Salma, Z., Hijón-Neira, R., & Pizarro, C. (2025). Designing co-creative systems: Five paradoxes in human–AI collaboration. *Information (Basel)*, *16*(10), 909. DOI: 10.3390/info16100909

Seerat, A. (2025). AI-powered reading support for multilingual learners in higher education: A critical review. *Journal for Social Science Archives Учредители: Ali Institute of Research & Skills Development*, *3*(1), 776–786. DOI: 10.59075/jssa.v3i1.158

Shafiee Rad, H. (2025). Reinforcing L2 reading comprehension through artificial intelligence intervention: Refining engagement to foster self-regulated learning. *Smart Learning Environments*, *12*(1), 23. DOI: 10.1186/s40561-025-00377-2

Silor, A. C., & Silor, F. S. (2025). Boosting reading comprehension through AI-based learning tools. *International Journal of Learning. Teaching and Education Research*, *24*(9), 61–79. DOI: 10.26803/ijlter.24.9

Tsao, J., Liang, C. X., Nogues, C., & Wong, A. (2025). Perceptions and integration of generative artificial intelligence in creative practices and industries: A scoping review and conceptual model. *AI & Society*, 1–20. DOI: 10.1007/s00146-025-02667-2

Wang, N., Kim, H., Peng, J., & Wang, J. (2025). Exploring creativity in human–AI co-creation: A comparative study across design experience. *Frontiers of Computer Science*, *7*, 1672735. DOI: 10.3389/fcomp.2025.1672735

Wei, X., Wang, L., Lee, L. K., & Liu, R. (2025). The effects of generative AI on collaborative problem-solving and team creativity performance in digital story creation: An experimental study. *International Journal of Educational Technology in Higher Education*, *22*(1), 23. DOI: 10.1186/s41239-025-00526-0

Yang, C., & Taele, P. (2025). AI for accessible education: Personalized audio-based learning for blind students. *arXiv preprint arXiv:2504.17117*. https://doi.org//arXiv.2504.17117DOI: 10.48550

Yim, I. H. Y., & Su, J. (2025). Artificial intelligence literacy education in primary schools: A review. *International Journal of Technology and Design Education*, *35*(5), 1–30. DOI: 10.1007/s10798-025-09979-w

Zafar, M. B., Ali, H., & Yasin, T. (2025). Reimagining human creativity and learning in the age of generative AI: A multi-method meta-thematic synthesis. *Next Research*, *100802*(4), 100802. Advance online publication. DOI: 10.1016/j.nexres.2025.100802

Zhou, M., & Peng, S. (2025). The usage of AI in teaching and students' creativity: The mediating role of learning engagement and the moderating role of AI literacy. *Behavioral Sciences (Basel, Switzerland)*, *15*(5), 587. DOI: 10.3390/bs15050587

Chapter 4
Education for the Future: Preparing Elementary Students for an AI-Driven World

Ramesh Kumar
http://orcid.org/0000-0003-2771-7274
Lovely Professional University, India

Raj Kumar Verma
Jiwaji University, Gwalior, India

Rohit Kumar Verma
Jiwaji University, Gwalior, India

Anand Pawar
http://orcid.org/0009-0005-4101-2985
Lovely Professional University, India

Tariq Abubakar Ally
Moshi Co-Operative University, Tanzania

ABSTRACT

In an era where artificial intelligence (AI) is reshaping industries, economies, and daily life, elementary education plays a crucial role in preparing young learners for an AI-driven future. This study explores the evolving landscape of education, highlighting the skills, knowledge, and competencies necessary for students to thrive in a technology-centric world. It examines the integration of AI-based tools in classrooms, the importance of digital literacy, problem-solving, and critical thinking skills, as well as the ethical considerations of AI education. Additionally, the research investigates the role of educators in adapting to AI advancements and the challenges of balancing technology with traditional learning methods. By analyzing

DOI: 10.4018/979-8-2600-2163-7.ch004

current trends and best practices, this study provides insights into how elementary education can be restructured to ensure students are not only consumers of AI but also capable contributors to future technological advancements. The findings emphasize the need for curriculum reforms, teacher training, and collaborative efforts.

INTRODUCTION

Artificial intelligence is increasingly being integrated into educational systems worldwide. Studies highlight that AI-powered tools such as adaptive learning platforms, intelligent tutoring systems, and automated assessments personalize learning experiences and improve student engagement (Luckin et al., 2018). AI also enhances real-time feedback, allowing teachers to address learning gaps more efficiently (Holmes et al., 2019). However, concerns remain regarding teacher dependency on AI and the ethical implications of data-driven education (Selwyn, 2020). Digital literacy is a fundamental skill for students in the 21st century. Research indicates that early exposure to digital tools fosters computational thinking, problem-solving abilities, and technological fluency (Wing, 2017). Studies suggest that integrating AI concepts, such as machine learning and automation, into elementary curricula helps students develop foundational knowledge for future careers (Touretzky et al., 2019). Furthermore, project-based learning and coding programs, such as Scratch and Code.org, have been shown to enhance students' logical reasoning and creativity (Grover & Pea, 2018). Beyond technical knowledge, preparing students for an AI-driven world requires fostering essential 21st-century skills, including critical thinking, creativity, collaboration, and adaptability (OECD, 2021). Research emphasizes that elementary education should prioritize interdisciplinary learning that combines AI literacy with social-emotional learning (SEL) to ensure that students can ethically and responsibly interact with AI technologies (Miao et al., 2021). Additionally, studies highlight the importance of inquiry-based and experiential learning approaches in developing these skills (Fullan et al., 2019). Despite its benefits, integrating AI into elementary education presents several challenges. Ethical concerns regarding data privacy, algorithmic bias, and the potential loss of human interaction in learning environments have been widely discussed (Baker & Smith, 2019). Researchers argue that while AI can enhance education, it should complement rather than replace human teachers (Williamson et al., 2020). Moreover, disparities in access to AI-based education tools raise concerns about the digital divide, particularly for students in underprivileged communities (Selwyn, 2021). Future research suggests that a balanced approach, incorporating AI while maintaining a human-centered educational framework, is essential for elementary education (Zawacki-Richter et al., 2019). Studies advocate for teacher training programs that equip educators with the skills needed to integrate AI into their teaching practices effectively (Wang & Woo, 2020). Additionally, policymakers and educators must collaborate to develop ethical guidelines and inclusive AI-driven learning models that ensure equal access for all students (UNESCO, 2022).

STATEMENT OF THE PROBLEM

As artificial intelligence (AI) continues to revolutionize various industries, the role of education, particularly at the elementary level, must evolve to prepare students for an AI-driven future. Traditional teaching methods often emphasize rote memorization and standardized testing, which may not adequately equip young learners with the critical thinking, problem-solving, and digital literacy skills necessary for success in a technology-driven world. Despite the increasing integration of AI in education, there remains a significant gap in the preparedness of elementary students to engage meaningfully with AI concepts. Many schools lack the necessary infrastructure, teacher training, and curriculum development to incorporate AI education effectively. Furthermore, disparities in access to AI-driven learning tools contribute to a growing digital divide, limiting opportunities for students in underprivileged communities. Ethical concerns, such as data privacy, algorithmic bias, and the role of human educators in AI-enhanced classrooms, further complicate the widespread adoption of AI in elementary education.

This study aims to examine the extent to which elementary education is preparing students for an AI-driven future. It seeks to identify existing challenges, explore best practices in AI-integrated learning, and propose strategies for developing a curriculum that fosters digital literacy, computational thinking, and ethical awareness. Addressing this problem is crucial to ensuring that future generations are not merely passive consumers of AI but active, informed contributors to a rapidly evolving technological landscape.

RESEARCH METHODOLOGY

This is a qualitative research study. The required tools, techniques and research methodology have been applied.

PURPOSE OF THE STUDY

The purpose of this study is to explore the role of elementary education in preparing students for an AI-driven future. As artificial intelligence continues to reshape industries, economies, and daily life, it is essential that young learners develop the necessary skills to navigate and contribute to this evolving technological landscape. This research aims to assess the current state of AI integration in elementary education, identify gaps in digital literacy and computational thinking, and propose strategies for equipping students with the knowledge and skills needed for future success. Evaluate the current state of AI education in elementary schools, including curriculum content, teaching methodologies, and available resources. Identify key competencies that elementary students need to develop in order to thrive in an AI-powered society, such as problem-solving, critical thinking, and digital literacy. Analyze the challenges faced by educators, schools, and policymakers in implementing AI-driven learning experiences, including issues related to teacher training, infrastructure, and ethical concerns. Examine best practices in AI education from leading educational institutions and technology-driven learning models. Recommend strategies for integrating AI education into elementary school curricula in a way that promotes inclusivity, ethical awareness, and equitable access to technological resources. By addressing these objectives, this study aims to contribute valuable insights into how elementary education can be transformed to foster AI literacy and prepare students for a future where AI is an integral part of everyday life and the workforce.

SIGNIFICANCE OF THE STUDY

This study is significant in addressing the urgent need for a reformed elementary education system that equips students with AI literacy and future-ready skills. By examining AI integration in early education, the research provides insights for educators, policymakers, and curriculum developers on how to create learning environments that foster innovation, critical thinking, and ethical awareness. Furthermore, the study highlights the importance of teacher training and the need to bridge the digital divide to ensure equitable access to AI-driven learning tools. The findings of this study will contribute to shaping a more inclusive and technologically advanced education system that prepares young learners to become informed and responsible participants in an AI-powered world.

RESEARCH GAP

While existing research explores AI integration in higher education and workforce training, there is a lack of comprehensive studies focused on AI preparedness at the elementary level. Most current literature emphasizes AI-driven learning tools but does not address the pedagogical shifts required to teach AI concepts effectively to young learners. Furthermore, research on AI ethics in early education remains limited, despite the increasing need to teach students about responsible AI usage. Additionally, disparities in access to AI resources, especially in underprivileged communities, are often overlooked in policy discussions. This study seeks to fill these gaps by examining how elementary education can be restructured to promote AI literacy, equitable access, and ethical awareness from an early age.

RESEARCH QUESTIONS

How well are elementary schools integrating AI-related concepts into their curricula?

What are the key skills and competencies that elementary students need to develop for an AI-driven future?

What challenges do educators face in implementing AI education at the elementary level?

How can AI tools enhance personalized and adaptive learning for young students?

What are the ethical implications of AI in elementary education, and how can they be addressed?

How can teacher training programs be improved to support AI literacy in elementary classrooms?

What policies and strategies can ensure equitable access to AI learning resources for all students?

What are the best practices in AI-integrated elementary education from leading institutions worldwide?

RESEARCH OBJECTIVES

To evaluate the current integration of AI-related concepts in elementary education.

To identify key skills and competencies essential for students to thrive in an AI-driven future.

To assess the challenges faced by educators in implementing AI education.

To explore the impact of AI tools on personalized and adaptive learning.
To analyze ethical considerations associated with AI in elementary education.
To recommend improvements for teacher training programs related to AI literacy.
To propose policies and strategies that ensure equitable access to AI education.
To identify best practices in AI-integrated elementary education worldwide.

INTERNATIONAL PERSPECTIVES

As artificial intelligence (AI) continues to revolutionize various industries, the education sector must adapt to prepare students for a future where AI-driven technologies play a central role. Countries worldwide are implementing diverse strategies to integrate AI literacy, critical thinking, and ethical considerations into elementary education. This paper explores international perspectives on preparing young learners for an AI-driven world, focusing on curriculum design, teacher training, and policy implementation. United States: STEAM and Computational Thinking-

The United States emphasizes Science, Technology, Engineering, Arts, and Mathematics (STEAM) education alongside computational thinking. Programs such as “AI for K-12” provide age-appropriate AI concepts, fostering problem-solving skills and creativity. Coding initiatives like code. org introduce elementary students to programming fundamentals, preparing them for future technological advancements. China: AI Integration and Government Policies-China has incorporated AI education into its national curriculum, starting from elementary levels. Government-driven initiatives support AI labs in schools, focusing on hands-on learning experiences. Platforms like Tencent’s “AI+ Education” promote interactive AI applications, helping students understand machine learning and automation principles early on.

Finland: Phenomenon-Based Learning-Finland adopts a phenomenon-based learning approach, integrating AI concepts across various subjects. Rather than standalone AI courses, Finnish students explore AI through interdisciplinary projects, emphasizing collaboration, ethical considerations, and societal impacts.

Singapore: Future-Ready Framework-Singapore’s Ministry of Education implements a structured approach to AI education, blending coding, data literacy, and digital ethics. Programs like Code for Fun engage elementary students in AI projects, ensuring they grasp fundamental AI concepts while developing problem-solving and analytical skills.

Canada: Inquiry-Based and Ethical AI Education-Canada prioritizes an inquiry-based learning approach, encouraging students to question AI’s role in society. Initiatives such as “AI4 Youth” integrate ethical discussions, ensuring children understand both AI’s capabilities and its potential biases or risks. Key Components for AI-Driven Education-Curriculum Development, Introducing AI literacy as a core competency, Incorporating age-appropriate coding and robotics, Emphasizing problem-solving, creativity, and digital citizenship, Teacher Training and Professional Development-Equipping educators with AI teaching resources, Providing continuous training on emerging AI trends, Encouraging interdisciplinary teaching approaches, Ethical Considerations and Digital Citizenship, Teaching students about AI biases and ethical implications, Encouraging responsible AI use, Fostering awareness of privacy, security, and data ethics, Collaborative International Efforts Sharing best practices through global partnerships, Encouraging cross-cultural AI education programs, Developing standardized AI literacy benchmarks, Preparing elementary students for an AI-driven world requires a forward-thinking, global approach. By integrating AI literacy, fostering ethical considerations, and equipping teachers with necessary skills, countries can ensure that young learners are prepared to navigate and contribute to an increasingly AI-powered society.

International collaboration will play a crucial role in shaping inclusive and effective AI education strategies for the future. Preparing elementary students for an AI-driven world requires a forward-thinking, global approach. By integrating AI literacy, fostering ethical considerations, and equipping teachers with necessary skills, countries can ensure that young learners are prepared to navigate and contribute to an increasingly AI-powered society. International collaboration will play a crucial role in shaping inclusive and effective AI education strategies for the future.

Advantages-Enhanced Problem-Solving Skills: AI education fosters critical thinking, creativity, and analytical skills, preparing students for complex problem-solving in the future workforce. Early Exposure to Technology: Introducing AI concepts at an early age equips students with fundamental digital literacy, ensuring they are prepared for a technology-driven world. Encourages Innovation: Learning about AI encourages students to explore new ideas and technological advancements, fostering innovation and entrepreneurship. Personalized Learning: AI-driven education tools can tailor lessons to individual learning styles and paces, improving student engagement and comprehension. Bridges the Digital Divide: Implementing AI education in diverse communities can help reduce technology gaps and create equitable learning opportunities. Disadvantages-Resource and Infrastructure Gaps: Many schools, especially in underprivileged areas, lack the resources and technology needed to implement AI education effectively. Teacher Training Challenges: Educators may not have the necessary AI knowledge or training, making it difficult to integrate AI concepts into the curriculum. Ethical Concerns and Biases: Without proper education on AI ethics, students may develop a skewed understanding of AI's impact, potentially reinforcing biases in AI systems. Over-Reliance on Technology: Excessive focus on AI-driven learning could reduce traditional learning methods and limit students' ability to develop social and emotional skills. Future Job Market Uncertainty: While AI education prepares students for the future, the rapid evolution of technology means that predicting which AI skills will be most valuable remains a challenge. The rapid advancements in artificial intelligence (AI) are transforming every facet of our lives, from how we work to how we communicate and learn. As AI continues to integrate into daily activities, the education system must evolve to ensure that young students are prepared for a future where AI plays a central role. Elementary education serves as the foundation for lifelong learning, and it is essential that it adapts to equip students with the necessary skills to thrive in an AI-driven world. This essay explores the importance of AI in the future, the skills students need to develop, and how educators can integrate AI literacy into elementary education.

IMPACT OF AI ON THE FUTURE

AI is reshaping industries and redefining job markets. Automation is replacing traditional tasks, and new career opportunities are emerging in fields such as data science, robotics, and AI ethics. The ability to work alongside intelligent machines and leverage AI for problem-solving will be crucial for future professionals. Moreover, AI-powered tools are revolutionizing education itself, with personalized learning platforms, intelligent tutoring systems, and adaptive assessments offering tailored educational experiences. Given AI's increasing influence, today's elementary students must be equipped with an understanding of how AI works and how they can responsibly interact with it.

Essential Skills for an AI-Driven Future- to prepare students for an AI-driven future, education must emphasize skills that go beyond traditional academic subjects. These skills include: Critical Thinking and Problem-Solving AI can process vast amounts of data, but human intuition and critical thinking remain indispensable. Students must learn how to analyze information, think logically, and approach problems with creativity. Digital Literacy and AI Awareness Understanding how AI functions, its applications, and its limitations is crucial. Early exposure to AI concepts can help students become responsible digital citizens who can critically assess AI-driven technologies.

Collaboration and Communication AI will complement, not replace, human teamwork. Future professionals will need to collaborate with AI systems and work effectively in diverse teams. Strong communication skills will remain a key asset.

Adaptability and Lifelong Learning the AI revolution will continuously reshape the workforce, requiring individuals to upskill and reskill throughout their lives. Instilling a growth mindset in students will help them embrace change and seek continuous learning opportunities.

Ethical Understanding and AI Responsibility as AI raises ethical dilemmas such as biases in algorithms and privacy concerns-students must be educated on AI ethics. They should understand the moral responsibilities associated with AI use and development.

Integrating AI Literacy into Elementary Education- educators can take several steps to ensure that AI literacy becomes an integral part of elementary education: Introducing AI Concepts Through Playful Learning Children learn best through interactive experiences. AI can be introduced using storytelling, hands-on activities, and simple coding exercises. Platforms like Scratch and blockily allow students to experiment with coding and logical thinking.

Encouraging Computational Thinking Computational thinking involves breaking down problems into manageable parts, recognizing patterns, and developing step-by-step solutions. These skills can be taught through coding exercises, puzzles, and games.

Using AI-Powered Educational Tools AI-driven tools like intelligent tutoring systems and adaptive learning platforms can provide personalized education, catering to individual learning needs and styles. This ensures that students receive customized instruction to strengthen their understanding of subjects.

Fostering Curiosity and Creativity Encouraging students to ask questions about how AI works and explore AI applications in art, music, and storytelling can stimulate their creativity. Open-ended projects allow students to experiment with AI in innovative ways.

Promoting Ethical Discussions on AI Use Simple discussions on topics like data privacy, bias in AI, and responsible AI use can be introduced in classrooms. Teaching students to think ethically about technology ensures they develop a sense of digital responsibility.

Despite the benefits of AI integration in education, challenges remain. Many schools lack access to advanced technology and trained educators who can effectively teach AI literacy. Additionally, concerns about screen time and data privacy must be addressed to ensure that AI tools are used responsibly in the classroom. To overcome these challenges, collaboration between educators, policymakers, and technology companies is essential. Providing professional development for teachers, investing in AI-related educational resources, and ensuring equitable access to technology can help bridge the gap. The future will be increasingly shaped by AI, and elementary education must evolve to prepare students for this new reality. By fostering critical thinking, digital literacy, collaboration, adaptability, and ethical awareness, educators can equip young learners with the skills they need to succeed in an AI-driven world. Through innovative teaching methods and responsible AI integration, we can empower the next generation to harness the power of AI while ensuring they remain at the forefront of technological progress.

ANALYSIS, DISCUSSION AND RESULTS

The literature review suggests that AI has the potential to revolutionize elementary education by enhancing personalized learning, fostering critical thinking, and preparing students for future technological advancements. However, it is crucial to address the ethical challenges and ensure that AI serves as a tool to support rather than replace traditional teaching methods. Future research should focus on creating equitable AI-integrated curricula and training educators to effectively implement AI in elementary classrooms.

The results indicate a systemic gap between the demands of an AI-driven future and the current structure of elementary education. First, while digital tools are increasingly used in classrooms, the focus remains on operational skills rather than conceptual understanding. AI education at the elementary level should prioritize foundational skills such as logical reasoning, pattern recognition, and ethical awareness instead of advanced technical programming. Second, the lack of teacher training emerges as a critical concern. Teachers play a pivotal role in shaping students' attitudes toward technology. Without structured professional development, AI integration risks becoming superficial or ineffective. Third, curriculum rigidity limits innovation. The absence of AI literacy within formal syllabi reflects a broader reluctance to adapt educational frameworks to technological change. This disconnect undermines long-term preparedness of students for future labor markets dominated by automation and intelligent systems. Fourth, inequitable access to technology threatens to widen the digital divide, creating unequal learning outcomes. Students from under-resourced schools are at a disadvantage, raising concerns about educational justice and inclusivity. The results reveal a structural disconnect between policy vision and classroom reality in elementary AI education. Curriculum-Reality Gap- Although policy frameworks recognize AI literacy as essential, elementary curricula remain overloaded with traditional content. AI integration often occurs as an add-on rather than a core pedagogical shift.

This indicates that: AI education is treated as technical exposure, not conceptual empowerment Ethical reasoning and societal impact of AI are insufficiently addressed Interdisciplinary integration remains underdeveloped A curriculum that prioritizes how AI thinks, learns, and affects society is still missing. Pedagogical Implications- the analysis shows that play-based, inquiry-driven, and experiential learning models are most effective for AI education at the elementary level. Successful approaches include: Storytelling to explain machine learning Games and simulations for pattern recognition Collaborative projects for human-AI interaction Traditional exam-oriented pedagogy is incompatible with AI literacy development. Teacher Capacity as a Determinant Factor- Teacher preparedness emerges as the single most decisive variable. Without: Continuous professional development AI-specific teaching toolkits Institutional incentives AI education risks becoming urban-centric and elitist, deepening the digital divide. Ethical and Humanistic Dimensions- the analysis underscores that AI education is not value-neutral. Elementary students are forming: Attitudes toward technology Ethical reasoning patterns social responsibility awareness Failure to integrate AI ethics, bias awareness, and data responsibility risks producing passive technology consumers rather than informed citizens.

DISCUSSION

The findings underscore the need for a paradigm shift in elementary education to align learning outcomes with the realities of an AI-driven society. Education for the future must move beyond rote learning toward fostering: Critical and creative thinking Ethical understanding of AI and technology Adaptability and lifelong learning skills International educational bodies such as UNESCO emphasize AI literacy, ethics, and human-centered learning as essential components of future education. The present study supports this approach, highlighting the importance of early exposure to AI concepts in age-appropriate ways. Teacher empowerment is central to this transformation. Continuous professional development, interdisciplinary teaching models, and institutional support mechanisms are necessary to ensure effective AI integration. Moreover, policy intervention is required to: Revise elementary curricula, invest in digital infrastructure, ensure equitable access to emerging educational technologies, Ethical considerations also assume significance. Introducing AI education at an early stage must include discussions on privacy, fairness, and human values, ensuring that technological advancement does not undermine social responsibility. The discussion situates the findings within global educational discourse and future-oriented learning paradigms. Elementary Education as the Foundation of AI Citizenship, Elementary education is not meant to produce programmers, but digitally conscious citizens. International frameworks, including guidance from UNESCO, emphasize: Human-centered AI Ethical literacy Inclusivity and equity The findings strongly support this humanistic approach. Reframing "AI Readiness" AI readiness must be understood as: The ability to question technology, Understanding AI limitations and biases, collaborating ethically with intelligent systems, Thus, success lies not in early technical mastery, but in critical and ethical engagement. Personalized Learning vs. Human Connection While AI-driven personalization enhances learning efficiency, the study reaffirms that: Emotional intelligence Empathy, Moral judgment remain irreplaceable human elements in education. AI must function within a "human-in-the-loop" educational model, supporting not substituting teachers. Equity and the Digital Divide The discussion highlights a critical concern: AI education without equity deepens inequality. Rural and under-resourced schools face infrastructural barriers Without policy intervention, AI literacy may become a privilege, Inclusive AI education is therefore both a technological and social justice issue.

The integrated findings establish that: AI integration in elementary education is inevitable but under-structured Teacher preparedness is the central success factor Ethical AI literacy is currently insufficient AI tools enhance learning only when human values remain central Preparing elementary students for an AI-driven world is not merely about teaching technology-it is about nurturing ethical judgment, critical inquiry, and human compassion alongside intelligent systems. The results, analysis, and discussion collectively demonstrate that while elementary education systems show potential readiness for an AI-driven future, significant structural, pedagogical, and policy-level reforms are required. Preparing students for the future is not merely a technological challenge but a holistic educational responsibility that integrates skills, ethics, and equity.

The qualitative analysis of curriculum frameworks, policy documents, pedagogical practices, and international models reveals a transitional phase in elementary education systems worldwide with respect to AI readiness. Status of AI Integration in Elementary Education- The findings indicate that AI education at the elementary level is emergent but uneven. While countries such as the United States, Singapore, Finland, and China have initiated structured AI-related programs, most elementary systems-including developing nations-remain at an introductory or experimental stage. AI concepts are not taught as standalone subjects at the elementary level. Integration primarily occurs through coding activities, digital literacy modules, robotics clubs, and STEAM projects. Ethical AI education remains largely implicit rather than explicit. In India, initiatives by CBSE demonstrate policy intent, but systematic implementation at the foundational level is limited Skills and Competencies Developed- The results show that current elementary education systems partially support 21st-century skills, but do not fully align with AI-era demands. Teacher Preparedness- The findings clearly indicate that teacher readiness is the weakest link in AI integration. Most elementary teachers lack formal training in AI or computational pedagogy AI teaching is often self-initiated rather than institutionally supported Educators express enthusiasm but face confidence and resource constraints This gap significantly affects classroom-level implementation. Role of AI Tools AI-based tools demonstrate strong potential for personalized and inclusive learning: Adaptive learning platforms improve learner pacing AI supports differentiated instruction for diverse learners Assistive AI enhances accessibility for children with disabilities However, concerns regarding over-reliance, data privacy, and emotional detachment were consistently noted. The study examined the preparedness of elementary education systems to equip students with competencies required in an AI-driven world. Data were collected through questionnaires administered to teachers, school administrators, and students, along with classroom observations and curriculum analysis. The results revealed that: Awareness of AI Concepts A majority of teachers possessed basic awareness of artificial intelligence but lacked formal training in AI-related pedagogy. Students demonstrated high curiosity toward technology but had limited conceptual understanding of AI. Curriculum Integration AI-related content was largely absent from the formal elementary curriculum. Digital literacy was present, but it focused mainly on device usage rather than computational thinking. Skill Development- Schools showed moderate success in developing problem-solving and creativity, but critical thinking, data literacy, and ethical reasoning were insufficiently addressed. Collaborative learning activities were found to positively influence students' adaptability to technology. Teacher Preparedness- Teachers expressed willingness to integrate AI concepts but cited lack of training, resources, and institutional support as major barriers. Equity and Access- Significant disparities were observed between urban and rural schools in terms of digital infrastructure and exposure to AI-based tools.

Analysis on Research Questions and Research Objectives- The research questions and objectives formulated for this study are well-structured, coherent, and methodologically sound, reflecting the multidisciplinary nature of AI education, pedagogy, ethics, and policy. When examined in the context of the uploaded manuscript, they demonstrate a strong logical alignment with the statement of the problem, research gap, and qualitative methodology. Alignment Between Research Questions and Objectives- A notable strength of the study is the direct correspondence between each research question and its respective research objective. This alignment ensures: Conceptual consistency, Methodological clarity, Ease of data interpretation, Strong validity of findings, each objective operationalizes a research question, transforming abstract inquiry into measurable and analyzable research components. Thematic Analysis of Research Questions- RQ 1: Integration of AI-Related Concepts in Elementary Curricula Research Question: How well are elementary schools integrating AI-related concepts into their curricula? Objective: To evaluate the current integration of AI-related concepts in elementary education. Analysis: This question directly addresses the core research gap identified in the literature review, namely the lack of structured AI education at the elementary level. The uploaded file demonstrates that AI integration is: Fragmented Policy-driven rather than pedagogy-driven Largely limited to digital literacy and coding This question is foundational, as it establishes the baseline status of AI education, without which further analysis of skills, ethics, or tools would lack context. RQ 2: Skills and Competencies for an AI-Driven Future Research Question: What are the key skills and competencies that elementary students need to develop for an AI-driven future? Objective: To identify key skills and competencies essential for students to thrive in an AI-driven future. Analysis: This question reflects a future-oriented and human-centered approach, consistent with the manuscript's emphasis on: Critical thinking Creativity Ethical awareness Collaboration and adaptability The uploaded study clearly establishes that AI readiness is not synonymous with early technical expertise, but with holistic competency development. This question elevates the study beyond technical discourse into educational philosophy and human development. RQ 3: Challenges Faced by Educators Research Question: What challenges do educators face in implementing AI education at the elementary level? Objective: To assess the challenges faced by educators in implementing AI education. Analysis: This question is empirically grounded and strongly supported by the uploaded file, which identifies: Lack of teacher training Curriculum overload Infrastructure gaps Ethical uncertainty The focus on educators aligns with the study's conclusion that teachers are the central agents of AI integration, making this question critical for actionable recommendations. RQ 4: Role of AI Tools in Personalized Learning Research Question: How can AI tools enhance personalized and adaptive learning for young students? Objective: To explore the impact of AI tools on personalized and adaptive learning. Analysis: This question reflects the technological dimension of the study while maintaining pedagogical balance. The uploaded manuscript demonstrates that AI tools: Improve differentiated learning Support inclusive education Enhance formative assessment However, the study also cautions against over-reliance, making this question analytically balanced and ethically informed. RQ 5: Ethical Implications of AI in Elementary Education Research Question: What are the ethical implications of AI in elementary education, and how can they be addressed? Objective: To analyze ethical considerations associated with AI in elementary education. Analysis: This question significantly strengthens the research by embedding normative and ethical inquiry. The uploaded file highlights concerns relating to: Data privacy Algorithmic bias, Surveillance Dehumanization of learning, by including ethics as a standalone question, the study aligns with global frameworks such as those advocated by UNESCO, reinforcing the study's academic and policy relevance. RQ 6: Teacher Training and AI Literacy Research Question: How can teacher training programs be improved to support AI literacy in elementary classrooms? Objective To recommend improvements for teacher training programs related to AI literacy. Analysis: This question translates diagnostic findings into solution-oriented inquiry. The uploaded manuscript repeatedly emphasizes that without teacher capacity building, AI education remains superficial. This question ensures the study contributes practical and policy-relevant recommendations. RQ 7: Equity and Access to AI Education Research Question: What policies and strategies can ensure equitable access to AI learning resources for all students? Objective: To propose policies and strategies that ensure equitable access to AI education. Analysis: This question situates AI education within the framework of social justice and educational equity. The manuscript clearly identifies the digital divide as a structural risk. Including this question ensures that the research does not privilege elite or urban contexts but addresses inclusive education, enhancing its societal relevance. RQ 8: Global Best Practices Research Question: What are the best practices in AI-integrated elementary education from leading institutions worldwide? Objective: To identify best practices in AI-integrated elementary education worldwide. Analysis: This question justifies the comparative and international perspective adopted in the study. The uploaded file's examination of the USA, Finland, Singapore, China, and Canada demonstrates how global models can inform local reforms. This question strengthens the study's generalizability and transferability.

FINDINGS, CONCLUSION, AND SUGGESTIONS

AI education is being integrated globally with varying degrees of success, influenced by policy frameworks, technological advancements, and national priorities. Countries with structured AI policies and dedicated AI curricula see better student engagement and learning outcomes. Teacher preparedness remains a major barrier, with many educators lacking the necessary AI knowledge and professional training. Ethical AI education is critical but often underemphasized, leading to concerns about bias, data privacy, and responsible AI use. Economic and social disparities significantly impact access to AI education, with underprivileged schools facing resource limitations and lack of technology infrastructure. International collaboration and knowledge-sharing are crucial in creating standardized AI literacy benchmarks and equitable access to AI education worldwide. Preparing elementary students for an AI-driven world requires a forward-thinking, global approach. By integrating AI literacy, fostering ethical considerations, and equipping teachers with necessary skills, countries can ensure that young learners are prepared to navigate and contribute to an increasingly AI-powered society. International collaboration will play a crucial role in shaping inclusive and effective AI education strategies for the future. Governments should implement standardized AI education policies. Increased investment in teacher training and AI-related professional development. Development of accessible AI learning resources for all socio-economic groups. Integration of ethical considerations and responsible AI use in curricula. Encouragement of partnerships between schools, industries, and AI experts to enhance learning experiences.

The study systematically examined the preparedness of elementary education systems to respond to the challenges and opportunities of an AI-driven world. Based on qualitative analysis of curricula, pedagogical practices, international models, and ethical considerations, the following key findings emerge: AI Integration in Elementary Education Is Nascent and Uneven -the research finds that AI education at the elementary level is globally emergent but inconsistently implemented.

AI-related learning is mostly limited to coding, robotics, and basic digital literacy, rather than conceptual understanding of AI. Only a few countries have introduced structured frameworks for AI literacy at the primary level. In most contexts, AI education remains policy-driven rather than classroom-driven, with limited translation into everyday pedagogy. This indicates a gap between policy intent and practical implementation, particularly in developing education systems. Curriculum Focuses on Tools, Not Understanding- elementary curricula emphasize technology usage over technological comprehension. Students are exposed to digital tools but rarely taught: How AI systems learn? How data influences decisions? How bias and ethics shape AI outcomes Ethical discussions on privacy, fairness, and accountability are largely absent at the foundational level. As a result, students risk becoming passive users of AI rather than informed and critical participants. Teacher Preparedness Is the Most Critical Bottleneck One of the most significant findings is the lack of teacher readiness to integrate AI education meaningfully. Most elementary teachers lack formal training in: AI concepts Computational thinking Ethical AI pedagogy AI teaching is often self-initiated, depending on individual teacher interest rather than institutional support. The study confirms that technology alone cannot transform education without empowered educators. AI Tools Enhance Personalization but Require Ethical Oversight-AI-powered educational tools demonstrate strong potential in: Personalized and adaptive learning Inclusive education for students with diverse needs Early identification of learning gaps. However, concerns were identified regarding: Student data privacy, Algorithmic bias, Over-reliance on automated feedback, reduced human interaction in learning environments, Thus, AI tools are effective only when guided by ethical frameworks and teacher mediation. Digital Divide Remains a Structural Barrier The findings reveal stark inequalities in access to AI-driven education. Urban and well-funded schools benefit disproportionately Rural and underprivileged schools face: Inadequate infrastructure Limited internet access Shortage of trained educators Without deliberate policy intervention, AI education risks deepening educational and social inequalities. Human-Centric Skills Are Underemphasized. While technical skills receive attention, the study finds insufficient emphasis on: Ethical reasoning Empathy and collaboration Critical and creative thinking Adaptability and lifelong learning These competencies are essential for human -AI coexistence, yet remain marginal in current elementary education models.

The study conclusively establishes that preparing elementary students for an AI-driven world is not merely a technological challenge, but a pedagogical, ethical, and social responsibility. Elementary education represents the most critical stage for shaping attitudes toward technology. The research demonstrates that while AI has begun to influence educational practices, its integration remains fragmented, tool-oriented, and unevenly accessible. The central conclusion of the study is that:

AI education must move beyond coding and devices The focus must shift toward conceptual understanding, ethical awareness, and human values Teachers- not machines-remain the cornerstone of meaningful AI education The findings align with global guidance from institutions such as UNESCO, which emphasizes human-centered and ethical AI in education. Unless education systems invest simultaneously in: Curriculum reform Teacher capacity building Ethical governance Equity-focused infrastructure AI education at the elementary level will remain symbolic rather than transformative. In essence, the future of education will not be determined by how early children learn AI, but by how wisely they learn to live with it.

Based on the findings and conclusions, the study offers the following in-depth, actionable, and policy-relevant suggestions: Curriculum Reform at the Elementary Level- Introduce age-appropriate AI literacy as a cross-curricular competency. Shift from tool-based learning to concept-based understanding of AI. Embed AI education within science, mathematics, social studies, and ethics. Emphasize inquiry-based and project-based learning. Mandatory Teacher Training and Professional Development- Establish continuous professional development programs on: AI fundamentals, Computational thinking, Ethical AI pedagogy, Create teacher-friendly AI toolkits and lesson plans. Encourage peer-learning communities and interdisciplinary collaboration. Ethical AI Education from an Early Age, introduce simplified discussions on Data privacy, Algorithmic bias, Fairness and accountability, Promote digital citizenship and responsible technology use. Ensure transparency in the use of AI tools in classrooms. Human-in-the-Loop Educational Models. Use AI as a supportive learning assistant, not a replacement for teachers. Preserve emotional connection, mentorship, and moral guidance. Balance screen-based learning with social and experiential activities. Bridging the Digital Divide, Invest in infrastructure for under-resourced schools. Provide subsidized access to AI-enabled educational tools. Ensure rural and marginalized communities are not excluded from AI education initiatives. Policy-Level Coordination and Governance, Develop national AI education policies specific to elementary education. Create standardized benchmarks for AI literacy. Foster collaboration between educators, policymakers, and technology experts. Future Research Directions- Longitudinal studies on the impact of early AI education. Empirical research on ethical AI awareness among children. Comparative studies across socio-economic and cultural contexts.

REFERENCES

Baker, T., & Smith, L. (with Anissa, N.). (2019). Educ-AI-tion rebooted? Exploring the future of artificial intelligence in schools and colleges. Nesta.

Fullan, M., Quinn, J., & McEachen, J. (2019). *Deep learning: Engage the world change the world*. Corwin Press. DOI: 10.4135/9781506368603

Grover, S., & Pea, R. (2018). Computational thinking: A competency whose time has come. In Sentance, S., Barendsen, E., & Schulte, C. (Eds.), *Computer science education: Perspectives on teaching and learning in school* (pp. 19–37). Bloomsbury Academic. DOI: 10.5040/9781350057142.ch-003

Holmes, W., Bialik, M., & Fadel, C. (2019). *Artificial intelligence in education: Promises and implications for teaching and learning*. Center for Curriculum Redesign.

Luckin, R., Holmes, W., Griffiths, M., & Forcier, L. B. (2018). *Intelligence unleashed: An argument for AI in education*. Pearson.

Miao, F., Holmes, W., Huang, R., & Zhang, H. (Eds.). (2021). *AI and education: Guidance for policy-makers*. UNESCO.

OECD. (2021). AI and the future of skills, Volume 1: Capabilities and assessments. OECD Publishing. DOI: 10.1787/5ee71f34-en

Selwyn, N. (2020). *Should robots replace teachers? AI and the future of education*. Polity Press.

Touretzky, D., Gardner-McCune, C., Breazeal, C., Martin, F., & Seehorn, D. (2019). A year in K–12 AI education. *AI Magazine*, *40*(4), 88–90. DOI: 10.1609/aimag.v40i4.5289

Wing, J. M. (2017). Computational thinking's influence on research and education for all. *Italian Journal of Educational Technology*, *25*(2), 7–14.

Zawacki-Richter, O., Marín, V. I., Bond, M., & Gouverneur, F. (2019). Systematic review of research on artificial intelligence applications in higher education—Where are the educators? *International Journal of Educational Technology in Higher Education*, *16*(1), 39. DOI: 10.1186/s41239-019-0171-0

Chapter 5
Revolutionizing Education With AI and ML in K-12 and Higher Education

Pooja Dehankar
Ajeenkya D.Y. Patil School of Engineering, India

Susanta Das
http://orcid.org/0000-0002-9314-3988
Ajeenkya D.Y. Patil University, India

ABSTRACT

Higher education as well as K–12 education are rapidly being impacted by AI & ML. They offer fresh resources and approaches to education. One crucial international strategic endeavor to prepare the next generation is incorporating AIML courses into K–12 curricula. Since AI education is still relatively new in both higher education and schools, there is a dearth of research to help teachers create AI curricula. Main goal of school systems' emphasis on diversity & inclusion is to increase the participation of underrepresented groups in the classroom. All activities that are purposefully designed & guided by teachers are included in the curriculum. Freedom of teachers influences their desire & commitment to deliver effective learning experiences for their students. It aids in administrative tasks and offers personalized learning experiences. Taking everything into account, they offer considerable opportunities to improve education overall. However, it is essential to consider ethical factors, ensure fair access, and cultivate suitable AI literacy for everyone involved.

DOI: 10.4018/979-8-2600-2163-7.ch005

INTRODUCTION

The swift progress of AI technologies comes with both benefits and drawbacks. Consequently, the significance of AI literacy as a key educational goal has been increasingly emphasized by scholars and professionals in education. The concept of AI literacy remains ambiguous, however. The term has been employed by scholars to characterize educational initiatives that vary based on school environments, learning goals, and the specific types of AI technologies utilized. Moreover, the emergence of generative AI is leading to significant progress in the area of AI literacy research. Therefore, it is essential to investigate the field and create a conceptual framework that considers the various interpretations of AI literacy (Gu & Ericson, 2025).

In both K–12 and higher education, AI technologies are actively utilized to offer educators and learners advanced tools and stimulating educational experiences. The incorporation of AI-driven adaptive and generative tools can significantly improve conventional teaching methods by offering engaging and personalized learning experiences. Adaptive AI technologies craft personalized learning paths for students, providing immediate feedback and support to ensure effective learning. Now widely used by both instructors and students, generative AI tools require practice to be as effective as possible. Teachers are essential in helping student's complete assignments that make use of these resources, clearing up any misunderstandings, and encouraging digital literacy (Khazanchi et al., 2025).

One of the most important strategic goals in global education is AI literacy. Despite this, there is limited understanding of the most effective methods for teaching AI. The findings indicate that there has been notable advancement in the promotion of AI literacy education over the last twenty years. This underscores that various intelligent tools, such as Google's Teachable Machine, Learning ML, and ML for Kids, are suitable for teaching AI literacy within K-12 environments. Young learners in kindergarten can gain from tools like PopBots, while programming platforms such as Scratch and Python, which facilitate the understanding of AI algorithms through computational thinking, can be introduced at both primary and secondary education levels. The findings suggest that project-based learning, computer-human collaboration, and game-based methods, which have a foundation in constructivism, are some of the techniques employed in AI literacy instruction. Cognitive, affective, and behavioral outcomes, as well as satisfaction with the course and soft skill acquisition, have all been demonstrated (Yim & Su, 2025).

The implementation of AI within education (AIEd) has increased immensely during the last decade, specifically within the sphere of ITSS (Information Technology Skill Standards). Despite the increasing use of ITSs and their capabilities to improve learning processes, the educational effects of AIEd continue to be unclear. While it appears that such effects might not be as pronounced as those of traditional tutoring systems, it has been demonstrated by researchers that ITSs can positively influence learning outcomes in the primary and secondary education sector. Nevertheless, further research is needed, involving longer time periods and a greater variety of participants. Additionally, there should be an exploration of the ethical aspects of AIEd (Létourneau et al., 2025).

The incorporation of AI-powered recommendation systems designed to cater to the needs of each individual student through EdTech can be attributed to personalized learning. This strategy, while effective, may give rise to biases in recommending educational material, thereby resulting in unfairness. In our research, we propose a K–12 student recommendation system that leverages matrix factorization and graph learning techniques to recommend activities such as volunteering, educational materials, and hobbies for students based on their interests. Our model incorporates a framework that is used to identify and mitigate any forms of biases through an analysis of the data collected from different categories of protected students (Drushchak et al., 2025).

K-12 EDUCATION

K–12 schooling encompasses all aspects of elementary and secondary schooling, from kindergarten (K) to twelfth grade. It encompasses the entire educational process from early childhood and progressing up to high school graduation. Students graduating from this system will possess academic, social, and emotional competencies for prospective employment, vocational training, and college attendance. To provide a well-rounded education, K–12 curricula cover a range of academic and extracurricular areas. It aims to promote not only academic achievement but also social and emotional development, helping students prepare for life after school. K-12 education establishes the foundation for lifelong learning, allowing students to thrive in higher education and face the challenges of today's world. Though the term K-12 is prevalent in the US and Canada, the idea of covering the entire range of primary and secondary education is widely recognized around the world, including in India. The K-12 model highlights the importance of interaction and communication between teachers and students during the learning process. The K-12 system is continually changing, with new technologies and methods being introduced to improve the learning experience and prepare students for the future. In many areas, there is an increasing focus on making K-12 education fair and accessible for all students, regardless of their socioeconomic situation (Sarvi et al., 2015).

AI LITERACY

Although teaching AI in K–12 classrooms is currently increasingly popular, creating curricula relating to AI has proven difficult for specialists and educators. Sustainable methodologies that can guide the construction of high-quality curricula are necessary because there haven't been many research that can advise practitioners on how to create and execute AI-related curriculum. In order to understand the new AI technology, teachers' viewpoints are crucial. a curriculum design paradigm that incorporates the four elements of praxis, process, produce, and content. Accordingly, the results identify six essential elements: student relevance, teacher-student communication, AI knowledge, AI processes, the impact of AI (content and product), and flexibility (process and praxis) (Chiu, 2021).

Various ML approaches and techniques employed in AI systems have made it possible to find patterns and trends in enormous, continuously growing amounts of data. Developments in this area continue to progress and have a growing impact on both our society and ourselves as people, permeating many facets of our life and impacting our decisions. Recent discussions regarding how to inform and teach AI in K–12 education have been sparked by the risks and unexpected consequences, such as bias from input data or algorithm design. Since AI is a novel subject for both teachers and K–12 students, new skill sets that facilitate critical engagement with AI are needed. The goal of AI literacy is to bridge the knowledge gap between research and the transmission of practical skills linked to AI. A key component of AI literacy is teachers' technological, pedagogical, and content knowledge (TPACK) in relation to AI. Nonetheless, teachers' opinions, convictions, and viewpoints influence how the curriculum is interpreted and implemented. Together with focus group talks, an anonymous questionnaire was used to obtain a thorough grasp of teachers' conceptions about AI. Teachers usually learn about AI through incidental learning, which often results in misconceptions and prejudices about the technology, according to the qualitative content analysis backed by the Intelligent TPACK theoretical framework (Velander et al., 2024).

PERSONALIZED LEARNING

With the fast-paced development of AI technology, there is increased interest in its use in the education sector. The introduction of AI-driven tutoring software is set to transform the field of education due to its ability to provide custom-tailored solutions depending on the learning styles and needs of every individual student. It has been noted from most research papers written that there was an analysis of the effectiveness, approaches to implementation, and design of the solutions. It was done through analyzing technologies that can be used to help in making these systems interactive according to the needs of the learners, for example, machine learning, natural language processing, and data mining (Rizvi, 2023).

The development and deployment of AI have brought about tremendous changes across different sectors. Personalized learning is one of the areas in education that is seeing increased use of AI technology. Personalized learning is the process of ensuring that the academic performance of students improves based on their personal needs and capabilities. AI technology is expected to bring about fundamental change to how education has always been practiced in the past through adaptive learning approaches. Some examples of the AI applications used in personalized learning include recommendation systems, adaptive tests, and intelligent tutoring systems. Using the processes involved in data analytics, natural language processing, and machine learning, these systems gather and analyze educational data to provide useful insight on how personalized teaching can be carried out. Adaptive learning through AI ensures that each learner studies based on their pace and capability. Intelligent tutoring systems encourage active participation through personalized feedback and suggestions based on the learner's level of involvement in learning. Recommendation engines that incorporate the use of artificial intelligence technology suggest appropriate learning materials for learners according to their interests, preferences, and learning level, thus making the learning process interesting. Although there are many advantages associated with personalized learning through the use of AI, it does have its own drawbacks as well. Privacy issues, ethical issues, and biases in the program need to be considered carefully (Kaswan et al., 2024).

AUTOMATION

Digital leadership is an essential driver of sustainable advancement in the context of higher education institutions. Through the deliberate integration of educational technology and nurturing of digital transformation, universities can eventually reduce their ecological impact, maximize the use of resources, and expand access to learning opportunities among diverse students. To more closely link business operations with sustainability goals like minimizing waste and reducing carbon footprints, it discusses how online learning platforms, virtual collaboration software, and analytics can reduce costs and improve operational effectiveness. It is one of the significant benefits of digital leadership that helps to ensure educational equity. Consequently, universities can instruct students from marginalized groups or areas via online education and digital platforms. Aligned with SDG 4: guarantee inclusive, equal, and high-quality education for everyone, there exists a way to tackle educational disparities. The purpose of such a study would be to highlight the flexible and affordable ways in which digital tools might be used to level the playing field in the educational process. Incorporating sustainability concepts into digital platform courses also serves to engage students and prepare them to address global sustainability challenges. Through virtual simulations and interactive digital technologies, students can interact with real-world problems that impact sustainability. These provide chances to develop critical thinking and problem-solving abilities, which are necessary for future leaders (Sharma et al., 2025).

ENHANCED ENGAGEMENT

The idea of virtual reality (VR) is transforming education by establishing a collaborative method that converts theoretical understanding into real-world application. Students can explore complex settings and situations pertaining to a range of subjects, including physics, engineering, and history. Because VR changes the paradigm from passive learning to active involvement through the manipulation of 3D models, it increases students' motivation for learning (Kwemoi, 2024).

These virtual reality-based systems encourage participation while also giving users a sense of accomplishment through the use of gamification. The idea of VR turns educational tasks into thrilling adventures by utilizing gaming components like prizes and even narrative (Analyti et al., 2024).

Another benefit of these immersive learning methods, which provide better memory encoding possibilities than traditional learning exercises, is increased knowledge retention. Compared to transient memory recall attained through conventional methods, immersive learning improves knowledge retention by utilizing several senses. Immersion training has been shown to improve recall by up to 75% compared to traditional approaches (McGovern et al., 2020).

Students can now leave the classroom due to increased access made possible by decreased expenses. VR breaks down geographical and financial boundaries by offering virtual field trips to far-off locations like the Louvre, ancient ruins, and the deep ocean (Kwemoi, 2024).

A number of facets of our life, including education, are being transformed by AI. Traditional educational systems emphasize memory and are teacher-centered. It has trouble meeting each person's unique demands and accommodating different learning styles. By offering intelligent tutoring programs, adaptive tests, and individualized learning experiences, AI can overcome these constraints. AI can improve learning outcomes and enable students to realize their full potential by customizing instruction to each student's preferences and speed. Interactive learning resources and gamification driven by AI are revolutionizing education. These tools support a variety of learning styles and improve cognitive capacities by turning education into interesting experiences. While interactive resources like learning management systems, educational apps, and simulations foster greater comprehension and retention, gamification tactics make learning enjoyable and memorable (Banik & Gullapelly, 2025).

EXAMPLES

AI has gained attention in education as it becomes more and more common. In addition to the implications on teaching and learning results, the use of AI in education raises a variety of challenging issues, such as those relating to particular student requirements and ethical concerns concerning personal data. The learning activities were divided into four categories: experience and practice; project-based learning with a variety of activities; apply, engage, interact, and use; and students serving as tutors. Cognitive, emotional, and psychomotor levels were the three levels of learning outcomes. Constructivism, experiential learning, AI-assisted learning, and project-based learning are the four categories into which AI tool pedagogy falls (Aravantinos et al., 2024).

AI devices are a part of everyday life for children. Giving them information about how AI functions is essential to empowering them to use AI sensibly and take an active role in their AI-driven future. Playful tools are frequently utilized in K–12 technology education to encourage motivation and participation. The most pertinent articles are categorized and examined according to the type of tools they employ, such as digital, partially digital, or unplugged instruments. The target age, the educational focus, and whether or not their impact is assessed are also taken into account in their study. Digital tools are the most researched, but there are resources for students at every grade level (Gennari et al., 2023).

Literacy in AI is a global strategic goal in education. Over the past 20 years, there has been a notable advancement in AI literacy instruction. This illustrates how K–12 environments can make use of age-appropriate AI literacy teaching resources like Google's Teachable Machine, Learning ML, and ML for Kids. While kindergarten students can benefit from learning tools like PopBots, primary and secondary schools can use software tools like Scratch and Python to promote the computational thinking of AI systems. The study claims that constructivist methods, play- and game-based approaches, project-based learning, and human-computer collaborative learning have all been widely used in AI literacy education. There have been reports of course satisfaction, the development of soft skills, and cognitive, emotional, and behavioral learning outcomes (Yim & Su, 2025).

AI AS A RESEARCH TOOL

The primary objective of the discipline of AI is to make clear the several ways that modeling and simulation are used to train AI systems, enhance algorithms, and enhance decision-making processes. The chosen articles cover a broad range of fields where modeling and simulation are essential to the development of AI applications. These include manufacturing, healthcare, environmental modeling, public sector decision-making, projecting energy use, and education. AI improves forecast accuracy, optimizes resource allocation, and increases decision-making across a variety of industries through modeling and simulation (Kumar, 2024).

The resurgence of interest in ML in recent decades has also affected engineering and the natural sciences. These days, ML techniques are used in data mining, processing, and scientific computing. It covers the use of ML to enhance or expedite simulation methods like molecular dynamics, computational fluid dynamics, and structural analysis. The ability of ML to fully eliminate the need for more expensive simulation techniques by producing computationally efficient stand-in models for real-world applications (Frank et al., 2020).

A novel machine modeling and simulation paradigm has been presented to complement the shortcomings of current simulation paradigms (digital twins, hybrid simulation, greater utilization of virtual and augmented reality) to address the challenges posed by Industry 4.0 paradigm. The most prominent advantages of the approach are the presence of more advanced models, more accurate visualized description, better product life cycle tracking, real-time integration of data, distant product servicing, and enhanced decision-making within processes. There are, however, drawbacks as well: Lack of standard languages and applications, modification of existing digitization processes, conversion of tacit knowledge into digital form, integration of future technologies like AI/CI, industrial synergy absence, and the need for higher implementation capabilities (Mourtzis, 2020; Chryssolouris et al., 2008; Mourtzis et al., 2014; Burczyński et al., 2020).

VIRTUALTA

Compared to previous learning chatbot systems, the VirtualTA system provides a more extensive and adaptable instructional support mechanism. Attention to academic honesty and learning analytics, support for varied question types, context awareness, and more advanced and effective educational support system is made possible by the integration of several components. Unlike other studies and applications in the field of education chatbots, the VirtualTA system has additional characteristics that assist in resolving certain problems encountered in higher education. In this way, it makes a substantial contribution to the advancement of educational technology and chatbot development. First of all, the VirtualTA system distinguishes itself from common chatbots because of the presence of such features as flashcards, quizzes, automatic assessment of homework, code playgrounds, and summarization. All these extra features constitute the integral component of the system, together with the basic functionality of question-and-answer chat. Second, the VirtualTA system pays special attention to such notions as academic integrity and learning analytics. Due to the presence of automatic homework assessment as well as the anti-cheating mechanisms, the system provides equal opportunity for each student in terms of assessment. Learning analytics enables the teachers to know how well their students perform in the class. The VirtualTA system intends to integrate with popular LMS such as Canvas, thus making its use more convenient for the users (Sajja et al., 2024).

AUTHENTIC ASSESSMENT

During an era characterized by rapid technological advancement and dynamic changes in job market requirements, one of the key problems facing higher learning institutions is the ability to equip learners with the relevant skills needed to thrive in the workplace environment. Real assessment refers to a relatively new educational framework that helps learners link the theoretical knowledge they acquire at institutions of higher learning to practical applications. This book captures some of the latest developments and best practices concerning real assessments, providing readers with four groundbreaking approaches. One of these methods, which is commonly referred to as patchwork assignments, entails carrying out a series of interrelated reflection exercises throughout a series of courses, culminating in one narrative. This approach promotes continuous learning and knowledge integration across various disciplines. The third strategy, role play through games, immerses students in gamified situations where they take on professional roles, work together to address challenges, and enhance their interpersonal and decision-making skills. Finally, e-portfolios are examined as online collections of student projects that demonstrate proficiency and monitor educational advancement, offering tangible proof of abilities for academic and career objectives (Vlachopoulos, 2025).

AI is changing society and the workplace. Human workers will increasingly need to have abilities like creativity, critical thinking, and adaptability as AI systems take on increasingly difficult cognitive tasks. In order to prepare pupils for an AI-dominated society, educational systems must change. To encourage skills like teamwork, computational thinking, problem-solving, and lifelong learning. Active, varied learning should be prioritized above rote memorizing. To critically examine how AI is changing society, students must have a firm understanding of ethics, philosophy, and the social sciences. The resilience and sophisticated problem-solving skills required to maintain AI systems are fostered by project-based and experiential learning. Automation, the future of labor, and the impact of AI on inequality should all be covered in the curriculum. Active learning activities must replace passive instruction in the classroom. For students to be motivated to continue honing their talents, they must be encouraged to cultivate growth mindsets. The interdisciplinary collaboration required for AI development is reflected in collaborative and team-based learning. Technology should not be used merely for its own sake, but rather in accordance with learning objectives. High-stakes tests are replaced by ongoing feedback through formative assessment. Mandates for standardized testing, deficiencies in teacher preparation, and opposition to pedagogical reform are some of the obstacles facing these initiatives. However, leaders in education must step up to the plate. Rethinking what is taught and how is necessary to develop the transdisciplinary competencies—creativity, communication, computational thinking, and lifelong learning—that are required in an AI era. Teaching methods and curricula based on the industrial paradigm of the 20th century will not sufficiently develop the adaptable, diverse skill sets that people need to work alongside AI systems and keep developing. To provide the learning environments children need to think critically, work creatively, and prosper in an AI-driven future, policymakers and education leaders must work together (George, 2023).

AI AS A CO-TEACHER

According to recent studies, AI has a great deal of promise to improve teaching methods in areas including performance evaluation, individualized teacher intervention and feedback, and lesson design. Understanding how educators creatively integrate and assess AI applications into their lesson plans is essential to maximizing the potential of AI in education. To support teachers' successful AI integration practices, there is a research need in understanding how teachers use different aspects of an AI-enabled system and how they perceive AI integration in the classroom (Shi et al., 2024).

The application of AI solutions in formal education, particularly in the classroom, has garnered attention recently as a potential solution to nearly all "problems." Students can receive individualized scaffolding and recommendations (Albacete et al. 2019; Tarus et al. 2018), as well as assistance with automatic or semi-automatic performance evaluation and progress tracking (Heffernan & Heffernan 2014; Luckin 2017).

ETHICAL CONCERNS

AI has revolutionized the education industry through data-driven analysis, evaluation, and customization of the learning process. Nonetheless, these advancements pose many ethical issues that require careful consideration. First, with all the student data collected and analyzed by educational organizations, there are issues of data security and abuse. In addition, it may happen that integrating AI into the teaching process will result in biased algorithms leading to unfair situations. What is more, the use of surveillance AI raises ethical questions about the balance between the right to privacy and maintaining academic integrity. Therefore, a comprehensive approach to addressing these concerns while embracing innovation is needed. It is imperative that stakeholders in this field promote AI ethics by ensuring that awareness of AI ethics issues is promoted and that AI decision-making is made public and regulated. Furthermore, advancements in technology may help address the issue of data security by utilizing privacy-preserving techniques like differential privacy and federated learning. However, a multidisciplinary cooperation among educators, legislators, and engineers should be encouraged in order to achieve the necessary equilibrium (Khan, 2024).

EQUITY AND ACCESS

The use of AI technology in many facets of social life has sparked both optimistic and pessimistic theories about how it will affect inequality. AI may worsen disparities in health care, education, employment, and service delivery, among other facets of social life. AI-based automation might cause income inequality and job losses, resulting in inequality among high-skilled and low-skilled workers. In addition, bias in AI algorithms may result in further discrimination against certain people, especially those in marginalized communities. New technological innovations using AI would help minimize inequalities concerning opportunities and resources in health care, education, and finances. They are more affordable and accessible due to greater efficiency. Moreover, initiatives to ensure ethical research and responsible governance in AI technology could address some of its negative consequences related to inequality. Depending on our choices about developing, applying, and governing AI systems, inequality either moves forward or recedes. By giving priority to social justice, equity, and human well-being in designing and using AI, we can harness its power of transformation to make our society more equitable and inclusive (Farahani & Ghasemi, 2024).

TEACHER TRAINING

Researchers, scholars, and practitioners are discussing the application of AI increasingly. Educators are being trained by schools now to implement AI within the classroom. However, there has been little research in preparing teachers to implement AI. The results indicated that the biggest challenge confronting trainers is the absence of enthusiasm from teachers for utilizing AI. Therefore, the training courses should be motivating, customized, and highlight the importance of AI. To provide the instructors with hands-on experience, the training sessions should also involve a test of the latest AI technology (Aljemely, 2024).

The expectation is that AI technology use in education will accelerate, necessitating teacher preparation programs to prepare instructors with the skills and knowledge needed to effectively harness AI in an increasingly changing world. Future educators will need to embrace new technologies, including developing AI literacy. Integrating AI into teacher preparation is one way to achieve that. This can be achieved through the use of strategies like building AI literacy, integrating AI into pre-service training of teachers, promoting collaborative learning of teachers in the future, providing continuous education opportunities, and promoting a supportive attitude towards the practical application of AI (Ismail et al., 2024).

TEACHER READINESS

There is a noticeable shift in education in terms of how teachers spend less time performing mundane chores that include grading and planning class schedules to develop advanced AI-based learning ecosystems instead. To facilitate this process, it is crucial for teachers to be well-versed in this field and undergo extensive training, as they should know how to work with such complex tools as adaptive learning systems within their classes. Additionally, there should be an analysis of psychological preparedness among educators who may be skeptical about the technology because of possible risks to students' welfare (Rojas & Chiappe, 2024).

The power of artificial intelligence lies in its ability to provide teachers with relevant insights based on performance data and give immediate and customized advice to underperforming learners. The new model of teacher-student interaction is based on the concept of a "teacher-co-pilot," where teachers leverage AI tools to boost the effectiveness of face-to-face instruction and mentor less experienced educators. However, this process poses several challenges to teachers, such as eliminating possible bias, ensuring data privacy, and addressing the digital divide (Almubarak et al., 2025).

PRACTICAL EXAMPLES

AI is transforming the way English for Specific Purposes (ESP) is taught. Authors discusses the revolutionary possibilities of state-of-the-art AI applications such as natural language processing (NLP) and big language models such as GPT-3 in creating extremely tailored, adaptive learning materials that are exactly customized to fit the varied professional and academic requirements of learners in disciplines such as engineering, finance, healthcare, and beyond. Teachers may create immersive, contextualized, interactive learning experiences that successfully target specialized linguistic, communicative, and domain-specific skills required in a variety of sectors and professions by carefully utilizing AI's capabilities. With the combination of human educators' knowledge in the relevant subject matter as well as pedagogical methods and AI technology in producing quality content that matches the needs of learners, it is possible to enhance the degree of motivation among learners, and make the process more effective as a result. In the long run, this will help increase the efficacy of language training within ESPs. The current use of AI in ESP will be analyzed in detail, with attention paid to creating dialogues and other material relevant to a certain job environment. It examines the deep educational ramifications, such as the potential for autonomous, exploratory learning and more comprehensive formative evaluation made possible by AI (Rudik & Onyshchuk, 2024).

The main goal is to demonstrate how students' learning in a higher education setting is improved by immediate, valid feedback and qualitative assessment. As online learning becomes more popular, particularly during the COVID-19 pandemic, the function of evaluation and feedback also shifts. As seen by the growth of online education, the paradigm has shifted toward assessing student activities that enhance learning outcomes. In HEIs, the evaluation aspect had not been regarded as the primary emphasis of teaching and learning. Extensive research has been conducted on developing assessment methods and strategies that can successfully enhance teaching and learning (Hooda et al., 2022).

Personalized learning approaches are bringing changes in field of math schooling through use of cognitive science and artificial intelligence for customized lessons for each learner. MATHia, one of Carnegie Learning's programs, is described as a one-to-one intelligent math tutoring program aimed at learners from grade 6 to 12 and which evaluates the process of solving tasks by the student instead of its result, offering skill-by-skill and timely feedback (Mustapha, 2025).

AI-based tutors are assisting the learner in their work and helping teachers in administrative tasks. Khanmigo, an AI-based tutorial program developed by Khan Academy with the help of OpenAI, does not offer answers but rather encourages the students to think analytically and come up with solutions. On the other hand, it works as a teacher's teaching assistant, helping in the planning of the course, developing a rubric, and differentiating, in most cases in cooperation with Microsoft (Shetye, 2024).

Differentiation tools help the educators tailor educational material to the appropriate reading level. Tools such as Diffit and ChatGPT allow the educators to easily adapt the same text to various Lexile levels or translate it into a specific language needed by the students to access the content successfully. They can also be used to create comprehension questions and summaries for the texts (Banerjee, 2024).

Interactive AI in education is creating opportunities to learn through practical means. For instance, Edu4AI is a project that aims to teach students in secondary schools about AI and ML in the context of project-based learning. Aim includes enabling the students to build machines that will change sound into visual indicators. Maker-based learning is an important process that encourages the development of skills required in the current world such as critical thinking and problem-solving (Papasarantou et al., 2002).

The tools designed to aid accessibility are allowing learners with disabilities to gain access to the material. Microsoft Immersive Reader provides several features that include text-to-speech, translations, and readability options (Agrahari, 2023).

The Read Aloud feature makes learning more accessible to everyone, especially to students who

have learning disabilities or who benefit from auditory learning. The technology reads the text out loud while also highlighting words at the same time, helping to improve the user's decoding abilities as well as their overall understanding (Batini & Toti, 2024).

The Readability Option allows users to personalize their experience when reading. It adjusts the font size, spacing between letters and lines, and even the page themes. This is especially helpful for students suffering from dyslexia and other visual disabilities because it provides the ideal conditions for faster reading and better concentration (Duranovic et al., 2018).

Translation and language options offer users the ability to translate any text into over 100 languages. This feature translates not only whole phrases but also words in order to improve users' understanding of the vocabulary used in other languages (Al-Awawdeh et al., 2025).

Grammar and Structural Assistance includes aids that help in the decoding and understanding process by segmenting words into syllables and showing particular grammatical parts of speech, such as nouns, verbs, and adjectives. Furthermore, there are features such as line focus which enable isolation of text and decrease distractions while aiding in tracking (Suranto, 2024).

Visual Assistance involves the use of a picture dictionary, whereby words are shown through images to improve their understanding, especially among young learners (Somba & Widyaningrum, 2024).

CONCLUSION

AI is regarded as capable of transforming education as a whole, especially within K-12 educational contexts. Today, AI has greatly changed K-12 education, converting conventional classrooms into learning environments enhanced by AI technology. Ethical considerations became crucial for people, making them pay attention to the development of regulations in relation to the usage of AI technology. Such problems as privacy, security, and bias became notable areas of consideration that require additional attention and development. Despite this, the future application of AI in higher education remained optimistic, with people dreaming about personalized approaches to learning, ethical implementation of AI technology, collaboration, and lifelong learning support.

More evaluation and analysis concerning the efficiency of the learning tools should be done in order to inform the parties concerned about the trends in this sphere, as well as pedagogical and professional development approaches.

Conclusive evidence is necessary to evaluate whether learning tools powered by artificial intelligence are efficient enough in regard to the risk-benefit assessment and how these tools can help implement the material effectively in classrooms. Educational contexts where particular tools can be used should be defined explicitly.

REFERENCES

Agrahari, S. K. (2023). The Crucial Role of Accessibility Tools and Software in Meeting the Needs of Individuals with Learning Disabilities. *Cutting Edge in Special Education, 121*.

Al-Awawdeh, N., Kaddum, M. M., Nasr, D., Merhye, N., & Nasr, M. (2025). The Correlation Between the Use of AI Translation Tools in Foreign Language Learning and the Positive Performance of Foreign Language Students. [TPLS]. *Theory and Practice in Language Studies*, *15*(12), 4117–4126. DOI: 10.17507/tpls.1512.31

Albacete, P., Jordan, P., Katz, S., Chounta, I. A., & McLaren, B. M. (2019). The impact of student model updates on contingent scaffolding in a natural-language tutoring system. In *International conference on AI in education* (pp. 37–47). Springer. DOI: 10.1007/978-3-030-23204-7_4

Aljemely, Y. (2024, October). Challenges and best practices in training teachers to utilize AI: A systematic review. []). Frontiers Media SA.]. *Frontiers in Education*, *9*, 1470853. DOI: 10.3389/feduc.2024.1470853

Almubarak, A., Alhalabi, W., Albidewi, I., & Alharbi, E. (2025). An AI-powered framework for assessing teacher performance in classroom interactions: A deep learning approach. *Frontiers in Artificial Intelligence*, *8*, 1553051. DOI: 10.3389/frai.2025.1553051 PMID: 40969168

Analyti, E., Charitou, R., Pesmatzoglou, E., Stavrogiannopoulou, M., Schoina, I., Travlou, C., & Mitroyanni, E. (2024). Virtual reality in education: Transforming learning through immersive technology. *Technium Education and Humanities*, *10*(October), 1–11. DOI: 10.47577/teh.v10i.11766

Aravantinos, S., Lavidas, K., Voulgari, I., Papadakis, S., Karalis, T., & Komis, V. (2024). Educational approaches with AI in primary school settings: A systematic review of the literature available in Scopus. *Education Sciences*, *14*(7), 744. DOI: 10.3390/educsci14070744

Banerjee, R. (2024, August). Education 4.0: Use of AI tools in classroom. In *ARTIFICIAL INTELLIGENCE IN EDUCATION* (p. 108).

Banik, B. G., & Gullapelly, A. (2025). AI-Powered gamification and interactive learning tools for enhancing student engagement. In *Driving Quality Education Through AI and Data Science* (pp. 283–310). IGI Global Scientific Publishing. DOI: 10.4018/979-8-3693-8292-9.ch013

Batini, F., & Toti, G. (2024). Shared reading aloud to enhance language and literacy. *Education 3-13, 52*(7), 946-962.

Burczyński, T., Kuś, W., Beluch, W., Długosz, A., Poteralski, A., & Szczepanik, M. (2020). *Intelligent computing in optimal design.* Springer. DOI: 10.1007/978-3-030-34161-9

Chiu, T. K. (2021). A holistic approach to the design of AI (AI) education for K-12 schools. *TechTrends, 65*(5), 796–807. DOI: 10.1007/s11528-021-00637-1

Chryssolouris, G., Papakostas, N., & Mavrikios, D. (2008). A perspective on manufacturing strategy: Produce more with less. *CIRP Journal of Manufacturing Science and Technology, 1*(1), 45–52. DOI: 10.1016/j.cirpj.2008.06.008

Drushchak, N., Tyshchenko, V., & Polyakovska, N. (2025, April). Towards Responsible AI in Education: Hybrid Recommendation System for K-12 Students Case Study. In *2025 IEEE/ACM International Workshop on Responsible AI Engineering (RAIE)* (pp. 61-68). IEEE. DOI: 10.1109/RAIE66699.2025.00015

Duranovic, M., Senka, S., & Babic-Gavric, B. (2018). Influence of increased letter spacing and font type on the reading ability of dyslexic children. *Annals of Dyslexia, 68*(3), 218–228. DOI: 10.1007/s11881-018-0164-z PMID: 30094714

Farahani, M., & Ghasemi, G. (2024). AI and inequality: Challenges and opportunities. *Int. J. Innov. Educ, 9*, 78–99.

Frank, M., Drikakis, D., & Charissis, V. (2020). Machine-learning methods for computational science and engineering. *Computation (Basel, Switzerland), 8*(1), 15. DOI: 10.3390/computation8010015

Gennari, R., Melonio, A., Pellegrino, M. A., & D'Angelo, M. (2023, September). How to playfully teach AI to young learners: a systematic literature review. In *Proceedings of the 15th Biannual Conference of the Italian SIGCHI Chapter* (pp. 1-9). DOI: 10.1145/3605390.3605393

George, A. S. (2023). Preparing students for an AI-driven world: Rethinking curriculum and pedagogy in the age of AI. *Partners Universal Innovative Research Publication, 1*(2), 112–136.

Gu, X., & Ericson, B. J. (2025, August). Ai literacy in k-12 and higher education in the wake of generative ai: An integrative review. In *Proceedings of the 2025 ACM Conference on International Computing Education Research* V. 1 (pp. 125-140). DOI: 10.1145/3702652.3744217

Heffernan, N. T., & Heffernan, C. L. (2014). The assistments ecosystem: Building a platform that brings scientists and teachers together for minimally invasive research on human learning and teaching. *International Journal of Artificial Intelligence in Education, 24*(4), 470–497. DOI: 10.1007/s40593-014-0024-x

Hooda, M., Rana, C., Dahiya, O., Rizwan, A., & Hossain, M. S. (2022). AI for assessment and feedback to enhance student success in higher education. *Mathematical Problems in Engineering, 2022*(1), 5215722.

Ismail, A., Aliu, A., Ibrahim, M., & Sulaiman, A. (2024). Preparing teachers of the future in the era of AI. *Journal of AI. MLand Neural Network, 44*, 31–41.

Kaswan, K. S., Dhatterwal, J. S., & Ojha, R. P. (2024). AI in personalized learning. In *Advances in technological innovations in higher education* (pp. 103–117). CRC Press. DOI: 10.1201/9781003376699-9

Khan, W. N. (2024). Ethical challenges of AI in education: Balancing innovation with data privacy. *AI EDIFY Journal, 1*(1), 1–13.

Khazanchi, R., Khazanchi, P., Warr, M., Mishra, P., Blankenship, R., Jacques, L., & Petit, J. (2025, March). Implications of AI in K-12 and Higher Education. In *Society for Information Technology & Teacher Education International Conference* (pp. 748-751). Association for the Advancement of Computing in Education (AACE).

Kumar, A. (2024). The role of simulation and modeling in AI: A review. *International Journal of Modeling, Simulation and Scientific Computing, 15*(03), 2430002. DOI: 10.1142/S1793962324300024

Kwemoi, K. C. (2024). The Integration of virtual reality and gamification in education. *Research Output Journal of Biological and Applied Science, 3*(1), 7–12.

Kwemoi, K. C. (2024). The Integration of virtual reality and gamification in education. *Research Output Journal of Biological and Applied Science, 3*(1), 7–12.

Létourneau, A., Deslandes Martineau, M., Charland, P., Karran, J. A., Boasen, J., & Léger, P. M. (2025). A systematic review of AI-driven intelligent tutoring systems (ITS) in K-12 education. *npj Science of Learning, 10*(1), 29.

Luckin, R. (2017). Towards AI-based assessment systems. *Nature Human Behaviour, 1*(3), 1–3. DOI: 10.1038/s41562-016-0028

McGovern, E., Moreira, G., & Luna-Nevarez, C. (2020). An application of virtual reality in education: Can this technology enhance the quality of students' learning experience? *Journal of Education for Business, 95*(7), 490–496. DOI: 10.1080/08832323.2019.1703096

Mourtzis, D. (2020). Simulation in the design and operation of manufacturing systems: State of the art and new trends. *International Journal of Production Research, 58*(7), 1927–1949. DOI: 10.1080/00207543.2019.1636321

Mourtzis, D., Doukas, M., & Bernidaki, D. (2014). Simulation in manufacturing: Review and challenges. *Procedia CIRP, 25*, 213–229. DOI: 10.1016/j.procir.2014.10.032

Mustapha, S. S. (2025). Personalized Learning with AI: Adapting Education to Learners' Needs.

Papasarantou, C., Alimisis, D., Geramani, K., & Ioannidis, G. (2002). Introducing Artificial Intelligence in school education: the Edu4AI project. *Proc. of the 17th Edition of the EUTIC–In the Intersection of Art, Science and Technology: Dialogos between Humans and Machines. Corfu, Greece: Department of Audio & Visual Arts, Ionian University*, 272-280.

Rızvı, M. (2023). Investigating AI-powered tutoring systems that adapt to individual student needs, providing personalized guidance and assessments. *The Eurasia Proceedings of Educational and Social Sciences, 31*, 67–73. DOI: 10.55549/epess.1381518

Rojas, M. P., & Chiappe, A. (2024). Artificial intelligence and digital ecosystems in education: A review. *Technology. Knowledge and Learning, 29*(4), 2153–2170. DOI: 10.1007/s10758-024-09732-7

Rudik, I. V., & Onyshchuk, I. Y. (2024). Artificial inteligence tools for developing educational resources: enhancing digital learning experience for teachers and learners.

Sajja, R., Sermet, Y., Cikmaz, M., Cwiertny, D., & Demir, I. (2024). AI-enabled intelligent assistant for personalized and adaptive learning in higher education. *Information (Basel), 15*(10), 596. DOI: 10.3390/info15100596

Sarvi, J., Munger, F., & Pillay, H. (2015). *Transitions to k–12 education systems: experiences from five case countries*. Asian Development Bank.

Sharma, M., Kumar, R. N., Sarkar, R., & Majumder, M. S. (2025). Transforming Higher Education for Sustainability: The Role of Digital Leadership in Innovation, Equity, and Resource Management. In *Digital Leadership for Sustainable Higher Education* (pp. 345-364). IGI Global Scientific Publishing.

Shetye, S. (2024). An evaluation of Khanmigo, a generative AI tool, as a computer-assisted language learning app. *Studies in Applied Linguistics and TESOL, 24*(1). Advance online publication. DOI: 10.52214/salt.v24i1.12869

Shi, L., Ding, A. C., & Choi, I. (2024). Investigating teachers' use of an AI-enabled system and their perceptions of AI integration in science classrooms: A case study. *Education Sciences, 14*(11), 1187. DOI: 10.3390/educsci14111187

Somba, S., & Widyaningrum, W. (2024). Visual dictionary for learning vocabulary for young English learners. *Dharmas Education Journal (DE_Journal), 5*(2), 1424-1433.

Suranto, S. (2024). The Analysis of Student's Ability to Identify Parts of Speech. *Global Journal of Social Science and Innovation, 1*(1), 18–26.

Tarus, J. K., Niu, Z., & Mustafa, G. (2018). Knowledge-based recommendation: A review of ontology-based recommender systems for e-learning. *Artificial Intelligence Review, 50*(1), 21–48. DOI: 10.1007/s10462-017-9539-5

Velander, J., Taiye, M. A., Otero, N., & Milrad, M. (2024). AI in K-12 Education: Eliciting and reflecting on Swedish teachers' understanding of AI and its implications for teaching & learning. *Education and Information Technologies, 29*(4), 4085–4105. DOI: 10.1007/s10639-023-11990-4

Vlachopoulos, D. (2025). Authentic assessment: Bridging higher education and real-world skills through diverse methodologies. In *INTED2025 Proceedings* (pp. 2225-2234). IATED.

Yim, I. H. Y., & Su, J. (2025). AI (AI) learning tools in K-12 education: A scoping review. *Journal of Computers in Education, 12*(1), 93–131.

Yim, I. H. Y., & Su, J. (2025). AI (AI) learning tools in K-12 education: A scoping review. *Journal of Computers in Education, 12*(1), 93–131.

Chapter 6
A Framework for an Educational Multi-Agent System

Janisha Sharma
http://orcid.org/0009-0004-0188-6795
Acharya Narendra Dev College, University of Delhi, India

Vibha Gaur
http://orcid.org/0000-0001-6668-9339
Acharya Narendra Dev College, University of Delhi, India

Shiva Saini
http://orcid.org/0009-0009-8619-8129
Acharya Narendra Dev College, University of Delhi, India

ABSTRACT

Modern digital learning environments struggle to deliver personalized, engaging, and scalable instruction. To address the gaps, the work presents a layered Multi-agent System (MAS) based framework for intelligent knowledge dissemination. The proposed MAS employs various autonomous software agents, such as the domain agent, the text-to-speech (TTS) agent, etc., with different functional roles. These software agents coordinate using standardized communication protocols to generate the multimodal instructional content in real time. A central coordination mechanism is used to handle task allocation, workflow sequencing, and multimodal synchronization. The framework adopts pedagogical reasoning, learner adaptation, and engagement for multimodal content generation. Formal communication standards, such as message primitives and state management strategies, are employed to make

DOI: 10.4018/979-8-2600-2163-7.ch006

the system scalable, and maintainable in the long term. This chapter integrates the advances in large language models (LLM), media production, and software agent theory for next-generation smart teaching systems.

INTRODUCTION

The introduction of artificial intelligence (AI) in the education sector is causing a massive paradigm shift. It has transformed the traditional way of teaching into a multimodal activity, where students enjoy learning through audio, video, and simulations. Existing digital learning involves linear content delivery that is static and passive and may cause disinterest of learners. Lack of communication with the teacher refrains them from effective learning.

Existing tools for e-education are designed for a single purpose. Problem-solving is facilitated by the tutor. Resources are recommended by the recommender systems. The chatbot answers questions. These tools work as separate pieces; as a result, the learner feels disconnected and disengaged. There exist gaps between the teaching, interaction, customization, and information presentation. This fragmentation does more than create a poor experience that prevents the growth and engagement of a critical learner. As a result, these systems fail to promote the growth of multimodal literacy by not showing coherent communication. Nowadays students expect the learning systems to adapt to their individual needs and pace. That is only feasible by using blended media of the digital world.

Recent advances in AI, particularly LLMs, allow the creation of an explanation system, dialogue, and response to the inputs of a learner. However, the majority of the AI-based educational tools are architecturally monolithic and interactionally constrained. They mostly work as isolated conversational bots, providing primarily textual responses without being heavily speech integrated, graphic, or embodied. Although the LLMs have good generative power, they do not possess an inherent structure for instructional learning. An educational intelligence system with specialized components that work in harmony towards a common instructional objective is the need of the hour.

This work presents an educational MAS framework that decentralizes intelligence among specialized agents that work together to achieve the common objective. This system is particularly suitable for education, where individualized yet coordinated agents contribute towards the pedagogical reasoning, personalization, content generation, and interaction management. An MAS is a collection of autonomous agents working together in a shared environment. All the agents perform certain tasks and synchronize with each other using structured communication. This modality has worked in multifaceted, dynamic disciplines that demand flexibility, robustness, and coordination. It also coincides with multimodal learning, in which various channels of communication can be produced, modulated, and coordinated by special agents.

The chapter presents a multi-agent educational system designed to improve multimodal learning in the era of AI. The system is constructed on a service-oriented architecture, with various agents executing particular functions. Some agents are responsible for creating subject-specific content, while others adapt lessons to individual learners. Some agents handle system conversations with the learners, while other agents manage text, speech, and visuals for effective learning. These agents are independent and autonomous. Students communicate with the education system using a central avatar, which provides an interface to them. The system can be used to provide interactive, flexible, inclusive, and transparent learning experiences making it more than mere tutoring. Its modular design also makes it scalable for diverse educational settings.

The chapter contributes to the educational field in three ways. First, it provides an evolutionary approach to educational MAS, positioning the proposed framework within more than twenty years of research. Second, it presents an adaptable and scalable framework that consolidates multimodal production, personalization, and accessibility on a system level. It offers a future-oriented framework that is capable of reimagining education in the era of AI. Third, it states how the multimodal literacy growth is supported directly by agent specialization and system coordination.

MULTIMODAL LITERACY IN THE AGE OF ARTIFICIAL INTELLIGENCE

The concept of literacy has traditionally been perceived as the ability to read and write a text. To establish how people acquire knowledge in the present era, ideas of literacy have been incorporated into a wider approach to include social and cognitive aspects. These practices entail the way people perceive and define meaning through representation forms. This extended perception is referred to as multimodal literacy. It recognizes the presence of communication and learning that occurs as a combination of different modes, such as the linguistic, the visual, the auditory, the spatial, or the gestural. Students constantly navigate and integrate information using these hybrid channels in digital learning environments.

Multimodality is a key feature of artificial intelligence-driven learning environments. Learners nowadays interact with digital tutors verbally as well. They interpret feedback provided with the help of different visual annotations. These learning experiences need a particular type of literacy skill. Learners should have the capacity to process numerous information streams at the same time. They need to understand how different modes of learning complement or contradict each other.

They also need to properly analyze and assess the reliability and validity of the AI-generated content. As a result, the aim of educational technology keeps evolving. Its main function is replaced from simply delivering information to supporting learners in the meaning-making process. The technology should therefore be designed to scaffold the learner's ability to work in multiple modes.

Artificial intelligence itself intensifies the urgency of the transformation to education. Powerful generative tools, like LLMs, have the capability to generate large amounts of audio and textual materials. But this characteristic of LLM models can be the source of major pedagogical challenges as well. Unstructured or excessive AI output can easily overwhelm a student. It can risk encouraging passive reception of information instead of active engagement of learners. That is the reason why multimodal literacy development should be thoroughly and thoughtfully designed. Any particular medium, be it video, an audio narrative, or an interactive model, should be purposefully selected. The choice of medium should directly serve a very clear learning objective. It must also consider the cognitive abilities of the diverse learners.

The embodied multimodal AI avatar is one of the technological methods to satisfy the needs of modern learners. They are used to simulate the presence of teachers by combining speech, facial expression, gesture, and contextual visuals. They have considerable potential for improving engagement and understanding of the learner. However, a few flaws exist in the current design. In many systems, multimodality is just a superficial feature. An interface layer is added to a system that is fundamentally text-based at the core. The different modes work in isolation, without a structural architecture that inherently provides proper synchronization, adaptation, and accessibility of the educational content.

This work suggests multimodal literacy as a basic structure of an education system. It cannot be an add-on feature acting at the interface level only. The deep integration is facilitated by a multi-agent system architecture. This MAS model achieves educational intelligence by specialized agents. Dedicated agents perform different pedagogical functions such as personalization, dialogue management, visual generation, and their coordination. These agents work together, directed by an instructional platform, with a shared conception of the learner. This architectural strategy can have several types of communication in a conscious, collaborative, and dynamic manner. It plays an active role in helping the learner become a competent and critical participant in a multimodal world.

The Evolution of Educational Multi-Agent Systems: A Twenty-Five Year Journey

Intelligent educational systems are being developed through a course of growing complexity. It reveals deeper insights about the way people learn as computer science advances. The idea of MAS is quite promising in the education field. In a MAS, intelligence and responsibility are distributed among a group of independent and collaborative software agents. For over a quarter-century, educational MAS have been developed beyond the mere tackling of problems of scale to the complexities of multimodal learning driven by AI. To trace the trajectory, this work presents a review of four overlapping research phases. This historical review discloses noteworthy technological advancements in MAS. It also pinpoints a persistent architectural gap that is summarized in Table 1. These gaps are the primary reasons why an integrated framework is proposed later in the chapter.

Table 1. Evolution of Educational Multi-Agent Systems (1999–2025)

S. No	Period	Core Focus	Representative Studies	Key Contributions	Persistent Limitations
1	**1999–2008**	Distributed & Modular Foundations	Riordan & Griffith (1999); Shi et al. (2000); Dorca et al. (2003); Sun et al. (2005); Longo et al. (2014)	Established scalable, modular, agent-based learning systems.	Text-based interaction; rule-driven behavior.
2	**2009–2018**	Personalization & Formalization	Braga Gago et al. (2006); Ahmad & Bokhari (2012); González et al. (2012); Hwang et al. (2013); Rodríguez et al. (2015); Estício et al. (2015); Armoni et al. (2015)	Introduced engineering rigor, security, and learner personalization.	Unimodal delivery; limited real-time adaptation.
3	**2019–2023**	Theory-Grounded & Affective Systems	Bandura & Wessels (1997); Cassidy (2015); Chi & Wylie (2014); Belland et al. (2017); Graesser et al. (2018); Hernández-Sells et al. (2019); Chen et al. (2020); Hamal et al. (2021); Viswanathan et al. (2022); Fang et al. (2022); Chen et al. (2024)	Integrated learning theory, affect, and empirical validation.	Adaptation remained non-embodied and non-multimodal.
4	**2024–2025**	LLM-Driven Agentic AI	Cress & Kimmerle (2023); Bansal et al. (2024); Jiang et al. (2024); Wang et al. (2024); Zhang et al. (2024); Yu & Zhao (2025); Gonnermann-Müller et al. (2025); Sun et al. (2025); Dai et al. (2024); Hare (2024); Kaur et al. (2025); Quarteroni et al. (2025)	Enabled reasoning, planning, and reflective agents.	Lacks integrated multimodal pipelines.

Phase I: Distributed & Modular Foundations (1999–2005)

The first educational MAS originated as a result of a practical limitation of the monolithic intelligent tutoring systems. They were unable to scale adequately in the newly created landscape of online and distance learning. Scholars, such as Riordan and Griffith (1999), suggested that the system coordination, teaching, and learner models should be handled using autonomous software agents. It made decentralization of tasks one of the core principles for achieving scalability. This idea was soon tested in practice. For example, Shi et al. (2000) presented a multi-agent framework for computer science education. They showed how instructional workflows can be managed using early agent communication protocols.

Another implementation was done by Dorca et al. (2003). Their design allocated different agents to instruction, evaluation, and learner modeling. This system was able to support large masses of students, proving that pedagogical roles could really be modularized. These technical architectures soon started to be linked to educational theory by researchers. Indicatively, Silveira and Vicari (2002) included models of learning styles into agent decision-making. Correspondingly, Sun et al. (2005) developed a system that incorporated learning objects and learning styles using an agent-based platform. Later theoretical work extended this vision of creating responsive, distributed learning spaces like smart environments by Longo et al. (2014). The initial step was a conclusive indication that MAS was capable of reasonable robustness and scale. However, these systems were text-based only. The process of adaptation remained procedural and lacked theory-informed personalization.

Phase II: Personalization & Formalization (2006–2018)

When MAS concepts left the laboratory to become a practical reality on the ground, there were two directions in which research efforts and activities took place. The first focused on the designing of reliable systems. The second aimed at rendering systems actually adaptive to the individual learners.

The stream of engineering dealt with how to construct trustworthy systems. Braga Gago et al. (2006) used Multiagent Systems Engineering (MaSE) methodology to introduce different structured engineering practices to MAS development. This period also saw advances in formalizing agent decision logic, such as the fuzzy inference system (FIS) of agent-dependency evaluation (Gaur & Soni, 2011) and the dynamic selection model in agent-mediated systems (Gaur & Sharma, 2011).

Later, Ahmad and Bokhari (2012) talked about security and encryption. They designed a framework where agent separation can be used to strengthen data protection. It was a very crucial step for making MAS viable in real-life e-learning systems. The stream of adaptive pedagogy was concerned with "who," the individual learner. Gonzalez et al. (2012) took it a step further by implementing Case-Based Reasoning (CBR) in multi-agent systems. This provided agents with some kind of institutional memory, helping them to reuse and implement solutions from previous learner interactions. Capdeferro and Romero (2012) said that frustration was one of the biggest barriers in the online learning system. Such a feeling was the result of isolation or unclear instructions. Hwang et al. (2013) revealed the effectiveness of personalized concept maps made by the agents. Estício et al. (2015) used a MAS to arrange and support pair programming sessions. Armoni et al. (2015) also showed the usefulness of agent-mediated environments for complicated transitions such as shifting learners between block-based programming and text-based programming.

Furthermore, MAS itself turned out to be a quite effective mediator of social learning. It dealt with issues pointed out by scholars like Capdeferro and Romero (2012). Rodríguez et al. (2015) presented recommendation as an important agent function. He used methods such as metadata clustering to match learners with resources. These ideas later influenced the roles allocated to agents and the inter-agent coordination.

Phase III: Theory-Grounded & Affective Systems (2012–2022)

MASs were quite influenced by the science of learning in this time period. The focus shifted from technical adaptation to personalization. Psychological foundational theories had a big role in guiding the overall agent design. This was based on the research by Bandura and Wessels (1997) on self-efficacy, which led to the design of motivational agents. The study of resilience by Cassidy (2015) offered an agent framework of helping learners to persevere.

The ICAP framework created by Chi and Wylie (2014) was one of the most prevailing blueprints. ICAP classifies learning activities and assists in shaping agent-based interaction, which results in more active and constructive learning. This theoretical direction was mainly reinforced by meta-analyses. The work reported by Belland et al. on the effectiveness of computer-based scaffolding is a prominent example (2017). Graesser et al. (2018) also mainly focused on the importance of interaction and deep engagement.

All these theories were used to build a basis for social and emotional aspects of learning. Hernandez-Sells et al. (2019) proposed emotion-sensitive agents that were capable of detecting and reacting to frustrations of the students. Chen et al. (2020) positioned MAS as a main architecture for achieving personalized support. Hamal et al. (2021) and Viswanathan et al. (2022) developed multi-agent systems using techniques like decision trees and collaborative filtering for improving their responsiveness. The MAS was useful in the development of computational thought (Fang et al., 2022). Chen et al. (2024) noticed that scaling such sophisticated adaptive systems brought new challenges related to maintaining performance and complexity.

Phase IV: LLM-Driven Agentic AI

LLMs are transforming educational multi-agent systems. Cress and Kimmerle (2023) presented generative AI as a very good source of collaborative knowledge building. It is the ideal representation of multi-agent architectures. Bansal et al.

(2024) proposed that LLMs should be treated as cognitive engines of a novel category of educational agents.

Jiang et al. (2024) designed a framework based on von Neumann architecture. Wang et al. (2024) proposed techniques of recursive introspection in which the agents were able to review their own reasoning process.

The use of such AI-powered agents and their implementation and applications are now proliferating in the education sphere. Zhang et al. (2024) studied how to replace a teacher using agents. Yu and Zhao (2025) extended such notions to the field of vocational education. Gonnermann-Muller et al. (2025) developed a teacher-centred LLM-based MAS to create personalized worksheets. The study of how learning takes place within these systems is still under research, as reported by Sun et al. (2025).

Intertwined with these technical inquisitions, the discipline is also coming of age with regard to the quality of designs and the practical impact on educational effectiveness. Dai et al. (2024) evaluated criteria for assessing adaptive learning systems. Hare (2024) explained how student experience can be conceptualized using iterative human-centred design. The engineering and quality assurance problems of these multi-agent systems were addressed by researchers Kaur et al. (2025) and Quarteroni et al. (2025).

Synthesis: The Unfinished Journey and the Architectural Imperative

The above-mentioned literature review demonstrates that there is substantial improvement in agent specialization, interaction, and multimodality. Educational MAS have evolved from distributed systems created on a scale to personal systems based on the learning theory to the present age of reasoning, agentic AI. However, the development is still far from reach.

There is a critical disconnection that persists even in the present, as can be seen in the last column of Table 1. The most advanced MAS on the basis of LLM are also architecturally focused on textual or semi-structured reasoning. Speech generation, expression generation, and contextual visual and approachable outputs are peripheral concerns. These multimodal components are the crux of modern communication, but they are not addressed as an architecture rule in an MAS design.

This gap indicates something beyond a set of missing features. It is one of the main deficits in facilitating the literacy needed today. When multimodal literacy involves making meaning from and across different media. Therefore, the educational systems should be built in such a way that they process, interpret, and generate meaning not just through text but also with the different modalities such as speech and visuals.

Even though multi-agent systems are becoming more mature in education contexts, the issue of ethical considerations has not been adequately discussed in most of the existing literature. Previous studies have indicated issues that pertain to the privacy of learner data, profiling, and ethical implications of learning analytics (Slade and Prinsloo, 2013). Some discussions on responsible artificial intelligence also highlights the transparency, responsibility, and governance issues in autonomous systems (Dignum, 2019; Floridi et al., 2018). All of these ethical dimensions of learning environments are defining the system design instead of being peripheral considerations. It also emphasizes the need to create multi-agent educational models that integrate both the principles of responsible design and technical innovation consciously.

Such a framework is introduced in the following chapters of this chapter. It is aimed at addressing the identified gaps by integrating LLM with a service-based, multi-agent system. The idea is to develop a system that can orchestrate coherent, adaptive, and inclusive multimodal learning experiences in direct support of the formation of multimodal literacy.

Proposed Multimodal LLM-Driven Educational Multi-Agent Framework

This section introduces a unified framework for an Educational Multi-Agent System (EMAS) particularly formulated to nurture multimodal literacy in an artificial intelligence-driven era. It is a direct answer to any of the constraints outlined in the historical review by synthesizing three major aspects, namely, enhanced reasoning using LLMs, pedagogical approaches rooted in learning science, and the coordination of several modes of communication. The framework leaves behind the traditional perception of agents as isolated tools. Instead, it represents the process of learning itself as a distributed cognitive activity. In the model, a society of dedicated software agents works together dynamically to develop, produce, customize, and assess education in real-time and offers a unified and responsive educational experience.

Foundational Design Principles

The proposed framework follows a set of five principles, which are derived from the synthesis of previous studies and their gaps:

1. **Dynamic Orchestration:** The agents are designed with pedagogical or computational expertise. But their cooperation is not dictated by strict workflow patterns. It has a central orchestration layer that dynamically activates agents and gives them priority according to real-time analysis of the context of the learner, instructional objectives, and system state.
2. **Multimodality as a First-Class Pedagogic Construct:** The text, speech, visual imagery, and their time-based correspondence are viewed as fundamental and

equally suitable qualities of teaching. Their combination does not come as an incidental feature but is a fundamental part of the design, which makes multimodal outputs pedagogically purposeful and coherent.

3. **Theory-driven Agent Behaviour:** The agents are directed by the decision-making logic based on the learning theories. The ICAP framework, helpful motivation, and collaborative cognition models are also some of the frameworks that are coded into agent rules to ensure pedagogically adequate interactions.
4. **Contextual and Cultural Adaptability:** The system is not just adaptive to the performance and knowledge gaps of a learner but also considers other factors of learners, such as supporting various language choices, technical limitations of the devices for using the system, and different needs of the learning environments.
5. **Comprehensive and repeatable evaluation:** A multi-faceted evaluation strategy is used to evaluate the effectiveness of the system. Measures include pedagogical quality, coherence and synchronization of multimodal outputs, and computational performance, so that results of assessment are comprehensive and consistent.

High-Level Architectural Overview

The EMAS system utilizes layered architecture to achieve modularity, scalability, and ease of integration. The system consists of four layers–Interaction layer, Coordination layer, Functional layer, and Knowledge and Model layer.

The interaction layer is responsible for providing a consistent and easy interface to the learner without exposing him to device-specific complexities. It receives all the inputs from the learner and delivers him the instructional content using different modalities like audio, video, and text.

The coordination layer is the core of the system. It is the executive controller that manages inter-agent dependencies, coordinates dynamic task allocation, synchronizes multimodal outputs, and optimizes system resources. The inter-agent communication in this layer uses the standardized messaging protocols to provide reliable coordination.

The Functional Agent Layer hosts the specialized autonomous agents to serve a particular educational or technical purpose. These agents are identified in the following section.

The knowledge layer combines the domain knowledge, the pedagogical rules, dynamic learner models, and LLMs required for the advanced reasoning.

The Functional Agent Ensemble

The EMAS framework shown in Figure 1 achieves its key goals through a group of nine specialized software agents. These agents work together to accomplish a dynamic and pedagogical process. Various agents and their roles are defined below in Table 2.

Table 2. Agents, Roles, and Enabling Technologies

S. No.	Agent	Core Function	Key Technologies
1	Coordinator Agent	Workflow orchestration and inter-agent coordination	FIPA-ACL, KQML
2	Domain Agent	Pedagogical reasoning and knowledge-grounded content generation	LLMs, Retrieval-Augmented Generation (RAG)
3	Personalization Agent	Learner modelling and adaptive instructional signalling	xAPI, engagement metrics
4	Question—Answering Agent	Interactive dialogue management and response generation	LLMs, dialogue state tracking
5	Text-to-Speech Agent	Natural and instructionally modulated speech synthesis	Bark, Coqui-TTS
6	Facial Animation Agent	Visual embodiment with synchronized facial expression	SadTalker, Wav2Lip
7	Background Generation Agent	Contextual visual scene generation for instructional grounding	Stable Diffusion XL (SDXL)
8	Subtitle Agent	Caption generation and temporal alignment	WhisperX
9	Compositor Agent	Multimodal stream synchronization and output packaging	FFmpeg

Figure 1. Proposed framework for an Educational Multi-Agent System

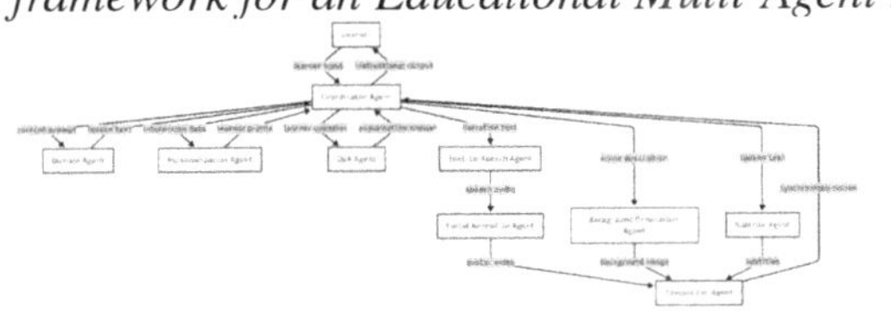

1. **Coordinator Agent:** It acts as the central command unit for the system. It controls the entire teaching-learning process. The agent takes decisions after evaluating the learner's progress, learning goals, and available system resources.

The precise mechanism by which agents communicate to achieve the inter-agent coordination is discussed in the following section.

2. **Domain Agent:** It functions as the primary teacher within the system. Its role is to provide correct and pedagogically effective content. This agent retrieves content from a structured, teacher-curated knowledge base. When the information sought by the learner is not available in the knowledge base, the agent relies on a powerful LLM to make an understandable and personalized explanation to clear the learner's doubt. It can create relevant examples and helpful analogies on the spot. However, to make sure that everything it says is factually accurate, it adopts a process called Retrieval Augmented Generation (RAG). The system will search a reliable and up-to-date knowledge base to obtain verified information through RAG before a final answer is generated. It may use systems like Haystack connected to a Pinecone database to perform the search quickly.
3. **Personalization Agent:** It is responsible for understanding the profile of an individual learner. It works as the memory of the system and its adaptation system. This agent collects information about each system-learner interaction. It records the answers and time taken by him to answer. It also takes note of instances when a learner seeks assistance. The agent organizes this complex information efficiently with the help of a modern specification named Experience API, also known as xAPI. A detailed and structured learning record is created for each learner using xAPI. These records are further analyzed by the Personalization agent to find out the strengths, weaknesses, and learning patterns of learners.
4. **Q&A Agent:** It takes care of the conversational part of learning. It maintains the communication with the learner in a natural and productive way. When the student asks a question, this agent interprets the purpose of the question and recalls the context of the whole conversation. Its greatest ability is not only to answer but also to ask the appropriate follow-up questions. It can also encourage the learner to explain their own reasoning or challenge them to think one step further. It simulates the Socratic style of teaching, where the student is led to find answers by guided dialogues. The fine-tuned interactive language models enable the agent to continue with coherent and focused conversation.
5. **Text to Speech (TTS) Agent:** It provides the system with the voice. The TTS agent converts the written text provided by the domain and the Q&A agents into articulate and easy-to-understand spoken words. The TTS agent uses tone, pace, and emphasis as teaching tools, e.g., it may reduce the speed of the speech to emphasize an important message or raise its inflection to state a query. To acquire the natural and controlled prosody, the TTS agent employs the latest technology in neural speech synthesis to create high-quality, human-like audio that is easily understandable. Systems like Bark or Coqui TTS enable the instructional purpose to be conveyed with the help of the sound or the voice itself.

6. **Facial Animation Agent:** It provides the system with a talking face. A facial agent generates a visual avatar that is able to speak and express feelings in accordance with the audio. This agent receives the speech audio from the TTS Agent and generates a corresponding video of a talking face. The lip movements are precisely matched to the words being spoken. Beyond lip sync, the avatar can show appropriate facial expressions. It may smile to motivate the learner or appear thoughtful while introducing any complicated topic. This kind of embodiment brings out a greater feeling of social presence of the teacher. Technologies like Opera's SadTalker and Wav2Lip are used directly to produce such realistic talking head avatars, making the learning process more personal and interactive.
7. **Subtitle Agent:** It is mainly used to make learning accessible to all the people by providing accurate, real-time captions for all spoken content. This precise synchronization is vital for learners who are deaf or hard of hearing and for anyone who prefers to read along.
8. **Background Generation Agent:** It prepares a visual environment in every lesson. It generates thematic pictures and scenes that support the subject of teaching in the background. Assuming it is a lesson on marine biology, this agent may create a picture of a coral reef. To teach a lesson about Shakespeare, it may make a setting of the Globe. These images are developed by the background agent with the help of strong generative AI, such as Stable Diffusion XL.
9. **Compositor Agent:** It is the multimedia editor of the system. This agent receives all the components, such as the audio, the talking avatar, the background image, and the subtitle files, from various agents. Its pivotal task is to integrate all the files into one complete, smooth video lesson. Also, it synchronizes all the files in frame-perfect precision so that the lips move with the audio and the captions appear at the right moment. Any kind of misalignment may distract the learner and hamper knowledge dissemination. To obtain the professional level of integration, the compositor agent uses a powerful and actively used multimedia platform known as FFmpeg. It is capable of encoding, mixing, and synchronizing all the media streams to create a finished and cohesive learning object.

Illustrative Instructional Scenario

Consider a learner called Sam who is studying a software engineering course. The EMAS interface is opened and presented to Sam that enable him to select one of the topics: the Waterfall Model. A virtual teaching avatar appears on the screen, which guides him through each and every step of the traditional software development method.

The avatar starts by taking Sam through each of the sequential stages of the model one by one, like requirements analysis, system design, implementation, testing, deployment, and maintenance. Sam is not simply listening, but he is watching a dynamic presentation. The expressions of the avatar keep changing to highlight important points. The background has relevant visuals, and subtitles keep running. The system presents the Waterfall model as a in-progress explanation, one that is tailored specially for him.

The coordinator agent is the one behind the scenes facilitating the information flow and pace and serves as the director of the entire learning experience. The Domain Agent provides the detailed explanation of the topic and makes sure it is accurate as well as pedagogically organized to increase the understanding of the learner.

As Sam watches the model, a question arises in his mind: Is it possible to go back to a previous stage of the Waterfall model? Sam paused the lesson and typed his query in the chat box. Instantly, the Q&A Agent addresses this question and keeps the conversation going. It then deciphers the query and asks the Personalization Agent, which creates the learner profile of Sam. The virtual instructor returns to Sam and provides a brief and specific explanation. It can make an analogy that Sam has previously responded well in the past without interrupting or interrupting the lesson. It seems to be an instinctive, passive teaching occasion to Sam and just not a system response.

A group of specialized autonomous agents interact to ensure that learning experience is smooth. The avatar gets the voice by the TTS Agent. The Facial Animation Agent makes sure that expressions of avatar are in sync with the speech. The Compositor Agent integrates all the files together to a unified video stream. At the end of the lesson, Sam is not just a consumer of information, but he interacts with the system and perceives it to be responsive and adaptive.

Inter-Agent Communication and Coordination Design

Inter-agent communication is the fundamental characteristic of a EMAS. It requires a strong communicative paradigm to organize the activities of various agents to create a well-integrated instructional experience. The EMAS design focuses on inter-agent coordination without reducing modularity that empowers the system to be scalable and adaptive.

The Communication Paradigm

The proposed educational system uses a standard multi-agent communication model for inter-agent coordination. Agents cooperate and interact with each other by exchanging messages. The framework utilises the communication architecture governed by a central coordinator agent that is responsible for sequencing and routing messages and the overall state of the system. Once each agent is assigned tasks by the coordinator agent, it remains autonomous with respect to the way it processes the received messages and accomplishes the tasks assigned to it.

The inter-agent communication is designed using principles of engineering multi-agent systems to achieve cross-system compatibility. These norms are required to achieve a standard system using a set of predefined interaction patterns.

Communication Protocols and Standards

Inter-agent communication using message passing is based on two standards– Foundation of Intelligent Physical Agents-Agent Communication Language (FIPA ACL) and Knowledge Query and Manipulation Language (KQML). FIPA ACL defines a full-fledged message structure that includes the sender, the receiver, a unique conversation identifier, and, most importantly, the communicative act or performative. These performatives state the intentions of the sender, like requesting some service, passing information, or making some commitment.

To organize the semantic content of messages, particularly the messages that contain pedagogical knowledge and instructional logic, the framework adopts the concepts of KQML. The language offers a higher-level vocabulary for expressing knowledge-oriented operations that involve querying, asserting, and subscribing to information streams.

All messages are serialized in an organized, machine-readable format. The structure of the framework can accommodate XML or other schemas. This makes messages self-describing, easily validated, and suitable for logging, debugging, and later analysis of system behavior.

Detailed Communicative Primitives

The system utilizes some fundamental basic set of communicative primitives, or performatives.

1. **Request primitive:** One agent requests another agent to perform a task. It carries all necessary parameters for the task. For example, the Domain Agent

is requested by the Coordinator Agent to create a lesson on a given topic at the appropriate difficulty level.

2. **Inform primitive:** It is used to convey information, data, or the result of a completed action. There is no implicit requirement for a subsequent act. After the Domain Agent obtains the complete information about the desired concept, it sends an Inform message back to the coordinator agent. This message contains the structured lesson plan.
3. **Query Ref:** It is a knowledge retrieval primitive. A Query Ref asks an agent to provide a given piece of information from its knowledge base. The Q&A agent makes use of this primitive to request the complete lesson from the Domain Agent.
4. **Propose primitive:** It is used for adaptive and collaborative planning. It is used by an agent to propose a possible action or change in the existing plan. The Personalization Agent may recommend to the coordinator agent that the explanation should be accompanied with a visual analogy due to high error rates reported by learners.
5. **Confirm and Acknowledge primitives:** These agents verify that they are in sync with each other. Confirm primitive is used to approve that there is understanding or consent on a lesson plan. Acknowledge primitive is a simple receipt for confirmation primitive.
6. **Failure and Refuse primitives:** These primitives are quite essential for robust error handling. When a Request cannot be fulfilled by an agent because of an internal error, or lack of data, the agent replies with a Failure message along with an error code. If an agent is designed to reject certain types of requests based on its roles, it sends a Refuse. This allows the coordinator to initiate contingency plans and actions.

Coordination Workflow and Feedback Integration

These primitives follow a dynamic workflow managed by the Coordinator Agent. Figure 2 represents the full orchestration process and coordination between agents with the help of a sequence-based interaction model

A typical instructional cycle starts with a question by the learner. The coordinator agent requests the Domain Agent to generate an explanation. When the Coordinator receives an Inform message containing the response content, then it analyses the structure. It then sends request to the corresponding rendering agents. Rendering agents consist of the Text to Speech Agent to narrate, the facial animation agent to form the avatar, the Background agent to display and the subtitle agent as shown in the figure.

Figure 2. Sequence diagram of inter-agent communication

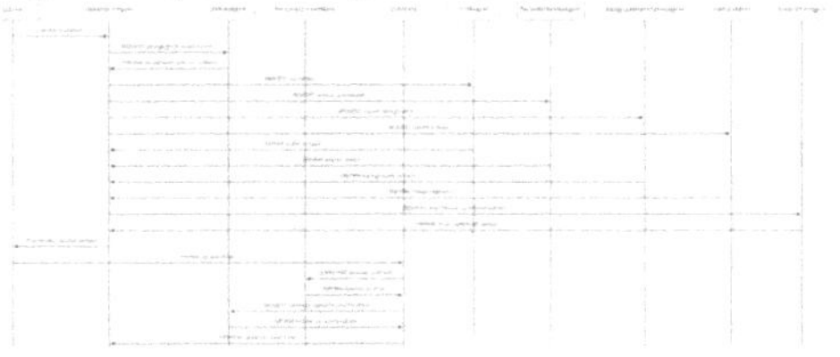

Each rendering agent is asynchronous in nature. An Inform message is sent by each of them back to the coordinator on completion. This message includes the produced media file and important timing metadata, like audio duration. These outputs are collected by the coordinator agent. It then forwards a Request to the Compositor Agent to ensure all the files are in sync. The Compositor agent integrates the components and an Inform message is sent to signal that the lesson is ready.

Learning however is a dialogic process that requires responsiveness. The system is adapted to the learner queries and misconceptions of learners in real time through a dedicated feedback loop, controlled by Q&A agent. This loop works simultaneously with the primary instructional loop, and provides the opportunity of dynamical intervention without reinitiating the whole process.

Feedback loop is activated when the learner asks a follow-up question or shows any sign of confusion. The learner input is taken by the system and then Q&A Agent comes into the picture.

The Q&A Agent passes on a Query-Ref to the Personalization Agent first. This query retrieves the profile that the learner is in at the current time, like learning history, error records and explanation demands. The Personalization Agent replies with an Inform message with this contextual information. It serves only a responsive purpose; it enriches the context of learners on-demand but does not interrupt the teaching process autonomously.

Armed with this learner context, the Q&A Agent then sends a request to the Domain Agent. It gives the exact position of the learner cycle that the learner is stuck at and integrates the learner parameters in the learner profile. This is passed on to the domain agent, who gives it a concise, pedagogically organized follow-up explanation as an Inform.

Lastly, this new content should be incorporated in the Q&A Agent. It sends a Propose message to the Coordinator Agent. In this proposal the new clarification and a proposed point of integration are like giving a break in the existing lesson, and inserting a micro-explanation, or including it as an additional note. The coordinator agent compares this proposal on the state of current instructional goals and sessions. Upon approval, the coordinator will easily add the new material to the workflow to announce and move on to a specific rendering cycle of the follow-up explanation without interfering with the flow of the rest of the learning session. This is a process that underpins the transformation of the system of a monolithic content deliverer to an interactive and a conversation partner.

Synchronization and State Management

The temporal alignment of the outputs produced by independent agents is one of the key technical problems. The educational framework addresses this issue through metadata in Inform messages, not through real time negotiation. By declaring the properties of their output, such as audio length, the rendering agents enable the Coordinator and Compositor agents to construct a feasible synchronization schedule. This declarative coordination reduces tight coupling and interdependencies.

The Coordinator Agent has a lightweight conversation state per session of the learner. This state is used to monitor the pending requests, requests that have been received and the current phase of instruction. This condition is necessary in order to properly route messages, deal with timeouts, and make the adaptive proposals of the Q&A Agent contextually relevant.

Extensibility and Interoperability

The educational framework is a growth-oriented communication architecture. New agents can be added to increase the functionality of the system. As inter-agent communication is standardized and decoupled from internal agent logic, the underlying technology of any agent can be upgraded independently. For example, swapping the current large language model in the Domain Agent for a newer version requires no changes to how it sends or receives Inform and Query Ref messages. This preserves the entire system's stability while allowing for continuous technological advancement.

Evaluation Strategy

Although the chapter proposes an architectural framework, the system is intended to facilitate an organized empirical evaluation of instructional and technical aspects. The learning effectiveness can be measured with the help of indicators such as conceptual understanding, task accuracy, and long-term retention. The learner engagement can be checked with interaction frequency, response time and number of queries.

Multimodal instructional output may also be assessed using objective quality measures such as Signal-to-Noise Ratio (SNR) and Short-Time Objective Intelligibility (STOI), which can be used to evaluate the clarity and intelligibility of speech. ROUGE-1 and ROUGE-L scores to assess subtitle quality. Structural Similarity Index (SSIM) and Peak Signal-to-Noise Ratio (PSNR) for video quality and synchronization accuracy are to make sure that the lips, audio, and subtitles move simultaneously.

In system terms, the performance indicators comprise inference time, or how fast the system can generate outputs, and real-time factor, or how much as compared to real playback time there is efficacy of processing time in order to find whether efficient content can be generated in real or near-real time instruction. Since the framework is modular, individual agents can be evaluated or disabled according to their individual contribution to the overall instruction performance.

Combined, these measures facilitate the holistic evaluation of the framework as a pedagogical system and as a multi-agent architecture that can be validated in the future.

Reimagining Multimodal Literacy development using MAS

This chapter has clearly examined that the current educational technologies fail to meet the standards to promote multimodal literacy needed in the modern learning settings. This work has proposed a multi-agent framework in which some specialized agents work together to create adaptive and coherent learning experiences. This proposal goes far beyond its technical architecture to an architectural change in the fabrication of systems in relation to the development of literacy.

To begin with, this framework redefines the main locus of literacy practices. Whereas literacy is commonly regarded as a skill used in relation to a static text or a prerecorded media. The proposed model develops literacy through active engagement of learners with a responsive system. The query of a student leads to a coordinated process of pedagogical reasoning, individualization, and multimodal representation. The learner does not merely read text or watch a video, but converses with an intelligent system that can explain, illustrate things graphically, highlight points by altering the voice, and ask questions to assess the learner.

In addition, the framework reinvigorates the goal of artificial intelligence in educational contexts. Widespread use of AI makes it a source of answers or a content generator. The large language model in the Domain Agent produces explanations, but this is guided by instructional rules based on verified knowledge. The AI in the Q&A Agent makes the dialogue more towards Socratic scaffolding than an open-ended conversation. In short, no single AI component governs the instructional experience. Their functions are managed by the Coordinator Agent and later refined by a learner model using Personalised agent. The design allows AI to serve as an enabling feature of a sound pedagogical process by modelling the way technology of advanced complexity could be used to develop critical skills instead of avoiding them.

Finally, the methodology offers a tangible way of achieving universally inclusive literacy teaching. The concept of accessibility is usually considered through feature additions to an existing system. The existing framework combines these capacities as core agent functions from inception. Subtitle Agent provides access with captioning, and the Personalization Agent dynamically changes the emphasis of modality depending on the profiles of the learners. As a result, neurodiversity and varied learning preferences are inherently implemented in the system. It proves that advanced AI-driven education can be inherently adaptable and equitable by design.

To sum up, the overall contribution of this multi-agent framework is both practical and conceptual. Practically, it offers a next generation architecture of learning systems that is detailed and implementable. Theoretically, it assumes that the future of literacy development lies in intelligence coordination. Such systems are modelled based on the framework and they change the paradigm of isolated digital tools to integrated, literacy-based learning.

The framework offers a conceptual design of a new type of learning environment which aims to transform a blueprint into a working system. It is very important at first to identify existing limitations and establish a well-defined and focused path for development of the system. The main weakness of the existing models is that they are theoretical which still needs empirical validation to support the instructional claims it makes. The other major challenge is the technical implementation of the system. Coordinated operation of multiple agents need high computational resources which can probably limit scalability in common educational settings. The design of the system is also dependent on the usage of other intelligent components that are themselves in a rapid and unpredictable state of evolution. Such dependencies may cause instability as AI models are rapidly growing and thus the system may require some significant changes in architecture after some time.

To overcome these limitations, the first thing in the future is to create an operational MAS prototype for education. This prototype won't be only assessed based on its technical performance but also would be evaluated on the basis of the competencies acquired by the learners. The future research may focus on integrating multiple AI agents in an effective way so that the system is a complimentary to the existing educational system not a replacement. In addition, the educational MAS should support a robust ethical governance to protect the privacy of leaners.

CONCLUSION

This study presents an educational MAS system to overcome the limitations of existing systems. Existing systems mainly lack flexibility and are not very equipped with aligning texts, audios, and visual effects to the study environment. So, the proposed system was designed to align the pedagogical coherence with synchronized system behaviour, using multimodal resources. The multi-agent learning environment seems a viable and ethical course for the future development of educational technology.

This chapter presented a historical background of intelligent systems to the proposed educational framework. The AI-based software agents focus on different pedagogical needs of the learners that enable them to focus and progress beyond monolithic educational tools. This framework utilizes guided LLM to address the advanced reasoning needs of the learners. An integrated lecture including text, speech, and visual content is presented to learners that supports their engagement across the various sessions.

This work supported and complemented the existing education in two ways. First, it provides a modular and extensible architecture that can be expanded by adding more agents or even upgrading the functionality of an isolated agent. Secondly, it assists learners to reason using Q&A, enhances their engagement using multimodal generation, and personalizes the learning. Such an AI-driven system in the field of education is needed to address the complex, multimodal needs of the contemporary world.

REFERENCES

Ahmad, S., & Bokhari, M. U. (2012). A new approach to multi-agent based architecture for secure and effective e-learning. *International Journal of Computer Applications*, *46*(22), 26–29. DOI: 10.5120/7098-9826

Armoni, M., Meerbaum-Salant, O., & Ben-Ari, M. (2015). From Scratch to "real" programming. *ACM Transactions on Computing Education*, *14*(4), 25. Advance online publication. DOI: 10.1145/2677087

Bandura, A., & Wessels, S. (1997). *Self-efficacy*. Cambridge University Press.

Bansal, G., Wu, T., Zhou, J., & Kim, J. (2024). Beyond chatbots: Large language models as educational agents. *Cognitive Computation*. Advance online publication. DOI: 10.1007/s12559-024-10235-1

Belland, B. R., Walker, A. E., Kim, N. J., & Lefler, M. (2017). Synthesizing results from empirical research on computer-based scaffolding. *Review of Educational Research*, *87*(2), 309–344. DOI: 10.3102/0034654316670999

Braga Gago, P., Silva, A., & Lucena, C. (2006). Formalizing multi-agent system design using the MaSE methodology. *Journal of Systems Architecture*, *52*(8–9), 501–517. DOI: 10.1016/j.sysarc.2006.02.003

Capdeferro, N., & Romero, M. (2012). Are online learners frustrated with collaborative learning? *International Review of Research in Open and Distance Learning*, *13*(2), 26–44. DOI: 10.19173/irrodl.v13i2.1127

Cassidy, S. (2015). Resilience building in students. *Frontiers in Psychology*, *6*, 1781. DOI: 10.3389/fpsyg.2015.01781

Chen, L., Chen, P., & Lin, Z. (2020). Artificial intelligence in education: A review. *IEEE Access : Practical Innovations, Open Solutions*, *8*, 75264–75278. DOI: 10.1109/ACCESS.2020.2988510

Chen, X. J., Wang, Y., & Li, S. (2024). Challenges of scaling intelligent tutoring systems. *Education and Information Technologies*, *29*, 1–22.

Chi, M. T. H., & Wylie, R. (2014). The ICAP framework. *Educational Psychologist*, *49*(4), 219–243. DOI: 10.1080/00461520.2014.965823

Cress, U., & Kimmerle, J. (2023). Generative AI as a catalyst for collaborative knowledge construction. *International Journal of Computer-Supported Collaborative Learning*, *18*(4), 607–614. DOI: 10.1007/s11412-023-09409-w

Dai, C. P.. (2024). Adaptive learning systems in AI-supported education. *Educational Psychology Review, 36*(1), 31. DOI: 10.1007/s10648-024-09855-4

Dignum, V. (2019). *Responsible artificial intelligence: How to develop and use AI in a responsible way*. Springer., DOI: 10.1007/978-3-030-30371-6

Dorca, F. A., Lima, L. V., Fernandes, M. A., & Lopes, C. R. (2003). Multi-agent tutoring systems for distance education. In *Proceedings of the International Conference on Artificial Intelligence in Education* (pp. 434–435).

Estício, B., Prates, R. O., & Magalhães, M. F. (2015). Supporting pair programming with multi-agent systems. In *Proceedings of the Brazilian Symposium on Software Engineering* (pp. 150–159).

Fang, J. W., Chang, C. C., & Hwang, G. J. (2022). Developing computational thinking through intelligent agents. *Journal of Educational Computing Research, 60*(5), 1301–1324. DOI: 10.1177/07356331211060470

Floridi, L., Cowls, J., Beltrametti, M., Chatila, R., Chazerand, P., Dignum, V., Luetge, C., Madelin, R., Pagallo, U., Rossi, F., Schafer, B., Valcke, P., & Vayena, E. (2018). AI4People- An ethical framework for a good AI society: Opportunities, risks, principles, and recommendations. *Minds and Machines, 28*(4), 689–707. DOI: 10.1007/s11023-018-9482-5

Gaur, V., & Sharma, N. K. (2011). A dynamic seller selection model for an agent mediated e-market. *Communications in Computer and Information Science, 191*(Part 2), 284–295. DOI: 10.1007/978-3-642-22714-1_30

Gaur, V., & Soni, A. (2011). Evaluating degree of dependency from domain knowledge using fuzzy inference system. *Communications in Computer and Information Science, 204*, 101–111. DOI: 10.1007/978-3-642-24043-0_11

Gonnermann-Müller, J., Haase, J., Fackeldey, K., & Pokutta, S. (2025). FACET: Teacher-centred LLM-based multi-agent systems. *arXiv preprint arXiv:2508.11401*.

González, M., Burguillo, J. C., & Llamas, M. (2012). Case-based reasoning in multi-agent intelligent tutoring systems. *Expert Systems with Applications, 39*(9), 8014–8023.

Graesser, A. C.. (2018). Complex learning environments. *Psychological Science in the Public Interest, 19*(2), 59–92. DOI: 10.1177/1529100618808244

Hamal, O., El Faddouli, N. E., & Harouni, M. H. A. (2021). Design and implementation of a multi-agent system in education. *World Journal on Educational Technology: Current Issues, 13*(4), 775–793. DOI: 10.18844/wjet.v13i4.6264

Hare, J. (2024). Enhancing student experience with iterative design. *British Journal of Educational Technology*. Advance online publication. DOI: 10.1111/bjet.13456

Hernández-Sells, N., Muñoz-Carril, P. C., & González-Sanmamed, M. (2019). Emotion-aware agents in collaborative learning. *Computers & Education, 138*, 1–12.

Hwang, G. J., Sung, H. Y., Hung, C. M., Huang, I., & Tsai, C. C. (2013). Development of a personalized concept map-based learning approach. *Computers & Education, 69*, 121–130. DOI: 10.1016/j.compedu.2013.07.008

Jiang, Y.-H., Li, R., Zhou, Y., Qi, C., Hu, H., Wei, Y., Jiang, B., & Wu, Y. (2024). AI agent for education: Von Neumann multi-agent system framework. *Proceedings of GCCCE, 2024*, 77–84.

Kaur, X., Yadav, Y., & Singh, Z. (2025). A novel approach to streamline requirements engineering for multi-agent systems. In *OASIcs*. ICPEC.

Longo, M.. (2014). Smart environments and agent-based learning. *Journal of Environmental Protection and Ecology, 12*(4A), 2225–2235.

Quarteroni, S.. (2025). Refining quality requirements in agent-mediated systems. In *Proceedings of AAMAS 2025*.

Riordan, R., & Griffith, N. (1999). Distributed multi-agent architectures for distance learning. In *Proceedings of CATE 1999*.

Rodríguez, P. A., Duque, N. D., & Ovalle, D. A. (2015). Multi-agent system for knowledge-based recommendation of learning objects. *Advances in Distributed Computing and Artificial Intelligence Journal, 4*(1), 80–89.

Shi, H., Shang, Y., & Chen, S.-S. (2000). A multi-agent system for computer science education. *Proceedings of ITiCSE, 2000*, 1–4. DOI: 10.1145/343048.343051

Silveira, I. F., & Vicari, R. M. (2002). Adaptive multi-agent systems with learning styles. In *Proceedings of AIED 2002*.

Slade, S., & Prinsloo, P. (2013). Learning analytics: Ethical issues and dilemmas. *The American Behavioral Scientist, 57*(10), 1510–1529. DOI: 10.1177/0002764213479366

Sun, S., Joy, M., & Griffiths, N. (2005). Learning objects and learning styles in a multi-agent system. *Proceedings of ED-MEDIA, 2005*, 3403–3410.

Sun, Y., et al. (2025). Learning processes in multi-agent tutoring systems. *Journal of Educational Technology Research*.

Viswanathan, N., Meacham, S., & Adedoyin, F. F. (2022). Enhancement of online education using a multi-agent approach. *Computers and Education: Artificial Intelligence, 3*, 100057. DOI: 10.1016/j.caeai.2022.100057

Wang, X., ... (2024). Recursive introspection: Teaching language model agents how to self-improve. In *Advances in Neural Information Processing Systems (NeurIPS 2024).*

Yu, H., & Zhao, L. (2025). LLM-based multi-agent chatbots for vocational education. *International Journal of Educational Technology in Higher Education, 22*(1).

Zhang, J., ... (2024). Multi-agent classroom frameworks with LLM-powered pedagogical roles. In *AIED 2024 Workshop Proceedings.*

ADDITIONAL READING

Baker, R. S., & Inventado, P. S. (2014). Educational data mining and learning analytics. In Larusson, J. A., & White, B. (Eds.), *Learning analytics* (pp. 61–75). Springer., DOI: 10.1007/978-1-4614-3305-7_4

Graesser, A. C., Chipman, P., Haynes, B. C., & Olney, A. (2005). AutoTutor: An intelligent tutoring system with mixed-initiative dialogue. *IEEE Transactions on Education, 48*(4), 612–618. DOI: 10.1109/TE.2005.856149

Graesser, A. C., Person, N. K., & Magliano, J. P. (1995). Collaborative dialogue patterns in naturalistic one-to-one tutoring. *Applied Cognitive Psychology, 9*(6), 495–522. DOI: 10.1002/acp.2350090604

Jennings, N. R., & Wooldridge, M. (1995). Intelligent agents: Theory and practice. *The Knowledge Engineering Review, 10*(2), 115–152. DOI: 10.1017/S0269888900008122

Kasneci, E., Seßler, K., Küchemann, S., Bannert, M., Dementieva, D., Fischer, F., & Kasneci, G. (2023). ChatGPT for good? On opportunities and challenges of large language models for education. *Learning and Individual Differences, 103*, 102274. DOI: 10.1016/j.lindif.2023.102274

Luck, M., McBurney, P., Shehory, O., & Willmott, S. (2005). *Agent technology: Computing as interaction.* AgentLink.

Stone, P., & Veloso, M. (2000). Multiagent systems: A survey from a machine learning perspective. *Autonomous Robots, 8*(3), 345–383. DOI: 10.1023/A:1008942012299

Sycara, K. P. (1998). Multiagent systems. *AI Magazine*, *19*(2), 79–92. DOI: 10.1609/aimag.v19i2.1370

Viswanathan, N., Meacham, S., & Adedoyin, F. F. (2022). Enhancement of online education using a multi-agent approach. *Computers and Education: Artificial Intelligence*, *3*, 100057. DOI: 10.1016/j.caeai.2022.100057

Wooldridge, M. (2009). *An introduction to multiagent systems* (2nd ed.). John Wiley & Sons.

KEY TERMS AND DEFINITIONS

Agent Coordination: It is the process by which coordination among various agents is established, actions synchronized, and interdependency between agents can be managed in complex educational settings.

Collaborative Learning: It is a pedagogical model used in which knowledge is built through teacher-learner interactions. Multi-agent systems facilitate the process of collaborative learning by mediation and monitoring of participation within the group.

Educational Agent: It is an independent or semi-independent software agent which helps facilitate learning and teaching, including tutoring, feedback development, assessment, or content modification.

Evaluation Metrics: Measures applied to determine the effectiveness, quality and performance of education systems such as learning outcomes, quality of interaction, and efficiency of the system.

Intelligent Tutoring System (ITS): It is a learning system that claims to offer personalized instruction and feedback without active human oversight. Multi-agent architectures are increasingly used by modern ITS in order to address the shortcomings of single-agent ITS.

Large Language Model (LLM): A data-driven language model which can understand and generate the English language at an advanced level. Recently, LLDMs have allowed more conversational and explanatory reasoning, and dialogue within educational agents.

Multi-Agent System (MAS): It is a system of computation, layered with multiple autonomous agents, which exchange and coordinate to reach common or complementary goals. In education MAS allow the apportionment of educational, adaptive, and assessment tasks among specialized agents enhancing scalability and elasticity.

Personalization: Adaption of the learning content, teaching methods, or pattern of interaction depending on the performance information, preferences, or patterns of interactions with a specific learner.

Scalability: It is the capability of an educational system to sustain performance and quality in instruction as the number of users, interactions or learning tasks increases.

Chapter 7
Exploring Reader Perceptions of Literary Narratives:
A Quantitative Study on Identity Construction, Social Impact, and Ecological Awareness

K. Hamna
University of Calicut, India

A. Ayyoob
http://orcid.org/0009-0003-2839-3598
University of Calicut, India

ABSTRACT

Reading literature shapes readers through the Identity Reflection through Literature (IRL), Narrative Impact on Social Awareness (NISA), and Ecological Consciousness via Literary Engagement (ECLE) processes. Despite strong theoretical support, quantitative evidence remains limited. In this study a total of 246 readers were surveyed (Jan–May 2025) and their responses were analyzed using descriptive statistics, t-tests, and ANOVA. The results revealed that readers experienced very high identity reflection and ecological awareness, but only moderate social awareness. Younger readers and females reported higher engagement across all dimensions. The findings confirm the multidimensional impact of literature and its potential for fostering self-reflection, empathy, and ecological thinking.

DOI: 10.4018/979-8-2600-2163-7.ch007

1. INTRODUCTION

In an era marked by still more fragmentation of societies, ecological crises, and tensions with identity, literature remained an uncanny mirror through which individuals and communities could examine their roles, responsibilities, and reflections. Narratives are not mere aesthetic manifestations—they could create consciousness, initiate empathy, or spur reflective action. Literary texts situate readers on a stage where they may dive into intricate questions about identity, power, justice, and ecological sustainability. Literature has been given fairly high esteem across disciplines; however, fewer empirical inquiries stand to substantiate the claims for the psychological and socio-cultural impact of literature.

Recent interdisciplinary research has highlighted literature's role in raising social awareness, facilitating the negotiation of identity, or deepening ecological consciousness. Scholars such as Sriratana (2008) and Holmes (2023) have considered literature to be a "laboratory of the mind," where personal and collective narratives may be recreated. This is a two-ended identity-related problem for individuals on the road to self-formation, which is usually influenced by storytelling—a process through which readers associate themselves with characters in conflict, oppression, or cultural hybridity (Sayuti, 2020; Aquino & Salvador, 2024). Conversely, ecocriticism scholars also stress establishing environmental awareness through literature, suggesting that the genre impresses ecological concerns on them with emotional immediacy (Rishma & Gill, 2024; Dorias, 2024). Nonetheless, small numbers of empirical studies investigated how contemporary readers respond to such literary engagements across different gender and age categories.

The problem under investigation in this research is the paucity of quantitative studies that elucidate the effect of literature on identity reflection, social awareness, and ecological consciousness. Much of the present conception remains within the theoretical or qualitative realms of discourse. As a matter of fact, even in fields where processes of real behavioural change are the name of the game-such as sustainability and CSR-the cognitive-emotional power of literature is rarely appreciated. Ayyoob and Sajeev (2024a) point out how dishonest corporate environmental narratives—the so-called 'greenwashing'—contaminate the public mind with misconceptions, suggesting that genuine narratives in literary constructs may correct these misconceptions. Similarly, Ayyoob and Sajeev (2024b) take on DEI in sustainable practices-a theme that corresponds to the textual inclusivity of literature as a force for raising social awareness, especially towards the display of marginalised voices.

Further, Ayyoob and Sajeev (2024c) put forth an emphatic statement that in modern times, calls for greater alignment between sustainability aspirations and narrative practices in corporate communication are simultaneously arguing for the need for clearer communication on environmental and social responsibility. These insights suggest the transformative power of narrative framing, which this study tries to apply in the context of literary engagement. The absence of integration between literary scholarship and sustainability-oriented behavioural- and organisational studies (e.g., CSR, social entrepreneurship) is a significant research gap. The second Ayyoob and Sajeev (2024d) opine that social entrepreneurship behaviour is created by two factors, strategy and context, and also moral reflection and storytelling, accounting for literature's subliminal pull. The authors also argue that innovation and CSR need to be analyzed as culturally and psychologically embedded processes-those exact kinds of integration that literature can develop by means of engagement both cognitively and emotively (Ayyoob and Sajeev 2025).

This research intends to empirically investigate three super-related constructs: Identity Reflection through Literature (IRL), Narrative Impact on Social Awareness (NISA), and Ecological Consciousness via Literary Engagement (ECLE). The study employs quantitative techniques in order to ascertain the mean levels of engagement in these spheres and also to identify the demographic influences from gender and age on literary interpretation. The significance of the study lies in how it can bring a rapprochement between theories of conceptualization and applied educational theories plus cultural development and sustainability awareness.

The research questions driving this work are (1) to what extent do readers engage with identity, social justice, and ecological themes in literature? (2) To what degree do gender and age affect these engagement levels? There are two objectives: first, to measure the intensity of all three dimensions in the reader's response, and second, to find differences at the group level. By addressing these questions, not only will the study address an evident empirical gap, but it will also suggest ways that pedagogues might develop these solutions to foster literature as a means of promoting reflection and cultivating socially responsible minds.

2. LITERATURE REVIEW AND RESEARCH GAP

Literature is not just a mirror reflecting the human experience, but it is a dynamic space for identity formation, social consciousness, and ecological awareness. Narratives have long been recognised as meaning-building machinery through which readers enter into the gaze of both personal and collective identities (Hogan, 2019; Sayuti, 2020). From the perspective of identity construction, a literary text thus becomes an interpretative space where individuals see their own lives reflected in the lives of the characters. This reflective nature of literature allows for self-recognition that feeds into the continuing construction of the self (Aquino & Salvador, 2024; Holmes, 2023). Through narrative empathy, readers find themselves navigating through their values, beliefs, and emotions in response to experiences encountered by characters.

Identity formation in literature is affected by socio-political and cultural intersections. As Sriratana (2008) puts it, literature is a “laboratory of the mind” where readers confront trauma and come to terms with a coherent sense of self through the medium of literature. Furthermore, accounts that speak of displacement, hybridity, and migration-the same themes presented in the works of Lahiri and Mistry-are involved in this finished investigation into the question of identity, particularly when it concerns multicultural and postcolonial matters (Akhtar, 2024; Qazi, 2022; Ray, 2024).

Along with the identity, literature raises consciousness on social concerns. It has been confirmed that literary works can stir strong emotional and moral engagement in themes such as gender, inequality, systemic oppression, and trauma (Nguy n, 2023; Lanser, 2016; Lewińska, 2024). Sachar (2024) reflects on how media and literature inform public ideas on gender constructions and marginalised voices. Loyola et al. (2023) show that narratives can build communal perceptions and promote public decisions even when policies in the transport sector are being decided, thus hinting at the more social applications of literature.

Thematic representations of resistance, social injustice, and trauma serve to provide readers with a window through which they may critically examine the structures of society. For example, novels such as Afterlives and Wild Thorns expose political repression and resistance under colonial systems, compelling readers to interrogate the bigger narratives (Mahmoud, 2019; Saxena, 2023). These narratives work in the line of Shyshkin (2024) and Alahou (2023), who speak of the interdisciplinary utility of narrative-the blending of literary aesthetics with sociological, psychological, and ethical discourse.

The other emergent and expanding domain within literary studies now becomes that of literature and ecological consciousness. Ecocriticism and the environmental humanities seek to analyze how texts engage with the tension between humans and the natural world. Rishma and Gill (2024) argue that literary narratives have a potential for remodeling ecological consciousness and engendering a certain set of sustainable behaviours. Indigenous storytelling traditions like Bukidnon's gauged (Dorias, 2024) and modern novels like Rahasia Pelangi (Insany et al., 2024) illustrate the power of storytelling to convey and critique environmental knowledge and destruction. As Sheetal and Kumar (2024) state, literature provides a unique framework to engage readers emotionally and morally about environmental issues, something rarely achieved through technical discourse. Despite ample interdisciplinary literature, empirical work seems to be lacking on how readers functionally perceive and internalize such literary thematic content. More often than not, scholarship remains mired in textual analyses and theoretical frameworks, with only a handful of efforts aft seeking to quantify the impact of literature in terms of the readers' self-construction, social awareness, and environmentally conscious behavior toward comparative lines such as gender and age, which would therefore point to significant differences in literary influence.

The works by Ayyoob and Sajeev (2024a–d; 2025) emphasize that organisations and education must employ evidence-based approaches to sustainability, diversity, and ethics. Applying similar evaluative frameworks to literary engagement could result in potential recommendations to practitioners, educators, curriculum designers, and social researchers. This study focuses on the act of reading, that is, quantitatively assessing how readers perceive identity, social awareness, and ecological engagement, thus filling a methodological and thematic gap.

The current research builds three interconnected theoretical frameworks that create the constructs of Identity Reflection through Literature (IRL) and Narrative Impact on Social Awareness (NISA) and Ecological Consciousness via Literary Engagement (ECLE). The first proposition of IRL establishes its foundation on narrative identity theory which states that people develop their identities by interacting with stories which present them with meaningful frameworks (Hogan, 2019; Holmes, 2023). Readers of literature use the text as a symbolic space to establish their self-concepts through the processes of identification and projection and reflection. The NISA framework establishes its foundation on social cognition and narrative persuasion theory which show that narrative exposure improves empathy and moral reasoning and social structure understanding through people learning to see things from the viewpoint of underrepresented communities (Nguy n 2023 Lanser 2016). The theoretical framework of ECLE exists within the fields of ecocriticism and environmental psychology because literary narratives function as tools which develop pro-environmental attitudes through their ability to create emotional bonds between readers and environmental issues (Rishma Gill 2024). The study develops a unified conceptual framework which connects literary engagement to three aspects of reader perception which include cognitive and social and ecological elements.

Therefore, this study aims to evaluate the perceived identity reflection, social awareness, and ecological consciousness of readers through narratives and to examine how gender and age intervene in the formation of these perceptions. In this way, an empirical contribution will be made to the verification of interdisciplinary effects of literature, setting the discipline of literature apart not only as an academic artifact but as a transforming force in several spheres of lay populations.

3. RESEARCH METHODOLOGY

A quantitative-empirical research design was used in this study to explore reader perceptions of literary narratives across the following three variables: Identity Reflection through Literature (IRL), Narrative Impact on Social Awareness (NISA), and Ecological Consciousness through Literary Engagement (ECLE). The primary objective was to provide that an analysis of the variables' levels be performed through descriptive statistics and that inferential statistical tests be applied to analyze the effect comparison of gender and age on the levels. The notion behind the research was to garner generalisable-lawful knowledge concerning how cognitive and emotional responses are instigated by literary narratives.

The sampling technique was purposive, guaranteeing that those who would say they actively engaged with literature would be included. Out of the sample, in addition to the teachers and literature enthusiasts, 246 respondents were both undergraduates and postgraduates, all of whom would have had at least some exposure to narrative fiction in English. Data were collected online with a structured questionnaire design from January to May 2025. The instrument comprised 15 items- five statements each for the three constructs measured on a 5-point Likert-type scale ranging from 1=Strongly Disagree to 5=Strongly Agree.

The selection of measurement items was guided by established theoretical definitions of the three constructs and prior literature on narrative engagement and reader-response theory. Each item was designed to capture specific dimensions of cognitive, emotional, and reflective engagement associated with three different methods which included IRL and NISA and ECLE. Construct validity required multiple stages which included expert assessment and initial testing and comparison with theoretical definitions. Content validity was established when each item mapped to its conduct domain which provided sufficient coverage of the domain without repeating elements. Internal consistency reliability assessment used Cronbach's alpha which showed all constructs achieved more than 0.70 threshold to demonstrate reliable measurement. The strict validation procedure establishes stronger study credibility through its development of the measurement instrument used in the research.

The instrument containing the survey was validated by means of expert face and content validation. A panel of three academic experts in literary studies and educational psychology reviewed the questionnaire for clarity, relevance, and its alignment with the research constructs. Some improvements were made for question wording and balance, as well as interpretability, based on their recommendations. Additionally, the questionnaire was administered to a pilot group of 20 participants to weed out items that might be ambiguous or confusing.

Normality assumptions were checked by running Kolmogorov–Smirnov (K–S) tests on the responses for each variable. The K-S results showed that the data met the normality assumption, which meant parametric tests could be used for the analysis. Descriptive statistics consisting of the mean and standard deviation were then calculated for each variable in order to determine central tendencies and variations in respondents' answers. The independent samples t-tests were used subsequently to check for gender differences, while the one-way ANOVA conducted across all three variables looked at differences between age groups.

Ethical standards were maintained throughout the research process. Participation was voluntary, and informed consent was sought and obtained from the participants. The survey was introduced with a statement declaring anonymity and confidentiality, with no personally identifiable information collected. Participants were informed that they could withdraw from the participation process at any time without penalty. Ethical approval was obtained from the Research Ethics Committee of the host institution before the commencement of data collection.

All data were analyzed using SPSS, version 25. Interpretation of the statistical findings was made at a significance level of $p < .05$. Variables such as gender and age were categorized for comparison in ways that made the group sizes consistent with the assumptions of ANOVA and t-tests.

This layout displays a solid quantitative base for the investigation of literature concerning self-reflection, social understanding, and ecological consciousness. Placing emphasis on statistical interpretation with respect to theory strengthens the reliability, generalisability, and practical utility of the findings.

4. DATA ANALYSIS AND INTERPRETATION

This chapter is devoted to presenting the findings of the analysis of the survey data collected from 246 participants, with the objective to ascertain the readers' perception of literary narratives relative to three primary variables, namely Identity Reflection through Literature (IRL), Narrative Impact on Social Awareness (NISA), and Ecological Consciousness via Literary Engagement (ECLE). The analysis is based on a structured approach that first uses descriptive statistics to investigate the level of each variable and then applies inferential statistics to identify differences by gender and age. Parametric tests' assumptions were met since the dataset followed a normal distribution according to the Kolmogorov–Smirnov testing.

4.1 Sample Profile

There were 135 females and 111 males in the sample, while respondents belonged to three different age groups: below 24 years, 24 to 35 years, and above 35 years. The below-24age group dominated in numbers with 95 participants, followed by

76 participants above 35 and 75 in the 24 to 35-age group. This distribution gave a balanced demographic profile for inferential comparisons. The cross-tabulation between age and gender ensured that the sample consisted of a diversity of views, thus enhancing the generalisability of the findings (Table 1 and Figure 1).

Table 1. sample profile (Cross tabulation)

		Gender		Total
		Female	**Male**	
Age	Below 24	57	38	95
	24 to 35	43	32	75
	Above 35	35	41	76
Total		135	111	246

Source: Field data, 2025

Figure 1. sample profile (Cross tabulation)

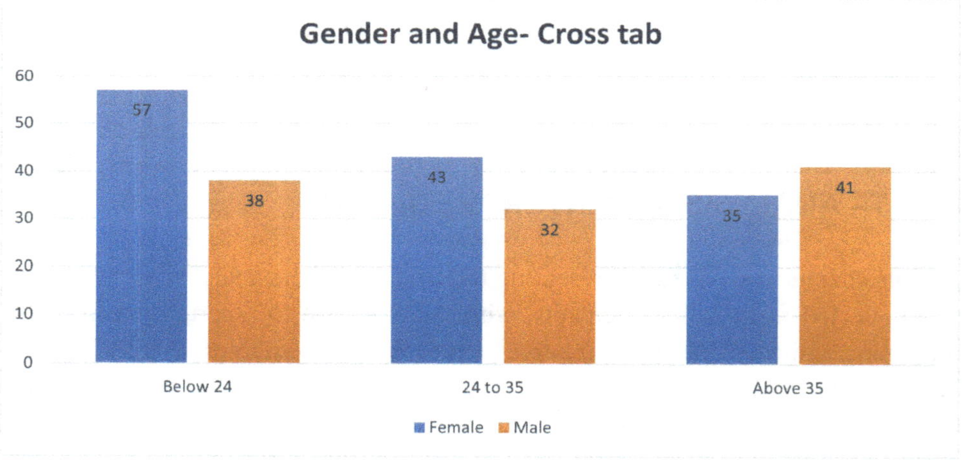

Source: Field data, 2025

4.2 Descriptive Statistics

Descriptive statistics indicated that participants scored higher on the identity reflection dimension. IRL had a mean of 4.03 and a standard deviation of 0.59, indicating that participants identify with literature where the main characters are identity-struggling or that they use literature to reflect on their own identities. NISA recorded a mean of 3.57 and a standard deviation of 0.67, suggesting moderate agreement with statements about how literature affects views on social issues like marginalisation and power dynamics. ECLE recorded a mean of 3.76 and a standard deviation of 0.64, suggesting that environmental themes in literature strongly resonate with many readers (Table 2).

Table 2. Descriptive statistics

		N	Mean	Std. Deviation
IRL1	I often relate to characters in literature who face cultural or personal identity struggles.	246	4.19	1.084
IRL2	Literature has helped me reflect more deeply on my own identity.	246	3.93	.996
IRL3	I find that narratives about displacement or hybridity resonate with my personal experiences.	246	4.59	.611
IRL4	Reading fiction has enhanced my understanding of how identities are shaped.	246	3.67	.970
IRL5	Literary texts have influenced how I perceive myself within a social context.	246	3.77	.981
Identity Reflection through Literature (IRL)			4.0309	.59331
NISA1	Literature has increased my awareness of social issues such as gender, oppression, or trauma.	246	3.89	1.143
NISA2	I believe stories can influence public opinion on important social matters.	246	3.50	1.124
NISA3	I feel more empathetic after reading narratives that portray marginalised voices.	246	2.86	1.056
NISA4	Literature helps challenge traditional views on power and resistance.	246	3.41	1.399
NISA5	Reading about characters facing social injustice makes me more socially conscious.	246	4.18	.514
Narrative Impact on Social Awareness (NISA)			3.5699	.66902
ECLE1	Stories featuring nature and environmental themes make me think critically about ecological issues.	246	3.44	1.186
ECLE2	I prefer reading books that explore human–nature relationships.	246	3.67	1.171
ECLE3	Literature has made me more aware of the environmental crisis.	246	3.57	.944
ECLE4	Fictional depictions of environmental destruction concern me more than news reports.	246	4.15	1.032
ECLE5	I believe literature can be a tool for promoting sustainable thinking.	246	3.98	1.088
Ecological Consciousness via Literary Engagement (ECLE)			3.7618	.64397

Source: Field data

Figure 2. Descriptive statistics

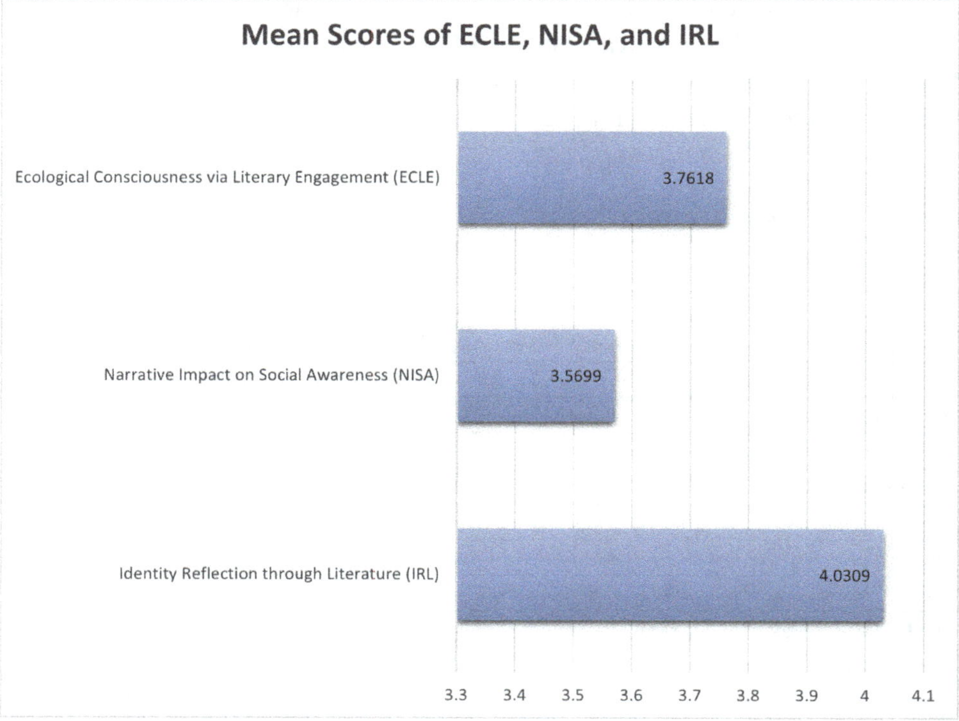

Source: Field data

4.3 Gender-Based Differences

To ascertain whether gender-based disparities were present, independent samples t-tests were conducted. It was revealed that, for all three variables, female respondents scored significantly higher than males. For IRL, females had an average of 4.12, whereas males had 3.91, with a p-value of .007 showing statistical significance.

Table 3. Descriptive statistics and independent sample t test

	Gender	N	Mean	Std. Deviation	t-test for Equality of Means		
					t	df	Sig. (2-tailed)
IRL	Female	135	4.1230	.54580	2.719	244	.007
	Male	111	3.9189	.63095			
NISA	Female	135	3.8059	.56301	6.613	244	.000
	Male	111	3.2829	.67768			
ECLE	Female	135	3.8607	.57265	2.692	244	.008
	Male	111	3.6414	.70536			

Source: Field data, 2025

The discrepancy was even larger for NISA, with females having an average of 3.80 in contrast to 3.28 for males and a very significant p-value of .000. For ECLE, females scored 3.86 while males averaged 3.64, with a p-value of .008. These results confirm that gender was one of the considerable factors that affected how respondents engaged with literary narratives, with females showing a higher level of reflective and empathetic engagement, by and large (see Table 3).

4.4 Age-Based Differences

A one-way ANOVA was further conducted to examine the influence of age on the dependent variables. The results revealed striking distinctions according to age. For IRL, younger readers in the below-24-years group obtained the highest average of 4.29, followed by the 24–35 group with 4.00 and the above-35 group with 3.72, with the F-values at a highly significant level of $p < .001$. A similar trend appeared in NISA, with younger participants scoring higher again. ECLE followed the same pattern of younger and middle-aged participants exhibiting higher perceptions of ecological issues than the older group. Therefore, an impact of age in literary engagement can be evidenced, pointing out that younger readers are more sensitive to matters of identity, social issues, and environmental concerns in literature (Table 4).

Table 4. Descriptive statistics and one-way ANOVA

		Descriptives			One way ANOVA	
		N	**Mean**	**Std. Deviation**	**F**	**Sig.**
IRL	Below 24	95	4.2926	.48097	22.742	.000
	24 to 35	75	4.0080	.45730		
	Above 35	76	3.7263	.68729		
	Total	246	4.0309	.59331		
NISA	Below 24	95	3.6968	.64831	10.405	.000
	24 to 35	75	3.6933	.57359		
	Above 35	76	3.2895	.70381		
	Total	246	3.5699	.66902		
ECLE	Below 24	95	3.8674	.65468	11.160	.000
	24 to 35	75	3.9093	.58198		
	Above 35	76	3.4842	.60774		
	Total	246	3.7618	.64397		

Source: Field data, 2025

These findings from data analysis confirm that literature plays an important role in shaping reader perceptions of multiple worlds. Gender and age remain the major factors that have determined the extent to which a reader engages with identity, social justice, and ecological themes in narrative literature. These findings provide a strong empirical foundation for making further pedagogical and literary interventions toward inclusive and socially responsive reading.

The statistical findings directly address the research questions outlined in the study. The first research question shows that readers exhibit high levels of identity reflection which researchers measured through IRL and readers showed high ecological awareness through ECLE while their social awareness showed moderate levels according to NISA. The data demonstrates that people understand literature better because it manifests itself through personal and environmental experiences than through societal interactions. The second research question shows that inferential analyses which include t-tests and ANOVA demonstrate that literary engagement changes according to both gender and age across all three constructs. The results show that both female and younger respondents exhibit higher engagement levels which indicates that demographic characteristics influence narrative perception and internalization. These findings provide empirical validation for the proposed relationships and reinforce the multidimensional impact of literary narratives.

5. DISCUSSION

The study focused on examining audience engagement with literature vis-à-vis three crucial dimensions: identity reflection (IRL), narrative impact on social awareness (NISA), and ecological consciousness via literary engagement (ECLE). The discussion of findings reveals significant patterns that fit into and extend the current interdisciplinary literature. Strong average scores for IRL suggest that literature continues to function as a mirror for persons to reflect inwardly and consequently develop a potential identity. These findings agreed with previous literature which claimed that literary narratives have an essential part in both individual and collective identity construction (Sriratana, 2008; Holmes, 2023). Characters in literature become, in a way, psychological mirrors for readers to project, negotiate, or otherwise reconstruct the contents of their own identity. This testified to Ayyoob and Sajeev's (2024d) findings that the narrative context has some transformative capacity for deepening introspection especially through educational and sociocultural paradigms. The aforementioned study also revealed significant differences with regard to gender and age, suggesting that younger readers and female readers are more prone to identifying with themes concerning identity within literature. This supports Hogan's (2019) assertion that stories operate cognitively and emotionally in aiding people in the processes of making sense of who they are.

The results for NISA revealed that literature does have consciousness-raising effects but less so than IRL and ECLE. In contradistinction, female readers appear to be more enamoured with socially reflective themes, such as those of oppression, gender, and resistance. This finding substantiates the view that feminist and postcolonial readings of literature enhance the awareness of marginalised voices (Nguy n, 2023; Mahmoud, 2019). At the same time, this supports Sachar's (2024) contention that media and literature can deconstruct traditional power structures by exposing intersecting forms of social exclusion. The relatively low scores on the gender scale further suggest a divergence in how males internalise social engagement through literature, a question worthy of further exploration. Again, younger readers indicated more social sensitivity through the stories, lining up with the conclusions of Ayyoob and Sajeev (2024c), who found similar trends in ESG and sustainability education where youth displayed greater value alignment and empathy.

The study needs to conduct further critical analysis of NISA because its current observed levels are measured at moderate value. The first possible explanation for this phenomenon arises from the fact that people display emotional engagement which differs from their ability to execute social cognitive processes. Although readers develop empathy toward characters who experience social injustice, this emotional connection does not lead to ongoing critical assessment or change in their future behavior. The gap exists because readers usually approach literary works through personal reading experiences which only enable them to achieve internal development without achieving external improvement. Social theme interpretation in different cultural and educational settings depends on various factors, especially in cases where educational systems do not prioritize teaching about inequality together with power structure systems. The lower mean score for empathy-related items further suggests that exposure to narratives alone may be insufficient without guided interpretation or pedagogical framing. The establishment of structured literary engagement methods needs to occur which enable readers to connect their narrative experiences with actual social problems. This process helps literature to develop social awareness through its capacity to create transformative experiences.

The peculiarity of this research resides in analyzing ecological conscience. There are moderate to high mean scores for the ECLE variable, with younger respondents once again being the most ecologically conscious as compared to the older ones. This supports the importance of ecocriticism and environmental humanities with their outlines as given by Rishma and Gill (2024), who state literature fosters ecological empathy by changing readers' conception of nature. Both indigenous narrative forms and contemporary fiction-the two cited in previous studies (Dorias, 2024; Insany et al., 2024)-show how literature can be an instrument of pedagogy for environmental discourse. These research results give a quantitative backing to that inference, promoting that fiction has far better emotional and cognitive awareness instilling capacity about environmental crisis compared to non-literary contents. The statistically significant gender and age-based differences across all three variables signify that demographic factors mediate how literature is received and interpreted. This view lends support to Ayyoob and Sajeev's 2025 view that sustainable engagement—be it social, ecological, or cultural—depends on the way narratives are internally received by different audience groups. The ramifications also apply to curriculum designers and educators when they aim to harness literature to assist individuals in becoming independent personal choices, good citizens, and ecologically literate people.

6. THEORETICAL AND MANAGERIAL IMPLICATIONS

The findings in this study contribute to the theoretical and practical domains. Theoretically, the study produced interdisciplinary views and perspectives by empirically validating the formation of identity reflection (IRL), narrative-induced social awareness (NISA), and ecological consciousness through literary engagement (ECLE). Such efforts to substantiate literary theory with empirical research give further credence to the earlier conceptual directions of identity construction (Sriratana, 2008; Holmes, 2023), narrative empathy (Aquino & Salvador, 2024), and ecocriticism (Rishma & Gill, 2024). These constructs, formed through qualitative or interpretative dimensions in the past, are now explored quantitatively, thus furthering the position of literature in creating perspectives of psychology, society, and environment. Managerially, this study sheds light on educators, planners of cultural policies, and sustainability communicators. Literature, when considered as a tool, is among the few avenues that can develop human-centered skills like empathy, reflexivity, and critical consciousness, which are consonant with corporate goals in sustainability and diversity (Ayyoob & Sajeev, 2025). Accordingly, training and educational programmes aimed at creating sustainable mindsets and responsible citizenship could benefit from thoughtfully selected literary materials. Further, from the perspective of target demographics the documented gender- and age-related differences provide an imperative. For example, given that younger and female participants more resonantly identified with identity and ecological themes, such findings would present a pathway to differentiated approaches to engagement in campaigns, CSR, or curriculum design. By linking the literary engagement with empirical study, this research invites all organizations, particularly those in education and advocacy, to consider literature as a cost-effective, high-impact intervention tool for sociocultural and environmental change in various populations.

7. CONCLUSION

The study aimed to explore empirically how literature differentiates consciousness in the individual versus collective domains: identity reflection, social awareness, and ecological engagement. Adopting a quantitative methodology, responses from 246 participants were analyzed to confirm that literary narratives significantly influence ways in which people think about identity formation, conceptualize social inequalities, and relate to the natural world. The main conclusion reveals that identity reflection (IRL) is a prevalent theme, with younger and female readers more likely to identify with characters faced with personal or cultural identity dilemmas. This supports previous theoretical arguments stating that literature facilitates deep engagement with the self and society (Holmes, 2023; Hogan, 2019). Social narratives—those about oppression, gender, or trauma—also ran a range of moderate impacts and differed, across demographic lines, in ways affirming feminist and postcolonial scholarship (Nguy n, 2023; Mahmoud, 2019). Accordingly, the ecological perspective presented in literature was warmly received, especially among the youth, an echo of ecocriticism that views the literary arts as bearing duty towards building environmental consciousness (Rishma & Gill, 2024; Dorias, 2024).

The findings provide both a theoretical underpinning and recommendations for teachers, educational institutions, and policymakers. Literature should not, it appears, be considered as belonging only to artistic and academic realms but must be seen as a powerful shaping tool that produces reflective and socially and environmentally conscious persons. Further research may advance investigations of longitudinal and cross-cultural dimensions of engagement with literary texts by employing a mixed-method model to deepen our grasp of how narratives work. Confronted with social fragmentation and the ecological crisis, the silent power of stories remains an important integrative force ready to be invested in by both scholars and institutions.

The study results provide educational professionals with concrete strategies that they can use to develop their teaching materials. Educators should use literature as a teaching tool which enables students to develop multiple educational skills through their identity development and social justice reading and environmental studies. The implementation of reflective writing tasks together with structured dialogue will lead to better results in internal listening tasks, while critical dialogue and debate-based learning methods will enhance NISA. The use of ecocritical texts together with interdisciplinary modules will create opportunities for ECLE development. Thematic and experiential approaches should guide curriculum designers to create programs which enable learners to experience their educational journey through direct experience of their learning activities. Such integration is particularly relevant in higher education, where literature can serve as a bridge between cognitive learning and societal responsibility.

REFERENCES

Akhtar, A. (2024). Cultural Crossroads and Subaltern Realities in Diasporic Discourse: Exploring the Sense of Belonging in Lahiri and Mistry's Narratives. *International Journal of English Literature and Social Sciences*, *9*(1), 238–245. DOI: 10.22161/ijels.91.32

Alahou, G. (2023). Thematic Analysis and its Interdisciplinary Interest: Advantage or a Disadvantage for Holton's Purpose? *Conatus -. The Journal of Philosophy*, *8*(1), 29–53. DOI: 10.12681/cjp.30938

Aquino, C. J., & Salvador, R. (2024). Exploring the Interrelated Roles of Text, Author, and Reader in Identity Formation through Literature. *Journal of Interdisciplinary Perspectives*, *2*(3). Advance online publication. DOI: 10.69569/jip.2024.0042

Ayyoob, A., & Sajeev, A. (2024a). Corporate Sustainability: The Role of Consumer Skepticism, Transparency, and Marketing in Greenwashing Practices. *Corporate Governance Insight*, *6*(2), 51–68. DOI: 10.58426/cgi.v6.i2.2024.51-68

Ayyoob, A., & Sajeev, A. (2024b). Diversity, Equity, and Inclusion: Employees Perspectives on Sustainable Business Practices. *Routledge EBooks*, 348–367. DOI: 10.4324/9781003487180-27

Ayyoob, A., & Sajeev, A. (2024c). Navigating Sustainability: Assessing the Imperative of ESG Considerations in Achieving SDGs. *ESG Frameworks for Sustainable Business Practices*, 53–84. DOI: 10.4018/979-8-3693-3880-3.ch003

Ayyoob, A., & Sajeev, A. (2024d). Role of Social Entrepreneurship in Sustainable Development. *Advances in Business Strategy and Competitive Advantage Book Series*, 193–224. DOI: 10.4018/979-8-3693-4338-8.ch008

Ayyoob, A., & Sajeev, A. (2025). Resilient and Sustainable Organizations. IGI Global EBooks, 35–58. DOI: 10.4018/979-8-3373-0608-7.ch003

Dorias, V. J. (2024). Ecological Themes in Human-Nature Relationships: An Ecocritical Analysis of Bukidnon's Gugud. *International Journal of Language and Literary Studies*, *6*(4), 561–576. DOI: 10.36892/ijlls.v6i4.1960

Hogan, P. C. (2019). Personal Identity and Literature. In *Routledge eBooks*. Informa., DOI: 10.4324/9780429265228

Holmes, T. R. (2023). Narrative Identity through a Constructivist Lens: Introduction. *Journal of Constructivist Psychology*, *1–3*(4), 427–429. Advance online publication. DOI: 10.1080/10720537.2023.2168808

Insany, F. D., Nur'ain, S., Utami, W. K., Januar, M. A., & Purwarno, P. (2024). Human-nature Relationship in Riawani Elyta and Shabrina Q. S.'s Novel Rahasia Pelangi: An Ecocritical Approach. [IJEAL]. *International Journal of English and Applied Linguistics*, *4*(1), 28–37. DOI: 10.47709/ijeal.v4i1.3698

Lanser, S. S. (2016). Gender and Narrative. *De Gruyter EBooks*, 206–218. DOI: 10.1515/9783110316469.206

Loyola, M., Nelson, J. D., Clifton, G., & Levinson, D. (2023). Narratives in transport research: A thematic and functional analysis. *Transportation Research Interdisciplinary Perspectives*, *17*, 100754. DOI: 10.1016/j.trip.2023.100754

Mahmoud, S. (2019). Resistance in Postcolonial Literature with Reference to Sahar Khalifeh's Wild Thorns. *International Journal of Language and Literary Studies*, *1*(2), 74–87. DOI: 10.36892/ijlls.v1i2.35

Qazi, K. A. (2022). Crossing Borders: Diasporic Identity and Cultural Displacement in Jhumpa Lahiri's The Namesake. *ShodhKosh: Journal of Visual and Performing Arts*, *3*(1). Advance online publication. DOI: 10.29121/shodhkosh.v3.i1.2022.3471

Ray, S. T.Dr Shobha Tiwari Ray. (2024). Diasporic Consciousness in Jhumpa Lahiri's Novel "The Namesake.". *Universal Research Reports*, *11*(1), 183–186. DOI: 10.36676/urr.v11.i1.28

Rishma, R. D., & Gill, R. (2024). Eco Criticism: Exploring the Interplay between Literature and Environment. *World Journal of English Language*, *14*(4), 563–563. DOI: 10.5430/wjel.v14n4p563

Sachar, S. (2024). Gender Representation in Film and Media. *Gender Representation in Film and Media*, *4*(3), 33–36. DOI: 10.59298/RIJRE/2024/433336

Saxena, P. (2023). The Politics of Power and Resistance in Gurnah's "Afterlives.". *International Journal for Multidisciplinary Research*, *5*(2), 1989. Advance online publication. DOI: 10.36948/ijfmr.2023.v05i02.1989

Sayuti, S. A. (2020, August 5). *Literature as a Field of Identity Construction*. Www .atlantis-Press.comAtlantis Press. DOI: 10.2991/assehr.k.200804.061

Sheetal, & Kumar, N. (2024). Human Nature Relationships in Ecocritical Context: A Study of Works by J. G. Ballard and Barbara Kingsolver. *International Journal for Research Publication and Seminar, 15*(4), 127–130. DOI: 10.36676/jrps.v15.i4.20

Shyshkin, M. (2024). Narrative as an Interdisciplinary Category: The History of Study. *Fìlologìčnì Traktati*, *16*(2), 133–139. DOI: 10.21272/Ftrk.2024.16(2)-13

Sriratana, V. (2008). Literature and the Construction of Identity in Alistair MacLeod's No Great Mischief. *Deleted Journal*, *1*, 136–151.

Waham, J. J. (2023). The Exploration of Trauma and Memory in Kazuo Ishiguro's Never Let Me Go and The Remains of the Day. *Journal of Critical Studies in Language and Literature*, *4*(3), 16–21. DOI: 10.46809/jcsll.v4i3.204

KEY TERMS AND DEFINITIONS

Cognitive Engagement: The level of intellectual involvement and mental processing a reader applies while interpreting and analyzing literary texts.

Critical Consciousness: The awareness of social inequalities and power structures, combined with the ability to critically reflect upon and challenge them.

Cultural Representation: The depiction and construction of cultural identities, norms, and values within literary narratives.

Ecocriticism: An interdisciplinary approach that examines the relationship between literature and the natural environment, emphasizing ecological themes and sustainability.

Ecological Consciousness via Literary Engagement (ECLE): The development of environmental awareness, ethical sensitivity, and sustainability-oriented thinking through engagement with ecologically themed literary texts.

Emotional Engagement: The affective involvement of readers, including feelings of empathy, connection, and emotional resonance with literary characters and narratives.

Empathy in Literature: The capacity of readers to emotionally identify with and understand the experiences, perspectives, and emotions of fictional characters.

Environmental Humanities: An interdisciplinary field that integrates humanities perspectives to explore human–environment relationships and ecological challenges.

Identity Reflection through Literature (IRL): The process through which readers interpret, negotiate, and reconstruct their personal and social identities through engagement with literary narratives.

Interpretative Agency: The reader's ability to actively construct meaning from a literary text based on individual experiences, cultural context, and subjective interpretation.

Literary Engagement: The multidimensional interaction between readers and literary texts encompassing cognitive, emotional, and reflective processes.

Literary Pedagogy: The use of literature as a teaching tool to develop critical thinking, empathy, social awareness, and ethical reasoning.

Marginalised Voices: The representation of perspectives and experiences of socially, culturally, or politically underrepresented groups within literary texts.

Moral Imagination: The ability to envision ethical possibilities and consequences through engagement with narrative experiences.

Narrative Engagement: The degree of cognitive, emotional, and imaginative involvement a reader experiences while interacting with a literary text.

Narrative Identity Theory: A theoretical framework suggesting that individuals construct and reconstruct their identities through internalized and evolving life stories shaped by narrative experiences.

Narrative Impact on Social Awareness (NISA): The extent to which literary texts influence readers' understanding of social issues, inequalities, and power dynamics.

Narrative Persuasion: The ability of narratives to influence beliefs, attitudes, and values through immersive and emotionally engaging storytelling.

Narrative Transportation: A psychological state in which readers become deeply immersed in a story, often leading to changes in attitudes and perceptions.

Postcolonial Narratives: Literary works that explore themes of colonialism, identity, displacement, cultural hybridity, and resistance.

Pro-environmental Attitudes: Positive orientations and behavioral intentions toward environmental protection and sustainability.

Reader-Response Theory: A literary theory that emphasizes the active role of the reader in interpreting and constructing meaning from a text.

Reflective Thinking: The process of introspection and critical evaluation triggered by engagement with literary narratives.

Social Cognition: The process through which individuals perceive, interpret, and respond to social information, often shaped by narrative exposure.

Sustainability Awareness: The recognition and understanding of environmental and social sustainability issues developed through cognitive and emotional engagement.

Chapter 8

Aesthetic Democracy in Practice: Student Agency Through Blackout Poetry

Siri Mohammad-Roe
http://orcid.org/0009-0002-5324-8731
Oslo Metropolitan University, Norway

Hilde Tørnby
Oslo Metropolitan University, Norway

ABSTRACT

This chapter examines a classroom-based blackout poetry project in lower secondary English, exploring how aesthetic text work can support literacy development, student agency, and democratic citizenship. Drawing on the Council of Europe's Competences for Democratic Culture, the study analyses students' multimodal poems, process artefacts, and reflections. Findings show that blackout poetry enables students to exercise agency by making deliberate linguistic and visual choices that express civic positioning, while engaging in critical reading and interpretation. The study concludes that structured creative constraints and transparent assessment criteria can foster equitable participation and agentic meaning-making, making abstract democratic competencies visible and assessable within everyday English instruction.

INTRODUCTION

The ability for young people to engage meaningfully in democratic processes depend not only on formal/civil knowledge, but also the sense of agency they expe-

DOI: 10.4018/979-8-2600-2163-7.ch008

rience in voicing their perspectives and shaping their environment. The International Civic and Citizenship Education study (ICCS) (Utdanningsdirektoratet 2022) reveals a worrying decline in democratic knowledge among Norwegian grade 9 students (students aged 14 – 15 years). Though their average scores remain above the international level, the Norwegian average fell by 35 scale points since the previous assessment in 2016. The proportion of students at the lowest performance level more than doubled (Utdanningsdirektoratet, 2023). Education plays a crucial role in shaping how young people see themselves as participants in a democracy. The role of schools goes beyond civic knowledge as they are also expected to enable students to take initiative and influence the world around them. This calls for pedagogical practices that fosters critical thinking, rooted in classrooms where students can exercise and experience agency.

In their reference Framework of Competencies for Democratic Culture, The Council of Europe highlights that *skills* are central to democratic competence, as they enable individuals to act thoughtfully and responsibly in democratic contexts (Council of Europe, 2018, p.32). Key skills include critical and analytical thinking, perspective-taking, communication, and autonomous learning skills. These skills help learners evaluate information, understand diverse viewpoints, express themselves, and participate actively in society. In the context of ESL (English as a second language) classrooms, creative activities like blackout poetry can provide students with opportunities to exercise these skills, fostering both agency and engagement with democratic practices.

This article explores how creative literary practices might function as a tool for experiencing agency in English as a second language and Arts and crafts. By examining the potential of blackout poetry as a mode of self-expression and exploring critical thinking, we argue that such arts-based practices may open opportunities for civic agency.

We explore the question: How do students describe their experiences of agency when engaging in blackout poetry based on newspaper articles in the EFL classroom, and in what ways might these experiences relate to dimensions of democratic competence?

The article extends earlier work on blackout poetry with novels (Mohammad-Roe & Tørnby, 2023) by shifting the textual basis from a novel chosen by the teacher, to authentic media discourses, linking students' voices more directly with democratic discourse. Rather than measuring the development of democratic competence, this study, based on interviews with four students and their teachers, explores how students articulate and make sense of agency while engaging in blackout poetry.

BACKGROUND

In our times, knowing what authentic news and alternative facts are, is of constant concern. To discern what can be trusted in the massive influx of information on a day-to-day basis is an essential skill and a fundamental part of a democratic society. Although young people frequently engage with digital media, it may still be challenging to detect what is real and what is fake due to naiveté, inexperience and lack of knowledge. Newspaper articles and their authenticity is a backdrop to this blackout poetry project. A self-chosen article found online from one of the larger newspaper houses like BBC and CCN served as the original text from which the blackout poems were created. Through selecting their own texts and transforming them into poems, students were invited to articulate their perspectives in a classroom context that supported democratic participation.

Against this backdrop, we investigate how blackout poetry can function in a lower secondary school in the Oslo area, and what kinds of learning and agency opportunities emerge when students work with current news stories in a multimodal writing process. To voice one's opinion is a basic democratic right and a basic feature of a democracy. "The argument is that democracy depends on a prior aesthetic event, or, to phrase it differently, democracy is impossible in a polity that degrades the arts." (Docherty, 2006, p. xiv). Drawing on Docherty's notion of aesthetic democracy, we explore whether the creative process of blackout poetry may be interpreted as an aesthetic site in which students negotiate voice and selfhood. In any democratic society there is a place for art because art fosters critical thinking and personal expression: "...it is in art and in aesthetics that we find a privileged site or paradigm of the very potentiality of selfhoods that establishes this democratic condition (Docherty, 2006, p. xviii). Thus, students' creation of blackout poems may be understood as ways of exploring expression and self which is seen as a premise in an aesthetic democracy. Furthermore, when connecting the creation of blackout poems to authentic newspapers, selfhood becomes the entryway in which the poem moves through. Also, the chosen original text becomes the steppingstone for students' aesthetic responses. The interaction between the source text and the student's aesthetic intervention becomes the analytical focus of this chapter. The making of blackout poetry discussed in this article entails the process of creating something visual regarding contemporary issues. Previously we have observed that creating blackout poems crystalize a challenging reading experience (Mohammad-Roe & Tørnby, 2023) in addition to fostering agency.

We set out to explore how creation of blackout poetry would look like in a school with low socio-economic status and resources in the greater Oslo area where there is a large population of students with immigrant backgrounds. In this context the work with blackout poems was a collaboration between the English teacher and the arts and crafts teacher in ninth grade. It should be noted that in ninth grade students do not have arts and crafts in the Norwegian system, but because the teachers felt that this was such an important project and in line with the new strategy *A more practical school* (Meld. Sto. 34 (2023-2024)) enhances that they wanted to find a way to integrate working with blackout poems in a cross-curricular way despite the fact that there were no class in arts and crafts. Also, this work was included to explore whether and how such work might relate to students' experiences of democratic competence. Persistent disparities in democratic competence across social groups can limit both individual and collective capacities for active participation in democratic processes (Milner, 2002; Swami et al., 2014; Barrett, 2018; Brattland & Storstad, 2025). Addressing these inequalities is a central aim of citizenship education, making schools in communities with lower socioeconomic resources and diverse student populations particularly relevant sites for exploring how students themselves describe experiences of agency in relation to democratic engagement.

THEORETICAL FRAMEWORK

For our project, previous work on blackout poetry and poetic enquiry is a natural starting point. Furthermore, framing the project within ideas of citizenship education and critical thinking seems relevant since such perspectives are vital in any education. Also, connecting the project to ideas of multimodality and remediation adds a new layer of understanding the student's blackout poems. Finally, in this part of the chapter we offer some contemplation on aspects of assessment of democratic skills and blackout poems.

Blackout Poetry

Blackout poetry is a creative literary practice where one (the student) takes an existing text, in the case of this study a newspaper article, (but can also be a book page, official document, poem etc) and blacks out or removes most of the words. The remaining visible words form a poem. It is a form of *found poetry* (Butler-Kisber, 2010) that transforms an original text by selecting and highlighting fragments to create new meaning. Through the act of removal, the student reshapes the source material, often revealing hidden stories or emotions, within the original text. This way of working, it can be argued, is a branch of *poetic inquiry*, in which researchers "use poetry in their work to re-represent the human experience in a more approachable, powerful, emotionally poignant form than prose research reports allow" (Falkner,

2021). This, Falkner argues, is a means to engage a political voice – a response to social issues a political commentary and call to action (2021).

Poetic inquiry, as described by Butler-Kisber (2010; 2018), involves using language in ways that capture meaning and emotion with nuance and depth. While it is often applied as a research method, its principles can also be used in teaching, for example as in this study where students create blackout poems based on already existing texts. Butler-Kisber's emphasis on reflexivity and expressive language provides a useful lens for understanding how this activity can shape students' comprehension of the articles and their ability to convey complex social issues through poetry.

Citizenship Education

Citizenship education is an important overarching perspective in the Norwegian curriculum from 2020, and it is specified that all subjects shall include this i teaching. Citizenship education in English (ESL) is connected to developing a conscious way of being in this world which leads to participatory actions. Furthermore, citizenship is understood to entail critical thinking, global awareness and intercultural competence. Thus, creating blackout poems from newspaper articles may be analysed as engaging with several dimensions of citizenship education. However, one main challenge for teachers in citizenship education is designing pedagogical practices and formative assessments that move beyond transmissions of factual knowledge towards values, attitudes, and self-reflection (Paaske et al., 2023). Blackout poetry can be argued as a didactic practice that engages particularly with these second- and third-order concepts. By erasing and reshaping existing texts, in the case of this study; newspaper articles, students are invited to examine dominant narratives/voices and construct new meanings and help the students position themselves. Using newspaper articles that many students deem as facts, they will also be analysing structures of power and positioning (second-order thinking). At the same time, the creative and personal nature of the activity encourages learners to position themselves in relation to current issues, fostering subjectification and reflexive awareness (third-order thinking). This way, blackout poetry exemplifies the type of innovative, formative practice that can address the pedagogical gaps identified by Paaske et al. (2023), offering teachers a tool to promote democratic citizenship competences through critical engagement and creativity.

Agency and Subjectification

Drawing on Biesta's (2010) notion of subjectification, blackout poetry can be understood as a pedagogical practice that foregrounds student agency and the emergence of voice. Subjectification refers to educational processes through which learners take critical distance from dominant orders of meaning and "become a subject to themselves and their learning lives" (den Heyer & van Kessel, 2015, p.2). Within this framework, *agency* can be understood as students' capacity to act meaningfully within, and sometimes against, existing structures of meaning. Drawing on Arendt (1998), agency is not reduced to individual choice or expression, but is constituted through *action,* that is, through interventions that introduce something new and unpredictable into the world (den Heyer & van Kessel, 2015, p.3). Den Heyer and van Kessel (2015) emphasise that such action involves interrupting routine practices in order to create new public spaces in which freedom can be "claimed or reclaimed" (p. 3). Blackout poetry can be analysed as a site where agency may be enacted by selecting texts, deciding what to erase, and determining which words are allowed to remain visible. These aesthetic choices can be analysed as sites where students negotiate positioning in relation to public issues. In this sense, the poems may be understood as engaging with dimensions of critical voice that are central to discussions of democratic competence.

Critical Thinking

As part of citizenship education and on its own critical thinking is seen as one of the most important skills in our times and it has been introduced in curricula in Norway specifically from 2020 onwards (Utdanningsdirektoratet, 2020). One way of understanding critical thinking is as "reasonable reflective thinking focused on deciding what to believe or do" (Ennis 2015, p. 32). A prolongation of this idea is that one should be able to make good and sensible decisions (Bailin & Siegel, 2003). Furthermore, the ability to take different perspectives (Lim, 2015) is of great importance when it comes to critical thinking. Also, unveiling power structures is vital in critical thinking (Fisher, 2011; Lim, 2015; Janks, 2010).

Janks (2010) sees critical thinking and literacy as closely connected to power and society, in addition to the ways meaning is created and challenged. A central idea in her work is the *redesign cycle*, which treats texts as carefully designed artefacts rather than neutral objects. The cycle has three main stages. First, in *design*, texts are produced with specific purposes and messages. Second, in *deconstruction*, readers critically examine the social, ideological, and linguistic structures that shape the text. Finally, in *redesign*, texts are transformed to offer new perspectives or question dominant assumptions. Janks' approach highlights that literacy is an active process, where understanding and creating texts involve both critical thinking and creative work. The model shows how learners can interpret, make choices, and engage with the power relations that are embedded in language, emphasizing that reading and writing are always socially and politically situated practices. In our context critical thinking is crucial to both the ability to see something from a different perspective, to deconstruct, to redesign as much as it is the ability to take justified choices in creating blackout poems.

Multimodality, Re-Mediation and Visual Literacy

Blackout poems consist of words and design elements such as drawings, colours and guiding lines (vectors) to suggest the reading sequence and communicate primarily through two modes, the written words and the visual affordances. Furthermore, the poems also construct meaning through the subordinate modes of colour and vectors (Kress & van Leuween, 2020). Discussing the meaning of composition and multimodal texts, Kress and van Leeuwen (2020) explain that composition relates to the representational and interactive meanings of the image through three systems: information, salience and framing (p. 177). Salience refers to the visual features included which attract the viewer and which constructs meaning. Numerous elements apply to the meaning-making process in multimodal text wherein color saturation (the quality) is one such element. Colour saturation refers to the quality, intensity and purity of colours.

Another fundamental aspect of the main difference between the written word and the visuals is that words narrate whereas visuals show (Kress, 2003). On this basis the interaction between words and visuals is given much attention in picturebook research regarding the relationship between the two modes to be either symmetrical, complementary or counterpointing (Nikolajeva & Scott, 2013). In our context this theoretical framework is useful for interpreting the student work and to extract meaning from all modes.

Additionally, when analysing the unique modes of the student blackout poems, ideas of remediation of texts (Bolter & Grusin, 1999) is relevant for our project. In the process of remediation what was original is altered, changed and reworked into a new form. Hence, the newspaper article stops being a newspaper article after the students have blacked out, crossed out, added colours and drawings and becomes a new text, a blackout poem. What signifies this process is that it is transformative (Østern, 2008) both for the text itself, but also for the creator. Using the aesthetic as pivot point for the transformation adds another layer, another materiality to the new text. Therefore, in this context transformative teaching and learning processes may open space for more student-driven interpretations of citizenship.

Using visual effects and devise meaning through visual affordances are understood as visual literacy (Kress and van Leeuwen, 2020). They choices made when it comes to colour palette, saturation and quality provide a sensed feeling of meaning in the reader. Moreover, the way elements are placed on the page communicates ideas of importance according to Stockwell (2005). The more important the more centred, is his point. Also, how much an element takes up of the space on the page, underscore its significance (Kress and van Leeuwen, 2020). These aesthetic choices are not merely matters of form; they make visible how students position themselves on public issues and exercise a critical voice, which is at the heart of competences for democratic culture.

Assesment Practice

A key challenge many teachers face when working with democratic skills concerns how such competencies should be assessed (Paaske et.al, 2023). With the shift from predominantly summative assessment practices towards more formative approaches, teachers often experience uncertainty in balancing the assessment of students' subject knowledge with the assessment of values that may emerge through work on democratic competence. This tension can lead to concerns about what is appropriate to assess and may result in some teachers avoiding explicit engagement with democratic skills in the classroom. However, when the criteria explicitly differentiate between language, interpretation, and visual structure, assessment becomes more transparent and fair for students with diverse linguistic and cultural backgrounds.

However, research by Mohammad-Roe et al. (2025) indicates that working with English as a second language can make this assessment work more manageable, as it allows teachers to place primary emphasis on linguistic aspects. When the language of assessment makes explicit what is being assessed, language use, reasoning, and connection to the source text, the risk that cultural and linguistic familiarity is favored is reduced, in line with the democratic principles of the Norwegian curriculum. In the context of this project, students are therefore not assessed on the topics they choose or the values they express, but on their ability to reason, argue, and explain the choices they make in their texts.

Using these concepts as analytical lenses, we designed an interdisciplinary unit in which students transformed selected news articles into blackout poems through a staged, multimodal process supported by brief mini-lessons and structured reflection. Below, we describe the participants, data sources, and analytic approach.

METHOD

As previously mentioned, this study explores how work with blackout poetry in the ESL classroom, combined with arts and crafts, can create new ways of reading and foster agency in grade 9 students. The project lasted for two weeks taking place in the ESL classes.

We approach this as a qualitative case study drawing on multiple data sources. First, we have access to the students' work: the articles made into poems. Secondly, we have conducted interviews with the students whose work was selected for further investigation. These works were strategically selected by the teacher to represent both high and low performing students from an ESL perspective. The selection was made in collaboration with the researchers and aimed to capture variation in thematic focus, and aesthetic expression. The purpose was not to identify representative cases, but to include contrasting examples that could illuminate different ways students engaged with the task. While the teacher's involvement in the selection process ensured pedagogical insight into variation in student performance, it may also have influenced which forms of engagement became visible in the data. The students were interviewed individually and were informed about the project in advance, which gave them the opportunity to withdraw if they did not wish to participate. The student interviews were unstructured in the sense that students were invited to speak freely about their own work, while we were able to prompt them to elaborate and reflect further. At the same time, we had a general understanding of the areas the interviews were intended to cover, including the choice of news article, aesthetic decisions, and the students' own perceptions of the method.

In addition, we conducted a semi-structured interview with both the English teacher and the arts and crafts teacher. The interview was conducted jointly, as some time had passed since the collaborative project was completed, allowing the teachers to complement and elaborate on each other's responses. Using a semi-structured interview format (Punch & Aonacea, 2014) enabled us to address questions that emerged during the student interviews and in the subsequent analysis of student texts, while also allowing the teachers to introduce new perspectives that we wished to explore further. All interviews were conducted in Norwegian in order to avoid placing additional linguistic demands on the students and teachers.

Teacher A is the English teacher involved in the project. At the time of the study, Teacher A was 30 years old and had been working at the school for five years, which also constituted his total teaching experience, apart from occasional substitute teaching. He is teacher educated from a university college in Norway. Teacher B is the arts and crafts teacher and was 62 years old at the time of the study. She had been working at the school for seven years and had no prior experience teaching arts and crafts in other schools. Her professional background is as a trained goldsmith, and she entered the teaching profession through a postgraduate certificate in education (PPU), based on a real competence assessment. In addition, she has studied German at the University of Oslo and has lived in Germany for five years, which informs her broader linguistic and cultural background.

It should be noted that the empirical data is limited to four student interviews and a small sample of student work. Thus, the findings are exploratory and intended to illustrate possible ways in which blackout poetry may support democratic competence, rather than to make broad generalizations. To enhance credibility, multiple data sources were used, including student texts, student interviews, and teacher interviews. The inclusion of teacher perspectives provided an additional interpretive layer and allowed for triangulation of student accounts. In the analysis, excerpts from interviews and visual representations of student work are used to support transparency and allow readers to follow the analytical reasoning.

Introduction of the Task

The idea of working with blackout poetry was introduced to the teachers by the researchers as a prolongation of a collaborative work between the school and one of the authors The school is known for its progressive profile, and the teachers were therefore open to participating in the project. As preparation for the classroom work, we introduced the two teachers to blackout poetry, demonstrating how the method can be applied to different types of texts and how it allows for a range of aesthetic expressions. The teachers then began to explore the method independently, and the arts and crafts teacher produced model texts that were later used to introduce the approach to the students. Whereas the English teacher focused on language aspects of the task.

The teachers described a gradual and exploratory approach to introducing the blackout poetry task. Initially, the concept was introduced step by step, with a focus on understanding what blackout poetry is and how meaning is created through selection rather than randomness. Example texts were used to support analysis and discussion, drawing in part on materials provided by the researchers. The task was then extended through guided practice, where students experimented with blackout poetry using different types of texts, such as song lyrics, before moving on to news articles. The work was organised across extended double lessons, allowing time for both instruction and experimentation. Towards the end of the process, students were given increased freedom to choose texts that interested them personally, a decision the teachers linked to student engagement and emotional involvement in the work. The teachers described this progression as an intentional move towards greater student autonomy,

Data

Our data consists of a collection of student blackout poems counting 24 texts created in ESL class. The texts were provided to us by the ESL teacher and in collaboration with him we selected four students to interview. The student's thoughts regarding their work are of importance to understand the thinking and planning that this work entails. For the purpose of this chapter, the four texts of the interviewed students and the data from the interviews are the focal point. According to the teacher, the selection was made to show the range of student texts. To further understand the work process of crafting these blackout poems, we interviewed the two teachers who were involved. The information from these interviews provides a meta perspective. All interviews followed a semi-structured interview guide (Brinkmann & Kvale, 2015).

The analysis was conducted in several stages. First, the material was read closely to identify recurring themes in how students described their choices and experiences with the blackout poetry task. In the next phase, these themes were examined in light of selected concepts from the theoretical framework, such as agency, positioning, and critical engagement.

The purpose of the analysis was not to determine whether students developed democratic competence, but to explore how they described experiences that could be understood in relation to such concepts. The interpretations were discussed among the authors throughout the process in order to consider different possible readings of the material.

As the researchers introduced the idea of blackout poetry to the teachers, we were attentive to how our own interests and assumptions might influence both the implementation of the project and the analysis. The poems and interviews are therefore treated as situated accounts rather than direct evidence of democratic competenc

Findings

In the following sections, each student example is presented as an illustrative case, combining visual analysis of the poem with the student's own reflections from the interview. The analysis draws on concepts from critical literacy and redesign theory to interpret how students engaged with the blackout poetry task. Furthermore, how these texts communicate through a poetic inquiry is also commented on. Later, in the discussion, ideas of citizenship education are discussed regarding student poems. Additionally, teacher perspectives are included to reflect their experiences of the project, which again gives a broader understanding. What is more, how elements of the text show signs of critical thinking are also addressed in the discussion. As two of the student examples address politically sensitive issues, it is important to contextualize them within the sociopolitical environment in which this study was conducted. In Norway, where the research took place, public support for Palestine in the Israeli–Palestinian conflict is relatively widespread. In Oslo, for example, demonstrations expressing support for Palestine occur regularly, and such perspectives are also represented in the mainstream press. We acknowledge, however, that this position may not be similarly prevalent or publicly expressed in other national or sociopolitical contexts.

In the subsequent presentations of the student work, we draw upon data from the interviews to inform and contextualize the descriptions of the blackout poems. These interview excerpts serve to foreground the students' intentions, interpretative frameworks, and creative processes. In addition, the researchers' analytical perspectives are incorporated into the discussion, offering a critical examination of what the poems convey and how they may be interpreted. This integrative approach enables a more nuanced reflection that combines participants' self-articulations with scholarly analysis.

Student Anna

Student Anna tells us that she wanted to find an article related to the Gaza conflict. The original newspaper article is a BBC article. As she talks about her text, Anna says that she is very much concerned about the situation on Gaza and that this work gave her a possibility to express her concern and focus on the situation. "There is a lot of talk about this war, we need to focus on what's important", she says. In the interview she elaborates on her work saying that the colors she chose bears the same colors as the Palestinian flag so that the readers immediately understand that this was about Palestine. About the work itself, she explains that the transformation from a black and white newspaper article to this blackout poem (figure 1) was challenging. She explains that the hardest part was to find and select words so that they correspond and give meaning. According to Anna this way of working felt important, and she very much liked it. This example illustrates how students exercised agency by making deliberate textual choices, a process that aligns with Janks' (2010) notion of redesign.

Figure 1. Blackout poem about the war on Gaza

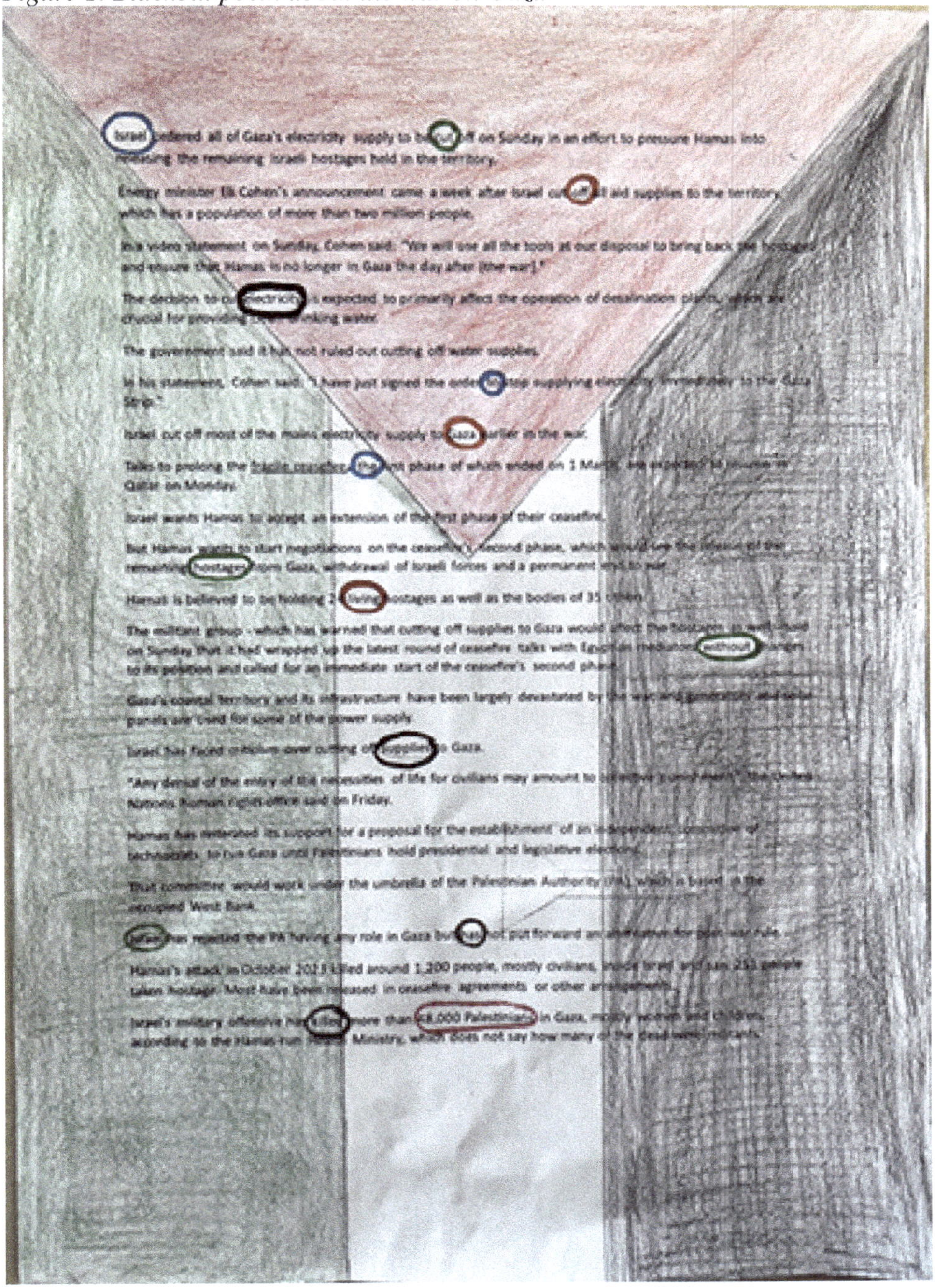

The transformation of the newspaper article in Anna's case is more than the selection of colors representing the Palestinian flag, it is in fact the flag itself. For many readers the flag imprints the reading process – this is the flag of the Palestinian people who lost their country and are forcefully removed from their homes. Form a rather neutral BBC article the student has added on a new layer which also stands in contrast to her own circled-out text due to the matter-of-fact like tone: "Israel cut off electricity to Gaza – the hostages living without supplies. Israel has killed 48000 Palestinians." In this work, the student explores an aesthetic transformation (Østern, 2008) through adding design and color to an otherwise bare text. What we see, is that something new arises in the aftermath: the new poem which cuts the original text down into the bare minimum, but which in this case is not a minimum: people live without electricity and 48000 have been killed. The flag that covers the entire text signals a deliberate prioritization of substance over form; in the interview, the student says, "I wanted the reader to know immediately what this was about," which shows both positioning and purposeful meaning-making.

Student Amir

Amir told us that he felt that Marcus Rashford was a very good football player and an example of a good sportsman. Being benched for quite some time in Manchester United, the student felt that this was very unfair. The newspaper reports on Rashford's reaction when he was bought by La Liga vlud Barcelona. In his original newspaper interview, Rashford gave thanks to Manchester United in a somewhat ironic way given that he was benched. So, the student blackout poem has a double bind – first it may be understood as a response to the way Rashford was treated, and secondly it turns something negative into something positive.

Figure 2. Blackout poem about Rashford

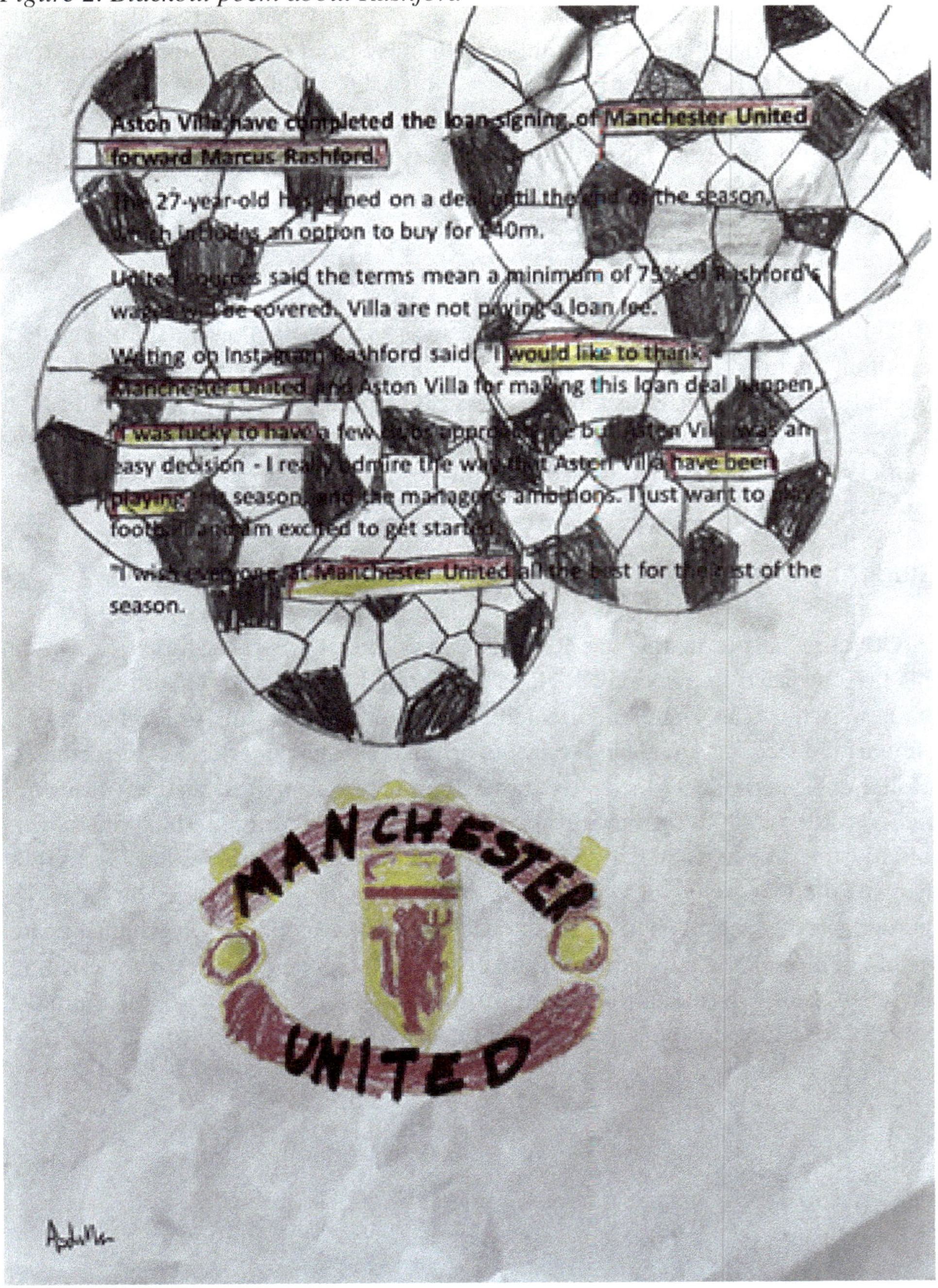

The design in this poem consists of six footballs in different sizes and there is an upward movement of footballs. Such an upward movement may underscore the movement in football games or in this case a move from one club to another, from being benched to being able to play games. Thus, the footballs are very effective and signify different layers of movement. Spreading out on the page the text behind feels cluttered and distant bringing forth the student text highlighted in Manchester's colors:

Manchester United
forward Marcus Rashford
would like to thank Manchester United.
I was lucky to have been playing Manchester United.

Through this poem the important part emerges, namely, how Rashford reacted to unfair treatment. The poem captures the irony in Rashford's words – that he would like to thank the ones who benched him. But it is Rashford's behavior that impressed the student. In the interview he told us that he was so impressed by this footballer and the way he expressed gratitude over something that had been a painful situation for him.

Student Olivia

Olivia reveals to us that she likes to read crime and murder stories. So, when this task surfaced in her English class, she wanted to find a text about murder in the news which she found and created a blackout poem out of (see figure three). Similarly to student Anna and Amir, the original newspaper article is re-mediated (Bolter & Grusin, 1999) into a new form, a new text. Through an aesthetic transformation (Østern, 2008) the new text takes flight and becomes something of its own. Initially, the student wanted to use stars to capture the chosen words, she tells us, but then she thought "why not blood?" The knife is added to underscore the theme of murder and the fact that by cutting into flesh, pools of blood appear which is quite visible in the student's remaking of the original newspaper article. As for creating the poem itself, Olivia said she felt it was rather challenging because it was almost impossible to turn this negative piece of news into something positive.

Figure 3. Murder story in the news

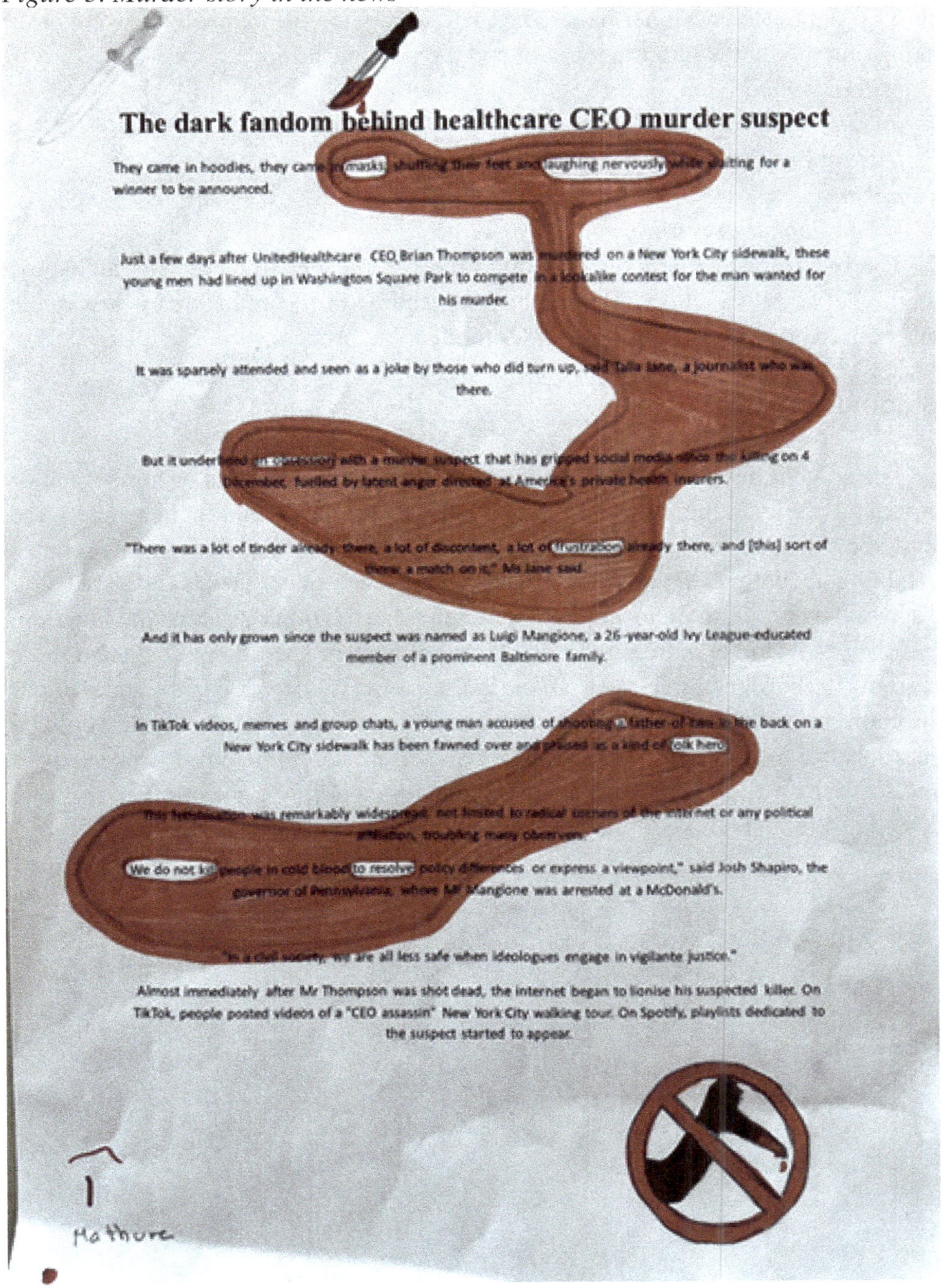

The dark fandom behind healthcare CEO murder suspect

They came in hoodies, they came in masks, shuffling their feet and laughing nervously while waiting for a winner to be announced.

Just a few days after UnitedHealthcare CEO Brian Thompson was murdered on a New York City sidewalk, these young men had lined up in Washington Square Park to compete in a lookalike contest for the man wanted for his murder.

It was sparsely attended and seen as a joke by those who did turn up, said Talia Jane, a journalist who was there.

But it underlined an obsession with a murder suspect that has gripped social media since the killing on 4 December, fuelled by latent anger directed at America's private health insurers.

"There was a lot of tinder already there, a lot of discontent, a lot of frustration already there, and [this] sort of threw a match on it," Ms Jane said.

And it has only grown since the suspect was named as Luigi Mangione, a 26-year-old Ivy League-educated member of a prominent Baltimore family.

In TikTok videos, memes and group chats, a young man accused of shooting a father-of-two in the back on a New York City sidewalk has been fawned over and praised as a kind of folk hero.

This fetishisation was remarkably widespread, not limited to radical corners of the internet or any political affiliation, troubling many observers.

"We do not kill people in cold blood to resolve policy differences or express a viewpoint," said Josh Shapiro, the governor of Pennsylvania, where Mr Mangione was arrested at a McDonald's.

"In a civil society, we are all less safe when ideologues engage in vigilante justice."

Almost immediately after Mr Thompson was shot dead, the internet began to lionise his suspected killer. On TikTok, people posted videos of a "CEO assassin" New York City walking tour. On Spotify, playlists dedicated to the suspect started to appear.

Her poem pinpoints the duality in the article that the murderer is seen as a folk hero by some. However, her punchline that "we do not kill to resolve" give a clear indication of what is important to her and the newspaper house:

Masks laughing nervously
an obsession
frustration
folk hero.
We do not kill to resolve.

The red color of the pools of blood greets the reader immediately, and some might feel as a distraction. Despite this, the reading of the embedded words in the piles of red adds movement and guides the reading process.

Student Sandra

The student has created a blackout poem of a person and his or her speech or thinking bubble. In the interview Sandra tells us that she is thinking a lot about the situation on Gaza and says that "there is an empty space in society when it comes to talking about this". By which she means that places where these issues are being discussed is non-existent. In the poem she depicts herself thinking about the situation, and she has included more words visible than the poem itself, to indicate that there is so much more than one reads about in the news. When we asked Sandra about the choice of using black and white only, her response was that she felt it would be disrespectful to use colors. The all black and white colors give resonance to pain and suffering, life and death. In a closing remark regarding her work, Sandra says: "One must talk about Gaza, people start to forget this situation."

Figure 4. Displacement

The use of black and white only is very effective and sets off a mood of sadness in the reader. Furthermore, drawing herself into the picture gives a feeling of intention and meaning. This blackout poem, this work, is of importance signalling that the student thinks about this deeply. So much of the original newspaper item is completely blacked out almost like a black wall or a black painting underscoring the intense sadness in the student leaving room for the few words that remain to imprint in the reader: *"Hundreds displaced. Gone back to what remains."*

Teacher's Perspectives

To fully comprehend the work on blackout poetry in grade 9, teachers' perspectives from the interviews carry valuable information from the insider point of view. Having grappled with the task in a real-life situation, their observations and thoughts are essential.

On the Positives

The teachers highlight several aspects they liked particularly well about the project, especially related to student engagement and interdisciplinarity. Both teachers emphasize that they were positively surprised by how engaged the students became, especially given that poetry can often be met with resistance. Teacher B describes a clear improvement over time and expresses surprise at how successful the final results were, saying: "I came in early in the process and thought this was complete chaos. Then I came back later, and it had become so much better. I really didn't think it would turn out as well as it did." Teacher A similarly points out that many students found the project enjoyable and meaningful, noting that it was encouraging to see that working with poetry did not trigger the expected negative attitudes. He reflects: "I thought there might be more resistance to working with poetry, but that wasn't really the case." Both teachers also appreciated the interdisciplinary nature of the project and the opportunity for students to choose their own texts and themes, which for some students led to a stronger sense of ownership and identity in their work. Overall, the teachers valued the project for its ability to motivate students and create meaningful connections between language, text, and visual expression.

On the Challenges

The teachers point to several challenges related to the project, both didactic and practical. First, Teacher A highlights that many students decide very early on a visual idea or message, which can cause the original text and textual analysis to become less important in the process. Instead of using the source text as a basis for interpretation, students tend to search for words that fit a pre-decided concept. Another challenge concerns the freedom of text choice, which both teachers describe as demanding for many students, as they lack experience in finding suitable texts and can feel overwhelmed by the large amount of available material. The teachers also emphasize large differences in students' language proficiency, making it difficult for all learners to achieve the same level of depth and reflection. In addition, time management and organisation are described as challenging, particularly in relation to double lessons, printing texts, and handling a large amount of physical materials. Overall, the teachers underline that while the project has strong learning potential, it requires careful scaffolding, clear structure, and sufficient time to work well in a heterogeneous classroom.

On Assessment

The teachers describe assessment in the project as mainly formative and dialogue-based, rather than focused on evaluating the final product. Teacher A explains that assessment in the follow-up subject conversations emphasized students' ability to reflect on their choices, justify why they made certain decisions, and use language to explain meaning, rather than judging the specific topic or "cause" they had chosen. Teacher A also stresses that it would be unfair to assess students based on their personal interests, and that students were clearly informed that they were not assessed on what they chose, but on how they reasoned about and reflected on their work. He explains: "on my part, when it comes to assessment in English, it was not very important to me whether the work was about a famine crisis or about being a specific athlete. What mattered more was whether the students were able to reflect on what they had done and why they had made the choices they did. Was there a reason behind their choices? And how they used language to explain this." Elements of text comprehension were still included, as students were asked to relate their final product to the original text and explain similarities and differences. Teacher B supports this view by highlighting that the project allowed for different strengths to emerge, reinforcing an understanding of assessment as supportive of learning processes rather than as a purely summative judgment.

DISCUSSION

While the analysis highlights moments where students engaged with issues of voice and choice, the small-scale nature of the study calls for caution. The findings are therefore discussed as indications of potential rather than evidence of fully developed democratic competence.

When remediating the original newspaper articles to blackout poems, the original text undergoes a transformation from being a neat straight forward article, to becoming a multimodal text with visual elements that overtake the impression of the newspaper article. In all the examples above, the news item is in the background, whereas the students' composition and creative work imprint the reader. Footballs, the Palestinian flag, pools of blood and a young girl meet the eye rather than the original text. The saturation (Kress and van Leeuwen, 2020) of the colours is unique in all four poems: from a soft use of pencil crayons in the flag, to a deep red marker in the blood puddles and to two diverse black colours in figure four. In the latter one of the black colours is almost like a see-through, covering parts of the article, whereas the other has a very distinct black added to the character in the picture. Such a contrast shows the interplay between the character involved and the heartbreaking news that has a weeping effect on the reader.

How the elements are placed on the page (Stockwell, 2005) differs in the four examples. In figure one the footballs rise from the page to the reader almost like a flight of birds out of the page. This movement stems from the different sizes of the footballs and their placement on the page. To the mind, they might represent a movement from something bound to freedom which supports the theme of the newspaper article. The blood puddles are placed in a manner that reminds of how puddles may distribute themselves on a surface. In this case, though, the placements also create a downward movement on the page supporting the reading sequence. When it comes to the placement of the flag, it covers the complete text indicating as the student told us in the interview, that she wanted the reader to know immediately what her poem was about. At last, in figure four a character is placed on the lefthand side of the page but extends to the right-hand side and to above the midline of the page. To the reader, one sees the character first and since the character is all coloured in black a sense of mourning overtakes the reader. In Stockwell's (2005) train of thought the figure is the more important part of the piece which corresponds to how the student talked about her work in the interview: she thinks about the situation on Gaza all the time. She places herself in the poem, because she feels so strongly about this situation and her composed verbal poem is depicted in her mind through a speech bubble.

These student works are examples of aesthetic transformation (Østern, 2008) entailing how students use visual literacy (Kress & van Leeuwen, 2020; Stockwell, 2005) in their compositions to support meaning-making in their blackout poems. The analyses presented here represent one possible interpretation of the data, and alternative readings could also be developed. Creating multimodal texts by blacking out, marking in and adding visual elements give students agency (Mohammad-Roe &

Tørnby, 2023) and may indicate the uncovering of students' critical thinking through a redesign circle (Janks, 2010). In this case the redesign circle means selecting the original text, choosing which words to keep and adding drawings or illustrations. Thus, the original text is redesign into a new format. Furthermore, students connect their work in ESL to work outside in the real world; thus, seeing the connections between the two (Lim, 2015). More than that, they involve their own perspective taking through remediation (Bolter & Grusin, 1999), aesthetic transformation (Østern, 2008) and redesign (Janks, 2010) enhancing new understandings and the potential for seeing new perspectives (Lim, 2015). The analysis suggests that blackout poetry may create spaces for a critical voice in an ESL setting. Voicing thought and contemplation may function as a basis for citizenship education competence. By testing it out in a classroom setting, students may dare voicing their interests and opinions in other settings outside school. Furthermore, by being given time to contemplate and redesign (Janks, 2010) one is given possibilities for thorough engagement with texts. In a larger scheme of things, it gives room for developing ideas and frame ones' identity. What I think about and how I react to these texts, may foster citizenship. The findings indicate that blackout poetry with newspapers may function as a bridge between literacy education and citizenship education.

Creative tasks such as blackout poetry offer students opportunities for personal expression and the exploration of individual interests. However, the open-ended nature of such tasks can create uncertainty regarding what aspects of the work are being assessed. Students may be unsure whether the focus is on the linguistic choices, the interpretation of the source text, or the overall creativity of the poem. However, in this specific project, assessment was facilitated by the fact that the task was conducted in an ESL context. Here, teachers could focus on evaluating the linguistic aspects, while using the poems and creative processes as a starting point for discussion. This approach aligns with Author et al. (2025), who highlight the potential of creative tasks to support language development when assessment is targeted.

At the same time, clear assessment criteria remain important for guiding students and ensuring fairness. Explicit expectations help students understand what quality looks like, supporting their learning without restricting creative freedom (Hattie, 2009). Formative assessment can further support students during the process, helping to balance the evaluation of both process and product. In black out poetry, for example, much effort goes into text selection, exploration, and experimentation, which can provide valuable insights into students' engagement and learning if process is considered alongside the final product.

Open, creative tasks may advantage students familiar with the language and cultural references teachers value, while others may struggle, making assessment less transparent and fair. From an equity perspective and in line with the Norwegian curriculum's emphasis on democratic principles, assessment should be both inclusive and understandable. While the ESL context in this project allowed a productive balance between language assessment and creative exploration, transferring this approach to other subjects would require careful consideration of the points discussed above, particularly regarding clarity and process-oriented assessment.

While student agency is often emphasised in creative writing tasks, research suggests that agency alone is not sufficient to support meaningful engagement for all learners. Kirschner, Sweller, and Clark (2006) argue that instructional approaches characterised by minimal guidance are generally ineffective, particularly for novice learners working with unfamiliar or complex tasks. The teachers in this project emphasised that although students appreciated being able to choose texts themselves and expressed pride in how the projects reflected their interests and identities, they also spent a considerable amount of time and attention searching for suitable websites, online newspapers, and texts. This suggests that the openness of the task, while supportive of student choice, may also have placed additional demands on learners. Rather, such frameworks can function as pedagogical support, enabling more students to exercise agency within a clearly defined task space. Providing clearer boundaries, such as directing students to a specific website from which to select an article, may therefore have reduced the time and effort spent on logistical decisions and allowed students to focus more fully on the creative and interpretive work involved in composing the poems.

Students clearly express positioning both visually and textually. Through colour choices, clear symbols (such as flags), and concrete images (knives, soccer balls), students aim to strengthen their poems and spark the reader's curiosity even before the text is read. Some of the poems lean more toward directly amplifying the original text rather than creating a literary piece, but this can also be seen as emphasizing the human dimension: students seek to highlight clear messages rather than obscure them and leave them open to interpretation.

The findings indicate a need to balance autonomy and support. This leads to three concrete design implications. This challenges teachers to balance autonomy and support. We therefore recommend three measures: (1) a limited text bank, (2) clear process requirements, (3) explicit assessment language that distinguishes between content, process, and language. By doing so students' keep real agency intact, they choose topic, stance, and design, while the teacher provide transparent scaffolds that ensure progress and fairness; this is minimal guidance in practice and it can be related to dimensions of democratic skills competences. These cases are illustrative of how blackout poetry may foster student agency and engagement, but conclusions should be drawn cautiously given the limited sample.

CONCLUSION

Students' exploration of newspaper articles through a redesign cycle (Janks, 2010) suggests that aesthetic transformation (Østern, 2008) may be present in their work and reflections, indicating potential pathways for engaging with democratic competencies. From the teacher perspective there a transformation is also visible – the chaotic classroom compared to the neatly organized ESL lesson including colours, paint, marker, scissors and more. But also at a different level, that this new approach provided new ideas and insights into ways of working to foster student engagement and agency.

Through the student interviews it is clear that the students have made intentional choices to construct meaning in the blackout poems. Furthermore, it is evident that students have chosen texts that speak to them in some way or another supporting their own interest or opinion about a matter. Being given this freedom provides agency in many layers: the original chosen text, the process of remediating or recycling the text, later to talk about the text in a subject conversation and in the interviews. All layers displaying student agency.

However, this outcome was not consistent across all students who participated in the blackout poetry project. Some students were, to varying degrees, unable to produce a coherent or meaningful new text derived from the original newspaper article. Several factors may account for this. First, some students may not have selected an article that aligned with their interests or prior knowledge, thereby limiting their engagement with the task. Second, difficulties in comprehending the original article may have hindered their ability to meaningfully remediate the text. Third, the aesthetic and creative methodology inherent in blackout poetry may have been unfamiliar to certain students, posing an additional challenge.

Another point of tension concerned the organizational demands of the project. According to the teacher's account, the activity generated considerable movement and material use in the classroom, resulting in a more chaotic physical environment. Furthermore, the necessity for the teacher to assist students in selecting appropriate texts introduced an additional layer of complexity that was perceived as burdensome.

Using the Council of Europe's Competences for Democratic Culture helped make it clear that learning goals go beyond just creating texts, they also include participating as citizens. In our study, students showed democratic values (like concern for human dignity and cultural diversity), attitudes (openness, respect, responsibility, and civic-mindedness), and skills (critical thinking and communication), as well as knowledge and understanding of media and public issues.

Based on our findings we encourage teachers to use creative, student-centred tasks foster agency, literacy, citizenship and democratic skills. In our previous work on blackout poems, we saw a higher degree of poetic language, but this could stem from many factors for instance that the original text was a literary text. This calls for more research into blackout poetry in education and maybe in other subjects than ESL. Blackout poetry as a method can serve as a bridge between literacy work and democratic citizenship by creating a space for voice, interpretation, and critique of systems, even in classrooms with limited resources.

REFERENCES

Bailin, S., & Siegel, H. (2003). Critical thinking. *The Blackwell guide to the philosophy of education*, 181-193.

Barrett, M. (2018). Young people's civic and political engagement and global citizenship. *UN Chronicle*, *54*(4), 44–46. DOI: 10.18356/11734699-en

Biesta, G. (2010). *Good education in an age of measurement: Ethics, politics, democracy*. Paradigm.

Bolter, J. D., & Grusin, R. (1999). *Remediation: Understanding new media R*. MIT Press.

Brattland, S. Ø., & Storstad, O. (2025). *2. Kan skolen kompensere for samfunnet? Kunnskapsforskjeller i et flerkulturelt utdanningslandskap. Unge medborgere i en ny tid*. Scandinavian University Press.

Brinkmann, S., & Kvale, S. (2015). *InterViews: learning the craft of qualitative research interviewing* (3rd ed.). Sage.

Butler-Kisber, L. (2010). *Qualitative inquiry: Thematic, narrative and arts-informed perspectives*. Sage. Publications., DOI: 10.4135/9781526435408

Butler-Kisber, L. (2018). Poetic inquiry. In *Qualitative inquiry: Thematic, narrative and arts- informed perspectives* (2nd ed., pp. 95–113). Sage Publications., DOI: 10.4135/9781526417978.n7

Council of Europe. (2018). Reference Framework of Competences for Democratic Culture, Context, concepts and model. (SBN 978-92-871-8573-0). Strasbourg Council of Europe Publishing.

Den Heyer, K., & van Kessel, C. (2015). Evil, agency, and citizenship education. *McGill Journal of Education*, *50*(1), 1–18.

Docherty, T. (2006). *Aesthetic democracy*. Stanford University Press. DOI: 10.1515/9781503625334

Ennis, R. H. (2015). Critical thinking: A streamlined conception. I M. Davies & R. Barnett (Eds.), *The Palgrave handbook of critical thinking in higher education* (pp. 31–47). Springer.

Falkner, R. (2021). *Environmentalism and global international society* (Vol. 156). Cambridge University Press. DOI: 10.1017/9781108966696

Fisher, A. (2011). *Critical thinking: an introduction* (2nd ed.). Cambridge University Press.

Hattie, J. (2009). *Visible learning: A synthesis of over 800 meta-analyses relating to achievement*. Routledge.

Janks, H. (2010). Language, power and pedagogies. In *N. H. Hornberger & S. L.* McKay.

Kirschner, P. A., Sweller, J., & Clark, R. E. (2006). Why minimal guidance during instruction does not work. *Educational Psychologist, 41*(2), 75–86. DOI: 10.1207/s15326985ep4102_1

Kress, G. (2003). *Literacy in the new media age*. Routledge.

Kress, G., & Van Leeuwen, T. (2020). *Reading images: The grammar of visual design*. Routledge. DOI: 10.4324/9781003099857

Lim, L. (2015). Critical thinking, social education and the curriculum: foregrounding a social

Meld. St. 34 (2023-2024). En mer praktisk skole [A More Pracitcal School]. Regjeringen [The Government]. Meld. St. 34 (2023–2024) - regjeringen.no

Milner, H. (2002). *Civic Literacy: How Informed Citizens Make Democracy Work*. University Press of New England.

Mohammad-Roe, S., Paaske, N., Van Hoof, N., & Amitai, A. (2025). Nurturing student engagement: Towards democratic values and attitudes. *Journal of Social Science Education, 24*(3). Advance online publication. DOI: 10.11576/jsse-7680

Roe-Mohammad, S., & Tørnby, H. (2023). "I wanted to freeze the moment". Blackout poetry and student agency during the covid lockdown. In *Using innovative literacies to develop leadership and agency: Inspiring transformation and hope*. IGI Global.

Nikolajeva, M., & Scott, C. (2013). *How picturebooks work*. Routledge. DOI: 10.4324/9780203960615

Østern, A.-L. (2008). Aktiv estetisk respons som utfordring i litteraturundervisning. In A.-L. Østern, A.-L., Otnes, H., & Hestnes, H. (Eds), Esteisk tilnærming til tekstarbeid i språkfagene (Vol 2). Tapir akademisk forlag.

Paaske, N., Mohammad-Roe, S., Smets, W., Amitai, A., Randazzo, N. A., & Huang, L. (2023). Challenges for European teachers when assessing student learning to promote democratic citizenship competences. *Journal of Social Science Education, 22*(3), 3–22. DOI: 10.11576/jsse-5978

Punch, P. F., & Aoancea, A. (2014). *Introduction to research methods in education* (2nd ed.). Sage.

Stockwell, P. (2005). *Cognitive Poetics: An Introduction*. Routledge. DOI: 10.4324/9780203995143

Swami, V., Voracek, M., Stieger, S., Tran, U. S., & Furnham, A. (2014). Analytic thinking reduces belief in conspiracy theories. *Cognition*, *133*(3), 572–585. DOI: 10.1016/j.cognition.2014.08.006 PMID: 25217762

Utdanningsdirektoratet The Norwegian Directorate for Education and Training (2020). The English Curriculum. Læreplan i engelsk (ENG01-05) | udir.no

Utdanningsdirektoratet, The Norwegian Directorate for Education and Training (2020). Cross-curricular Curriculum. Tverrfaglige temaer | udir.no

Utdanningsdirektoratet, The Norwegian Directorate for Education and Training (2023). *ICCS 2022: Rapport om medborgerskap*.

Chapter 9

EMI in STEM:
A Pathway to Global Competence

Pooja Dehankar
Ajeenkya D.Y. Patil School of Engineering, India

Susanta Das
http://orcid.org/0000-0002-9314-3988
Ajeenkya D.Y. Patil University, India

ABSTRACT

The increasing use of English in higher education in non-English-speaking nations has given rise to new standards of linguistic ideology & practices. It gives a general overview of EMI, a study of Higher Education laws, & an analysis of how teachers & students are affected by them. To comprehend how EMI aids in our understanding of pedagogical techniques & challenges, it focuses on studying & critically analyzing pertinent literature. It establishes the foundation for qualitative/quantitative future approaches to EMI success in Higher Education. EMI pedagogy techniques allow instructors & students to benefit from EMI education philosophy. It aims to map out teachers' attitudes, beliefs, & classroom practices of teachers about the use of English as primary language of teaching. It argues that EMI in STEM fosters global competency. EMI in STEM education plays a critical role in forming next generation of scientists who can address global challenges & contribute to international advancements by providing students with the skills they need to navigate & thrive in an interconnected world.

INTRODUCTION

STEM was first used at the National Science Foundation (NSF) in the 1990s. Since then, it has been a catch-all term for any activity, rule, initiative, or procedure

DOI: 10.4018/979-8-2600-2163-7.ch009

that involves one or more STEM disciplines. The awareness of the interconnected disciplines of science, technology, engineering, and mathematics education is stressed by the use of the phrase STEM today. The importance of science, and by extension, technology and engineering, in school curricula, could be emphasized by reauthorizing the Elementary and Secondary Education Act (ESEA). It is rare for STEM to have anything to do with technology or engineering and is typically considered to refer to science or math (Bybee, 2010).

The four walls of a classroom in an educational institution represent the walls on which teachers and students are supposed to collaborate in order to produce human resources that will benefit all people. But as things stand right now, "India's destiny is being shaped both inside and outside the walls." The general public, as well as educationists, have a strong belief and faith that education has a significant impact on society overall. Education institutions serve as hubs for the development of human resources, and graduates are expected to contribute to society and assume various responsibilities, including those in business. Good human resources with moral and ethical standards will grow good businesses, and successful businesses will eventually provide good services to the community. Consequently, there are links and dependencies between business and society. Good educational institutions must assume the duty of creating excellent human resources in order to shape business and society in the future (Gonda, 2014).

The increasing use of English has led to a rise in the significance of English-language education globally as well as English-based education. Universities all throughout the world have been becoming more international in recent years, and higher education institutions (HEI) now prioritize this. Higher education institutions are eager to internationalize their courses, establish a global footprint, and compete for the enrollment of students from around the world. There are numerous ways to do this, including as internationalization policies, branch campus establishments abroad, staff and student exchanges, joint degree programs and courses, and recruitment drives for foreign workers and students (Chapple, 2015).

Higher education institutions, junior colleges, and even elementary schools are using EMI more and more. The education of young people is significantly impacted by this phenomena. However, not much empirical research has been done to determine the introduction date and purpose of EMI as well as its delivery method. Regarding the effects of using English instead of one's native tongue (L1) on instruction, learning, assessment, and teacher preparation, we don't know enough. The overall goal of the Oxford University Department of Education's Center for Research and Development on EMI Oxford is to conduct research on the locations, methods, and results of the implementation of EMI (Dearden, 2014).

Building STEM literacy and 21st century skills, creating a workforce prepared for STEM fields, and increasing interest and involvement in STEM are among the objectives stated in the framework. In terms of results, the framework takes into account learning and accomplishment, enrollment in STEM courses, employment connected to STEM fields, creation of a "STEM identity," and the capacity to transfer knowledge between STEM subjects. The framework discusses which disciplines are prominent, which subjects are connected, the magnitude, complexity, and duration of an initiative, as well as the type and breadth of integration. In terms of execution, the framework concentrates on problem-based learning and engineering design instructional designs; the kind of educator supports that are in place, like professional development for pre- and in-service teachers and the creation of professional learning communities; and modifications to the learning environment (Honey et al., 2014).

Modern EMI pedagogy techniques have been shown to reduce undue pressure, allowing instructors and students to benefit from the EMI education philosophy and educate one another. To comprehend how EMI aids in our understanding of pedagogical techniques and education-related challenges, this chapter focuses on studying and critically analyzing pertinent literature. It establishes the foundation for more in-depth qualitative or quantitative future approaches to EMI success in Higher Education.

BACKGROUND

Research shows that English Medium Instruction (EMI) frequently results in unequal educational outcomes, supporting the claim that EMI in Indian STEM education poses substantial hurdles despite its goal of globalization. Even while EMI is meant to improve employment and global competitiveness, its execution often faces pedagogical difficulties, linguistic barriers, and the widening of socioeconomic gaps (Borooah & Sabharwal, 2017).

One of the main issues is that both students and instructors have poor English proficiency, which makes it difficult to understand the material and prevents students from deeply engaging with scientific ideas. The active learning necessary for STEM topics may be hampered by lecturers' frequent use of conventional, passive teaching techniques (Islam & Stapa, 2021).

EMI functions as a type of "linguistic capital" that favors students from affluent, metropolitan homes who have previously encountered English, frequently excluding pupils from rural or disadvantaged backgrounds (Sah & Li, 2018). Regional languages are frequently marginalized by the quick, top-down introduction of EMI, endangering India's linguistic diversity and alienating pupils (Kumar, 2025). Many teachers themselves struggle with language, and there is a severe shortage of qualified STEM educators who can instruct in English (Aziz et al., 2024).

English [as the] Medium of Instruction (EMI) has emerged in tandem with the current global economy's growing internationalization of education. It has established a solid foundation in higher education systems where English is not the primary language and is still trending upward. As universities react to growing competition over global resources and in an environment where global careers operate almost entirely in English, the motivations, or a nation's strategic agenda, for establishing EMI programs are dynamic but primarily driven by economic and political forces (Wilkinson, 2013).

The expansion of English as a foreign language instruction in higher education systems across Europe and Asia, or in nations within the Expanding Circle, has been noted to be strengthening EMI's status as a new "colonial frontier" (Doiz et al., 2012). English's globalization is often viewed and promoted as a universally applicable educational medium. The promotion of imperial languages is achieved through linguicism (discrimination based on the language one speaks), of which many modern initiatives are examples. A macro-sociolinguistic tension between national linguistic capital accumulation or dispossession arises from increased use of English. Because of this, EMI is relentlessly sold, blindly supported, and approved by decision-makers in these areas despite arguments to the contrary—for instance, that students and teachers react more critically and creatively when thinking in their first language (Phillipson, 2017).

The method to language and content integration in learning is known by the acronym CLIL (Content and Language Integrated Learning). Typically interpreted as a catch-all phrase, this all-encompassing method of language acquisition denotes the process of acquiring the target language via course material in traditional schooling. Despite having strong ties to its American-Canadian equivalent, content-based instruction, or CBI, CLIL originated in Europe in response to demands for the multilingual and intercultural education of EU citizens. A variety of approaches with the option of collaborative teaching emerged as CLIL was introduced into regular education, from elementary school through university. The language-content integration in these paradigms can be thought of as a continuum. Regarding language, one example would be an English instructor illustrating specific terminology and the use of the present tense to express processes in a topic-based lecture centered around volcanoes. In terms of substance, we may find a biology teacher instructing the course in English. No matter which model is used, CLIL encourages team teaching, in which a language teacher and a content teacher collaborate. Since CLIL has been widely used in Europe and, more recently, other parts of the world, since the 1990s, there has been a demand for a book that explains the benefits of this novel method, provides implementation models, and addresses classroom considerations (Coyle et al., 2010).

According to Dearden (2014), EMI is commonly understood to be the use of English in academic topic instruction while teaching English as a foreign language. For Inner Circle nations where English is the primary language, it appears inconsequential (Kachru et al., 1985). Instead, for the nations in the Expanding and Outer Circles, it comes up as important "business" that reflects their dedication to a neoliberal economy. Thus, it is possible to interpret EMI as an indicator of the globalization of English colonization becoming more entrenched. The United States, the United Kingdom, Australia, Canada, and New Zealand are among the countries in the Inner Circle that continue to reap the benefits of having English as their national language, including its hegemonic status and profit and convenience.

CENTRAL PROBLEM

The main issue is the "double pressure" (or dual challenge) for both teachers and students, as the quick, sometimes forced, introduction of EMI in STEM education (Science, Technology, Engineering, and Mathematics) due to internationalization strategies happens too quickly for the linguistic preparation of the participants. Students experience academic difficulties, such as a lack of understanding of scientific concepts, as the language of instruction is not their native language.

Teachers are asked to teach complex subject matter in a foreign language without proper training, which results in pedagogical constraints, identity crises, and a possible simplification of the subject matter.

OBJECTIVE

The chapter seeks to critically assess the application of EMI in STEM fields with the aim of offering evidence-based insights and recommendations for improving its effectiveness. Some of the key objectives of the chapter include: Examining the perspectives of students, staff, and administrators on EMI. Pointing out the challenges associated with lecture comprehension, assessment, and participation. Offering solutions in terms of improving pedagogy through techniques such as scaffolding and translanguaging, among others.

MAJOR GUIDING QUESTIONS

A series of guiding questions that center on the conflict between language proficiency, topic mastery, and pedagogical adaptability are frequently used in chapters studying English Medium Instruction (EMI) in STEM (Science, Technology, Engineering, and Mathematics), according to recent research. Higher education settings in "expanding circle" nations (where English is a foreign language) like Korea, China, Kazakhstan, and Algeria are often the setting for these studies (Macaro, 2022).

There are many unexplored concerns that require careful attention since English-Medium Instruction (EMI) has become a significant area of policy and research. A fundamental question for a chapter on EMI in the field of STEM is: "To what extent does English-medium instruction in STEM disciplines facilitate content learning while supporting language development, and what pedagogical strategies are necessary to overcome challenges in content comprehension and student interaction?" (Sah, 2022).

STEM

STEM disciplines (Science, Technology, Engineering, and Mathematics), which are known for their dense technical terminology, intricate, abstract ideas, and need for precise language (Yang et al., 2023).

Mainly concerned with non-Anglophone settings (EFL settings), especially in Asia (South Korea/KAIST, Kazakhstan, Thailand) and the Middle East (Oman, Saudi Arabia) (Meurant, 2010).

Rapidly internationalizing Higher Education Institutions (HEIs) often driven by government policies mandating the need for "English-only" education to improve international rankings (Fenton-Smith et al., 2026).

HIGHER EDUCATION LAWS

The Indian University Grants Commission (UGC), which was founded soon after independence, has the authority to control academic standards and distribute funding that come from the national government. Regretfully, despite the fact that these obligations are enshrined in law, the UGC has declined to carry them out, which has had detrimental effects on academic standards in Indian universities. The collegiate structure of the University of London served as the model for the Indian university system. As a result, the enormous growth in student enrollment in the 1950s and 1960s caused an unchecked rise in the number and size of colleges, which in turn came to dominate the university system. Once more, the UGC made the decision to remain silent and made no effort to coordinate the expansion of universities (Singh, 1984).

The first part of the twentieth century saw a sharp increase in state authority over teacher certification. Alongside this, state education departments became larger and gained more control over schools in rural areas. The transformation of regular schools into teacher colleges, the raising of admission standards to the point of high school graduation, the decline of exams and teachers institutes as the main means of certifying teachers for the country schools, the vast expansion of the number, types, and specificity of certificates issued, the growth of these institutions' graduate programs and degrees, and—perhaps most importantly—the unification of professional opinion around a single, highly unified ideology of what made a good teacher and good preparation program were all witnessed during this period (Angus, 2001).

In recent decades, higher education institutions in Asia have benefited from increased autonomy from numerous governments. It was anticipated that increased autonomy would improve institutions' operational efficiency and give rise to new governance structures. Research based on studies conducted in Cambodia, China, Indonesia, Japan, and Vietnam shows that autonomy has increased institutional independence by giving them the freedom to plan ahead, hire staff, mobilize resources, launch new academic initiatives, set up new governance frameworks, and implement significant changes to the way decisions are made both academically and administratively. Due to the state's diminished involvement in the administration of institutions and the professoriate's diminished influence and collective bargaining power in the institutional decision-making process, autonomy did, however, also bring with it a certain amount of financial uncertainty (Varghese & Martin, 2014).

The intricate network of relationships, institutions, and rules that exist above the level of a single institution makes up the higher education system's superstructure. The nature of the relationship between the state and higher education institutions is a central issue in system-level governance; however, in multiinstitutional systems, this level of authority frequently includes mechanisms to relate the various components of the system to one another as well as different regulatory arrangements for different sectors or institutional types (Amaral et al., 2002).

Student, staff, and offshore delivery are the three main forces for internationalization in higher education. This raises concerns about quality and equity on a national, institutional, and personal level. It could be difficult for non-Anglophone nations to draw in and keep the "brightest and best" at the national level. Institutions' financial stability and ability to protect their intellectual property are both impacted by the linguistic skewed market. Ultimately, the ability to function in a foreign language and academic culture may limit an individual's ability to achieve in school. Hence, institutions that lack a strong language strategy, sufficient pre-training, and continuous assistance risk causing more harm than good instruction or their own international reputation (Hughes, 2008).

Higher education has had the greatest internationalization of all educational levels. The international character of universities' activity has been evident from their founding, therefore this internationalization is not a recent development. Actually, the concept of the traveling scholar existed before colleges were established as formal educational establishments. Foreign scholars and students had a crucial role in the founding of the first universities in the mediaeval West (Welch, 2005). However, modern colleges are distinguished by an unparalleled emphasis on internationalization, which has an impact on the makeup of academic staff and student body, the courses that are taught, and the kinds of learning opportunities that are provided to students (Källkvist & Hult, 2016; Liddicoat, 2003).

OUTER/EXPANDING CIRCLES

In Outer Circle countries, English is commonly maintained from colonial times for administrative and higher education purposes. English is the prevalent language of instruction in engineering, science, and professional programs. In Singapore English is the official and strictly enforced language of instruction in all tertiary institutions. In India English is the prevalent language of instruction in STEM fields, especially in top universities. In Malaysia Although the national language (Bahasa Malaysia) is promoted, the government allows widespread EMI in public and private universities, especially in STEM fields. In Philippines English is the largely unchallenged language of instruction in science and engineering.

Although prevalent, issues include variable student and faculty proficiency in English, as well as the challenge of maintaining English alongside national language policies. In Expanding Circle countries, English has traditionally been a foreign language. The motivation for EMI is to improve international rankings and attract global talent. The explosive rise of EMI, with top institutions such as KAIST (Korea Advanced Institute of Science and Technology), where EMI is widely adopted in STEM fields to promote global competitiveness. In China while Putonghua is the default language, many universities have established English-medium programs, particularly in business, engineering, and medicine to attract international students. Japan government initiatives encourage EMI, but programs are sometimes criticized for attracting foreign students rather than preparing local students. Taiwan actively promoting EMI in STEM to improve Chinese-English bilingualism. "Hasty implementation" has led to serious pedagogical problems, including adverse effects on students' comprehension of complex technical concepts, low proficiency levels, and reduced student engagement.

ESSENCE OF MODERN-DAY HIGHER EDUCATION

A vital institution for social and economic advancement in a knowledge-intensive society is the research university. Research universities are increasingly becoming more globally focused, with an emphasis on new knowledge discovery and the training of the next generation of academics. The Emerging Global Model (EGM) represents a new paradigm for research universities that has evolved over the last few decades. These universities are at the forefront of the acceptance of globalization in higher education. Their research intensity is significantly higher than what has been seen in the past. They work in a context where conventional political, linguistic, and access borders are becoming increasingly porous; they are competing globally for students, professors, staff, and financing. When defining their scope as trans-national in nature, these prestigious universities look beyond national borders (Mohrman et al., 2008).

The goal of higher education, which stands at the pinnacle of the Indian educational system, is to produce responsible human resources for society. To shape the destiny of the country, the sole resource required are knowledgeable individuals with moral and ethical beliefs. Furthermore, higher education has a duty to produce informed citizens for their nation. A small number of nations have achieved global development as a result of higher education's demonstrated value in the past. Developing nations, like India, have come to understand the significance of higher education in the process of creating human resources, which is necessary for the advancement of their countries (Gonda, 2014).

ENGLISH-MEDIUM INSTRUCTION

The phrase "English-medium instruction" (EMI), which refers to any type of formal education where instruction is conducted in English, may seem self-explanatory. In environments where English is a foreign or second language for at least some of the professors and/or students, "EMI refers to the use of the English language to teach academic subjects, other than English itself" (Dafouz & Gray, 2022). The reality of EMI, however, is more complicated in terms of the geographic location, educational level and orientation, impacted individuals, and languages involved, reflecting the complicated history and worldwide dissemination of English (Pecorari & Malmström, 2018)..

Three fundamental components are necessary for EMI to occur: (1) English-medium instruction; (2) academic subjects other than the English language to L2 English users; and (3) these components must both be present. All of them, however, permit some change and therefore distinct realizations of EMI: (1) There are many different academic subjects, each with its own educational and linguistic affordances; (2) language learning is intricately linked to learning content; and (3) the linguistic repertoires of student and teacher groups vary in terms of the languages they speak and the proficiency levels at which they speak them. English is one of these mediums of instruction (Smit, 2023).

The phenomena known as EMI in non-Anglophone regions has coincided with an increase in the amount of research produced on the subject, making it a significant and well-established area of study. Research on the views of the main players in this type of education—teachers, students, and policy makers—has been heavily focused. However, a number of other significant questions remain unanswered, the most significant of which is: What are the results of this kind of instruction? What are EMI's effects on society and the economy? How can EMI instructors enhance their instruction? And how can students better themselves so they can learn more effectively? In the EMI educational system, students are taught subjects in English as a second or foreign language. In the education market, EMI has grown significantly in value as a result of recent trends toward internationalization, particularly in higher education (Macaro, 2022).

Three different approaches exist for implementing EMI programs. In certain countries, including Saudi Arabia and Turkey, there is a program called the Preparatory Year Model (PYP) wherein university students who have completed their secondary education are required to study English for a full year before beginning an EMI program. A university support model might be the second kind, in which all prospective students have access to EMI but no PYP, however it is anticipated that they will also receive simultaneous support from English language experts. A selection mechanism of some kind is used in the third model to grant admission to EMI courses. Those whose English proficiency is deemed adequate are admitted, while those whose proficiency is insufficient are directed to get education in their native tongue. By offering their children private language instruction, affluent parents may guarantee that their children attain the necessary English proficiency, making this model the least equitable and potentially socially controversial one (Macaro, 2018).

ENGLISH MEDIUM INSTRUCTION (EMI) IN INDIA

Globalization and the desire for "linguistic capital" are driving the fast growth of English Medium Instruction (EMI) in India. But under the National Education Policy (NEP) 2020, which promotes mother-tongue-based education while also pushing for the globalization of higher education, it is undergoing a dramatic change. As a result, there is a "linguistic paradox" whereby foundational education shifts toward regional languages while postsecondary education increases its emphasis on English, underscoring long-standing difficulties in multilingual classrooms (Kalyanpur, et al., 2022). The policy's "Multilingual Turn" asserts that proficiency in English and other languages can be attained without required English Medium Instruction (EMI) in the foundational levels, using multilingualism as a cognitive and pedagogical resource rather than a hindrance. This method places a great emphasis on developing a solid foundation through training in one's mother tongue or native tongue (Manan et al., 2023). On the other hand, the policy seeks to internationalize higher education in order to make India a "global knowledge superpower". In order to portray EMI as crucial for higher education and competitive global jobs, this entails attracting prestigious foreign colleges to India, growing Indian institutions overseas (like IIT Delhi in Abu Dhabi), and promoting foreign languages (Setty, 2013).

The policy serves as a "Bridge to EMI," recognizing the possible gap between home languages and comprehensive English instruction, in order to balance these methods. In order to prevent pupils from being disadvantaged, it promotes a bilingual, transitional approach to education, which eventually manages a gradual, successful change in the medium of instruction (Escamilla, 2010).

According to research, there are a number of significant obstacles to implementing a uniform English Medium Instruction (EMI) policy throughout India's heterogeneous linguistic terrain. The growing English-vernacular divide is one of the main problems, as EMI favors urban, privileged students while posing significant challenges to those from rural or lower socioeconomic backgrounds, especially Dalit children who might not have had any prior exposure to English. Due to this discrepancy, many people find English to be an obstacle rather than an opportunity in the educational system (Ramamoorthy & Dinesh, 2025).

EMI also results in substantial conceptual and cognitive deficits. When students are taught technical, scientific, or abstract material in a language they do not completely understand, it restricts their ability to comprehend and think critically, which frequently leads to worse educational outcomes than when instruction is given in the mother tongue. This method frequently leads to rote learning instead of in-depth comprehension, which makes it difficult for students to interact with difficult subjects (Feng et al., 2023).

Another significant obstacle is teacher readiness, since the majority of Indian educators lack the particular knowledge and training needed to instruct non-native English speakers in multilingual classrooms. This results in the widespread practice of "translanguaging," in which many educators and learners naturally turn to bilingual or translation techniques to guarantee understanding despite formal "English-only" standards (Manju, 2024).

There are serious resource limitations, such as a severe lack of excellent regional language learning resources and textbooks. These shortages underscore the practical challenges of delivering egalitarian education throughout the nation and make it challenging to fully follow the NEP's instructions to teach in local languages (Rajbanshi, 2025).

TEACHERS' BELIEFS

The opinions of teachers have always been an interesting subject because of the valuable insights they may provide to enhance English language instruction. Because of the choices they make and how they convey their views on language instruction and acquisition, it has a significant influence on classroom principles (Gilakjani & Sabouri, 2017). When examining the impact of professional background on teachers' beliefs, practices, and attitudes, which can have varying causal interpretations, is a more accessible perspective from the perspective of education policy (Klieme & Vieluf, 2009).

Initially, educators held the view that using English as a teaching language for content-area courses was beneficial. Secondly, educators exhibited their convictions in line with the methods used in the classroom. Third, when teaching topic areas in English as a medium of instruction, teachers had to deal with issues related to language barriers, participation in class discussions, and lesson planning. The results point to the possibility of initially implementing EMI in Indonesian schools, particularly at the primary level, as it is a very helpful program. Secondly, schools and educators must be aware of the sources of the views held by their teachers, as these sources may have an impact on how those beliefs are reflected in classroom procedures. Third, because overcoming the obstacles will have an impact on the execution of EMI, teachers cannot ignore them and must take further action.

Few people who work in higher education today—as managers, professors, or administrators—aware of the growing significance of the English language as a crucial—and, some would argue, contentious—issue in the field are unaware of this, especially in an era of globalization and ever-increasing student mobility. As universities strive to gain a piece of what is now the global education industry, the number of English-medium universities—where all or part of the curriculum is provided via the English language—is increasing. The guarantee that overseas students from non-English speaking backgrounds may flourish in an English-medium teaching setting is necessary for university admission offices, who are responsible for assessing and admitting students. The certification of English language ability is a major issue (Murray, 2016).

Educating students in English gives them a high degree of education, challenges them, makes them competitive in a global market, and encourages them—these are the top five reasons why teachers believe EMI is useful. In the current study, secondary teachers felt substantially and substantively more strongly than tertiary teachers about the reasons that EMI is helpful to their students, especially when it comes to enlivening the lesson, inspiring students, and simplifying the concepts. The majority of EMI teachers across all phases think that EMI helps students. Teachers of EMI do not firmly believe that EMI hinders pupils' ability to acquire languages, while some worry about content learning. In terms of how EMI affects the content subject, the sample is less in agreement.

There was no discernible variation based on the institutional level, with 53.4% of the sample as a whole believing that EMI influences academic subject material. The qualitative findings in this respect indicate that the teaching approach and the English language competence level of the students may be factors that lead to a negative influence of EMI (Briggs et al., 2018).

Engaging students in learning can be achieved through a variety of teaching tactics, such as using audio and visual aids (like YouTube videos), individual and group work, hands-on activities (like creating, building, and testing the Medical Mission kit), and more. While opinions about individual and group work varied, two teaching strategies—visual aids and role play, according to Killen (2013)—came out as favorable by both the teacher and the students in this study. Students' attitudes toward their learning appeared to be positively impacted, for example, by role-playing the three states of matter. They reported that the activity was "fun learning" and "helped me understand how the different molecules and particles worked." Scholarly works have acknowledged role play's value as a teaching approach (McSharry & Jones, 2000).

The key components of active, collaborative, cooperative, and problem-based learning seem to have "broad but uneven support," (Prince, 2004). According to this study's findings, group and individual work can help target students' learning needs because some students need group work to get ideas and motivation, while individual learners can solve problems on their own (Gokhale, 1995). This is because students can develop their skills and attitudes through individual and group work. This approach may offer a means of simulating the work of engineers, who perform both solo and group projects at different times. In general, both the instructor and the pupils reported that the instructional techniques used in the STEM classes encouraged students to approach ideas and assignments with a positive attitude.

Discussions over STEM instructors' capacity to fulfill the requirements of English Language Learners (ELLs) have been spurred by the rise of ELLs in the K–12 educational system. According to reports from STEM educators, they frequently lack professional development opportunities and don't feel ready to meet these demands (Janzen, 2008; Ballantyne et al., 2008; August & Shanahan, 2010).

Teachers need to be able to reflect on their practice and make the necessary adjustments because of the limitations and demands that come with adopting EMI for both students and teachers. Reflective practice often entails EMI instructors critically analyzing their beliefs, practices, and philosophy of practice in order to become more accountable for their activities. Teachers of EMI are able to operate purposefully and deliberately because of reflective practice. Reflective practice is EMI teachers methodically examining what they do, how they do it, why they do it, the results they get in terms of students' learning, and the actions they will take after learning all of this. As a result, professional development can result from experience paired with methodical reflection, making us better language instructors (Farrell, 2020).

According to Hargreaves (1998), teaching has traditionally been regarded as an "emotional practice." During their working day, teachers face a wide range of emotions from people in the wider educational community, including students, administrators, guardians, administrative staff, policy makers, and so forth. These emotions are felt by teachers everywhere and at all educational levels. Education is crucial to one's life and is fundamental to a country. Therefore, emotions become even more intense when we add another layer to it—that of teaching and learning a second language. For the most part, this language is English. The use of the English language to teach academic courses in nations or jurisdictions where the majority of the population does not speak English as their first language (L1) is known as English-medium instruction (EMI) and is a worldwide phenomenon (Dearden, 2014). In higher education, however, one may argue that "English-medium" refers to much more. In recent years, there has been a significant surge in its use as the primary language for international communication, projects, publishing, research, and education (Wächter & Maiworm, 2014).

CONCLUSION

An increase in English-medium instruction (EMI) in higher education (HE) is essential to the sector's expansion and internationalization in multilingual Asia Pacific countries. The character of academic English has received insufficient attention in discussions and implementation of language in education policy in the region, despite mirroring global trends and solidifying the language's standing as the global academic language. Currently, governments and institutions must find a way to promote local languages in academic activities while also implementing EMI rules in a cogent manner.

Internationalization initiatives have brought about significant changes to higher education institutions around the world. Internationalization of curricula (or internationalization at home) is just one of the many activities that these institutions may take part in as part of the impending internationalization process, according to Knight (2016). EMI, a pedagogical technique that advocates for teaching classes in English, is a significant and essential component of the internationalization process.

The phrase "internationalization" is broad. Knight (2005) defined it as encompassing global endeavors like teacher and student mobility, collaborations, projects, or the export of education through franchises or branch campuses. Conversely, according to Knight (2005), it can also refer to "the inclusion of an international, intercultural, or global dimension in the curriculum and the teaching / learning process" (p. 2).

In STEM education, English as a Medium of Instruction (EMI) is an essential tool for developing global competency in the connected world of today. Students are better prepared to interact with international information resources, communicate in the scientific community worldwide, and work together on cross-border initiatives when EMI is incorporated into STEM curriculum. Additionally, EMI improves students' job chances by training them to participate in academic mobility, work in multinational settings, and advance global science.

Despite obstacles like language hurdles, EMI in STEM is an important tactic for developing the next generation of globally competent scientists, engineers, and innovators because of its long-term advantages, which include improved international communication and academic and professional mobility.

REFERENCES

Amaral, A., Jones, G. A., & Karseth, B. (2002). Governing higher education: Comparing national perspectives. In *Governing Higher Education: National perspectives on institutional Governance* (pp. 279–298). Springer Netherlands. DOI: 10.1007/978-94-015-9946-7_14

Angus, D. L. (2001). Professionalism and the Public Good: A Brief History of Teacher Certification.

August, D., & Shanahan, T. (2010). Response to a review and update on developing literacy in second-language learners: Report of the national literacy panel on language minority children and youth. *Journal of Literacy Research*, *42*(3), 341–348. DOI: 10.1080/1086296X.2010.503745

Aziz, M. A., Azizullah, A., & Baloch, S. (2024). Emerging trends and issues in English language teaching: A bibliometric analysis. *Journal of Asian Development Studies*, *13*(1), 1004–1016. DOI: 10.62345/jads.2024.13.1.83

Ballantyne, K. G., Sanderman, A. R., & Levy, J. (2008). *Educating English Language Learners: Building Teacher Capacity. Roundtable Report*. National Clearinghouse for English Language Acquisition & Language Instruction Educational Programs.

Borooah, V. K., & Sabharwal, N. S. (2017). English as a medium of instruction in Indian education: Inequality of access to educational opportunities. *CPRHE research papers, 7*, 1-33.

Briggs, J., Dearden, J., & Macaro, E. (2018). English medium instruction: Comparing teacher beliefs in secondary and tertiary education. *Studies in Second Language Learning and Teaching*, *8*(3), 673–696. DOI: 10.14746/ssllt.2018.8.3.7

Bybee, R. W. (2010). Advancing STEM education: A 2020 vision. *Technology and engineering teacher, 70*(1), 30.

Chapple, J. (2015). Teaching in English is not necessarily the teaching of English. *International Education Studies*, *8*(3), 1–13. DOI: 10.5539/ies.v8n3p1

Coyle, D., Hood, P., & Marsh, D. (2010). *CLIL: Content and language integrated learning* (Vol. 9). Cambridge University Press. DOI: 10.1017/9781009024549

Dearden, J. (2014). English as a medium of instruction–A growing global phenomenon. *British Council*. https://www.britishcouncil.es/sites/default/files/british_council_english_as_a_medium_of_instruction.pdf

Doiz, A., Lasagabaster, D., & Sierra, J. M. (Eds.). (2012). *English-medium instruction at universities: Global challenges*. Multilingual Matters., https://www.researchgate.net/publication/285573621_English-Medium_Instruction_at_Universities_Global_Challenges DOI: 10.21832/9781847698162

Escamilla, K. (2010). Bilingual education programs: Maintenance, transitional, and dual language. *Encyclopedia of Cross-Cultural School Psychology*, 145-149.

Farrell, T. S. (2020). Professional development through reflective practice for English-medium instruction (EMI) teachers. *International Journal of Bilingual Education and Bilingualism, 23*(3), 277–286. DOI: 10.1080/13670050.2019.1612840

Feng, L., He, L., & Yiganmu, A. (2023). Determinants of students' academic success in English as a medium of instruction (EMI) classes: A systematic review. *Heliyon, 9*(10), e20421. DOI: 10.1016/j.heliyon.2023.e20421 PMID: 37790980

Fenton-Smith, B., Zhou, J., & Galloway, N. (2026). Unpacking the English Medium Instruction (EMI) boom: Exploring student enrolment and driving forces in China and Japan. *Research Papers in Education*, 1–25. DOI: 10.1080/02671522.2026.2633628

Gilakjani, A. P., & Sabouri, N. B. (2017). Teachers' Beliefs in English Language Teaching and Learning: A Review of the Literature. *English Language Teaching, 10*(4), 78–86. DOI: 10.5539/elt.v10n4p78

Gokhale, A. A. (1995). Collaborative learning enhances critical thinking. *Journal of Technology Education, 7*(1). Advance online publication. https://jte-journal.org/articles/10.21061/jte.v7i1.a.2. DOI: 10.21061/jte.v7i1.a.2

Gonda, M. G. (2014). Role of educational institutions in shaping the future of business and society. *Procedia Economics and Finance, 11*, 635–641. DOI: 10.1016/S2212-5671(14)00229-9

Hargreaves, A. (1998). The emotional practice of teaching. *Teaching and Teacher Education, 14*(8), 835–854. DOI: 10.1016/S0742-051X(98)00025-0

Honey, M., Pearson, G., & Schweingruber, H. A. (Eds.). (2014). *STEM integration in K-12 education: Status, prospects, and an agenda for research* (Vol. 500). National Academies Press.

Hughes, R. (2008). Internationalisation of higher education and language policy: Questions of quality and equity. *Higher Education Management and Policy, 20*(1), 1–18.

Islam, M. S., & Stapa, M. B. (2021). Students' low proficiency in spoken English in private universities in Bangladesh: Reasons and remedies. *Language Testing in Asia*, *11*(1), 22. DOI: 10.1186/s40468-021-00139-0

Janzen, J. (2008). Teaching English language learners in the content areas. *Review of Educational Research*, *78*(4), 1010–1038. DOI: 10.3102/0034654308325580

Kachru, B. B., Quirk, R., & Widdowson, H. G. (1985). Standards, codification and sociolinguistic realism. *World Englishes. Critical Concepts in Linguistics*, 241-270.

Källkvist, M., & Hult, F. M. (2016). Discursive mechanisms and human agency in language policy formation: Negotiating bilingualism and parallel language use at a Swedish university. *International Journal of Bilingual Education and Bilingualism*, *19*(1), 1–17. DOI: 10.1080/13670050.2014.956044

Kalyanpur, M., Boruah, P. B., Molina, S. C., & Shenoy, S. (2022). *The politics of English language education and social inequality: Global pressures, national priorities and schooling in India*. Routledge. DOI: 10.4324/9781003125488

Klieme, E., & Vieluf, S. (2009). Teaching practices, teachers' beliefs and attitudes. *Creating Effektive Teaching and Learning Environments. First Results from TALIS, 2009*, 87–135.

Knight, J. (2005). An internationalization model: responding to new realities and challenges. *Higher Education in Latin America: The International Dimension*, 1-38.

Knight, J. (2016). Transnational education remodeled: Toward a common TNE framework and definitions. *Journal of Studies in International Education*, *20*(1), 34–47. DOI: 10.1177/1028315315602927

Kumar, P. (2025). *Language Barriers in Education: Challenges and Opportunities for Marginalized, Rural, and Lower Caste Students in India*. https://www.researchgate.net/publication/388817366_Language_Barriers_in_Education_Challenges_and_Opportunities_for_Marginalized_Rural_and_Lower_Caste_Students_in_India

Liddicoat, A. J. (2003). Internationalisation as a concept in higher education: Perspectives from policy. *Australian Perspectives on Internationalising Education*, 13-26.

Macaro, E. (2018). English medium instruction: A research agenda for a worldwide phenomenon. *La didattica delle lingue nel nuovo millennio: Le sfide dell'internazionalizzazione*, 15-20.

Macaro, E. (2022). English Medium Instruction: What do we know so far and what do we still need to find out? *Language Teaching*, *55*(4), 533–546. DOI: 10.1017/S0261444822000052

Manan, S. A., Channa, L. A., & Haidar, S. (2023). *1 Fostering the multilingual agenda in EMI*. English-Medium Instruction Pedagogies in Multilingual Universities in Asia. DOI: 10.4324/9781003173137-3

Manju, D. (2024). Challenges of teaching English language in India: A comprehensive analysis. *International Journal of Emerging Technologies and Innovative Research*, *11*(6), c549–c554.

McSharry, G., & Jones, S. (2000). Role-play in science teaching and learning. *The School Science Review*, *82*, 73–82.

Meurant, R. C. (2010). EFL/ESL textbook selection in Korea and East Asia-Relevant issues and literature review. In *International Conference on Ubiquitous Computing and Multimedia Applications* (pp. 89-102). Springer Berlin Heidelberg. DOI: 10.1007/978-3-642-13467-8_9

Mohrman, K., Ma, W., & Baker, D. (2008). The research university in transition: The emerging global model. *Higher Education Policy*, *21*(1), 5–27. DOI: 10.1057/palgrave.hep.8300175

National Education Policy (NEP). (2020). https://www.education.gov.in/en/nep/about-nep

Pecorari, D., & Malmström, H. (2018). At the crossroads of TESOL and English medium instruction. *TESOL Quarterly*, *52*(3), 497–515. DOI: 10.1002/tesq.470

Prince, M. (2004). Does active learning work? A review of the research. *Journal of Engineering Education*, *93*(3), 223–231. DOI: 10.1002/j.2168-9830.2004.tb00809.x

Rajbanshi, S. (2025). Recasting methodologies in English language classrooms: Teachers' roles and challenges in the context of NEP 2020. *DLC IMAGE: PRATIBIMBO, 3*(2), 01-06.

Ramamoorthy, S., & Dinesh, A. (2025). *English Medium Instruction (EMI), Challenges, and Coping Strategies: Stances of Dalit Students and Teaches in Institutes of HE in India*. https://www.researchgate.net/publication/394986048_English_Medium_Instruction_EMI_Challenges_and_Coping_Strategies_Stances_of_Dalit_Students_and_Teaches_in_Institutes_of_HE_in_India

Sah, P. K. (2022). A research agenda for English-medium instruction: Conversations with scholars at the research fronts. *Journal of English-Medium Instruction*, *1*(1), 124–136. DOI: 10.1075/jemi.21022.sah

Sah, P. K., & Li, G. (2018). English medium instruction (EMI) as linguistic capital in Nepal: Promises and realities. *International Multilingual Research Journal, 12*(2), 109–123. DOI: 10.1080/19313152.2017.1401448

Setty, R. (2013). Indian education in the 21st century: More than money, manpower, and materials. *Knowledge Cultures, 1*(03), 65–75.

Singh, A. (1984). The Indian university grants commission. *Higher Education, 13*(5), 517–533. DOI: 10.1007/BF00128562

Smit, U. (2023). English-medium instruction (EMI). *ELT Journal, 77*(4), 499–503. DOI: 10.1093/elt/ccad018

Varghese, N. V., & Martin, M. (2014). *Governance reforms in higher education: A study of institutional autonomy in Asian countries*. International Institute for Educational Planning.

Wächter, B., & Maiworm, F. (2014). English-taught programmes in European higher education. *The State of Play In, 15*.

Welch, A. (2005). From peregrinatio academica to global academic: The internationalisation of the profession. In *The professoriate: Profile of a Profession* (pp. 71–96). Springer Netherlands. DOI: 10.1007/1-4020-3383-4_5

Wilkinson, R. (2013). English-medium instruction at a Dutch university: Challenges and pitfalls. *English-medium Instruction at Universities: Global Challenges, 324*(10.21832), 9781847698162-005.

Yang, D., Wu, X., Liu, J., & Zhou, J. (2023). CiteSpace-based global science, technology, engineering, and mathematics education knowledge mapping analysis. *Frontiers in Psychology, 13*, 1094959. DOI: 10.3389/fpsyg.2022.1094959 PMID: 36704670

Chapter 10

Media and Technology Literacy in the Age of AI

Deepak Gupta
http://orcid.org/0000-0003-3929-1362
Institute of Technology and Management, Gwalior, India

Karimov Abror
Karshi State Technical University, Uzbekistan

Temur Eshchanov
Urgench State University, Urgench, Uzbekistan

Dilnoza Butanova
Mamun University, Khiva, Uzbekistan

Khudaybergen Kochkarov
Tashkent State University of Economy, Tashkent, Uzbekistan

Melikov Otabek Maxmadaminovich
Denov Institute of Entrepreneurship and Pedagogy, Uzbekistan

Divyang Pankajbhai Raval
GTU-Institute of Technology and Research, India

Deepak Dharrao
Symbiosis Institute of Technology, Symbiosis International (Deemed to be) University, Pune, India

ABSTRACT

The integration of artificial intelligence (AI) into educational contexts has fundamentally transformed the landscape of media and technology literacy requirements for higher education. This chapter examines the evolving competencies necessary for students to navigate, critically evaluate, and ethically engage with AI-driven media ecosystems. Drawing on recent empirical research and theoretical frameworks (2021-2025), we analyze the intersection of digital literacy, critical thinking, and AI awareness as essential components of 21st-century education. The chapter presents a comprehensive framework integrating technical competencies, ethical consider-

DOI: 10.4018/979-8-2600-2163-7.ch010

ations, and pedagogical strategies for developing AI literacy. Through examination of current challenges including misinformation, algorithmic bias, and the digital divide, we propose evidence-based interventions and assessment methodologies.

INTRODUCTION

The rapid proliferation of artificial intelligence technologies across educational, professional, and social domains has precipitated an urgent need to reconceptualize media and technology literacy for the 21st century. As generative AI systems such as ChatGPT, Claude, and multimodal AI platforms become increasingly integrated into daily life, higher education institutions face unprecedented challenges in preparing students to navigate this transformed landscape (Chan & Hu, 2023; Dempere et al., 2023). The traditional frameworks of digital literacy, while foundational, prove insufficient for addressing the unique complexities introduced by AI-mediated information ecosystems.

Contemporary students encounter AI technologies not merely as passive tools but as active agents shaping content creation, information curation, and knowledge production. This paradigmatic shift necessitates expanded literacy frameworks that encompass technical understanding, critical evaluation capabilities, ethical reasoning, and adaptive learning strategies (Long & Magerko, 2020; Hwang et al., 2020). The convergence of media literacy and AI competency represents a critical educational imperative, particularly as misinformation, algorithmic bias, and digital inequality intensify in AI-augmented environments (Buckingham, 2019; Guess et al., 2020).

HISTORICAL CONTEXT AND EVOLUTION

The concept of media literacy has evolved substantially since its inception in the mid-20th century, transitioning from print-based critical analysis to encompass digital, multimodal, and now AI-generated content. Early digital literacy frameworks focused primarily on technical proficiency and information retrieval skills (Valtonen et al., 2019). However, the emergence of social media, algorithmic curation, and generative AI has necessitated more sophisticated competency models that integrate technical, cognitive, and socio-emotional dimensions (Reddy et al., 2023).

The 'post-truth' era has further complicated media literacy education, as students must navigate increasingly complex information landscapes characterized by algorithmic amplification of misinformation and sophisticated manipulation techniques (Breakstone et al., 2022; Buckingham, 2019). Recent research demonstrates that traditional fact-checking approaches alone prove inadequate; students require comprehensive frameworks for evaluating AI-generated content, understanding algorithmic systems, and recognizing emerging forms of digital manipulation (Bewersdorff et al., 2023).

THE AI DISRUPTION IN HIGHER EDUCATION

Generative AI technologies have introduced transformative possibilities and challenges for higher education. Students increasingly utilize AI systems for writing assistance, research support, coding, and creative production (Kang & Yi, 2023; Cope & Kalantzis, 2024). This widespread adoption necessitates institutional responses that move beyond prohibition toward thoughtful integration and critical engagement (Michel-Villarreal et al., 2023). The challenge lies in developing pedagogical approaches that leverage AI's potential while cultivating essential human capacities for critical thinking, creativity, and ethical reasoning.

Figure 1. Research Publications on AI Literacy in Education (2019-2025)

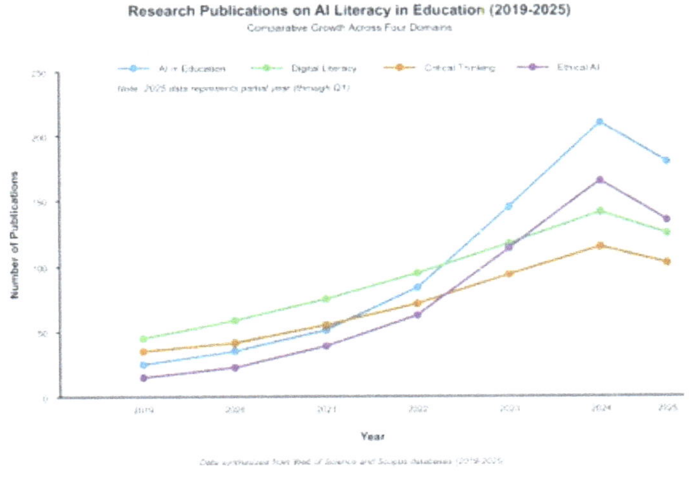

Figure 1 Illustrates The convergence of these research streams—evidenced by simultaneous growth across all four domains—underscores the multidimensional nature of AI literacy discussed throughout this chapter. The relative acceleration of ethical AI research (purple line) compared to more established digital literacy scholarship (green line) signals growing awareness that technical competencies alone prove insufficient without robust ethical frameworks. This pattern supports our argument that effective AI literacy education must integrate technical understanding, critical evaluation capabilities, ethical reasoning, and practical application skills.

Research indicates diverse student perceptions regarding AI in education, ranging from enthusiasm about efficiency gains to concerns about academic integrity and skill atrophy (Chan & Hu, 2023; Ríos Hernández et al., 2024). These varied perspectives underscore the importance of comprehensive AI literacy initiatives that address both opportunities and risks, preparing students for responsible engagement with AI technologies throughout their academic and professional careers (Mustafa et al., 2024).

THE EVOLVING RESEARCH LANDSCAPE ON AI IN EDUCATION

The scholarly literature examining AI in education has expanded exponentially in recent years, reflecting both the urgency of addressing AI's educational implications and the field's rapid maturation. Early research focused primarily on technical possibilities and implementation challenges, often approaching AI as simply another educational technology requiring integration strategies. However, contemporary scholarship increasingly recognizes AI's transformative nature, examining not merely how to incorporate AI tools but how AI fundamentally reshapes learning, knowledge production, and educational purposes.

This scholarly evolution reflects broader patterns in educational technology research, where initial techno-optimism giving way to more nuanced, critical perspectives examining both affordances and constraints. Current research demonstrates sophisticated understanding that AI technologies are not neutral tools but rather systems embedding particular values, assumptions, and power relations. This critical turn proves essential for developing educational responses that cultivate informed agency rather than uncritical adoption or fearful rejection.

Empirical research examining student AI use reveals complex patterns of adoption and resistance. While some students embrace AI tools enthusiastically, viewing them as efficiency enhancers and creative partners, others express concerns about dependency, authenticity, and potential skill degradation. These varied responses reflect different educational backgrounds, disciplinary contexts, prior technology experiences, and underlying beliefs about learning and knowledge. Understanding this heterogeneity proves crucial for developing literacy initiatives serving diverse learner populations effectively.

Faculty perspectives on AI integration similarly demonstrate complexity. Some educators view AI as opportunity for pedagogical innovation, enabling new forms of personalized learning, automated feedback, and authentic assessment. Others perceive AI as threat to academic integrity, educational quality, and professional autonomy. These divergent views reflect different epistemological commitments, pedagogical philosophies, and practical experiences. Effective institutional responses must engage this diversity rather than imposing uniform approaches that fail to address varied concerns and contexts.

Institutional research examining AI literacy program implementation provides valuable insights into effective practices and common pitfalls. Successful initiatives typically feature strong administrative support, adequate resources, faculty development opportunities, and iterative refinement based on assessment data. Failed or struggling initiatives often suffer from insufficient planning, inadequate stakeholder engagement, resource constraints, or misalignment between stated goals and actual practices. These patterns suggest that successful AI literacy implementation requires treating it as comprehensive institutional change rather than simple curricular addition.

CHAPTER OBJECTIVES AND STRUCTURE

This chapter aims to:

- Synthesize current research on media and technology literacy in the context of AI integration
- Develop a comprehensive framework for AI literacy in higher education
- Examine critical challenges including misinformation, bias, and digital inequality
- Propose evidence-based pedagogical strategies and assessment approaches
- Offer practical recommendations for curriculum development and institutional policy

THEORETICAL FOUNDATIONS OF AI LITERACY

Understanding AI literacy requires examination of its theoretical foundations, which draw from multiple disciplinary perspectives including education technology, media studies, critical pedagogy, and computer science. This section explores key frameworks that inform contemporary AI literacy education.

Defining AI Literacy

Long and Magerko (2020) provided a foundational definition of AI literacy as the set of competencies enabling individuals to critically evaluate AI technologies, communicate and collaborate effectively with AI, and use AI as a tool while understanding ethical implications. Their framework identifies seventeen core competencies organized across five dimensions: recognizing AI, understanding AI, using AI, evaluating AI, and ethical AI. This multidimensional approach acknowledges that AI literacy extends beyond technical knowledge to encompass critical thinking, ethical reasoning, and practical application skills.

Recent scholarship has refined and expanded this foundational work. Hackl et al. (2025) proposed the AI Literacy Heptagon, a structured approach specifically designed for higher education contexts. This framework identifies seven interconnected domains: technical knowledge, critical thinking, creative application, ethical awareness, social-emotional competencies, practical skills, and adaptive learning. The heptagonal model emphasizes the dynamic, evolving nature of AI literacy and the necessity for continuous learning as technologies advance.

Kong et al. (2021) demonstrated through empirical research that AI literacy can be effectively developed across diverse academic backgrounds, challenging assumptions that such competencies require extensive technical prerequisites. Their evaluation of an AI literacy course for university students reveals that structured, multidisciplinary approaches successfully develop both conceptual understanding and practical capabilities across varied student populations.

Digital Media Literacy Foundations

Digital media literacy provides essential grounding for AI literacy development. Reddy et al. (2023) proposed a comprehensive digital literacy model addressing the skills gap through four primary dimensions: technical proficiency, cognitive capabilities, social-emotional awareness, and creative-productive competencies. This holistic framework recognizes that effective digital engagement requires integration of multiple competency domains.

Nguyen and Habók (2023) contributed to this foundation through their systematic review of teacher digital literacy assessment tools, identifying critical components including technological, pedagogical, content, and ethical knowledge. Their work emphasizes that effective digital literacy education requires careful attention to assessment methodologies that capture the multifaceted nature of these competencies. Similarly, Lukitasari et al. (2022) demonstrated that well-constructed digital literacy instruments significantly correlate with learning outcomes, validating the importance of systematic competency development.

The relationship between digital literacy and technology acceptance proves particularly relevant for AI integration. Kabakus et al. (2023) found that digital literacy levels significantly predict technology acceptance among administrative staff, suggesting that literacy development serves as a prerequisite for successful technology adoption. This finding has important implications for institutional AI implementation strategies.

Critical Media Literacy in the Digital Age

Critical media literacy emphasizes the power dimensions inherent in media systems and the importance of developing critical consciousness alongside technical skills. Buckingham (2019) argued that media literacy education must explicitly address 'post-truth' phenomena, including fake news, algorithmic bias, and ideological manipulation. This critical perspective challenges purely skills-based approaches, insisting that media literacy must engage with political, economic, and cultural contexts shaping information ecosystems.

Albardía et al. (2025) extended this critical framework to technology education more broadly, examining how critical media literacy can address challenges posed by digital technologies. Their work emphasizes the importance of developing student capacities to question technological neutrality assumptions and recognize how technologies embed particular values, interests, and power relations.

Empirical research demonstrates the effectiveness of critical media literacy interventions. Guess et al. (2020) showed that digital media literacy interventions significantly increase discernment between mainstream and false news sources, with effects persisting across diverse cultural contexts. Their randomized controlled trial provides robust evidence that targeted literacy education can improve critical evaluation capabilities. Similarly, Breakstone et al. (2022) revealed substantial deficiencies in college students' source evaluation skills, underscoring the urgent need for enhanced critical literacy education in higher education.

Integration of AI and Media Literacy Frameworks

The synthesis of AI literacy and media literacy frameworks reveals essential interconnections and mutual reinforcement. Sergeeva et al. (2025) demonstrated empirically that digital media literacy significantly influences attitudes toward generative AI acceptance in higher education, establishing a causal relationship between foundational literacy competencies and openness to emerging technologies. This finding suggests that robust media literacy education serves as essential preparation for AI integration.

Figure 2. AI Literacy Framework for Higher Education

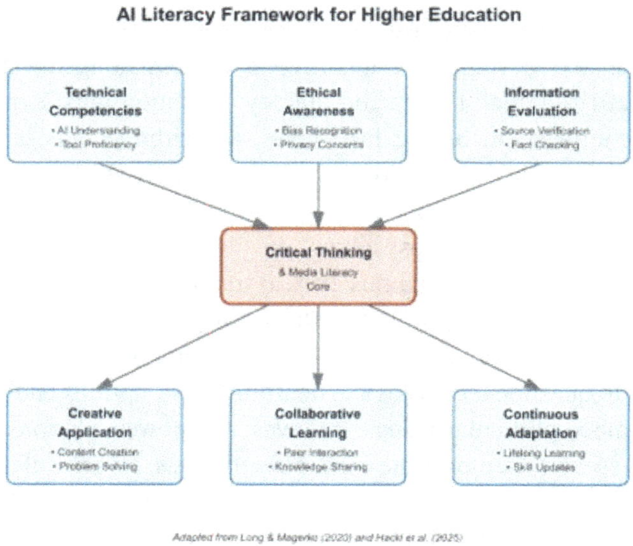

Figure 2 presents an integrated AI literacy framework synthesizing key theoretical contributions discussed above. The model positions critical thinking and media literacy as the foundational core, from which technical competencies, ethical awareness, and information evaluation capabilities develop. These elements subsequently enable higher-order applications including creative production, collaborative learning, and continuous adaptation.

Moravec et al. (2024) provided empirical support for this integrated approach, demonstrating that digital literacy significantly predicts both ChatGPT adoption and utilization patterns. Their research reveals that individuals with higher digital literacy levels exhibit more sophisticated, purpose-driven AI usage rather than superficial experimentation. This finding reinforces the importance of comprehensive literacy education as a foundation for effective AI engagement.

CORE COMPETENCIES FOR AI-ENHANCED MEDIA LITERACY

Building on theoretical foundations, this section examines specific competencies essential for effective engagement with AI-mediated information environments. These competencies span technical, cognitive, ethical, and creative domains, reflecting the multidimensional nature of contemporary literacy requirements.

Technical Understanding and AI System Awareness

Fundamental AI literacy requires basic understanding of how AI systems function, including machine learning principles, training data dependencies, and model limitations. Students need not become computer scientists, but they must grasp essential concepts including pattern recognition, statistical prediction, and algorithmic decision-making (Long & Magerko, 2020). This technical foundation enables more sophisticated critical evaluation of AI outputs and recognition of system capabilities and constraints.

Cardon et al. (2023) emphasized that AI literacy for business and professional communication requires understanding specific characteristics of AI-assisted writing tools, including their strengths in generating drafts and suggestions alongside limitations in contextual understanding and originality. Their framework identifies key competencies including recognizing AI-generated content, understanding appropriate use cases, and developing effective human-AI collaboration strategies.

Recent research on multimodal AI extends technical literacy requirements beyond text-based systems. Kang and Yi (2023) explored how multimodal generative AI transforms second language writing, identifying new competencies needed to effectively leverage image-text integration, voice-to-text capabilities, and multilingual translation features. Similarly, Cope and Kalantzis (2024) developed a multimodal grammar for analyzing AI systems, providing frameworks for understanding how different AI modalities (text, image, audio, video) function and interact.

Critical Evaluation and Information Assessment

Critical evaluation capabilities represent perhaps the most essential competency for navigating AI-mediated information landscapes. Students must develop sophisticated skills for assessing source credibility, recognizing potential biases, identifying manipulation techniques, and verifying factual claims. These traditional media literacy competencies require substantial adaptation for AI-generated content, which often lacks conventional source indicators and may exhibit subtle forms of bias or fabrication (Bewersdorff et al., 2023).

Mabini and Gallardo (2024) demonstrated significant relationships between digital literacy and critical thinking skills among learners, providing empirical evidence that literacy education enhances analytical capabilities. Their research suggests that structured literacy interventions can effectively develop the critical evaluation competencies necessary for engaging with complex information environments.

Meirbekov et al. (2022) examined how specific digital education tools can foster critical thinking development, identifying pedagogical approaches that effectively promote analytical reasoning, evidence evaluation, and argument construction. Their work emphasizes the importance of explicit critical thinking instruction within technology-rich learning environments rather than assuming critical capacities emerge naturally from technology exposure.

Ethical Reasoning and Responsible AI Use

Ethical competencies constitute a critical dimension of AI literacy, encompassing understanding of privacy implications, recognition of algorithmic bias, awareness of intellectual property considerations, and commitment to responsible technology use. Bond et al. (2024) conduct a comprehensive meta-systematic review of AI in higher education, identifying a critical need for increased ethical attention in AI implementation. Their analysis reveals that many existing AI educational initiatives inadequately address ethical dimensions, potentially perpetuating harmful practices.

Sarrionandia et al. (2025) examined AI training for media professionals, emphasizing the importance of addressing both technical and ethical challenges. Their research with journalists reveals particular concerns about AI-generated misinformation, source verification in automated content production, and maintaining editorial integrity in AI-augmented newsrooms. These professional concerns translate directly to educational contexts, where students must develop ethical frameworks for responsible AI engagement.

Bewersdorff et al. (2023) identified numerous misconceptions about AI that impede ethical reasoning, including overestimating AI capabilities, misunderstanding bias sources, and underestimating privacy risks. Their systematic review of AI preconceptions reveals that many students harbor fundamental misunderstandings about how AI systems function, leading to potentially harmful usage patterns. Effective ethics education must therefore combine conceptual correction with normative guidance about appropriate AI engagement.

Privacy and Data Literacy in AI Contexts

Privacy and data literacy constitute critical components of ethical AI engagement that warrant particular attention. As AI systems increasingly depend on vast datasets for training and operation, students must understand how their personal information feeds algorithmic systems and shapes AI outputs. The widespread adoption of generative AI platforms has intensified concerns about data privacy, as users often input sensitive information—including academic work, personal communications, and proprietary data—without fully comprehending retention policies, usage rights, or potential disclosure risks.

Contemporary AI systems operate through complex data pipelines that collect, process, store, and sometimes share user information in ways that may not be immediately transparent. Students require competencies for evaluating privacy policies, understanding terms of service, recognizing data collection mechanisms, and making informed decisions about what information to share with AI platforms. This data literacy extends beyond personal privacy to encompass broader societal implications including surveillance capitalism, algorithmic profiling, and the commodification of human behavior data.

The European Union's General Data Protection Regulation (GDPR) and similar privacy frameworks worldwide establish important legal protections, yet many students lack awareness of their rights or practical strategies for exercising them. Educational initiatives must therefore address both conceptual understanding of privacy principles and practical competencies for privacy protection. This includes teaching students to evaluate AI platforms' data practices, use privacy-enhancing technologies, recognize consent manipulation techniques, and understand the long-term implications of data sharing decisions made during their educational careers.

Furthermore, students must develop critical awareness of how training data shapes AI system biases and outputs. Understanding that AI models reflect patterns in their training data helps students recognize that AI-generated content may perpetuate historical biases, underrepresent certain perspectives, or reproduce problematic associations present in source materials. This awareness proves essential for critical evaluation of AI outputs and informed decisions about when AI assistance proves appropriate versus potentially harmful.

Creative and Productive Competencies

Beyond critical consumption, contemporary literacy encompasses creative production capabilities. Students must learn to effectively harness AI tools for content creation, problem-solving, and innovation while maintaining human agency and creative control. This balance proves essential as AI systems become increasingly capable of generating sophisticated outputs across multiple modalities (Cope & Kalantzis, 2024).

Kang and Yi (2023) explored how L2 writers can leverage multimodal generative AI for enhanced composition, identifying strategies for effective human-AI collaboration in writing processes. Their research demonstrates that when students develop appropriate competencies for AI-assisted writing, they can achieve improved outputs while maintaining authentic voice and critical engagement. The key lies in viewing AI as a collaborative tool rather than a replacement for human creativity.

Jiang et al. (2024) contributed to understanding creative competencies through conceptualization of multimodal feedback literacy for writing teachers in the digital age. This framework emphasizes the importance of developing sophisticated strategies for interpreting, evaluating, and acting upon diverse forms of feedback, including

AI-generated suggestions. Such meta-cognitive competencies enable learners to maintain critical distance while productively engaging with AI assistance.

CHALLENGES AND BARRIERS TO AI LITERACY DEVELOPMENT

Despite growing recognition of AI literacy's importance, significant challenges impede effective implementation in higher education. This section examines key barriers including misinformation proliferation, digital inequality, assessment difficulties, and resistance to change.

Misinformation and AI-Generated Content

The increasing sophistication of AI-generated content presents unprecedented challenges for information verification and critical evaluation. Generative AI systems can produce plausible but factually incorrect information, often with high confidence and sophisticated presentation (Bewersdorff et al., 2023). This 'hallucination' phenomenon complicates traditional fact-checking approaches and requires new verification strategies.

Buckingham (2019) argued that post-truth conditions demand fundamental reconceptualization of media literacy education. Traditional approaches emphasizing source credibility and fact-checking prove insufficient when content can be generated with no clear source attribution and when verification requires technical expertise beyond typical student capabilities. Educational responses must therefore emphasize process-based verification strategies, lateral reading techniques, and healthy skepticism toward all digital content regardless of apparent sophistication.

Sarrionandia et al. (2025) documented specific concerns among media professionals about AI's role in misinformation propagation. Their interviews reveal worries about automated generation of fake news, sophisticated deepfakes, and the potential for AI-powered disinformation campaigns. These professional concerns underscore the importance of preparing students to recognize and resist various forms of AI-mediated manipulation.

Digital Divide and Equity Concerns

Access to AI technologies and opportunities for literacy development remain unevenly distributed across socioeconomic, geographic, and demographic lines. Brata et al. (2022) demonstrated that students' digital literacy levels correlate significantly with technology access, internet costs, and prior exposure to digital tools. These disparities risk creating a new digital divide where advantaged students develop AI literacy while disadvantaged populations lack opportunities for competency development.

Timotheou et al. (2023) provided comprehensive analysis of factors influencing schools' digital capacity and transformation, identifying resource limitations, infrastructure gaps, and professional development deficiencies as critical barriers. Their work emphasizes that successful technology integration requires addressing systemic inequalities rather than simply providing access to tools. Without intentional equity-focused interventions, AI literacy initiatives risk exacerbating existing educational disparities.

International perspectives reveal particular challenges in Global South contexts. Ríos Hernández et al. (2024) examined Latin American students' perceptions of AI in higher education, documenting concerns about access limitations, language barriers (most AI systems optimize for English), and cultural appropriateness of predominantly Western-developed technologies. These findings underscore the importance of culturally responsive, equitable approaches to AI literacy education.

Pedagogical and Assessment Challenges

Educators face substantial challenges in teaching about rapidly evolving AI technologies while lacking formal training in AI literacy pedagogy. Nguyen and Habók (2023) revealed significant gaps in teacher digital literacy assessment, suggesting that many educators lack preparation for teaching advanced technology competencies. This preparation deficit becomes particularly acute for AI literacy, which requires specialized knowledge and continuous learning to remain current.

Assessment presents particular difficulties. Traditional evaluation methods prove inadequate for measuring complex, multidimensional AI literacy competencies. Lukitasari et al. (2022) demonstrated the importance of well-designed digital literacy instruments, but acknowledge challenges in capturing higher-order competencies such as ethical reasoning and creative application. The rapid evolution of AI technologies further complicates assessment development, as evaluation tools may become outdated before validation processes complete.

Academic integrity concerns add complexity to pedagogical decision-making. Dempere et al. (2023) examined ChatGPT's impact on higher education, identifying tensions between leveraging AI for learning enhancement and preventing academic misconduct. Educators struggle to distinguish between appropriate AI use and plagiarism, particularly as AI assistance becomes increasingly sophisticated and integrated into standard writing processes.

The Tension Between Innovation and Regulation

Higher education institutions face a fundamental tension between encouraging innovative AI use and establishing necessary guardrails to prevent harm. This tension manifests across multiple dimensions: promoting student experimentation with AI tools while ensuring academic integrity, supporting faculty exploration of AI-enhanced pedagogy while maintaining educational quality standards, and embracing AI's transformative potential while protecting against exploitation and inequity.

The rapid pace of AI technological development exacerbates this challenge. By the time institutions develop comprehensive policies addressing particular AI capabilities, new tools with different affordances emerge, potentially rendering existing guidelines obsolete or insufficient. This temporal mismatch between institutional policy cycles and technology evolution creates ongoing uncertainty for faculty and students attempting to navigate appropriate AI use.

Different disciplinary contexts further complicate policy development. What constitutes appropriate AI assistance varies substantially across fields: AI code generation tools may be valuable learning aids in computer science education while potentially undermining learning objectives in introductory programming courses; AI writing assistance might enhance research productivity in some contexts while compromising assessment validity in others. Developing policies sufficiently nuanced to address disciplinary variation while maintaining institutional consistency proves extraordinarily difficult.

Moreover, institutions must balance local autonomy with broader coordination. Individual faculty members require flexibility to make pedagogically sound decisions about AI integration in their courses, yet institution-wide consistency helps students understand expectations and promotes equity. Accreditation requirements, professional standards, and transfer agreements add additional layers of complexity, as institutions cannot operate in complete isolation from external stakeholders and requirements.

The innovation-regulation tension also reflects deeper philosophical questions about education's purposes. If education aims primarily to develop general capabilities like critical thinking and adaptive learning, AI tools that handle routine tasks while students focus on higher-order thinking may align well with educational goals. Conversely, if education values demonstration of specific competencies including routine skills that AI can now automate, greater regulation may be warranted. These foundational questions lack clear consensus, complicating efforts to develop coherent AI policies.

Institutional and Systemic Barriers

Beyond individual and classroom-level challenges, systemic barriers impede AI literacy implementation. Bond et al. (2024) identify insufficient collaboration, limited ethical frameworks, and inadequate research rigor as critical deficiencies in current AI education initiatives. Their meta-systematic review calls for increased coordination across disciplines, stronger ethical foundations, and more robust empirical investigation of effective practices.

Institutional resistance to change presents additional obstacles. Faculty may resist adopting AI literacy initiatives due to concerns about workload, lack of support, or skepticism about necessity. Administrative priorities may not align with literacy development goals, particularly when faced with competing demands and limited resources. Successful implementation therefore requires strategic change management, stakeholder engagement, and sustained institutional commitment (Timotheou et al., 2023).

PEDAGOGICAL STRATEGIES AND INTERVENTIONS

Effective AI literacy education requires thoughtfully designed pedagogical approaches that address the multidimensional nature of required competencies while responding to identified challenges. This section examines evidence-based strategies for curriculum design, instructional methods, and learning environment organization.

Integrated Curriculum Approaches

Rather than treating AI literacy as a separate add-on, effective approaches integrate competency development across existing curricula. Kong et al. (2021) demonstrated successful AI literacy course implementation for students with diverse academic backgrounds, revealing that multidisciplinary approaches effectively serve varied learner populations. Their course model combines technical foundations, ethical reasoning, practical applications, and critical reflection within a cohesive framework.

Su and Yang (2022) examined AI integration in early childhood education, identifying developmentally appropriate approaches for introducing AI concepts. While focused on younger learners, their scoping review provides insights applicable to higher education, including the importance of hands-on experiences, scaffolded complexity, and explicit connection between technical understanding and real-world applications. These principles translate to university contexts through project-based learning, case studies, and authentic assessment tasks.

Figure 3. Digital Media Literacy Competency Model in the AI Era

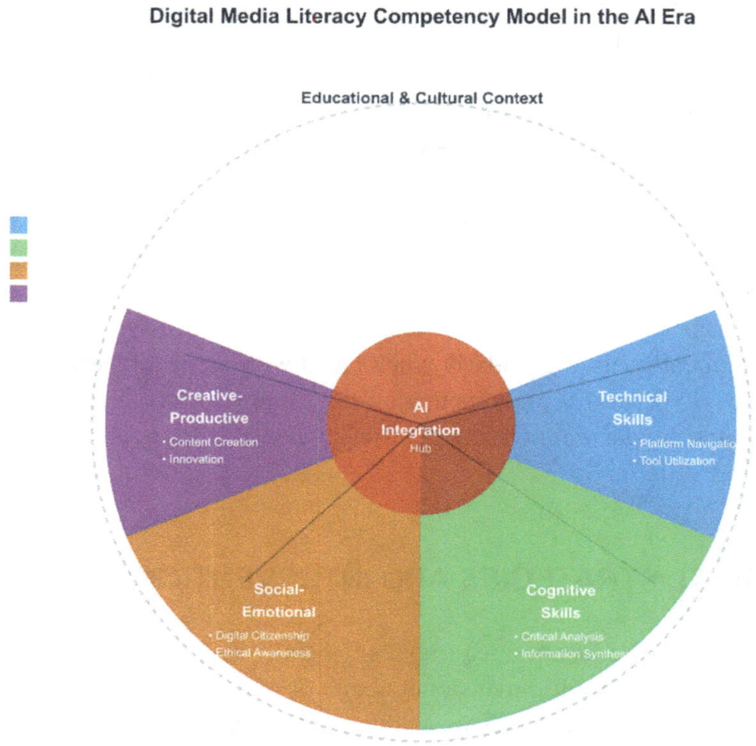

Figure 3 illustrates a comprehensive digital media literacy competency model adapted for the AI era. This framework positions AI integration as a central hub connecting technical skills, cognitive capabilities, social-emotional competencies, and creative-productive applications within broader educational and cultural contexts.

Active Learning and Experiential Approaches

Active engagement with AI technologies proves essential for developing genuine literacy. Passive instruction about AI systems cannot substitute for hands-on experience with tools, critical analysis of outputs, and reflective examination of usage practices. Chan and Hu (2023) documented students' preferences for experiential learning opportunities that allow exploration of AI capabilities while developing critical evaluation skills.

Effective experiential approaches might include: comparative analysis of AI outputs from different systems, identification of biases or errors in AI-generated content, collaborative projects leveraging AI tools, documentation of AI usage processes and decision points, and reflection on ethical dilemmas encountered during AI use. These activities promote active construction of understanding rather than passive reception of information (Hwang et al., 2020).

Meirbekov et al. (2022) demonstrated the effectiveness of specific digital tools for critical thinking development, emphasizing the importance of carefully selected technologies that promote analysis and reasoning rather than mere consumption. Their work suggests that tool selection should prioritize those requiring active cognitive engagement over passive information reception.

Collaborative Learning and Peer Interaction

Collaborative approaches enhance AI literacy development by enabling peer learning, diverse perspective sharing, and collective problem-solving. Students bring varied experiences with and perceptions of AI technologies; structured collaboration can productively harness this diversity. Discussion-based activities examining ethical dilemmas, group analysis of AI-generated content, and collaborative projects requiring coordinated AI tool use all promote deeper learning than individual instruction alone.

Chan and Hu (2023) documented the value students place on opportunities to discuss AI experiences with peers, share discovery of useful applications, and collectively navigate challenges and uncertainties. These informal learning opportunities complement formal instruction and contribute to development of shared norms and practices around AI use.

Bond et al. (2024) emphasized the critical need for increased collaboration in AI education initiatives, both among students and across institutional boundaries. Their meta-systematic review reveals that isolated, siloed approaches prove less effective than coordinated, collaborative efforts that leverage collective expertise and resources.

Critical Reflection and Metacognitive Development

Metacognitive competencies—thinking about one's own thinking and learning processes—prove essential for navigating rapidly evolving AI landscapes. Students must develop capacities for self-directed learning, critical self-reflection, and adaptive strategy development. These higher-order competencies enable continued literacy development beyond formal educational experiences.

Jiang et al. (2024) contributed valuable frameworks for developing metacognitive feedback literacy, emphasizing the importance of teaching students to critically evaluate, interpret, and act upon diverse forms of input including AI-generated suggestions. This metacognitive orientation promotes active agency rather than passive acceptance of AI outputs.

Structured reflection activities might include: learning journals documenting AI usage patterns and decision-making processes, comparative analyses of work produced with and without AI assistance, peer review examining appropriate versus problematic AI use, and case-based discussions of ethical dilemmas. These activities promote critical consciousness about AI engagement and support development of principled usage practices.

ASSESSMENT AND EVALUATION FRAMEWORKS

Effective assessment of AI literacy requires multidimensional evaluation approaches capturing technical understanding, critical thinking, ethical reasoning, and practical application capabilities. This section examines frameworks and methods for assessing AI literacy competencies.

Competency-Based Assessment Approaches

Competency-based assessment emphasizes demonstration of specific skills and knowledge rather than mere exposure to content. Lukitasari et al. (2022) demonstrated that well-constructed digital literacy instruments significantly correlate with learning outcomes, validating competency-based approaches. Their work provides guidance for instrument development, including attention to construct validity, reliability, and alignment with intended learning outcomes.

Effective AI literacy assessment should evaluate multiple competency dimensions including: technical understanding (conceptual knowledge of AI systems), critical evaluation (analysis of AI outputs and identification of limitations), ethical reasoning (recognition of ethical issues and application of principled frameworks), and practical application (effective use of AI tools for authentic purposes). Table 1 presents a comprehensive assessment framework aligned with these dimensions.

Table 1. Multidimensional AI Literacy Assessment Framework

Competency Domain	Assessment Methods	Key Indicators	Evidence Sources
Technical Understanding	Concept mapping, technical quizzes, system comparison analyses	Accurate explanation of AI mechanisms, recognition of capabilities/limitations	Written explanations, presentations, discussion contributions
Critical Evaluation	Output analysis tasks, error identification exercises, bias detection activities	Identification of errors, recognition of biases, appropriate skepticism	Analytical reports, annotated examples, peer review
Ethical Reasoning	Case study discussions, ethical dilemma responses, policy development	Recognition of ethical issues, application of frameworks, principled decision-making	Reflection papers, discussion forums, position statements
Practical Application	Project work, portfolio development, usage documentation	Effective tool selection, appropriate usage, quality outputs	Completed projects, process documentation, self-assessment

Performance-Based and Authentic Assessment

Performance-based assessment requires students to demonstrate competencies through authentic tasks reflecting real-world AI engagement. Rather than testing decontextualized knowledge, these approaches evaluate integrated application of skills in meaningful contexts. Examples include analyzing real AI-generated content for accuracy and bias, developing ethical guidelines for AI use in specific professional contexts, creating projects that appropriately leverage AI tools, and documenting decision-making processes when using AI assistance.

Portfolio assessment provides particularly valuable approaches for capturing development over time. Students might compile examples of their AI tool usage, reflections on learning progression, evidence of ethical reasoning development, and demonstrations of improved critical evaluation capabilities. This longitudinal approach recognizes that AI literacy develops gradually through sustained practice rather than emerging fully formed from single instructional interventions (Valtonen et al., 2019).

Authentic assessment approaches require students to demonstrate competencies in contexts closely resembling real-world AI engagement scenarios. Rather than decontextualized tests measuring abstract knowledge, authentic assessments present realistic challenges requiring integrated application of technical understanding, critical evaluation, ethical reasoning, and creative problem-solving. For example, students might analyze actual AI-generated content from their discipline, evaluate competing AI tools for specific purposes, or develop guidelines for responsible AI use in particular professional contexts. These authentic tasks provide richer evidence of competency than traditional testing while also serving learning purposes by engaging students in meaningful application of developing knowledge and skills.

Rubric development for AI literacy assessment presents particular challenges given the multidimensional nature of competencies and rapid technological evolution. Effective rubrics must capture both technical and critical dimensions, distinguish between levels of sophistication in AI engagement, and remain flexible enough to accommodate emerging tools and capabilities. Collaborative rubric development involving faculty across disciplines, students, and external stakeholders can enhance validity while building shared understanding of AI literacy expectations. Regular rubric review and revision ensures continued alignment with evolving competency requirements and technological contexts.

Formative Assessment and Feedback

Formative assessment throughout learning processes proves essential for supporting AI literacy development. Regular feedback helps students calibrate their understanding, identify misconceptions, and refine practices. Jiang et al. (2024) emphasizes the importance of multimodal feedback literacy, suggesting that students must learn to effectively interpret and respond to varied forms of input including instructor comments, peer feedback, self-assessment insights, and AI-generated suggestions.

Effective formative assessment strategies might include: low-stakes quizzes providing immediate feedback on conceptual understanding, peer review activities promoting collaborative learning and diverse perspectives, self-assessment reflections encouraging metacognitive development, and instructor feedback on draft work supporting iterative improvement. These ongoing assessment activities complement summative evaluation and contribute more directly to learning progression.

INSTITUTIONAL IMPLEMENTATION STRATEGIES

Successful AI literacy implementation requires coordinated institutional efforts extending beyond individual courses or instructors. This section examines strategic approaches for institutional change, faculty development, and policy formulation.

Strategic Planning and Institutional Commitment

Effective implementation begins with strategic planning that articulates clear vision, goals, and implementation pathways. Timotheou et al. (2023) identified strategic leadership as a critical factor influencing successful technology integration, emphasizing the importance of aligned vision, adequate resources, and sustained commitment. Institutional leaders must recognize AI literacy as a core competency rather than optional enhancement, integrating it into strategic plans, resource allocation decisions, and accountability structures.

Strategic planning should address multiple dimensions including: curriculum integration across disciplines, faculty development and support, infrastructure and resource provision, assessment and evaluation systems, and policy development regarding acceptable AI use. Comprehensive approaches prove more effective than piecemeal initiatives addressing isolated components.

Faculty Development and Support

Faculty constitute the frontline of AI literacy education, yet many lack preparation for this role. Nguyen and Habók (2023) documented significant gaps in teacher digital literacy, suggesting widespread need for professional development. Effective faculty development programs should combine technical training in AI tools, pedagogical guidance for teaching AI literacy, opportunities for experimentation and practice, collegial support networks, and ongoing learning opportunities recognizing continuous technological evolution.

Sarrionandia et al. (2025) emphasized the importance of addressing both technical and ethical dimensions in professional development for media practitioners. This balanced approach applies equally to faculty development, where educators must understand AI technologies while developing sophisticated ethical frameworks for guiding student engagement. Professional development should model the pedagogical approaches expected in classrooms, emphasizing active learning, critical reflection, and collaborative exploration.

Policy Development and Academic Integrity

Clear institutional policies regarding AI use prove essential for providing guidance while avoiding either overly restrictive prohibitions or laissez-faire approaches lacking ethical guardrails. Dempere et al. (2023) examined academic integrity challenges posed by ChatGPT, identifying tensions between preventing misconduct and enabling legitimate AI assistance. Effective policies should articulate principles for responsible AI use, provide specific guidance for different contexts, establish expectations for disclosure and attribution, outline consequences for policy violations, and commit to regular review and updating as technologies evolve.

Bond et al. (2024) called for increased ethical attention in AI implementation, emphasizing the necessity of robust frameworks guiding institutional decision-making. Policy development should involve diverse stakeholders including faculty, students, administrators, and ethics experts, ensuring multiple perspectives inform guidelines. Transparency about policy rationales and decision-making processes promotes community buy-in and facilitates productive dialogue about appropriate AI engagement.

Infrastructure and Resource Provision

Adequate infrastructure and resources prove essential for supporting AI literacy initiatives. Brata et al. (2022) demonstrated that access limitations significantly constrain digital literacy development, a finding with direct implications for AI literacy implementation. Institutions must ensure: equitable access to AI tools and technologies, adequate technical support for faculty and students, learning spaces conducive to technology-rich pedagogy, digital resources including tutorials and guides, and financial support for ongoing tool access and professional development.

Equity considerations should guide resource provision. Institutions must address disparities in student access to personal devices, reliable internet connectivity, and private study spaces suitable for AI tool usage. Without intentional attention to equity, AI literacy initiatives risk exacerbating existing educational inequalities (Timotheou et al., 2023).

FUTURE DIRECTIONS AND EMERGING TRENDS

The rapid evolution of AI technologies ensures that literacy requirements will continue developing. This section examines emerging trends and future directions for AI literacy education in higher education.

Multimodal and Embodied AI

Current AI literacy frameworks focus primarily on text-based systems, but emerging multimodal AI technologies integrate text, image, audio, and video modalities in increasingly sophisticated ways. Cope and Kalantzis (2024) developed multimodal grammars for analyzing AI systems, providing frameworks for understanding cross-modal integration. Future literacy education must address competencies for engaging with multimodal AI including understanding how different modalities interact, evaluating multimedia AI outputs, and creating multimodal content using AI assistance.

Embodied AI and robotics introduce additional dimensions requiring literacy development. As AI systems become physically instantiated in robots, autonomous vehicles, and smart environments, new competencies emerge around physical safety, spatial awareness, and human-machine interaction in shared physical spaces. Educational initiatives must expand beyond screen-based AI engagement to address these emerging contexts.

The integration of multimodal AI capabilities raises important questions about literacy assessment and competency evaluation. How do we assess student capabilities for engaging with AI systems that seamlessly integrate text, image, audio, and video? What frameworks help evaluate ethical reasoning about AI systems operating across multiple modalities simultaneously? These questions demand ongoing research and pedagogical innovation as multimodal AI technologies continue advancing. Educational institutions must develop assessment approaches capturing not merely technical proficiency with individual modalities but sophisticated understanding of cross-modal integration, emergent capabilities from multimodal systems, and critical evaluation of complex AI-generated multimedia content.

Personalized and Adaptive Learning Systems

AI-powered personalized learning systems promise customized educational experiences adapted to individual learner needs, preferences, and progress. Hwang et al. (2020) envisioned AI's transformative potential for education, including adaptive content delivery, intelligent tutoring, and automated assessment. However, these systems introduce new literacy requirements including understanding how personalization algorithms function, recognizing potential biases in adaptive systems, maintaining agency in personalized learning environments, and critically evaluating AI-recommended learning pathways.

Mustafa et al. (2024) provided comprehensive analysis of AI in education research, identifying adaptive learning as a critical emerging area. Their systematic review of literature reviews reveals both promise and concern regarding personalized AI systems, emphasizing the necessity of critical literacy that enables learners to productively engage with these technologies while recognizing limitations and potential harms.

Global and Cross-Cultural Perspectives

AI literacy education must attend to global and cross-cultural dimensions, recognizing that AI technologies embed particular cultural assumptions and power dynamics. Ríos Hernández et al. (2024) examine Latin American student perspectives on AI in higher education, revealing region-specific concerns about technological colonialism, language barriers, and cultural appropriateness. Future initiatives must develop culturally responsive approaches that acknowledge diverse contexts and values.

International collaboration proves essential for developing globally relevant AI literacy frameworks. Different regions face distinct challenges regarding access, regulation, cultural norms, and educational priorities. Collaborative efforts can identify universal core competencies while respecting contextual variations in implementation approaches (Bond et al., 2024).

Lifelong Learning and Professional Development

The rapid pace of AI technological change ensures that literacy development must extend beyond formal education into lifelong learning. Students graduating today will encounter AI technologies throughout their careers that do not yet exist or remain in early development stages. Educational institutions must therefore emphasize meta-learning competencies enabling continued adaptation including strategies for independent learning about new technologies, frameworks for evaluating emerging AI systems, professional networks supporting ongoing development, and dispositions toward continuous learning and adaptation.

Professional development initiatives must similarly embrace continuous learning models. Faculty, staff, and administrators require ongoing opportunities to update knowledge, refine practices, and engage with emerging technologies and pedagogies. One-time training proves insufficient; sustained, iterative development better serves institutional needs.

CONCLUSION

The integration of artificial intelligence into educational and social contexts has fundamentally transformed literacy requirements for the 21st century. This chapter has examined the evolving landscape of media and technology literacy in the AI age, synthesizing recent research to develop comprehensive frameworks, identify critical challenges, and propose evidence-based interventions for higher education.

Key Findings and Contributions

Several key findings emerge from this analysis. First, AI literacy represents a multidimensional construct encompassing technical understanding, critical evaluation capabilities, ethical reasoning, and creative application competencies. Effective literacy education must address all these dimensions rather than focusing narrowly on technical skills alone (Long & Magerko, 2020; Hackl et al., 2025).

Second, AI literacy builds upon but extends beyond traditional digital media literacy. While foundational competencies in information evaluation, critical thinking, and ethical reasoning remain essential, AI technologies introduce novel challenges requiring expanded frameworks (Reddy et al., 2023; Sergeeva et al., 2025). The relationship proves synergistic: strong media literacy foundations facilitate AI literacy development, while AI engagement provides new contexts for exercising critical capabilities.

Third, significant challenges impede effective AI literacy implementation including misinformation proliferation, digital inequality, pedagogical gaps, and institutional barriers. Addressing these challenges requires coordinated efforts across individual, institutional, and systemic levels (Bond et al., 2024; Timotheou et al., 2023). Isolated interventions prove insufficient; comprehensive approaches integrating curriculum development, faculty support, policy formulation, and infrastructure provision yield better results.

Fourth, evidence-based pedagogical strategies emphasize active learning, collaborative approaches, critical reflection, and authentic assessment. Passive instruction about AI systems cannot develop the sophisticated competencies required for responsible engagement. Students must actively explore AI tools, critically analyze outputs, engage in ethical deliberation, and apply learning in meaningful contexts (Chan & Hu, 2023; Kong et al., 2021).

Practical Implications

These findings generate several practical implications for higher education institutions. Curriculum designers should integrate AI literacy across disciplines rather than confining it to computer science or specialized programs. All students require foundational competencies regardless of major, with discipline-specific applications building upon common cores.

Faculty development initiatives must prioritize AI literacy, providing educators with technical understanding, pedagogical strategies, and ongoing support. Professional development should model effective teaching approaches including active learning, collaborative exploration, and critical reflection.

Institutional policies should provide clear guidance while avoiding either prohibition or uncritical acceptance. Policies must articulate principles for responsible AI use, establish expectations for transparency and attribution, and commit to regular review as technologies evolve.

Assessment approaches should employ multidimensional, performance-based methods capturing technical understanding, critical thinking, ethical reasoning, and practical application. Portfolio assessment, project-based evaluation, and formative feedback prove particularly valuable for documenting development over time.

Finally, equity considerations must inform all implementation decisions. Institutions must ensure equitable access to technologies, learning opportunities, and support resources, recognizing that AI literacy initiatives risk exacerbating existing inequalities without intentional equity focus.

Future Research Directions

Several areas merit additional research attention. Longitudinal studies examining AI literacy development over time would provide valuable insights into learning progression, retention, and transfer. Current research predominantly employs cross-sectional designs; sustained investigation would better illuminate developmental trajectories.

Comparative studies examining different pedagogical approaches could identify most-effective strategies for various contexts and populations. Experimental and quasi-experimental designs would strengthen causal claims about intervention effectiveness.

Investigation of assessment methodologies would advance understanding of how to effectively evaluate multidimensional AI literacy competencies. Research examining validity, reliability, and practical utility of different assessment approaches would inform practice.

Cross-cultural research exploring how AI literacy manifests across different contexts would support development of globally relevant but culturally responsive frameworks. Current literature predominantly reflects Western, developed country perspectives; expanding geographic and cultural diversity would enrich understanding.

Finally, research examining equity implications of AI literacy initiatives would help ensure interventions reduce rather than exacerbate educational disparities. Critical examination of how different student populations experience and benefit from literacy education would inform more inclusive practices.

Concluding Thoughts

AI technologies will continue evolving rapidly, ensuring that literacy requirements remain dynamic rather than static. Educational institutions face the challenge of preparing students for engagement with technologies that do not yet exist, requiring emphasis on adaptable competencies and lifelong learning dispositions rather than fixed skill sets.

The stakes prove high. AI systems increasingly mediate access to information, shape public discourse, influence decision-making, and structure social interactions.

Without robust literacy enabling critical engagement, individuals risk becoming passive consumers rather than active agents in AI-mediated environments. Higher education institutions bear responsibility for equipping students with competencies necessary for informed, ethical, and effective participation in an AI-augmented world.

This responsibility extends beyond individual skill development to encompass broader democratic and civic goals. Media and technology literacy education serves not merely private interests in career preparation but public interests in informed citizenship, democratic participation, and social justice. As AI systems shape information landscapes, educational initiatives promoting critical consciousness, ethical reasoning, and collective agency become essential for sustaining democratic societies.

The transformative potential of AI technologies extends across virtually all domains of human activity, from healthcare and scientific research to creative arts and social services. Students graduating today will encounter AI systems throughout their professional lives in forms and applications not yet imagined. This reality necessitates educational approaches emphasizing adaptability, continuous learning, and fundamental understanding of AI principles rather than narrow training in particular tools or platforms that may quickly become obsolete.

Higher education's unique position enables institutions to serve as crucial sites for developing societal capacity for critical AI engagement. Universities bring together diverse disciplinary expertise, research capabilities, and educational missions that position them well to address AI literacy challenges comprehensively. Computer scientists can explain technical mechanisms, philosophers can illuminate ethical dimensions, social scientists can analyze societal impacts, and educators can develop effective pedagogical approaches. This multidisciplinary integration proves essential for addressing AI literacy's inherently complex, multifaceted nature.

Moreover, universities serve public good missions that extend beyond individual student benefit. Research universities generate knowledge about AI systems, their impacts, and effective educational approaches. Teaching institutions prepare future educators who will carry AI literacy initiatives into K-12 schools and community colleges. Professional schools train lawyers, journalists, healthcare providers, and business leaders who will shape AI governance and implementation across sectors. This multilevel impact amplifies higher education's contributions to broader societal AI literacy.

The challenge of developing AI literacy amid rapid technological change requires humility about limitations alongside confidence in core educational missions. We cannot predict exactly what AI capabilities will emerge in coming years, which specific tools will dominate, or how regulatory frameworks will evolve. However, we can confidently assert that critical thinking, ethical reasoning, collaborative problem-solving, and adaptive learning will remain essential regardless of particular technological trajectories. Educational initiatives building these foundational competencies while developing specific AI literacy skills serve students well across multiple possible futures.

International collaboration and knowledge sharing will prove increasingly important as AI technologies and their educational implications transcend national boundaries. Different nations face distinct challenges regarding AI governance, digital infrastructure, cultural values, and educational systems. Yet common needs for developing AI literacy competencies create opportunities for productive international exchange. Scholarly networks, policy forums, and resource-sharing platforms can facilitate learning across contexts while respecting local adaptation needs.

Finally, we must acknowledge that AI literacy education occurs within broader contexts of educational inequality, technological access disparities, and social justice concerns. Without intentional attention to equity, AI literacy initiatives risk exacerbating existing gaps between privileged and marginalized populations. Educational institutions must therefore approach AI literacy with explicit commitment to inclusive access, culturally responsive pedagogy, and recognition that literacy development requires not just individual effort but structural support including adequate resources, qualified instruction, and supportive environments.

The path forward requires sustained commitment, thoughtful innovation, and collaborative effort across institutions, disciplines, and contexts. By embracing this challenge with intellectual rigor, pedagogical creativity, and ethical purpose, higher education can fulfill its mission of preparing students not merely to navigate but to shape the AI-augmented future.

REFERENCES

Albardía, M. S., Peña-Fernández, S., & Agirreazkuenaga, I. (2025). Technology, education and critical media literacy: Potential, challenges, and opportunities. *Frontiers in Human Dynamics*, *7*, 1608911. Advance online publication. DOI: 10.3389/fhumd.2025.1608911

Bewersdorff, A., Zhai, X., Roberts, J., & Nerdel, C. (2023). Myths, mis- and preconceptions of artificial intelligence: A review of the literature. *Computers and Education: Artificial Intelligence*, *4*, 100143. Advance online publication. DOI: 10.1016/j.caeai.2023.100143

Bond, M., Khosravi, H., De Laat, M., Bergdahl, N., Negrea, V., Oxley, E., Pham, P., Chong, S. W., & Siemens, G. (2024). A meta systematic review of artificial intelligence in higher education: A call for increased ethics, collaboration, and rigour. *International Journal of Educational Technology in Higher Education*, *21*(1), 4. Advance online publication. DOI: 10.1186/s41239-023-00436-z

Brata, W. W. W., Padang, R. Y., Suriani, C., Prasetya, E., & Pratiwi, N. (2022). Student's digital literacy based on students' interest in digital technology, internet costs, gender, and learning outcomes. *International Journal of Emerging Technologies in Learning*, *17*(3), 138–151. DOI: 10.3991/ijet.v17i03.27151

Breakstone, J., Smith, M., Ziv, N., & Wineburg, S. (2022). Civic preparation for the digital age: How college students evaluate online sources about social and political issues. *The Journal of Higher Education*, *93*(6), 963–988. DOI: 10.1080/00221546.2022.2082783

Buckingham, D. (2019). Teaching media in a 'post-truth' age: Fake news, media bias and the challenge for media/digital literacy education. *C&E, Cultura y Educación*, *31*(2), 213–231. DOI: 10.1080/11356405.2019.1603814

Cardon, P. W., Fleischmann, C., Aritz, J., Logemann, M., & Heidewald, J. (2023). The challenges and opportunities of AI-assisted writing: Developing AI literacy for the AI age. *Business and Professional Communication Quarterly*, *86*(3), 257–295. DOI: 10.1177/23294906231176517

Chan, C. K. Y., & Hu, W. (2023). Students' voices on generative AI: Perceptions, benefits, and challenges in higher education. *International Journal of Educational Technology in Higher Education*, *20*(1), 43. Advance online publication. DOI: 10.1186/s41239-023-00411-8

Cope, B., & Kalantzis, M. (2024). A multimodal grammar of artificial intelligence: Measuring the gains and losses in generative AI. *Multimodality & Society*, *4*(1), 6–32. DOI: 10.1177/26349795231221699

Dempere, J., Modugu, K., Hesham, A., & Ramasamy, L. K. (2023). The impact of ChatGPT on higher education. *Frontiers in Education*, *8*, 1206936. Advance online publication. DOI: 10.3389/feduc.2023.1206936

Guess, A. M., Lerner, M., Lyons, B., Montgomery, J. M., Nyhan, B., Reifler, J., & Sircar, N. (2020). A digital media literacy intervention increases discernment between mainstream and false news in the United States and India. *Proceedings of the National Academy of Sciences of the United States of America, 117*(27), 15536–15545. DOI: 10.1073/pnas.1920498117 PMID: 32571950

Hackl, V., Mueller, A., & Sailer, M. (2025). AI Literacy Heptagon: A structured approach to AI literacy in higher education. arXiv preprint arXiv:2509.18900v1. https://doi.org//arXiv.2509.18900DOI: 10.48550

Hwang, G. J., Xie, H., Wah, B. W., & Gašević, D. (2020). Vision, challenges, roles and research issues of Artificial Intelligence in Education. *Computers and Education: Artificial Intelligence*, *1*, 100001. Advance online publication. DOI: 10.1016/j.caeai.2020.100001

Jiang, L., Lee, I., & Yu, S. (2024). Conceptualizing multimodal feedback literacy for L2 writing teachers in the digital age. *International Journal of Applied Linguistics*, *34*(3), 987–1003. DOI: 10.1111/ijal.12578

Kabakus, A. K., Bahcekapili, E., & Ayaz, A. (2023). The effect of digital literacy on technology acceptance: An evaluation on administrative staff in higher education. *Journal of Information Science*, *51*(4), 512–533. DOI: 10.1177/01655515231160028

Kang, J., & Yi, Y. (2023). Beyond ChatGPT: Multimodal generative AI for L2 writers. *Journal of Second Language Writing*, *62*, 101070. Advance online publication. DOI: 10.1016/j.jslw.2023.101070

Kong, S. C., Cheung, W. M. Y., & Zhang, G. (2021). Evaluation of an artificial intelligence literacy course for university students with diverse study backgrounds. *Computers and Education: Artificial Intelligence*, 2, 100026. Advance online publication. DOI: 10.1016/j.caeai.2021.100026

Long, D., & Magerko, B. (2020). What is AI literacy? Competencies and design considerations. *Proceedings of the 2020 CHI Conference on Human Factors in Computing Systems*, 1-16. DOI: 10.1145/3313831.3376727

Lukitasari, M., Murtafiah, W., Ramdiah, S., Hasan, R., & Sukri, A. (2022). Constructing digital literacy instrument and its effect on college students' learning outcomes. *International Journal of Instruction, 15*(2), 171–188. DOI: 10.29333/iji.2022.15210a

Mabini, H., & Gallardo, R. (2024). Digital literacy and critical thinking skills among Grade 5 learners. *International Journal of Innovative Science and Research Technology, 9*(6), 1589–1597. DOI: 10.38124/ijisrt/IJISRT24JUN413

Meirbekov, A., Maslova, I., & Gallyamova, Z. (2022). Digital education tools for critical thinking development. *Thinking Skills and Creativity, 44*, 101023. Advance online publication. DOI: 10.1016/j.tsc.2022.101023

Michel-Villarreal, R., Vilalta-Perdomo, E. L., Salinas-Navarro, D. E., Thierry-Aguilera, R., & Gerardou, F. S. (2023). Challenges and opportunities of generative AI for higher education as explained by ChatGPT. *Education Sciences, 13*(9), 856. Advance online publication. DOI: 10.3390/educsci13090856

Moravec, V., Hynek, N., Gavurova, B., & Rigelsky, M. (2024). Who uses it and for what purpose? The role of digital literacy in ChatGPT adoption and utilisation. *Journal of Innovation & Knowledge, 9*(2), 100602. Advance online publication. DOI: 10.1016/j.jik.2024.100602

Mustafa, M., Tlili, A., Lampropoulos, G., Huang, R., Sampson, D. G., & Ifenthaler, D. (2024). A systematic review of literature reviews on artificial intelligence in education (AIED): A roadmap to a future research agenda. *Smart Learning Environments, 11*(1), 59. Advance online publication. DOI: 10.1186/s40561-024-00350-5

Nguyen, L., & Habók, A. (2023). Tools for assessing teacher digital literacy: A review. *Journal of Computers in Education, 10*(2), 257–297. DOI: 10.1007/s40692-022-00257-5

Reddy, P., Chaudhary, K., & Hussein, S. (2023). A digital literacy model to narrow the digital literacy skills gap. *Heliyon, 9*(4), e14878. Advance online publication. DOI: 10.1016/j.heliyon.2023.e14878 PMID: 37025876

Ríos Hernández, I. N., Mateus, J. C., Rivera Rogel, D., & Rosa Ávila Meléndez, L. (2024). Percepciones de estudiantes latinoamericanos sobre el uso de la inteligencia artificial en la educación superior. *Austral Comunicación, 13*(1), e01302. Advance online publication. DOI: 10.26422/aucom.2024.1301.rio

Sarrionandia, B., Peña-Fernández, S., Ángel Pérez-Dasilva, J., & Larrondo-Ureta, A. (2025). Artificial intelligence training in media: Addressing technical and ethical challenges for journalists and media professionals. *Frontiers in Communication*, *10*, 1537918. Advance online publication. DOI: 10.3389/fcomm.2025.1537918

Sergeeva, M. G., Tala, M. L., & Zhirnova, A. M. (2025). Impact of digital media literacy on attitude toward generative AI acceptance in higher education. *Frontiers in Education*, *10*, 1563148. Advance online publication. DOI: 10.3389/feduc.2025.1563148

Su, J., & Yang, W. (2022). Artificial intelligence in early childhood education: A scoping review. *Computers and Education: Artificial Intelligence*, *3*, 100049. Advance online publication. DOI: 10.1016/j.caeai.2022.100049

Timotheou, S., Miliou, O., Dimitriadis, Y., Villagrá Sobrino, S., Giannoutsou, N., Cachia, R., & Ioannou, A. (2023). Impacts of digital technologies on education and factors influencing schools' digital capacity and transformation: A literature review. *Education and Information Technologies*, *28*(6), 6695–6726. DOI: 10.1007/s10639-022-11431-8 PMID: 36465416

Valtonen, T., Sointu, E., Kukkonen, J., Kontkanen, S., Lambert, M. C., & Mäkitalo-Siegl, K. (2019). TPACK updated to measure pre-service teachers' twenty-first century skills. *Australasian Journal of Educational Technology*, *35*(3), 1–13. DOI: 10.14742/ajet.3518

KEY TERMS AND DEFINITIONS

Artificial Intelligence Literacy: Artificial intelligence literacy is the ability to understand, evaluate, and responsibly use AI technologies. It involves knowledge of AI concepts, applications, limitations, and ethical implications, empowering individuals to engage critically with AI-driven systems.

Critical Thinking: Critical thinking is the disciplined process of analyzing, evaluating, and synthesizing information to form reasoned judgments. It involves questioning assumptions, identifying biases, and applying logic to solve problems or make informed decisions.

Digital Media Literacy: Digital media literacy is the skill of accessing, analyzing, creating, and sharing digital content responsibly. It emphasizes critical evaluation of online information, awareness of misinformation, and effective communication across diverse digital platforms.

Ethical AI: Ethical AI is the design and use of artificial intelligence systems guided by fairness, transparency, accountability, and respect for human rights. It seeks to prevent bias, misuse, and harm while promoting trust and social good.

Generative AI: Generative AI refers to AI models that create new content such as text, images, music, or code. It learns patterns from large datasets and produces original outputs, enabling creativity, automation, and innovation across industries.

Higher Education: Higher education refers to advanced learning beyond secondary school, typically offered by universities, colleges, and institutes. It focuses on specialized knowledge, research, and skill development, preparing individuals for professional careers and intellectual growth.

Technology Integration: Technology integration is the effective use of digital tools and systems within educational, business, or social contexts. It enhances learning, productivity, and communication by embedding technology seamlessly into everyday practices and workflows.

Chapter 11
AI-Driven Media Literacy in National Identity Coverage:
Ethics, Manipulations, and Challenges in Kazakhstan

Bogdan Petrov
http://orcid.org/0000-0001-9773-8914
Astana IT University, Kazakhstan

Ainur Abiltayeva
http://orcid.org/0009-0002-5456-463X
L.N. Gumilyov Eurasian National University, Kazakhstan

Amangeldy Shurentayev
http://orcid.org/0000-0002-8953-0010
L.N. Gumilyov Eurasian National University, Kazakhstan

ABSTRACT

This chapter explores the role of contemporary media in shaping national identity, using Kazakhstan case. Drawing on theories of mediatization, agenda-setting, imagined communities, and symbolic nation-building, it demonstrates how media actively construct identity through language, framing, stereotypes, and value-based representations rather than merely reflecting social reality. The analysis highlights key ethical challenges, including hate speech, stigmatization, clickbait, and manipulative framing, which can distort public perceptions and reinforce social divisions. Particular attention is given to the growing influence of algorithmic platforms and

DOI: 10.4018/979-8-2600-2163-7.ch011

generative AI, which increasingly function as de facto editors and interpreters of national narratives. The chapter illustrates both the constructive and manipulative potential of AI-generated content.

INTRODUCTION

The relevance of this study lies in the growing importance of issues of national identity and civic unity in an increasingly globalized AI-driven world, as well as in the expanding influence of the media on public consciousness. Society is undergoing a process of mediatization, in which media become embedded in the structure of social institutions and exert a direct impact on their functioning (Hjarvard, 2008).

The rapid integration of artificial intelligence into media production, distribution, and consumption has fundamentally altered the ways in which national identity is represented, interpreted, and contested in contemporary societies. Traditional media literacy frameworks, which primarily focused on the critical reading of texts and the evaluation of journalistic credibility, are no longer sufficient in an environment where algorithms curate information flows and generative AI systems autonomously produce content (Djumanova, 2025). In AI-driven media ecosystems, national identity becomes not only a cultural or ideological construct but also a technological output shaped by data, code, and platform logics.

In this chapter, AI-driven media literacy is defined as a set of analytical and civic competencies that enable individuals to critically interpret identity-related media content in environments shaped by recommendation algorithms, generative AI systems, and platform governance (Sarkar & Ghosh, 2024). AI-driven media literacy requires understanding how algorithmic ranking, personalization, synthetic media generation, and opaque data-driven optimization shape what becomes visible, credible, and emotionally persuasive. It includes

1) the ability to recognize AI-generated or AI-assisted content;
2) awareness of algorithmic amplification and engagement-based optimization;
3) basic understanding of how training data and model biases affect cultural representation;
4) knowledge of platform governance mechanisms and accountability gaps;
5) civic skills for ethical participation and countering manipulation.

In Kazakhstan, where national identity is formed at the intersection of multilingualism, post-Soviet transformation, and digital globalization, these changes are particularly evident.

In the era of information technology development, the concept of "media reality" has emerged - a reality constructed by mass media. People spend a significant part of their lives immersed in media images, adopting the habits of media characters as well as the opinions and information presented by the media. This leads to the effect of a confused or blurred reality. In his psychological model, Comstock et al. (1978) describes the direct impact of mass communication on individuals. The essence of this model lies in the idea that the behavior of television characters influences the behavior of viewers; that is, viewers internalize the behavior demonstrated on the screen. One of the key variables determining the intensity of media influence is the credibility of the imagined reality.

While studying the influence of mass media on public opinion, the German scholar Noelle-Neumann (1996) identified the spiral of silence effect. The essence of this phenomenon lies in the manipulative influence of the media on the population, dividing it into a majority and a minority. The internal motivating factor is the fear of social isolation: minorities are more likely to remain silent or join the majority. This mechanism also explains the motivation behind "bandwagon" behavior in voting processes - no one wants to be isolated or to end up on the losing side.

This logic of silence driven by perceived social risk becomes even more pronounced in AI-mediated environments. Recent survey-based research among young female social media users shows that perceived deepfake threat is positively associated with online self-censorship, primarily through psychological mechanisms such as reduced perceived control and a shift toward more passive platform use (Lee, 2026).

Today, new media are capable not so much of reflecting objective reality as of creating their own realities that better correspond to individual needs. Nevertheless, the thesis that "a properly constructed agenda can steer public opinion in a desired direction" remains relevant and in demand within the system of new media (Dyakova, 2003). Mass media today represent the most powerful instrument for shaping civic identity and patriotic sentiment. It is precisely new media that possess the functionality enabling direct dialogue with youth audiences.

Many scholars define national identity as "a sense of the nation as a coherent whole, represented by unique traditions, culture, and language" (Velilayeva & Abdullaeva, 2020). The foundation of Kazakhstan's national identity lies in deep Kazakh culture and mythology, as well as historical preconditions in the form of polyethnicity (Urozbayeva, 2020).

Researchers Insebayeva & Insebayeva (2021), in their article, use the state anthem and national currency to explain the nature of Kazakh national identity. They describe these symbols as key attributes of statehood and economic independence, as well as essential elements of nation-building.

N. Mkrtchyan (2014) concludes that the relocation of the capital and the adoption of new state symbols during Kazakhstan's independence following the collapse of the Soviet Union became key milestones in the creation of symbolic spaces for the formation of a new national consciousness. He analyzes the architectural design of Astana and state symbols, referring to them as the principal symbols of "Kazakhness".

Mass media play an enormous role in shaping national identity, as they contribute to the creation of the so-called "imagined community" described by B. Anderson (1991). According to Anderson's concept, since the decline of religion and the emergence of print culture, it has become possible and necessary for an "imagined community" to arise, through which a sense of immortality can be awakened - a sense with which anonymous individuals can identify. Through printed texts, people unfamiliar with one another can share homogeneous time and recognizable space, belonging to an imagined community and to future generations.

Over time, the perception of mass media as merely "informative" has become outdated; depending on perspective, they are now described as "shaping," "entertaining," and so forth. The development of feedback mechanisms - that is, the formal possibility for audiences to influence or express opinions - has transformed mass media into a form of communication that is no longer strictly one-directional.

It is evident that mass media today exert greater influence on the formation of human consciousness and behavior than ever before and have become a powerful instrument of influence on both the state and society. They actively participate in the natural process of expanding and deepening communication, mutual influence, and mutual enrichment among peoples, resulting in the overcoming of national isolation across all spheres of life and the emergence of shared features of interethnic community. Today, the media constitute a large, branched, and stable system that strives to objectively reflect the rich and diverse life of society, significant phenomena, and events at national and global levels, while shaping public opinion around pressing social, economic, and political issues related to national development (Grivennaya, 2018).

More than 100 different ethnic groups live in Kazakhstan. The republic has developed a model of national harmony recognized worldwide. Current geopolitical changes influence Kazakhstani society, raising issues of ethnic and linguistic tolerance. Mass media and social networks demonstrate the relevance of these issues and influence the formation of public opinion.

This topic remains constantly in the focus of scholars worldwide. In particular, Marinovich (2015) devoted her academic article to the role of the internet in mobilizing and uniting the public, as well as to social media as a platform facilitating the formation of ethnic identity, using the example of political transformations during revolutionary movements in the Arab region. The author concludes that social movement theories enable scholars to model revolutionary processes and better understand the role of mass media in shaping ethnic identity.

Nevokshanova and Stefanchikov (2019) studied the role of print media in the formation of Uruguayan national identity in the first third of the twentieth century. They argue that discursive strategies are employed in the press during nation-building, including the postulation of the nation's existence, presuppositions of internal national similarity, emphasis on interethnic differences, highlighting national exclusivity, positive self-representation, positive representation of the "other," and negative representation of the "other."

European scholars, examining various aspects of social life in Central and Eastern European countries, point to the specificity of state–church relations in the region, its multireligious heritage, cultural religiosity, and the authority of religious tradition. Religion is also important for national identity in Central Europe and is perceived as an expression of moral judgments and collective identity in political disputes. The authors argue that residents of the region place religious identity along a continuum with civic identity. Historical diversity is viewed as "traditional pluralism," where the "dominant" and "national" are expected to be supported by the state and to clearly dominate in publicly proclaimed values and media representation. The strengthening of equality and tolerance is often considered unnecessary - a perspective that resonates with conservative and nationalist circles and certain populist sentiments (Moddelmog-Anweiler et al., 2022).

Arab scholar T. Asharari (2023) analyzes a secondary-level social studies curriculum within a joint program in the Kingdom of Saudi Arabia aimed at raising awareness of the concept of Saudi national identity, as included in the Saudi Vision 2030 framework. Using educational units across five domains and drawing on the principles of Vision 2030, the program prepares students to understand Saudi national identity in all its dimensions - national, Arab, and international - and emphasizes the authors' ability to employ activities and assessment messages linking academic content to national identity.

Another study by Arab scholars examines social media use among Saudi youth and its influence on the strength of their national and cultural identity. The findings indicate that social media contribute to strengthening intellectual, cultural, legal, and educational activities, as well as to building a high level of trust in the competence and capabilities of youth.

Finnish scholars Nortio et al. (2022) argue that discussions of national identity, like political debates in general, increasingly take place online. They find that narratives of origin and continuity of the nation do not exclude one another but are intertwined with stories of transformation, change, and anticipation. Spatial, territorial, and local dimensions also play a significant role in the discursive construction of national identity. Their analysis shows that identity construction relied on references to historical memory of wars glorifying national resilience, successful neutrality during the Cold War, and future-oriented dimensions of identification.

Thus, national identity is clearly both deeply personal and socially significant. For each individual, awareness of belonging to a nation is not an abstract category but a vital element of self-identification associated with a sense of home, cultural memory, language, and symbols through which one recognizes oneself.

Mass media play a key role in representing national identity by transmitting ideas, values, historical narratives, and cultural images. Media influence can be both constructive and destructive. Positive contributions include:

- the formation of a sense of "shared destiny" and "common future";
- promotion of ethno-confessional harmony and diversity;
- presentation of ethnocultural richness as a national value;
- expansion of knowledge about one's own culture and those of other ethnic groups in Kazakhstan;
- support for state and civic initiatives aimed at strengthening identity.

However, biased media representations may distort or even undermine national identity. Particularly concerning practices include hate speech, manipulation, and stereotyping, which can foster distrust, fear, marginalization, and social tension.

Journalists bear professional and ethical responsibility for the ways in which they construct images of ethnic groups, nations, and cultures. The use of hate speech, unreliable generalizations, or deliberate omissions not only violates professional ethical standards but may also become a factor contributing to social tension. A conscious, critical, and respectful approach to issues of identity allows journalists not merely to "reflect" reality, but to contribute to its harmonious development.

The contradictions in the development of contemporary journalism have been extensively analyzed by Steven Pinker, a well-known American scholar and professor. His research focuses on media coverage of democracy, language, civil rights, and freedoms in mass communication. Pinker reflects on the development of journalism in the context of shaping public moods and individual opinions.

Pinker rightly notes that modern media increasingly contain negative content depicting the cruelty of the world, crime, injustice, and related issues. However, he makes an important clarification: the growing number of such publications does not necessarily indicate that life itself has become more saturated with negative events, but rather that the media tend to focus on these topics. It is often easier for journalists to report on problems, failures, or mistakes of authorities, institutions, or individuals than to disseminate positive news. In this respect, it is difficult to disagree with the professor, as in the pursuit of hype and audience attention some media actors do not hesitate to "dig into dirty laundry," distort facts, or even replicate fake information.

It is also common for journalists to focus on a single detail of a major news event without revealing its broader context. For example, in 2019, nearly 200 fewer students were admitted to Kozybayev North Kazakhstan University compared to the previous year. This was stated by the executive secretary of the admissions committee during a press conference summarizing the summer admissions campaign. Some media outlets immediately disseminated headlines such as "In northern Kazakhstan, the number of applicants wishing to study at local universities has decreased" (Vaitovich, 2019). However, this information was taken out of context, as the admissions officer later explained that the decrease was due to a reduction in the number of secondary school graduates in the North Kazakhstan region that year. Evidently, the journalists aimed to generate likes and comments and therefore framed the story from a different angle.

Such examples are abundant in both the Kazakhstani and international media landscapes. It is important to emphasize that no one argues against reporting negative events; on the contrary, people should be informed of the truth, regardless of how harsh it may be. However, if journalists consistently focus exclusively on problems and broadcast them as the dominant narrative, audiences may develop a distorted perception of reality, experience reduced motivation for positive change, and lose trust in one another. It is equally important to remember that there is also much good in the world that deserves attention.

Pinker (2021) aptly notes: "If the press gives the impression that there is not a single functioning institution left in our society, that democracy does not work, that the United Nations does not work, and that the modern economy as a whole does not work, it encourages radicalism. There arises a desire to destroy everything at its roots". Under such conditions, specific social groups may emerge that trust only these media sources while rejecting all others. Their worldview becomes one of a bleak present surrounded by darkness: the government does not work, people are hostile, and survival is uncertain. From this perspective, civil servants appear as complete idlers, university lecturers as people who allegedly bought their diplomas, and doctors as incompetent individuals motivated solely by money.

In this context, Pinker's assertion is particularly relevant: "Journalists should reflect on the picture of the world they are creating for their readers, even if unintentionally".

HATE SPEECH

In contemporary scholarship, researchers identify the concept of "communicative aggression," which emerges when acute social contradictions manifest within the media environment, leading to conflicts of opposing opinions and evaluations. This process results in media-driven stigmatization, understood as the consolidation of images and perceptions that frame certain individuals or groups as alien, threatening, or fundamentally different, preventing their identification as members of the broader society. Public reactions to stigmatized groups often involve exclusion, isolation, and the normalization of restrictions on their rights or discriminatory practices. One of the simplest media techniques contributing to stigmatization is the dissemination of false myths and manipulation of feelings of security and fear. More complex techniques include the division into "us" and "them" and the construction of an image of the "enemy" (Blokhin, 2016).

An irreconcilable conflict of interest for journalists arises from the desire to produce sensational content while simultaneously being required to comply with the law and ethical standards. Under such conditions, media materials often exhibit elements of hate speech. In addition to the aforementioned divisions between "us" and "them," "good" and "bad," hate speech includes the use of discriminatory language or implicit discrimination, calls to action against specific individuals or groups, and manipulation of facts through selective presentation, fragmentation, or overgeneralization.

Scholars distinguish three forms of hate speech: soft, medium, and hard. Soft hate speech involves the construction of a negative image of individuals or groups, references made in a derogatory or humiliating manner, claims of inferiority, publication of xenophobic statements, or the presentation of authors' discriminatory views without editorial commentary separating personal opinion from journalistic position. Medium hate speech includes justification of historical cases of discrimination and violence, dissemination of information questioning well-established historical facts of violence and discrimination, attribution of blame to specific ethnic groups, allegations of connections to foreign states, claims of criminality, and accusatory discourse regarding disproportionate dominance in wealth, political power, or social influence. Hard hate speech entails direct and explicit calls for violence, violent actions, or discrimination (Ismanov et al., 2023).

When covering issues of national identity, hate speech in the media may manifest through unnecessary emphasis on the ethnic or religious affiliation of criminals, the use of divisive rhetoric opposing one ethnic group to another, the marginalization or exclusion of certain ethno-confessional groups, and the reinforcement or creation of stereotypes.

It is important to note that Article 14, Paragraph 2 of the Constitution of the Republic of Kazakhstan (1995) states that "no one shall be subject to any discrimination for reasons of origin, social, official or property status, sex, race, nationality, language, attitude to religion, beliefs, place of residence, or any other circumstances". Criminal liability for such actions is established in Article 174 of the Criminal Code of the Republic of Kazakhstan (2014), which provide punishment for intentional actions aimed at inciting discord, insulting national honor and dignity or religious feelings, as well as promoting exclusivity, superiority, or inferiority of citizens when committed publicly or through mass media, telecommunications networks, or online platforms.

Administrative liability is also provided. Article 453 of the Code of Administrative Offenses of the Republic of Kazakhstan (2014) establishes penalties for the production, storage, import, or distribution of mass media products containing materials that promote violent change of the constitutional order, violation of territorial integrity, undermining state security, war, or incitement of social, racial, national, religious, class, or clan hatred.

In practice, however, this legal framework most often applies only to manifestations of hard hate speech. Other forms are regulated primarily through the Code of Professional Ethics of Journalists. According to Section 1 of the Code of Ethics of the Journalist of the Republic of Kazakhstan (2012), "a journalist must act in the interests of the profession, freedom of speech, interfaith and interethnic harmony." Section 2 emphasizes the obligation to strengthen moral and ethical principles in society and avoid inciting social discord.

ETHNIC STEREOTYPES IN THE MEDIA

Journalists often, consciously or unconsciously, rely on stereotypical images to simplify or enliven content, which ultimately leads to the reinforcement and reproduction of biased perceptions in society. To avoid this, it is important to understand how media stereotypes function and what risks they pose to social harmony and national identity.

In the works of the prominent scholar Walter Lippmann, the concept of the "pseudo-environment" is introduced. Individuals possess a mental image of the world and adapt not to reality itself, but to this pseudo-environment. Since most of the world remains inaccessible to direct verification, audiences are unable to independently check information received through the media. As a result, mass media have extensive opportunities to construct particular worldviews. Lippmann (2004) also notes that media are compelled to use stereotypes by selecting standards familiar to audiences, as they operate under conditions of overwhelming information flows. Without standardization and simplification, he argues, journalists would be unable to function effectively.

Stereotypes are stable, simplified, and often distorted representations of social groups, events, or phenomena. They may relate to ethnic, religious, gender, age, or other characteristics. In media discourse, stereotypes are reproduced through recurring images, clichés, and formulaic expressions that shape public attitudes and influence collective perceptions.

Journalists resort to stereotypes for various reasons, including the simplification of complex topics for rapid presentation, reliance on familiar narratives to capture audience attention, pursuit of sensational and replicable headlines, insufficient media literacy, or lack of ethical oversight within editorial teams. However, the danger of stereotypes lies in their impact on public consciousness: they reinforce biased images, foster prejudice and discriminatory practices, intensify divisions between "us" and "them," and may serve as catalysts for social tension or conflict.

Ethnic stereotypes are particularly significant. Examples include common generalizations such as "punctual Germans," "reserved Englishmen," or "hospitable Kazakhs." Similar patterns exist with religious stereotypes. In media coverage of national identity, common stereotypes include portraying certain ethnic or linguistic groups exclusively through negative or marginalized images; reducing cultural diversity to folkloric clichés; constructing oppositions between "indigenous" and "outsiders," especially in discussions of migration or language policy; and using stigmatizing metaphors or labels when covering interethnic issues.

While traditional media manipulation often operates through conscious framing choices and discursive strategies, AI-driven systems may reproduce bias at a deeper structural level. For example, corpus-based cognitive-linguistic analyses of AI-generated content have shown systematic metaphorical and semantic patterns that construct People With Disabilities as vulnerable and unequal, relying on medicalized and bodily frames (Abdelzaher & Alshammari, 2026). Such findings indicate that AI does not merely reflect language use but may reinforce hierarchical identity constructions through implicit conceptual metaphors and evaluative markers. Similar mechanisms may affect representations of national, ethnic, or linguistic identities, particularly in multilingual and politically sensitive contexts.

If humans construct identity through lived and embodied storytelling, LLMs generate narratives based on learned statistical patterns. Empirical research shows that AI-generated interpretations of personal narratives often rely on culturally dominant redemptive structures, which may feel "uncanny" or inauthentic (Mansfield et al., 2026). In the context of national identity, this suggests that AI may unintentionally standardize and homogenize identity narratives, privileging certain symbolic templates over others.

Stereotypes in media content can be identified through generalized statements, absence of factual data or sources, emotionally charged or derogatory language, and the lack of alternative perspectives. To avoid stereotyping, journalists must critically reflect on their own biases, rely on verified facts and sources, present diverse viewpoints, and avoid emotionally loaded or demeaning language. An essential guiding question should be whether a particular image helps audiences understand the issue or merely reinforces prejudice.

MANIPULATIVE TECHNIQUES IN COVERING NATIONAL IDENTITY IN THE AGE OF AI

Manipulative practices in media content can amplify stereotypes, construct false images, and provoke conflicts. Media manipulation involves the conscious or unconscious use of information framing techniques designed to influence audience perception and elicit desired emotional responses such as fear, aggression, sympathy, or outrage.

Typical manipulative techniques include taking facts out of context, selective emphasis, overgeneralization, emotional labeling, dramatization, and conceptual substitution - for example, conflating migration with terrorism or patriotism with nationalism. Clickbait represents a particularly widespread form of manipulation in online journalism, relying on sensationalist or misleading headlines to attract attention, often at the expense of accuracy (Silverman, 2015).

Finally, national identity today is shaped not only by editorial decisions but also by recommendation algorithms on platforms such as TikTok, YouTube, and Instagram, as well as by generative AI systems and automated SMM tools. As a result, users increasingly encounter algorithmically constructed versions of identity rather than social reality itself.

In addition to synthetic images and video, large language models enable the rapid production of persuasive textual mis/disinformation. Recent computational research shows that even when linguistic distinctions exist between AI-generated and authentic content, the intrinsic detection capabilities of LLM-based systems remain limited, and linguistic feature patterns may cause automated detectors to fail. This suggests that information governance cannot rely solely on technical detection tools, especially in multilingual environments (Ma et al., 2026).

A major ethical challenge arises from the fact that AI systems effectively perform editorial and interpretive functions while remaining outside traditional frameworks of journalistic responsibility. In Kazakhstan's media system, where issues of national identity are particularly sensitive, this creates risks of reproducing culturally and historically loaded meanings without expert verification or ethical assessment.

At the same time, experimental artistic projects using GenAI highlight its capacity to re-visualize erased or underrepresented histories that were excluded from official archives due to political, social, or urban transformations. When guided by archival research and intentional design, AI-generated imagery may operate as a form of digital memory reconstruction, raising important questions about authorship, authenticity, and the politics of visual representation in the age of algorithmic media (Chen, 2026). However, when similar technologies are adopted within commercial media logic, the outcomes may differ. The dissemination of AI-generated images and videos stylized as "historical reconstructions" of the Kazakh past illustrates this influence. Despite their visual realism, such materials often combine artistic imagination, popular myths, and fragmented historical knowledge. While perceived by audiences as restoring historical justice and strengthening national pride, they contribute to the formation of simplified and aestheticized versions of identity. For example, an article with a headline "Photos of Kazakh intelligentsia reinterpreted with the help of AI" (2024) published on the popular online media TengriNews.

The issue of deepfakes and synthetic speech deserves special attention. The potential ability to generate video appearances of historical or contemporary public figures speaking on behalf of the "nation" or "tradition" poses a serious threat to trust in visual and audio evidence. Some scholars have expressed concern that the rapid spread of generative AI may contribute to "epistemic pollution" - the gradual degradation of the information and knowledge ecosystem through the production and circulation of low-quality, misleading, or fabricated content (Acquier & Cossey, 2026).

A positive example of the AI usage in Kazakhstan is the creation of the digital influencer AILA by the International Artificial Intelligence Center Alem.AI in Astana. Her appearance reproduces the image of a Kazakh girl wearing clothing consistent with traditional Kazakh national dress. Within just a few days after the publication of the first posts on AILA's Instagram page (2025), tens of thousands of views, likes, and positive comments were recorded.

A contrasting example illustrates the risks associated with AI-generated personas in digital media. In January 2026, a blogger known as Aileen rapidly gained popularity in Kazakhstani social media. Presenting herself as a young woman from Ust-Kamenogorsk with vitiligo, she shared emotionally engaging stories about childhood bullying, self-acceptance, and resilience. Within four days, the account accumulated over 22,000 followers, more than 9.3 million video views, and numerous advertising offers. Influential public figures and bloggers reacted to her content, and she was even invited to appear on television programs. However, it was later revealed that "Aileen" was not a real person but a highly realistic AI-generated model created as an experiment by a digital content producer (Smagulov, 2026). After the disclosure, user reactions shifted dramatically. While some admired the technical sophistication of the project, many expressed feelings of deception and emotional manipulation. Comments such as "I believed her and gave compliments," "It feels like I was deceived," and "Now it is unclear where reality ends" reflected a sense of betrayal and epistemic uncertainty. This case demonstrates how AI-generated identities can exploit affective engagement mechanisms typical of social media environments. Unlike openly declared digital influencers such as AILA, whose artificial nature is part of the project's concept, the Aileen case involved an implicit claim to authenticity. The emotional narrative about discrimination and self-acceptance functioned as a powerful trigger for empathy, which amplified audience involvement. When the artificial origin of the persona was revealed, the collapse of perceived authenticity resulted in distrust not only toward the specific account but also toward the broader digital environment.

Another illustrative case concerns the AI-generated persona Aderinke, presented as an "Afro-Kazakh" woman with a Nigerian father and a Kazakh mother (Muratbekov, 2026). A video narrating her origin story emphasizing her mixed heritage received approximately 80,000 likes and significant engagement. In the comments, users expressed admiration and romantic interest: "What a beautiful combination!", "Your mother is beautiful, and so are you," "We would have beautiful children," and similar remarks. Many commenters appeared to believe in the authenticity of the character. At the same time, the discussion was not uniformly positive. The sociocultural implications of such a case are particularly sensitive in the Kazakhstani context. Interethnic marriages remain a debated and emotionally charged topic in public discourse. A considerable segment of society maintains conservative views regarding endogamy, arguing that ethnic Kazakhs should marry within their own ethnic group to preserve cultural continuity and symbolic notions of "Kazakh blood" (Zhylkybayeva, 2022; Sanzharova, 2022). These attitudes are closely tied to broader processes of post-Soviet nation-building and ethnocultural consolidation. Scholars examining national identity formation in Kazakhstan (e.g., Kazakhstan in the Making) note that questions of ethnicity, lineage, and cultural preservation remain central to public debates about belonging and authenticity.

Research on AI-generated traditional cultural narratives further indicates that generative models can be trained to produce semantically consistent and culturally resonant content when guided by explicit stylistic and identity-oriented parameters. This highlights the dual potential of AI: while capable of distortion, it may also function as a tool for cultural preservation and symbolic reconstruction (Liu & Wang, 2026).

In the context of Kazakhstan's public discourse, where issues of language, cultural heritage, and national values are actively debated, such technologies may be used to manipulatively reinforce certain ideological positions, creating the illusion of their historical or social legitimacy.

Recent systematic reviews emphasize that deepfake technologies are evolving rapidly and becoming increasingly accessible, while detection remains an ongoing "arms race" between generation and verification tools. Importantly, contemporary detection systems are often vulnerable to adversarial attacks and may fail outside benchmark conditions, which makes deepfakes a persistent challenge for media credibility. This reinforces the need for combined approaches: technical safeguards, newsroom protocols, and policy-level regulation (Sharma & Selwal, 2026).

In Kazakhstan, media organizations are already integrating artificial intelligence technologies into journalistic production and visual content creation. For example, large media company Qazcontent, which unites several of the most popular Kazakhstani digital news platforms, including Baigenews.kz, El.kz, Kazinform, and other affiliated media resources, conducted experiments in 2025 on the use of AI tools for news production. In this experiment, AI was applied to assist with illustration generation, image editing, and support of editorial workflows as part of broader digital transformation efforts in state-supported media ecosystems (Ruzmatova, 2025).

The adoption of AI technologies has significantly simplified journalistic production processes. In particular, AI-generated visual materials reduce operational costs by eliminating the need to maintain full-time design staff, purchasing stock images, or resolving complex copyright issues, since neural networks can automatically generate illustrations tailored to news content. At the same time, the use of AI introduces new challenges related to media authenticity and audience trust.

Empirical data suggest that Kazakhstani audiences demonstrate a relatively high level of sensitivity toward AI-generated media content. According to survey findings ("How Kazakhstanis relate to artificial intelligence," 2025), in social networks approximately four to five posts out of ten are perceived as AI-generated. Textual content is identified as artificial more frequently than visual material: 80% of respondents reported being able to recognize AI-generated text, while 70% indicated the ability to identify AI-produced video. Respondents associate AI-generated texts with specific stylistic and structural markers, including overly long and syntactically overloaded sentences, excessive use of colons and segmented structuring, formulaic rhetorical constructions (e.g., "this is no longer…, this is…"), inflated or overly elevated vocabulary, and repetitive argumentative patterns. Such linguistic characteristics contribute to perceptions of inauthenticity and mechanical production in digital media discourse.

The issue of declining trust may also be linked to the lack of transparency regarding the use of AI in media production. When media organizations do not clearly disclose where and how AI tools are applied, audiences may perceive such practices as manipulative or deceptive. Conversely, transparency can have a positive effect on credibility. If audiences are informed that AI was used as an assisting tool rather than as a full replacement for human editorial judgment, trust levels may increase, since openness about technological mediation reduces uncertainty in content interpretation. In this context, transparency regarding AI-generated or AI-assisted content is gradually becoming a new standard of ethical media communication.

These developments are further reinforced by recent legislative regulation. Starting in January 2026, Kazakhstan will enforce the law "On Artificial Intelligence" (2025) signed by the President of the Republic. One of the key provisions of this law is the mandatory labeling of AI-generated or AI-modified content. Synthetic outputs, including images, videos, audio, and textual materials created using artificial intelligence, must be clearly marked if they imitate real people, voices, or events that did not actually occur. Distribution of such content is permitted only under conditions of visible and understandable labeling. The law applies to individuals, companies, media organizations, bloggers, and AI system operators who distribute AI-generated content. Responsibility for non-compliance primarily rests with AI system owners and operators rather than individual users of AI tools. The law does not prescribe a strict universal format for labeling; instead, it allows flexibility, including visual marks such as "Created with AI," textual disclaimers placed before materials, or audio notifications during content playback. Particular attention is given to regulating deepfake technologies and synthetic representations of real individuals. Administrative penalties for non-compliance include fines, with increased penalties and possible suspension of AI systems in case of repeated violations within one year. The implementation of this legislation reflects Kazakhstan's broader strategy of digital transformation and responsible AI governance.

To minimize the ethical, legal risks and manipulative potential of artificial intelligence in the coverage of national identity in Kazakhstan, a systemic approach is required, combining educational, professional, and institutional measures. First and foremost, it is necessary to reconsider the very concept of media literacy in light of the algorithmic nature of the contemporary media environment. AI-driven media literacy should be integrated into educational programs in journalism, communication studies, and digital media as a separate module focused on the analysis of recommendation algorithms, generative models, and their influence on the symbolic production of identity.

Particular attention should be paid to the development of critical analysis of AI-generated content related to history, cultural heritage, and national symbols. Recent experimental research comparing humans and machine-learning systems suggests that detection accuracy depends strongly on the format of the deepfake: while automated systems may perform well on static images, both humans and machines face substantial difficulties when dealing with dynamic video deepfakes. Importantly, human detection performance has been linked to factors such as analytical thinking and internet skills, reinforcing the relevance of AI-driven media literacy as a practical competence rather than a purely theoretical concept (Pehlivanoglu et al., 2026).

Training should include case studies of deepfakes, synthetic visuals, and texts in which students and practicing journalists analyze not only the accuracy of information, but also the mechanisms of aestheticization, mythologization, and ideological simplification of the national narrative. This approach shifts the focus from formal fact-checking to an understanding of how AI constructs plausibility itself.

Within the professional media environment, it is advisable to develop ethical guidelines for the use of artificial intelligence in the production of content addressing issues of national identity. These guidelines should include requirements for labeling AI-generated content -especially when synthetic images, video, and speech are used - as well as the mandatory involvement of experts such as historians, cultural scholars, and linguists in the interpretation of sensitive topics. Such measures would help maintain a balance between innovation and editorial responsibility.

A separate area of focus is the support of Kazakh-language digital content and the creation of local datasets for training and fine-tuning language models. Without targeted investment in the development of the Kazakh language within the AI domain, there is a risk of reinforcing algorithmic asymmetry, whereby Kazakhstani identity is represented primarily through external, simplified, or exoticized models. In this context, state and academic institutions may act as initiators of open text corpora and multimodal datasets that reflect the country's contemporary cultural diversity.

Finally, at the level of public policy and societal dialogue, it is important to recognize artificial intelligence as a full-fledged participant in media processes that influence the formation of public consciousness and national identity. This entails the development of framework principles for regulating the use of AI technologies in media and culture, aimed not at prohibition but at increasing algorithmic transparency and accountability for social consequences. Incorporating AI-driven media literacy into Kazakhstan's digital development strategies and cultural policy may become an important step toward building a sustainable and inclusive media environment.

REFERENCES

Abdelzaher, E., & Alshammari, S. (2026). Learning from machinery misspeaks: Cognitive basis of ableism and bias in AI-generated content. *Corpus Pragmatics : International Journal of Corpus Linguistics and Pragmatics*, *10*(1), 8. Advance online publication. DOI: 10.1007/s41701-025-00216-2

Acquier, A., & Cossey, J. (2026). Generative AI, academic deepfakes, and epistemic pollution. *Business & Society*, *65*(3), 538–543. DOI: 10.1177/00076503251406457

Alem.AI. (2025). AILA digital influencer profile. Instagram. https://www.instagram.com/reel/DPGjxKfDCgt/

Anderson, B. (1991). *Imagined communities: Reflections on the origin and spread of nationalism*. Verso.

Asharari, T. M. H. (2023). An analytical study of the social studies course at the secondary education stage (course system): The joint program in the Kingdom of Saudi Arabia in promoting awareness of national identity in line with Vision 2030. *Information Sciences Letters*, *12*(2), 757–773. DOI: 10.18576/isl/120218

Blokhin, I. N. (2016). Understanding in the system of mass communication effects. In S. G. Korkonosenko (Ed.), The age of information: Media in the modern world. St. Petersburg readings: Proceedings of the 55th International Forum (April 21-22, 2016). Higher School of Journalism and Mass Communications.

Chen, J. (2026). AI photography and cultural memory: Revisualizing the queer histories of Bugis Street in Singapore through layered gazes. *Humanities & Social Sciences Communications*, *13*(1), 172. Advance online publication. DOI: 10.1057/s41599-025-06473-5

Code of Administrative Offenses of the Republic of Kazakhstan. (2014, July 5). https://adilet.zan.kz

Code of Ethics of the Journalist of the Republic of Kazakhstan. (2012, October 30). https://online.zakon.kz

Constitution of the Republic of Kazakhstan. (1995, August 30). https://adilet.zan.kz

Criminal Code of the Republic of Kazakhstan. (2014, July 3). https://adilet.zan.kz

Djumanova, S. B. (2025). AI-driven media literacy skills of Uzbek journalists: Key indicators and challenges. Scientific Electronic Journal. *Foreign Languages in Uzbekistan*, *11*(6), 198–215. DOI: 10.36078/1767696698

Dyakova, E. G. (2003). Mass political communication in agenda-setting theory: From effect to process. *Political Science (Wellington, N.Z.)*, (3), 42–44.

Grivennaya, L. A. (2018). *National identity: Theory and practice*. Publising House of Kozybayev North Kazakhstan University.

Hjarvard, S. (2008). *The mediatization of religion: A theory of the media as agents of religious change*. Northern Lights. *Film and Media Studies Yearbook*, *6*(1), 9–26. DOI: 10.1386/nl.6.1.9_1

How Kazakhstanis relate to artificial intelligence: trust, irritation and hope. (2025, November 13). *Tribune.kz*. https://tribune.kz/kak-kazahstantsy-otnosyatsya-k-iskusstvennomu-intellektu-doverie-razdrazhenie-i-nadezhdy/

Insebayeva, S., & Insebayeva, N. (2021). The power of ambiguity: National symbols, nation-building, and political legitimacy in Kazakhstan. *Europe-Asia Studies*, *74*(4), 660–682. DOI: 10.1080/09668136.2021.1912296

Ismanov, A., Kupuyeva, N., Stanalieva, G., Toktogulova, M., & Turdubaeva, E. (2023). *From hate speech to nonviolent communication*. Prevention Media.

Law "On Artificial Intelligence" of the Republic of Kazakhstan. (2025, November 230). https://adilet.zan.kz

Lee, J.-Y. (2026). Silenced by non-consensual deepfakes? Perceived threat and online self-censorship among female users: Mediating roles of perceived control, belief in a just world, and passive SNS use. *Telematics and Informatics Reports*, *21*, 100279. Advance online publication. DOI: 10.1016/j.teler.2025.100279

Lippmann, W. (2004). *Public opinion*. Institute of the Public Opinion Foundation.

Liu, Y., & Wang, H. (2026). Application of deep learning for transformation of Chinese traditional cultural narrative patterns and enhancement of cultural identity empowered by AIGC. *Scientific Reports*, *16*(1), 2505. Advance online publication. DOI: 10.1038/s41598-025-32302-5 PMID: 41444384

Ma, Y., Zhang, X., Ren, J., Wang, R., Wang, M., & Chen, Y. (2026). Linguistic features of AI mis/disinformation and the detection limits of LLMs. *Nature Communications*, *17*(1), 456. Advance online publication. DOI: 10.1038/s41467-025-67145-1 PMID: 41372163

Mansfield, C. D., Bauer, J. J., Booker, J., Grysman, A., Singer, J., & Fivush, R. (2026). What might we learn about autobiographical narrative processing from artificial intelligence? *Humanities & Social Sciences Communications*, *13*(1), 182. Advance online publication. DOI: 10.1057/s41599-025-06426-y

Marinovich, A. (2015, March 21). The role of social media in shaping ethnic identity during the political transformations of the Arab Spring. *Electronic Scientific Archive.* https://elar.urfu.ru/bitstream/10995/35366/1/iimvmm_2015_21.pdf

Mkrtchyan, N. (2014). The notion of "Kazakhness" behind the symbolic nation-building of Kazakhstan. *SSRN*, *9*(1–2), 16–38. DOI: 10.2139/ssrn.2458368

Moddelmog-Anweiler, E., & Mach, Z. (2022). Religious identities and religious pluralism in Central and Eastern Europe. In *Religion in the public sphere in Central and Eastern Europe* (pp. 13–61).

Muratbekov, B. (2026, February 12). "Beautiful, but not real": how AI bloggers are taking over the Internet and why it can be dangerous. TengriNews. https://tengrinews.kz/curious/krasivyie-nenastoyaschie-ii-blogeryi-zahvatyivayut-kaznet-592449/

Nevokshanova, A. A., & Stefanchikov, I. V. (2019). The role of print media in shaping Uruguayan national identity in the first third of the 20th century. *Litera*, (2), 78–96. DOI: 10.25136/2409-8698.2019.2.29945

Noelle-Neumann, E. (1996). *The spiral of silence: Public opinion—Our social skin.* Progress-Akademiya; Mir.

Nortio, E., Jasinskaja-Lahti, I., Hämäläinen, M., & Pakkasvirta, J. (2022). Fear of the Russian bear? Negotiating Finnish national identity online. *Nations and Nationalism*, *28*(3), 861–876. DOI: 10.1111/nana.12832

Pehlivanoglu, D., Zhu, M., Zhen, J., Gagnon-Roberge, A. A., Kern, R. K., Woodard, D., Cahill, B. S., & Ebner, N. C. (2026). Is this real? Susceptibility to deepfakes in machines and humans. *Cognitive Research: Principles and Implications*, *11*(1), 3. Advance online publication. DOI: 10.1186/s41235-025-00700-y PMID: 41501543

Photos of Kazakh intelligentsia reinterpreted with the help of AI. (2024, January 31). *TengriNews.* https://tengrinews.kz/curious/foto-kazahskoy-intelligentsii-pereosmyislili-s-pomoschyu-ii-524824/

Pinker, S. (2021). *Enlightenment now: The case for reason, science, humanism, and progress.* Alpina Publisher.

Ruzmatova, M. (2025, April 4). Qazcontent JSC conducted an experiment on the introduction of AI in media production. *El.kz.* https://el.kz/ru/ao-qazcontent-provelo-eksperiment-po-vnedreniyu-ii-v-mediaproizvodstvo_400018594/?utm

Sanzharova, D. (2022, November 12). Karakat Abden proposed imposing a higher tax on Kazakh women who marry foreign nationals. *NewTimes.kz.* https://newtimes.kz/vybory2022/159529-karakat-abden-predlagaet-oblozhit-bolshim-nalogov-kazashek-za-brak-s-inostrancami

Sarkar, S., & Ghosh, A. (2024). *Leveraging artificial intelligence to enhance media literacy and combat misinformation.* SSRN Electronic Journal. DOI: 10.2139/ssrn.4991258

Sharma, S., & Selwal, A. (2026). Potential of artificial intelligence in deepfake media: From generation to detection mechanisms, state-of-the-art, and challenges. *Computer Science Review, 60,* 100866. Advance online publication. DOI: 10.1016/j.cosrev.2025.100866

Silverman, C. (2015). *Lies, damn lies, and viral content.* Tow Center for Digital Journalism, Columbia University. DOI: 10.7916/D8Q81RHH

Smagulov, A. (2026, January 8). The blogger who conquered Kaznet turned out to be an AI model. *Kursiv.media.* https://kz.kursiv.media/2026-01-08/assm-zamerzshee-ozero-na-severe-kazakhstana-priznali-idealnym-dlya-kataniya-na-konkakh-2

Urozbaeva, D. (2020). Nation-building in Kazakhstan: The role of national symbols. *Bulletin of the Kazakh-German University,* (2), 32–38.

Vaitovich, O. (2019, August 2). In northern Kazakhstan, the number of applicants wishing to study at local universities has decreased. *Petropavlovsk.News.* https://xn--80aeaj2aesddcjte.news/na-severe-kazakhstana-umenshilos-kolichestvo-zhelayushhikh-uchitsya-v-mestnom-vuze

Velilaeva, L. R., & Abdullaeva, N. R. (2020). The concept of "national identity": Theoretical and literary aspects of research. *Universum: Philology and Art Studies, 6*(73), 26–28.

Zhylkybayeva, D. (2022, February 14). Social media users demanded the revocation of citizenship from Kazakh women who married foreign nationals. *Caravan.kz.* https://www.caravan.kz/news/v-socsetyakh-potrebovali-lishit-grazhdanstva-kazashek-vyshedshikh-zamuzh-za-inostrancev-816312/

Chapter 12
Media and Technology Literacy in the Age of AI: Frameworks, Competencies, and Educational Imperatives

Deepak Gupta
http://orcid.org/0000-0003-3929-1362
Institute of Technology and Management, Gwalior, India

Anbarjon Kurbanboeva
Mamun University, Khiva, Uzbekistan

Nurullaeva Shakhlo
Karshi State University, Uzbekistan

Yusubov Jaloliddin
National University of Uzbekistan, Uzbekistan

Guljahon Ozodova
Urgench State Pedagogical Institute, Urgench, Uzbekistan

Nilufar Samandarova
Urgench State University, Uzbekistan

Farkhod Egamberdiyev
University of Information Technologies and Management, Karshi, Uzbekistan

ABSTRACT

This chapter examines the evolving landscape of media and technology literacy in the context of artificial intelligence integration in education. Drawing on interdisciplinary frameworks and empirical research, it explores how digital competencies, critical media literacy, and AI literacy converge to form essential 21st-century skills. The chapter analyzes current challenges in technology adoption, including digital divides, misinformation, and the need for adaptive pedagogical approaches. It presents comprehensive frameworks for developing AI literacy among students and educators, emphasizing the importance of ethical considerations, human rights implications, and sustainable practices.

DOI: 10.4018/979-8-2600-2163-7.ch012

1. INTRODUCTION

The rapid advancement of artificial intelligence technologies has fundamentally transformed the educational landscape, creating unprecedented opportunities and challenges for learners, educators, and institutions worldwide. As AI systems become increasingly integrated into daily life and educational practices, the need for comprehensive media and technology literacy has never been more critical. This chapter explores the intersection of traditional media literacy, digital competence, and emerging AI literacy frameworks, examining how these interconnected domains shape contemporary educational paradigms.

The contemporary educational environment demands a reconceptualization of literacy that extends beyond conventional reading and writing skills to encompass critical engagement with digital media, technological tools, and artificial intelligence systems. Media literacy, traditionally focused on understanding and critically analyzing media messages, has evolved to address the complexities of digital environments where information flows continuously, algorithms shape content exposure, and AI-generated materials blur the boundaries between human and machine-created content (Turner et al., 2025; Albardía et al., 2025). These developments necessitate new pedagogical approaches that prepare learners to navigate algorithmically mediated information ecosystems while maintaining critical autonomy and ethical judgment.

Technology literacy encompasses a broader spectrum of competencies, including the ability to effectively use digital tools, understand technological systems, and adapt to evolving technological landscapes. As Tinmaz et al. (2022) note in their systematic review, digital literacy represents a multifaceted construct that integrates technical skills, cognitive abilities, and socio-emotional competencies necessary for meaningful participation in digital society. The integration of AI into educational contexts adds another layer of complexity, requiring learners to understand not only how to use AI tools but also how these systems function, their limitations, and their societal implications. This multidimensional understanding forms the foundation for what we term integrated literacy in the age of AI.

The emergence of generative AI technologies, such as large language models and multimodal AI systems, has accelerated the urgency of developing comprehensive literacy frameworks. These technologies possess capabilities that can enhance learning experiences, automate routine tasks, and provide personalized educational support. However, they also raise critical questions about academic integrity, information reliability, algorithmic bias, and the preservation of human agency in learning processes. As Chiu (2024) emphasizes, transforming higher education with generative AI requires careful consideration of pedagogical approaches, ethical frameworks, and institutional policies. The challenge lies not in rejecting these powerful tools but in developing the literacy competencies necessary to use them wisely and ethically.

This chapter addresses several key questions that frame the current discourse on media and technology literacy in the age of AI. First, how do traditional media literacy frameworks adapt to incorporate AI-specific competencies? Second, what are the essential components of AI literacy for both students and educators? Third, how do factors such as self-efficacy, anxiety, and attitudes influence technology acceptance and effective use? Fourth, what role do cultural contexts and global perspectives play in shaping literacy initiatives? Fifth, how can educational institutions develop sustainable, ethical, and inclusive approaches to technology and media literacy education? These questions guide our examination of the evolving literacy landscape and inform our recommendations for educational practice.

Beyond these foundational questions, the chapter examines how educational institutions can balance the integration of AI technologies with the preservation of critical thinking, human creativity, and ethical reasoning. The rapid deployment of AI tools in educational settings often outpaces the development of appropriate pedagogical frameworks and literacy curricula. This temporal gap creates challenges for educators who must navigate the integration of powerful new technologies while ensuring that students develop the competencies necessary to use these tools responsibly and effectively. Addressing this gap requires coordinated efforts among educators, administrators, policymakers, and technology developers to create coherent approaches to literacy education.

The democratization of AI technologies has made powerful computational capabilities accessible to broader populations, yet this accessibility does not automatically translate into meaningful literacy. Students may interact with AI systems daily through recommendation algorithms, virtual assistants, and automated services without understanding the underlying mechanisms or implications of these interactions. Developing AI literacy therefore requires intentional educational interventions that make visible the invisible processes shaping digital experiences and empower learners to engage critically with AI-mediated environments. This visibility is essential for developing informed citizenship in increasingly AI-dependent societies.

Furthermore, the chapter recognizes that literacy education cannot be divorced from considerations of equity and social justice. Digital divides persist globally, creating disparities in access to technology, quality literacy education, and opportunities to develop advanced digital competencies. These divides intersect with existing social inequalities based on socioeconomic status, geography, gender, race, and other factors. Addressing these equity concerns requires comprehensive approaches that attend to infrastructure development, culturally responsive pedagogy, and systemic barriers that prevent equitable literacy development. As we will explore, the challenge is not simply providing access to technology but ensuring that all learners have opportunities to develop meaningful competencies.

Figure 1. Integrated Model of Media and Technology Literacy in the AI Age

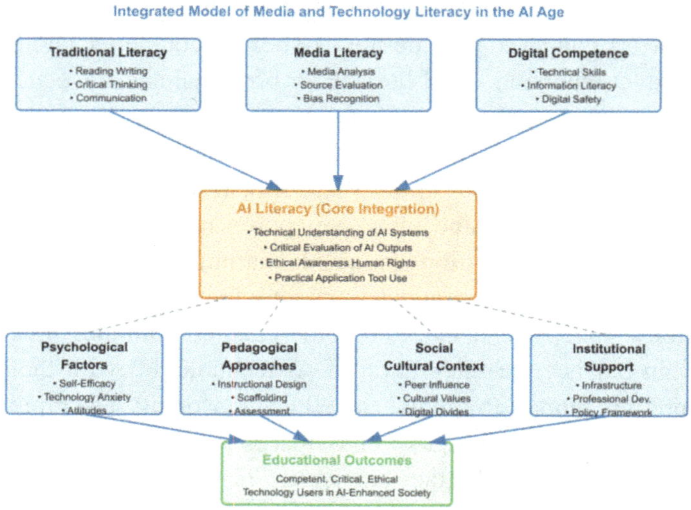

Figure 1 presents an integrated model that synthesizes traditional literacy, media literacy, and digital competence as foundational elements that converge into AI literacy as the core competency for the contemporary era. This model illustrates how psychological, pedagogical, social, and institutional factors interact to shape literacy development and educational outcomes. The model emphasizes that effective AI literacy education requires attention to all these dimensions simultaneously, rather than focusing narrowly on technical skills or isolated competencies.

The chapter is structured to provide a comprehensive examination of these questions through six major sections. Following this introduction, Section 2 presents theoretical frameworks and conceptual foundations that underpin contemporary approaches to media and technology literacy. Section 3 explores AI literacy frameworks and competencies, drawing on recent research to identify essential knowledge domains and skills. Section 4 examines factors influencing technology acceptance and adoption, including psychological, pedagogical, and institutional dimensions. Section 5 addresses global perspectives and contextual considerations, highlighting the importance of culturally responsive approaches. Section 6 discusses challenges, opportunities, and future directions for research and practice. The chapter concludes with practical recommendations for educators, policymakers, and researchers working to advance literacy education in the age of AI.

2. THEORETICAL FRAMEWORKS AND CONCEPTUAL FOUNDATIONS

2.1 Evolving Definitions of Literacy

The concept of literacy has undergone significant transformation in response to technological advancement and changing communication practices. Traditional literacy, defined primarily as the ability to read and write text, has expanded to encompass multiple modes of meaning-making and communication. Kalantzis and Cope (2024) argue that literacy in the time of artificial intelligence requires a fundamental reconceptualization that recognizes how AI technologies mediate human communication, knowledge production, and cognitive processes. This expanded view positions literacy as a dynamic, socially situated practice that adapts to technological contexts while maintaining core critical thinking competencies.

The evolution of literacy definitions reflects broader shifts in how societies produce, distribute, and consume information. In pre-digital eras, literacy focused primarily on decoding printed text and producing written communication. The emergence of mass media expanded literacy to include critical analysis of television, radio, and print journalism. Digital technologies further broadened literacy to encompass navigation of hypertext, evaluation of online sources, and creation of multimedia content. Each technological shift has not replaced previous forms of literacy but rather layered new competencies onto existing foundations, creating increasingly complex literacy demands.

Media literacy, as conceptualized by contemporary scholars, extends beyond simple media consumption to encompass critical analysis, evaluation, and creation of media messages across various platforms and formats. Turner et al. (2025) emphasize that digital media literacy represents an essential component of children's development in screen-based environments, requiring competencies in understanding media construction, recognizing persuasive techniques, identifying bias, and evaluating source credibility. These competencies become increasingly important as media ecosystems grow more complex and AI-generated content becomes more prevalent. The challenge for educators is teaching students to apply critical frameworks to content whose origins and production processes may be obscured or deliberately concealed.

Digital literacy represents another crucial dimension of contemporary literacy frameworks. As Tinmaz et al. (2022) document in their systematic review, digital literacy encompasses technical skills, information literacy, communication competencies, and the ability to navigate digital environments safely and ethically. The integration of these various literacy domains reflects a recognition that effective participation in digital society requires multifaceted competencies that span technical, cognitive, and social dimensions. Moreover, digital literacy is not simply about using technology but about understanding how technology shapes social practices, power relations, and knowledge structures.

Multimodal literacy has emerged as a particularly relevant framework for understanding communication in AI-enhanced environments. Lam and Ni (2024) demonstrate how AI-assisted portfolio assessment can support multiliteracies development, enabling students to engage with texts, images, videos, and interactive media in integrated ways. This approach recognizes that meaning-making in contemporary contexts often involves simultaneous engagement with multiple modes of representation and communication, requiring learners to develop sophisticated interpretive and productive capacities. AI technologies both facilitate and complicate multimodal communication, offering new tools for creation while raising questions about authenticity and authorship.

2.2 Critical Media Literacy and Misinformation

Critical media literacy has gained particular urgency in an era characterized by information abundance, algorithmic content curation, and sophisticated misinformation campaigns. Gaultney et al. (2022) examine the intersection of political polarization, misinformation, and media literacy, demonstrating how partisan media ecosystems and confirmation bias create environments where misinformation flourishes. Their research underscores the importance of developing critical thinking skills that enable individuals to recognize manipulative techniques, verify information sources, and resist emotional manipulation. In AI-mediated information environments, these skills become even more essential as algorithmic amplification can rapidly spread false or misleading content to vast audiences.

The challenge of misinformation has been compounded by the emergence of AI-generated content, including deepfakes, synthetic media, and algorithmically optimized disinformation. Traditional media literacy approaches, which focused primarily on identifying human-created bias and manipulation, must now contend with content generated by systems that can mimic human communication patterns with increasing sophistication. This necessitates new frameworks for evaluating information authenticity and understanding the mechanisms through which AI systems can be weaponized for misinformation purposes. Educators must help students develop not only skepticism about questionable content but also strategies for verification and fact-checking in environments where traditional markers of credibility may be unreliable.

Mustapha et al. (2024) highlight a critical misconception among students in Anglophone West African countries regarding the relationship between media literacy and critical thinking in combating misinformation. Their research reveals that many students view media literacy tools as mere technical instruments rather than cognitive frameworks that support critical evaluation and analysis. This finding emphasizes the need for educational approaches that explicitly connect technological competencies with critical thinking practices, ensuring that learners understand how to apply analytical frameworks to digital media environments. The misconception that technology itself provides protection against misinformation without the application of critical judgment represents a significant vulnerability that educators must address.

Albardía et al. (2025) explore the potential, challenges, and opportunities of technology in developing critical media literacy, arguing that educational technologies can serve as powerful tools for teaching critical analysis when integrated with appropriate pedagogical frameworks. Their work emphasizes that technology itself is not sufficient for developing critical media literacy; rather, educators must design learning experiences that leverage technological affordances while maintaining focus on critical thinking, ethical reasoning, and civic engagement. This pedagogical integration requires careful planning and ongoing professional development to ensure that technology enhances rather than supplants critical literacy instruction.

2.3 Technology Acceptance Models and Behavioral Frameworks

Understanding technology adoption and acceptance represents a crucial component of technology literacy research. The Technology Acceptance Model (TAM) and its extensions provide theoretical frameworks for understanding the psychological and contextual factors that influence how individuals engage with technological systems. Chen et al. (2024) extend TAM to examine college students' use of AI for second language learning, identifying self-efficacy, anxiety, and attitude as key factors that mediate technology acceptance and use. Their research demonstrates that technology adoption is not simply a matter of availability or mandates but depends fundamentally on users' psychological readiness and perceptions of value.

Figure 2. Technology Acceptance Framework: Factors Influencing AI Adoption in Education

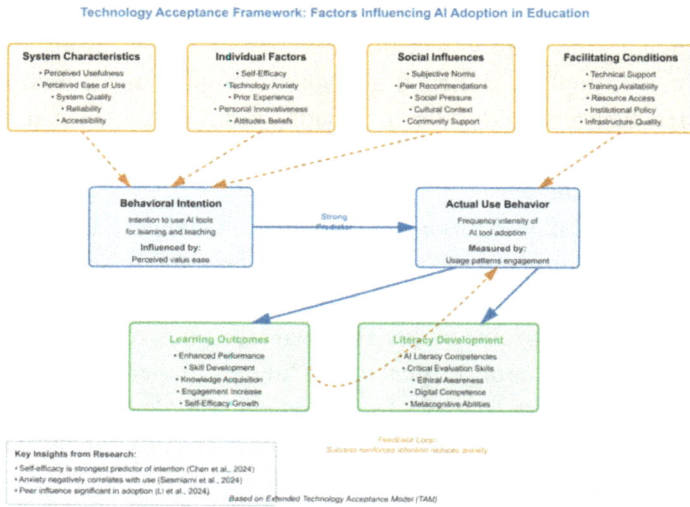

Figure 2 illustrates a comprehensive technology acceptance framework that synthesizes multiple factors influencing AI adoption in educational contexts. The model shows how system characteristics, individual factors, social influences, and facilitating conditions collectively shape behavioral intentions and actual use behaviors, which in turn affect learning outcomes and literacy development. The bidirectional arrows represent feedback loops through which successful experiences reinforce positive attitudes and reduce anxiety, creating virtuous cycles of engagement and competence development.

Self-efficacy, defined as an individual's belief in their capacity to use technology effectively, emerges as a particularly influential factor across multiple studies. Sesmiarni et al. (2024) demonstrate how self-efficacy influences adoption of learning management systems in the Education 4.0 era, showing that students with higher technology self-efficacy are more likely to engage with digital learning platforms and persist through technical challenges. This finding has important implications for literacy education, suggesting that building confidence and competence should proceed in tandem. Effective literacy instruction must attend not only to skill development but also to the development of self-efficacy through scaffolded experiences, constructive feedback, and opportunities for successful technology engagement.

Technology anxiety represents the inverse of self-efficacy, manifesting as apprehension, stress, or fear associated with technology use. Research by Chen et al. (2024) reveals that anxiety about AI technologies can significantly impede learning outcomes and technology adoption, particularly when students lack adequate support or preparation. Addressing technology anxiety requires careful pedagogical design that provides scaffolding, builds confidence gradually, and creates safe environments for experimentation and learning from mistakes. The reduction of anxiety is not merely about making students comfortable with technology but about developing genuine competence that provides rational grounds for confidence.

Li et al. (2024) examine college students' acceptance of translation technologies, revealing how perceived usefulness, ease of use, and subjective norms influence adoption patterns. Their research demonstrates that technology acceptance varies significantly based on task contexts, prior experiences, and social influences. These findings suggest that literacy education must attend not only to technical skills but also to shaping attitudes, perceptions, and social norms around technology use. Creating learning communities where productive technology use is modeled and valued can significantly influence individual adoption decisions and ongoing engagement patterns.

3. AI LITERACY FRAMEWORKS AND COMPETENCIES

3.1 Defining AI Literacy: Core Dimensions and Components

AI literacy represents an emerging domain that extends traditional technology literacy to encompass understanding of artificial intelligence systems, their capabilities, limitations, and societal implications. Chiu et al. (2024) propose a comprehensive framework that defines AI literacy as encompassing multiple dimensions: technical understanding of AI systems, critical evaluation of AI outputs, ethical awareness of AI implications, and practical skills for effective AI use. This multidimensional approach recognizes that AI literacy involves both conceptual understanding and practical application, requiring learners to develop capabilities across cognitive, technical, and ethical domains.

Table 1. Framework for AI Literacy Competencies in Education

Competency Domain	Key Components	Educational Implications
Technical Understanding	Machine learning concepts, algorithms, training data, model limitations	Requires conceptual explanations balanced with hands-on experiences; avoid overly technical jargon
Critical Evaluation	Assessing AI output reliability, recognizing bias, evaluating appropriateness for context	Integrate with critical thinking curricula; use authentic evaluation tasks and case studies
Ethical Awareness	Privacy, bias, accountability, human rights implications, societal impact	Embed ethical discussions throughout curriculum; use real-world case studies and dilemmas
Practical Application	Using AI tools effectively, prompt engineering, integrating AI into workflows	Provide authentic practice opportunities; scaffold skill development progressively
Metacognitive Awareness	Monitoring learning processes, evaluating tool effectiveness, decision-making about AI use	Encourage reflection on learning; teach decision-making frameworks for tool selection

Note: This framework synthesizes findings from Chiu et al. (2024), Allen and Kendeou (2023), and Ng et al. (2023).

Allen and Kendeou (2023) present an interdisciplinary framework for AI literacy in education (ED-AI lit) that integrates insights from education, psychology, computer science, and information science. Their framework emphasizes four core components: understanding AI capabilities and limitations, recognizing AI applications in various contexts, evaluating AI-generated information critically, and using AI tools responsibly and ethically. This interdisciplinary approach reflects the complex nature of AI literacy, which requires knowledge that spans multiple domains. The framework acknowledges that AI literacy cannot be reduced to technical knowledge alone but must encompass broader understandings of how AI affects cognition, learning, social interactions, and societal structures.

The technical dimension of AI literacy involves understanding fundamental concepts such as machine learning, neural networks, training data, algorithms, and model limitations. However, as Ng et al. (2023) emphasize in their review of AI literacy education in secondary schools, technical knowledge should be balanced with critical understanding of how AI systems are developed, deployed, and regulated. Students need to understand not only what AI can do but also how it works at a conceptual level and what constraints govern its operation. This understanding need not involve deep mathematical or programming knowledge but should provide sufficient conceptual grasp to support informed reasoning about AI capabilities and limitations.

Critical evaluation represents another essential component of AI literacy. As AI-generated content becomes increasingly sophisticated and widespread, learners must develop skills for assessing the reliability, accuracy, and appropriateness of AI outputs. This includes understanding how training data influences AI behavior, recognizing potential biases in AI systems, and evaluating whether AI-generated information is suitable for specific contexts and purposes. The challenge is that AI systems can produce content that appears authoritative and well-reasoned while being factually incorrect, biased, or contextually inappropriate. Developing the discernment to identify these issues requires both technical understanding and critical thinking skills.

3.2 Essential Competencies for Students

Students in AI-enhanced educational environments require a diverse set of competencies that enable them to engage productively with AI technologies while maintaining critical thinking and ethical awareness. Lo et al. (2025) examine how generative AI impacts essay revision and student engagement, finding that students who possess strong foundational writing skills combined with AI literacy achieve superior outcomes compared to those who rely on AI without critical evaluation. This research underscores the importance of developing traditional academic competencies alongside AI-specific skills. AI tools are most valuable when used by learners who understand the domains in which they are working and can critically evaluate AI-generated suggestions or content.

Digital competence emerges as a foundational requirement for effective AI use. Pan et al. (2024) investigate the impact of digital competence and personal innovativeness on learning behavior, revealing that students with strong digital skills demonstrate greater adaptability when engaging with AI-enhanced learning environments. Their research emphasizes that digital competence serves as a prerequisite for AI literacy, providing the foundational skills necessary for navigating complex technological systems. This finding suggests that AI literacy education cannot begin from scratch but must build on existing digital literacy foundations, requiring coordinated curriculum development across educational levels.

Metacognitive awareness represents another crucial competency domain. Students must develop the ability to monitor their own learning processes, evaluate the effectiveness of AI tools for specific tasks, and make informed decisions about when and how to use AI assistance. Guo and Li (2024) demonstrate how electronic portfolio-based writing instruction enhances metacognitive awareness alongside writing self-efficacy, suggesting that well-designed technological interventions can support development of both domain-specific skills and higher-order thinking competencies. Metacognitive skills enable students to approach AI tools strategically, recognizing when AI assistance is beneficial and when it might impede learning or development of essential skills.

Ethical reasoning and responsible use constitute essential components of student AI competencies. Students must understand issues related to privacy, intellectual property, algorithmic bias, and the societal implications of AI deployment. As Chan and Lo (2025) argue in their study on human rights impact with AI advancement, educational programs must explicitly address how AI technologies affect fundamental rights and freedoms, preparing students to engage thoughtfully with these complex ethical dimensions. This ethical education cannot be abstract but must engage students with concrete scenarios and dilemmas that help them develop practical ethical reasoning capabilities applicable to real-world AI use contexts.

3.3 Educator Competencies and Professional Development Needs

Educators play a pivotal role in fostering AI literacy among students, yet many lack adequate preparation for this responsibility. Qian et al. (2025) examine the influence of artificial intelligence on higher education reform and talent cultivation, identifying faculty development as a critical factor in successful AI integration. Their research reveals significant gaps between the AI competencies educators possess and those they need to effectively guide student learning in AI-enhanced environments. This gap is particularly concerning given that educators must not only use AI tools themselves but also help students develop critical perspectives on AI technologies.

Pedagogical AI literacy represents a specialized form of AI literacy focused on understanding how AI can enhance teaching and learning. Chiu (2024) provides recommendations for transforming higher education with generative AI, emphasizing that educators need competencies in designing AI-enhanced learning experiences, evaluating AI tools for pedagogical purposes, and supporting students in developing critical AI literacy. This pedagogical dimension extends beyond personal AI use to encompass facilitating student learning about and with AI. Educators must understand not only how to use AI tools but also how these tools affect learning processes, student motivation, and educational outcomes.

Professional development programs for educators must address multiple dimensions simultaneously. Technical training should equip educators with practical skills for using AI tools in their teaching, including understanding different types of AI systems, their appropriate applications, and their limitations. Pedagogical preparation should focus on designing effective learning experiences that integrate AI meaningfully, maintaining learning objectives while leveraging AI affordances. Critical literacy development should enable educators to evaluate AI systems, recognize their limitations, and address ethical implications with students. Finally, professional learning should support educators in developing confidence and reducing anxiety around AI adoption through hands-on experiences and peer support.

Godsk and Møller (2024) examine strategies for engaging students in higher education with educational technology, finding that educator attitudes and competencies significantly influence student engagement and learning outcomes. Their research suggests that professional development programs must attend not only to skill development but also to shaping educator beliefs, attitudes, and self-efficacy regarding technology use. This holistic approach recognizes that effective technology integration depends on both competence and confidence. Educators who feel overwhelmed or skeptical about AI technologies are unlikely to integrate them effectively or to foster positive student attitudes toward AI literacy development.

4. FACTORS INFLUENCING TECHNOLOGY ACCEPTANCE AND USE

4.1 Psychological Factors: Self-Efficacy and Anxiety

Psychological factors play a crucial role in determining how individuals engage with technology and AI systems. Self-efficacy, particularly technology self-efficacy, emerges consistently across research as a primary predictor of technology acceptance and effective use. Rodafinos et al. (2024) explore the impact of digital competence and technology acceptance on academic performance in physical education and sports science students, demonstrating that students with higher technology self-efficacy demonstrate greater persistence, achieve better outcomes, and report higher satisfaction with technology-enhanced learning. This relationship between self-efficacy and outcomes creates either virtuous or vicious cycles depending on initial experiences with technology.

The relationship between self-efficacy and technology use operates through multiple mechanisms. First, individuals with high technology self-efficacy are more likely to attempt challenging tasks and persist through difficulties, viewing obstacles as learning opportunities rather than evidence of incompetence. Second, they experience less anxiety when confronting new technologies, creating a positive feedback loop that reinforces engagement and learning. Third, they demonstrate greater metacognitive monitoring, enabling them to evaluate their progress and adjust strategies effectively. These mechanisms collectively contribute to more successful technology adoption and skill development, highlighting the importance of building self-efficacy alongside technical competencies.

Technology anxiety represents a significant barrier to effective technology use and literacy development. Chen et al. (2024) examine college students' use of AI for second language learning, finding that anxiety about AI technologies correlates negatively with usage frequency and learning outcomes. Students experiencing high AI anxiety tend to avoid using AI tools, limiting their opportunities to develop competence and reduce their anxiety through successful experiences. Breaking this cycle requires careful instructional design that reduces anxiety while building confidence. This may involve starting with simpler applications, providing extensive support, creating low-stakes practice environments, and celebrating small successes to build momentum.

Strategies for building self-efficacy and reducing anxiety include providing graduated challenges that build competence progressively, offering abundant support and scaffolding during initial learning stages, creating safe environments where mistakes are viewed as learning opportunities, and highlighting success experiences that demonstrate growing competence. Guo and Li (2024) demonstrate how electronic portfolio-based instruction enhances writing self-efficacy, suggesting that well-designed technological interventions can simultaneously develop domain skills and technology confidence. The key is ensuring that technology use provides genuine opportunities for competence development while managing challenge levels to maintain engagement without overwhelming learners.

4.2 Pedagogical and Institutional Factors

Pedagogical approaches significantly influence technology acceptance and literacy development. Chasubuta et al. (2024) examine technological literacy in using learning management systems among students in Tanzanian higher education institutions, finding that pedagogical integration quality predicts student engagement more strongly than technology features or availability. Their research demonstrates that technology adoption depends not merely on access but on how educators integrate technology into meaningful learning experiences. Technology becomes valuable when it serves clear learning objectives, supports authentic tasks, and enhances rather than complicates learning processes.

Effective pedagogical integration requires alignment between learning objectives, instructional activities, and technology affordances. Technology should support and enhance learning goals rather than serving as an end in itself. Levido (2024) explores media literacy and the concept of technologies in primary school classrooms, arguing that education must move beyond technical skills to emphasize critical understanding of how technologies shape communication, knowledge, and social relationships. This approach positions technology as a subject of inquiry rather than simply a tool for instruction, encouraging students to develop metacognitive awareness of how technology affects their thinking and learning.

Institutional factors create enabling or constraining contexts for technology literacy development. Infrastructure availability, technical support quality, professional development opportunities, and institutional policies all influence how technology is adopted and used. Sesmiarni et al. (2024) examine adoption of learning management systems in the Education 4.0 era, identifying institutional support as a critical mediating factor between individual readiness and actual technology use. Institutions that provide robust support systems, adequate resources, and clear policies facilitate more effective technology integration. Conversely, institutions that deploy technology without adequate support infrastructure often see poor adoption and suboptimal outcomes regardless of individual user motivation or competence.

Assessment and evaluation practices also shape technology adoption patterns. When assessment systems reward technology use without evaluating learning quality, students may engage with technology superficially, focusing on demonstrating technology use rather than leveraging technology for deep learning. Conversely, when assessment focuses on deep learning outcomes enabled by technology, students are more likely to develop meaningful competencies. Lam and Ni (2024) demonstrate how AI-assisted portfolio assessment can support multiliteracies development when assessment criteria emphasize critical thinking, creativity, and multimodal communication rather than mere technology use. The design of assessment systems thus plays a crucial role in shaping how students approach and value technology in learning contexts.

4.3 Social and Cultural Influences on Technology Adoption

Social and cultural contexts fundamentally shape how individuals and communities engage with technology. Technology acceptance varies significantly across cultural contexts, influenced by cultural values, social norms, educational traditions, and technological infrastructure. Pan et al. (2024) examine the role of digitalization in higher education quality, finding that cultural attitudes toward innovation and change significantly moderate the relationship between digital competence and learning outcomes. In cultures that embrace technological innovation, students may approach new technologies with enthusiasm and optimism. In cultures that emphasize traditional approaches or express skepticism about technological change, students may be more cautious or resistant.

Peer influence and social norms play particularly important roles in technology adoption among students. Li et al. (2024) investigate college students' acceptance of translation technologies, revealing that subjective norms and peer recommendations strongly influence whether students adopt and continue using translation tools. This finding highlights the importance of cultivating positive technology cultures within educational communities where productive technology use is normalized and supported. When students observe peers using technology effectively and receiving recognition for technology-enabled achievements, they are more likely to adopt similar practices. Educational institutions can leverage this social influence by creating communities of practice, showcasing exemplary technology use, and fostering peer learning around technology integration.

Digital divides represent persistent challenges that intersect with social, economic, and geographic factors. Boshoff and Fafowora (2025) examine digital media literacy in Africa, identifying significant disparities in technology access, infrastructure quality, and literacy education opportunities. These divides create unequal opportunities for developing technology literacy, potentially exacerbating existing educational inequalities. Students from well-resourced backgrounds may have extensive experience with diverse technologies, high-quality devices, reliable internet access, and supportive learning environments. Students from disadvantaged backgrounds may face limited access, outdated equipment, unreliable connectivity, and lack of technical support. These disparities in access create cumulative advantages and disadvantages that widen over time without intentional intervention.

Cultural responsiveness in technology literacy education involves recognizing that technology is not culturally neutral. Different communities have varying relationships with technology, distinct technological traditions, and diverse perspectives on appropriate technology use. Almakaty (2025) analyzes emerging trends in communication and media education globally, demonstrating how different cultural contexts shape media literacy curricula and pedagogical approaches. Effective literacy education must honor cultural diversity while ensuring all learners develop essential competencies. This requires understanding local contexts, engaging community stakeholders in curriculum development, and adapting pedagogical approaches to align with cultural values and communication practices.

5. GLOBAL PERSPECTIVES AND CONTEXTUAL CONSIDERATIONS

5.1 Digital Divides and Equity Issues in Global Context

Digital divides manifest in multiple forms, including disparities in technology access, internet connectivity, device quality, technical support, and educational opportunities. Boshoff and Fafowora (2025) propose a research agenda for digital media literacy in Africa, highlighting how infrastructure limitations, economic constraints, and policy gaps create barriers to meaningful technology literacy development. Their work emphasizes that addressing digital divides requires comprehensive approaches that tackle technological, educational, and systemic challenges simultaneously. Simple provision of devices or internet access proves insufficient without corresponding investments in technical infrastructure, educator preparation, curriculum development, and ongoing support systems.

Figure 3. Comparative Analysis of Digital Competence Levels Across Educational Contexts

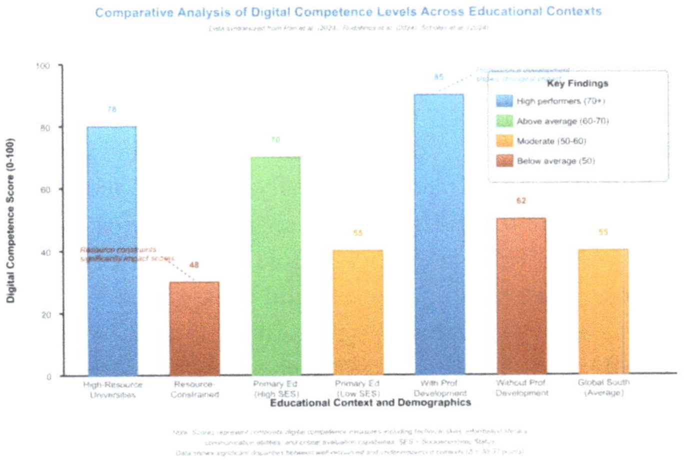

Figure 3 presents comparative data on digital competence levels across diverse educational contexts, illustrating the substantial disparities that exist between high-resource and resource-constrained institutions. The data shows that students in well-resourced environments with professional development support achieve digital competence scores approximately 30-37 points higher than students in resource-constrained contexts. These disparities highlight the urgency of equity-focused interventions that address systemic barriers to literacy development.

Beyond basic access issues, second-level digital divides involve disparities in digital skills, technology self-efficacy, and ability to leverage technology for meaningful purposes. Scholes et al. (2024) examine video gaming and digital competence among elementary school students, finding that children from disadvantaged backgrounds demonstrate lower digital competence despite having technology access. This research reveals that access alone is insufficient; students need guidance, support, and structured learning opportunities to develop sophisticated digital competencies. The quality of access matters as much as the fact of access, with factors such as device quality, internet speed, technical support, and educational guidance significantly affecting literacy development outcomes.

The emergence of AI technologies risks creating new forms of digital divide. Access to advanced AI tools, quality AI literacy education, and opportunities to develop AI competencies may be concentrated among privileged populations, potentially exacerbating existing educational inequalities. Chasubuta et al. (2024) document technological literacy gaps among students in Tanzanian universities, demonstrating how resource constraints limit opportunities for developing advanced technological competencies. Ensuring equitable AI literacy development requires intentional efforts to provide access and support to underserved communities, including investments in infrastructure, professional development for educators, curriculum resources, and ongoing technical support.

Equity-oriented approaches to technology literacy education must address multiple dimensions simultaneously. First, infrastructure development must ensure reliable technology access across diverse contexts, including rural and underserved urban areas. Second, curriculum design must be culturally responsive and relevant to diverse learner populations, recognizing different starting points and learning needs. Third, professional development must prepare educators to work effectively with diverse student populations, understanding how cultural backgrounds, prior experiences, and socioeconomic factors affect technology learning. Fourth, assessment practices must recognize and value diverse forms of technological competence rather than privileging particular cultural or socioeconomic approaches to technology use. Finally, policy frameworks must prioritize equity in technology literacy initiatives, allocating resources based on need rather than existing advantage.

5.2 Cultural and Regional Variations in Literacy Education

Cultural contexts significantly shape how media and technology literacy are conceptualized, taught, and evaluated. Almakaty (2025) provides a global analysis of communication and media education, revealing substantial variations in curriculum emphasis, pedagogical approaches, and learning outcomes across different regions. These variations reflect diverse educational philosophies, cultural values, technological infrastructures, and societal priorities. For example, some cultural contexts emphasize collaborative technology use and collective knowledge construction, while others focus on individual competence and competitive achievement. Some prioritize critical analysis and questioning of technology, while others emphasize practical skills and instrumental use.

Mustapha et al. (2024) examine students' misconceptions about media literacy and critical thinking in Anglophone West African countries, revealing how cultural contexts influence understanding of these concepts. Their research demonstrates that students often perceive media literacy as technical skill acquisition rather than critical analytical practice, a misconception that reflects both educational traditions and available resources. These findings underscore the importance of culturally grounded literacy education that addresses local contexts while developing universal competencies. Effective literacy education must start from learners' existing understandings and cultural frameworks, building bridges to broader competencies rather than imposing external frameworks without regard for cultural context.

Regional variations also emerge in how technology is integrated into education. In some contexts, technology serves primarily to expand access to educational resources, bringing quality content to remote or underserved areas. In others, technology supports transformation of pedagogical practices and learning environments, enabling new forms of interaction, assessment, and knowledge construction. Chasubuta et al. (2024) document how Tanzanian universities navigate technological literacy development amid resource constraints, developing innovative approaches that leverage available technologies while building toward more comprehensive digital transformation. These examples demonstrate that effective technology integration need not wait for ideal conditions but can proceed thoughtfully with available resources while working toward systemic improvements.

Respecting cultural diversity while promoting universal literacy competencies requires careful balance. Literacy frameworks should establish core competencies that apply across contexts while allowing for cultural adaptation and local relevance. Lo (2024) explores the confluence of digital literacy and eco-consciousness, arguing that digital literacy education should harmonize with local values and priorities, including environmental sustainability, social justice, and cultural preservation. This approach positions literacy education as culturally responsive while addressing global challenges. The goal is not cultural homogenization but rather ensuring that all learners develop competencies necessary for full participation in increasingly globalized and technologically mediated societies while maintaining cultural identities and values.

5.3 Sustainable and Ethical Technology Use

Sustainability represents an increasingly important dimension of technology literacy. Lo (2024) examines the confluence of digital literacy and eco-consciousness, arguing that technology literacy education must incorporate awareness of environmental impacts, resource consumption, and sustainable technology practices. This expanded view recognizes that technology choices have environmental consequences that literate users should understand and consider. AI systems in particular require substantial computational resources and energy, raising questions about their environmental sustainability. Students need to understand these environmental dimensions and consider them alongside other factors when making decisions about technology use.

Ethical considerations extend beyond environmental sustainability to encompass human rights, privacy, algorithmic fairness, and social justice. Chan and Lo (2025) examine human rights impact with the advancement of artificial intelligence, identifying how AI systems can affect fundamental rights including privacy, freedom of expression, non-discrimination, and access to information. Their research emphasizes that AI literacy must include understanding of these human rights dimensions and capacity to evaluate AI systems through ethical lenses. Students must learn to recognize when AI systems threaten rights or freedoms and to advocate for ethical AI development and deployment.

Privacy and data protection represent particularly pressing ethical concerns in AI-enhanced education. Educational AI systems collect extensive data about student learning, behavior, and performance, often without students fully understanding what data is collected, how it is used, or who has access to it. Students need literacy competencies that enable them to understand data collection practices, evaluate privacy policies, recognize data misuse risks, and make informed decisions about technology use. Developing these competencies requires explicit instruction about data privacy, digital rights, and informed consent, helping students understand both technical and legal dimensions of privacy protection.

Algorithmic bias and fairness constitute another critical ethical dimension. AI systems can perpetuate and amplify existing biases when trained on biased data or designed without adequate attention to fairness. Students need to understand how bias enters AI systems, recognize potential discriminatory outcomes, and advocate for fair and equitable AI development and deployment. This requires literacy education that addresses both technical aspects of bias—such as how training data affects model behavior—and broader social justice implications—such as how algorithmic bias affects different communities. The goal is developing students' capacity to critically evaluate AI systems and participate meaningfully in debates about AI governance and regulation.

6. CHALLENGES, OPPORTUNITIES, AND FUTURE DIRECTIONS

6.1 Current Challenges in Literacy Education

Contemporary literacy education faces numerous challenges that complicate efforts to prepare learners for AI-enhanced futures. First, rapid technological change creates moving targets for literacy curricula. By the time educational programs develop and implement new literacy frameworks, technologies may have evolved substantially, requiring continuous curriculum revision and educator professional development. This challenge demands flexible, adaptive approaches that emphasize foundational concepts and transferable skills rather than technology-specific competencies. Educators must learn to balance teaching about current technologies with developing generalizable capabilities that will remain relevant as technologies evolve.

Second, resource constraints limit many institutions' capacity to provide comprehensive technology literacy education. Inadequate infrastructure, limited access to current technologies, insufficient professional development opportunities, and competing curricular demands create barriers to effective literacy instruction. These constraints affect disadvantaged communities disproportionately, potentially widening existing achievement gaps. Addressing these challenges requires creative solutions that maximize available resources while advocating for necessary investments. This may involve leveraging free or low-cost tools, developing shared resources across institutions, creating peer learning networks, and building partnerships with technology companies or community organizations.

Third, balancing multiple literacy domains presents pedagogical challenges. Students need traditional academic literacies, digital competencies, media literacy, AI literacy, and critical thinking skills, all while mastering subject-specific content. Integrating these domains coherently while respecting curricular time constraints requires careful instructional design. Pei et al. (2021) examine multimodal learning analytics, suggesting that integrated approaches that leverage technology to support multiple literacy development simultaneously may offer promising solutions. Rather than treating literacies as separate subjects, educators can design learning experiences that develop multiple competencies in integrated ways through authentic, complex tasks.

Fourth, assessment of technology literacy presents significant challenges. Traditional assessment methods may not capture sophisticated digital competencies or critical technology engagement. Developing valid, reliable assessment approaches that measure meaningful literacy competencies rather than superficial technology use requires ongoing research and innovation. Rodafinos et al. (2024) demonstrate complexities in measuring digital competence and its relationship to academic performance, highlighting needs for more sophisticated assessment frameworks. Effective assessment must evaluate not only technical skills but also critical thinking, ethical reasoning, creativity, and metacognitive awareness in technology-mediated contexts.

6.2 Emerging Opportunities for Innovation

Despite challenges, significant opportunities exist for advancing media and technology literacy education. Generative AI technologies offer unprecedented capabilities for personalized learning, adaptive instruction, and immediate feedback. Chiu (2024) identifies numerous opportunities for transforming higher education with generative AI, including enhanced student support, innovative assessment approaches, and new forms of collaborative learning. Realizing these opportunities requires thoughtful implementation that centers learning goals and maintains critical engagement. AI tools can provide scaffolding, generate practice materials, offer multiple explanations of concepts, and adapt to individual learning needs in ways that were previously impossible or prohibitively resource-intensive.

Multimodal learning environments enabled by advanced technologies provide opportunities for engaging diverse learners and supporting multiple forms of literacy development simultaneously. Lam and Ni (2024) demonstrate how AI-assisted portfolio assessment can support multiliteracies development, enabling students to work with text, images, video, and interactive media in integrated ways. These multimodal approaches align with how students engage with media and communication in their daily lives, potentially increasing relevance and engagement. Furthermore, multimodal learning can accommodate diverse learning preferences and styles, making education more inclusive and accessible.

Collaborative and networked learning opportunities expand possibilities for literacy development across geographic and cultural boundaries. Technology enables students to engage with diverse perspectives, participate in global learning communities, and develop intercultural competencies alongside technology literacy. These networked learning experiences can support development of critical media literacy by exposing students to multiple viewpoints and requiring them to navigate information from diverse sources. Global collaboration also helps students understand that technology is not culturally neutral and that different communities approach technology in different ways, developing cultural competence alongside technological competence.

Open educational resources and technology-enhanced professional development create opportunities for expanding literacy education access. Online courses, digital learning materials, and collaborative professional learning networks can reach educators and students who lack access to traditional educational resources. These opportunities are particularly important for addressing equity concerns and reducing digital divides, though they require careful attention to quality, accessibility, and cultural appropriateness. Open resources can democratize access to high-quality educational materials while also creating opportunities for educators to share innovations and learn from colleagues globally.

6.3 Future Research Directions and Priorities

Future research must address several critical areas to advance understanding of media and technology literacy in the age of AI. First, longitudinal studies are needed to examine how literacy competencies develop over time and how they relate to long-term outcomes. Most existing research relies on cross-sectional designs that cannot capture developmental processes or sustained impacts. Understanding how literacy competencies evolve, how they interact with one another, and how they affect long-term educational and career trajectories requires sustained investigation over extended periods. Such research could identify critical periods for literacy development, optimal sequencing of skill instruction, and factors that support transfer of learning across contexts.

Second, research must investigate effective pedagogical approaches for integrated literacy education. How can educators most effectively develop traditional literacies, digital competencies, and AI literacy simultaneously? What instructional strategies support transfer of literacy skills across contexts? How can assessment capture complex, integrated literacy competencies? Godsk and Møller (2024) call for research on engaging students with educational technology, suggesting that pedagogical innovation requires empirical support. Research should examine specific instructional approaches, compare their effectiveness, and identify conditions under which different approaches work best. This includes understanding how to design learning tasks that develop multiple literacies, how to provide effective feedback on literacy development, and how to support metacognitive awareness.

Third, cross-cultural research is essential for understanding how literacy education can be both culturally responsive and universally effective. Comparative studies examining literacy education across diverse contexts can identify successful approaches, cultural variations in literacy conceptualization, and strategies for addressing context-specific challenges. Boshoff and Fafowora (2025) propose research agendas for specific regions, but coordinated international research efforts could provide broader insights. Such research should examine not only what works in different contexts but also why particular approaches succeed or fail, identifying underlying principles that can inform adaptation across contexts.

Fourth, research on ethical dimensions of AI in education requires expansion. How do AI systems affect student privacy, autonomy, and rights? What frameworks support ethical AI use in educational contexts? How can students develop ethical reasoning about AI technologies? Chan and Lo (2025) examine human rights implications of AI advancement, but more research is needed on how to operationalize ethical frameworks in educational practice. This includes understanding how to teach ethics in ways that affect actual behavior, how to create educational AI systems that respect rights and dignity, and how to prepare students for ethical decision-making in AI-mediated environments.

Finally, research must investigate how to prepare educators for literacy education in AI-enhanced environments. What competencies do educators need? What professional development approaches prove most effective? How can institutions support ongoing educator learning as technologies evolve? Qian et al. (2025) identify faculty development as critical for educational transformation, but specific strategies require further investigation and validation. Research should examine both initial preparation and ongoing professional learning, understanding how to support educators at different career stages and with varying levels of technological experience.

7. CONCLUSION

This chapter has examined the evolving landscape of media and technology literacy in the age of artificial intelligence, drawing on interdisciplinary research to identify essential competencies, effective pedagogical approaches, and critical challenges. The integration of AI into educational contexts demands expanded conceptions of literacy that encompass technical understanding, critical evaluation, ethical reasoning, and practical application. Traditional media literacy frameworks must adapt to address AI-generated content, algorithmic curation, and the complex information ecosystems that characterize contemporary digital environments.

Several key themes emerge from the research reviewed in this chapter. First, effective literacy education requires integration across multiple domains rather than treating media literacy, digital competence, and AI literacy as separate subjects. Students need cohesive frameworks that connect technical skills, critical thinking, and ethical awareness. The integrated model presented in Figure 1 illustrates how traditional literacy foundations, media literacy, and digital competence converge into AI literacy, supported by psychological, pedagogical, social, and institutional factors. This integration is not merely additive but transformative, creating new forms of literacy that exceed the sum of their component parts.

Second, psychological factors including self-efficacy and anxiety significantly influence technology acceptance and effective use, requiring pedagogical approaches that build confidence alongside competence. As demonstrated in Figure 2, technology acceptance depends on complex interactions among system characteristics, individual factors, social influences, and facilitating conditions. Educators must attend to these multiple dimensions, recognizing that technical training alone is insufficient. Building positive attitudes, reducing anxiety, and fostering self-efficacy require intentional pedagogical strategies including graduated challenges, abundant support, safe learning environments, and celebration of success.

Third, equity considerations must be central to literacy initiatives, ensuring that all learners have opportunities to develop essential competencies regardless of socioeconomic status, geographic location, or cultural background. Graph 1 starkly illustrates the substantial disparities in digital competence levels across different educational contexts, with gaps of 30-37 points between well-resourced and resource-constrained environments. These disparities reflect systemic inequalities that literacy education alone cannot solve but must actively work to mitigate. Equity-oriented approaches require addressing infrastructure, professional development, curriculum quality, and assessment practices simultaneously.

The comprehensive frameworks presented by researchers such as Chiu et al. (2024), Allen and Kendeou (2023), and Ng et al. (2023) provide valuable foundations for developing AI literacy education. Table 1 synthesizes these frameworks, identifying five core competency domains: technical understanding, critical evaluation, ethical awareness, practical application, and metacognitive awareness. Implementing these frameworks requires coordinated efforts involving curriculum development, professional development, resource allocation, and policy reform. No single intervention will suffice; rather, systematic change across multiple levels is necessary.

Educator preparation emerges as a critical factor in successful literacy education. Teachers need not only technical competencies but also pedagogical knowledge for integrating technology meaningfully into learning experiences. Professional development programs must address multiple dimensions simultaneously: technical skills, pedagogical approaches, critical literacy, and confidence building. Institutions bear responsibility for providing ongoing support, resources, and opportunities for educator learning as technologies continue to evolve. This support must be sustained rather than episodic, recognizing that technology learning is an ongoing process rather than a one-time event.

Cultural and contextual considerations require careful attention in literacy education. Technology is not culturally neutral, and literacy frameworks must be adapted to local contexts while maintaining core competencies. Research from diverse global contexts, including studies from Africa, Asia, and other regions, demonstrates that effective literacy education respects cultural diversity, addresses local challenges, and builds on existing strengths rather than imposing standardized approaches. The goal is developing globally relevant competencies while honoring cultural identities and values, recognizing that there are multiple valid approaches to technology use and literacy development.

Ethical and sustainable technology use constitutes an essential component of literacy education that has sometimes received insufficient attention. Students need to understand how AI systems affect privacy, rights, and social justice. They need frameworks for evaluating algorithmic bias and advocating for fair technology development and deployment. Environmental sustainability must also be incorporated into technology literacy, helping students understand resource consumption and environmental impacts of technology choices. These ethical dimensions cannot be treated as separate topics but must be woven throughout literacy education, informing all aspects of technology learning.

Looking forward, several priorities emerge for advancing media and technology literacy education. First, research must continue examining effective pedagogical approaches, assessment methods, and professional development strategies. Longitudinal studies are particularly needed to understand how literacy competencies develop over time and how they relate to long-term outcomes. Such research should examine not only what competencies develop but also how they develop, identifying optimal developmental pathways and critical periods for intervention.

Second, equity must remain central to literacy initiatives, with intentional efforts to address digital divides and ensure all learners develop essential competencies. This requires not only providing access to technology but also ensuring access to high-quality literacy education, supportive learning environments, and opportunities to develop advanced competencies. Equity work must be ongoing and systematic, attending to how seemingly neutral policies and practices may perpetuate or exacerbate existing inequalities.

Third, collaboration across disciplines, institutions, and national boundaries can accelerate progress and share effective practices. Literacy challenges are too complex for any single discipline, institution, or nation to solve independently. Productive collaboration requires building shared understanding across different perspectives, creating mechanisms for knowledge exchange, and developing collective action agendas. International cooperation is particularly important for addressing global challenges such as misinformation, algorithmic bias, and environmental sustainability of technology.

Fourth, adaptive frameworks are needed that can evolve alongside technological change. Rather than developing rigid curricula that quickly become outdated, literacy education should emphasize foundational concepts, transferable skills, and metacognitive awareness that enable ongoing learning. Students need to learn how to learn about new technologies, developing confidence in their ability to master unfamiliar tools and critical frameworks for evaluating new technological developments. This meta-literacy—literacy about literacy—may be the most enduring competency education can develop.

Finally, technology literacy education must maintain focus on human flourishing, ensuring that technological competence serves broader educational goals of developing thoughtful, ethical, engaged citizens. Technology is a means, not an end. The ultimate purpose of literacy education is empowering individuals to participate fully in society, contribute to collective well-being, and live meaningful lives. Technology literacy serves these purposes by enabling effective communication, informed decision-making, creative expression, and critical engagement with the systems that shape contemporary life.

The challenges facing media and technology literacy education are substantial, but so are the opportunities. AI technologies offer powerful capabilities for enhancing learning, personalizing instruction, and supporting diverse learners. Realizing these opportunities while addressing ethical concerns and maintaining critical engagement requires thoughtful implementation guided by research, informed by diverse perspectives, and centered on student learning and wellbeing. This chapter has sought to synthesize current understanding and provide foundations for continued progress in this vital educational domain, recognizing that the work of developing

REFERENCES

Albardía, M. S., Peña-Fernández, S., & Agirreazkuenaga, I. (2025). Technology, education and critical media literacy: Potential, challenges, and opportunities. *Frontiers in Human Dynamics*, *7*, 1608911. DOI: 10.3389/fhumd.2025.1608911

Allen, L. K., & Kendeou, P. (2023). ED-AI lit: An interdisciplinary framework for AI literacy in education. *Policy Insights from the Behavioral and Brain Sciences*. Advance online publication. DOI: 10.1177/23727322231220339

Almakaty, S. S. (2025). Emerging trends in communication and media education in the digital age: A global analysis and comparative study. *Preprints*. DOI: 10.20944/preprints202410.1022.v2

Boshoff, P., & Fafowora, B. (2025). Digital media literacy in Africa: Towards a research agenda. *African Journalism Studies*, *45*(4), 259–269. DOI: 10.1080/23743670.2025.2478460

Chan, H. W. H., & Lo, N. P. K. (2025). A study on human rights impact with the advancement of artificial intelligence. *Journal of Posthumanism*, *5*(2), 490. DOI: 10.63332/joph.v5i2.490

Chasubuta, A. R., Ndibalema, P. M., & Loisulie, P. (2024). Technological literacy in using learning management system among students in higher education institutions Tanzania: The case of two selected universities. *Educational Technology Quarterly*, *2024*(1), 76–96. DOI: 10.55056/etq.695

Chen, D., Liu, W., & Liu, X. (2024). What drives college students to use AI for L2 learning? Modeling the roles of self-efficacy, anxiety, and attitude based on an extended technology acceptance model. *Acta Psychologica*, *249*, 104442. DOI: 10.1016/j.actpsy.2024.104442

Chiu, T. K. F. (2024). Future research recommendations for transforming higher education with generative AI. *Computers and Education: Artificial Intelligence*, *6*, 100197. DOI: 10.1016/j.caeai.2023.100197

Chiu, T. K. F., Ahmad, Z., Ismailov, M., & Sanusi, I. T. (2024). What are artificial intelligence literacy and competency? A comprehensive framework to support them. *Computers and Education Open*, *6*, 100171. DOI: 10.1016/j.caeo.2024.100171

Gaultney, I. B., Sherron, T., & Boden, C. (2022). Political polarization, misinformation, and media literacy. *The Journal of Media Literacy Education*, *14*(1), 59–81. DOI: 10.23860/JMLE-2022-14-1-5

Godsk, M., & Møller, K. L. (2024). Engaging students in higher education with educational technology. *Education and Information Technologies*. Advance online publication. DOI: 10.1007/s10639-024-12901-x

Guo, H., & Li, D. (2024). The effect of electronic portfolio-based writing instruction on the second language writing performance and writing self-efficacy of EFL learners: A mixed methods study. *SAGE Open*, *14*(2), 21582440241257697. Advance online publication. DOI: 10.1177/21582440241257697

Kalantzis, M., & Cope, B. (2024). Literacy in the time of artificial intelligence. *Reading Research Quarterly*. Advance online publication. DOI: 10.1002/rrq.591

Lam, R., & Ni, Y. (2024). Students' perceptions of multiliteracies development using AI-assisted portfolio assessment. *Pedagogies*, *60*(1), 1–28. Advance online publication. DOI: 10.1080/1554480X.2025.2545212

Levido, A. (2024). Media literacy and the concept of 'technologies' in primary school classrooms: Moving beyond technical skills. *Learning, Media and Technology*, *50*(4), 560–572. DOI: 10.1080/17439884.2024.2308609

Li, X., Gao, Z., & Liao, H. (2024). An empirical investigation of college students' acceptance of translation technologies. *PLoS One*, *19*(2), e0297297. DOI: 10.1371/journal.pone.0297297

Lo, N., Wong, A., & Chan, S. (2025). The impact of generative AI on essay revisions and student engagement. *Computers and Education Open*, *22*, 100249. DOI: 10.1016/j.caeo.2025.100249

Lo, N. P. K. (2024). The confluence of digital literacy and eco-consciousness: Harmonizing digital skills with sustainable practices in education. *Platforms*, *2*(1), 15–32. DOI: 10.3390/platforms2010002

Mustapha, M. J., Lasisi, M. I., & Barabash, V. V. (2024). Are they tools? Anglophone West African countries' students' misconception of media literacy and critical thinking for combating misinformation. *The Journal of Media Literacy Education*, *16*(1), 94–103. DOI: 10.23860/JMLE-2024-16-1-7

Ng, D. T. K., Su, J., Leung, J. K. L., & Chu, S. K. W. (2023). Artificial intelligence (AI) literacy education in secondary schools: A review. *Interactive Learning Environments*. Advance online publication. DOI: 10.1080/10494820.2023.2255228

Pan, L., Haq, S., Shi, X., & Nadeem, M. (2024). The impact of digital competence and personal innovativeness on the learning behavior of students: Exploring the moderating role of digitalization in higher education quality. *SAGE Open*, *14*(2), 21582440241265919. Advance online publication. DOI: 10.1177/21582440241265919

Pei, B., Xing, W., & Wang, M. (2021). Academic development of multimodal learning analytics: A bibliometric analysis. *Interactive Learning Environments*, *31*(6), 3543–3561. DOI: 10.1080/10494820.2021.1936075

Qian, L., Cao, W., & Chen, L. (2025). Influence of artificial intelligence on higher education reform and talent cultivation in the digital intelligence era. *Scientific Reports*, *15*(1), 6047. DOI: 10.1038/s41598-025-89392-4

Rodafinos, A., Barkoukis, V., Tzafilkou, K., Ourda, D., Economides, A., & Perifanou, M. (2024). Exploring the impact of digital competence and technology acceptance on academic performance in physical education and sports science students. *Journal of Information Technology Education*, *23*, 19. DOI: 10.28945/5309

Scholes, L., Rowe, L., Mills, K. A., Gutierrez, A., & Pink, E. (2024). Video gaming and digital competence among elementary school students. *Learning, Media and Technology*, *49*(2), 200–215. DOI: 10.1080/17439884.2022.2156537

Sesmiarni, Z., Hoque, M. E., Susanto, P., Islam, M. A., & Hendrayati, H. (2024). Adoption of SPACE-learning management system in education era 4.0: An extended technology acceptance model with self-efficacy. *Frontiers in Education*, *9*, 1457188. DOI: 10.3389/feduc.2024.1457188

Tinmaz, H., Lee, Y. T., Fanea-Ivanovici, M., & Baber, H. (2022). A systematic review on digital literacy. *Smart Learning Environments*, *9*(1), 21. DOI: 10.1186/s40561-022-00204-y

Turner, K. H., Jolls, T., & Hagerman, M. S.. (2025). The importance of digital media literacy. In Christakis, D. A., & Hale, L. (Eds.), *Handbook of children and screens* (pp. 1305–1325). Springer., DOI: 10.1007/978-3-031-69362-5_74

KEY TERMS AND DEFINITIONS

AI Literacy: The ability to understand, use, and critically evaluate Artificial Intelligence. It involves knowing how AI models function, recognizing their limitations (like bias or "hallucinations"), and ethically applying AI tools to solve problems or enhance productivity.

Critical Thinking: The disciplined process of actively analyzing, synthesizing, and evaluating information gathered from observation or communication. It is the mental "filter" used to determine whether a claim is true, logical, or backed by credible evidence.

Digital Competence: A broad set of skills required to confidently and safely use digital technologies for work, learning, and leisure. It encompasses everything from basic hardware operation to data management, online collaboration, and maintaining a secure digital identity.

Educational Technology (EdTech): The combined use of computer hardware, software, and educational theory to facilitate learning. It aims to improve student performance and engagement by creating managed technological processes and resources tailored to diverse learning environments.

Media Literacy: The capacity to access, analyze, and create messages in various forms. It focuses on questioning the source, purpose, and perspective of media content—from news reports to social posts—to understand how they shape our perception of reality.

Misinformation: False or inaccurate information that is spread regardless of an intent to deceive. Unlike *disinformation*, which is intentionally malicious, misinformation often spreads through honest mistakes or social sharing by people who believe the content is true.

Technology Acceptance: A psychological concept describing how users come to accept and use a new technology. It is primarily influenced by two factors: perceived usefulness (how much it helps) and perceived ease of use (how hard it is to learn).

Compilation of References

Abdelzaher, E., & Alshammari, S. (2026). Learning from machinery misspeaks: Cognitive basis of ableism and bias in AI-generated content. *Corpus Pragmatics : International Journal of Corpus Linguistics and Pragmatics*, *10*(1), 8. Advance online publication. DOI: 10.1007/s41701-025-00216-2

Acquier, A., & Cossey, J. (2026). Generative AI, academic deepfakes, and epistemic pollution. *Business & Society*, *65*(3), 538–543. DOI: 10.1177/00076503251406457

Agaoglu, F. O., Bas, M., Tarsuslu, S., Ekinci, L. O., & Agaoglu, N. B. (2025). The mediating digital literacy and the moderating role of academic support in the relationship between artificial intelligence usage and creative thinking in nursing students. *BMC Nursing*, *24*(1), 484. DOI: 10.1186/s12912-025-03128-3

Agrahari, S. K. (2023). The Crucial Role of Accessibility Tools and Software in Meeting the Needs of Individuals with Learning Disabilities. *Cutting Edge in Special Education, 121.*

Ahmad, S., & Bokhari, M. U. (2012). A new approach to multi-agent based architecture for secure and effective e-learning. *International Journal of Computer Applications*, *46*(22), 26–29. DOI: 10.5120/7098-9826

Ahmed, F. (2024). The digital divide and AI in education: Addressing equity and accessibility. *AI EDIFY Journal*, *1*(2), 12–23.

Akhtar, A. (2024). Cultural Crossroads and Subaltern Realities in Diasporic Discourse: Exploring the Sense of Belonging in Lahiri and Mistry's Narratives. *International Journal of English Literature and Social Sciences*, *9*(1), 238–245. DOI: 10.22161/ijels.91.32

Alahou, G. (2023). Thematic Analysis and its Interdisciplinary Interest: Advantage or a Disadvantage for Holton's Purpose? *Conatus -. The Journal of Philosophy*, *8*(1), 29–53. DOI: 10.12681/cjp.30938

Al-Awawdeh, N., Kaddum, M. M., Nasr, D., Merhye, N., & Nasr, M. (2025). The Correlation Between the Use of AI Translation Tools in Foreign Language Learning and the Positive Performance of Foreign Language Students. [TPLS]. *Theory and Practice in Language Studies*, *15*(12), 4117–4126. DOI: 10.17507/tpls.1512.31

Alazemi, A. F. T. (2024). Formative assessment in artificial integrated instruction: Delving into the effects on reading comprehension progress, online academic enjoyment, personal best goals, and academic mindfulness. *Language Testing in Asia*, *14*(1), 44. DOI: 10.1186/s40468-024-00319-8

Albacete, P., Jordan, P., Katz, S., Chounta, I. A., & McLaren, B. M. (2019). The impact of student model updates on contingent scaffolding in a natural-language tutoring system. In *International conference on AI in education* (pp. 37–47). Springer. DOI: 10.1007/978-3-030-23204-7_4

Albardía, M. S., Peña-Fernández, S., & Agirreazkuenaga, I. (2025). Technology, education and critical media literacy: Potential, challenges, and opportunities. *Frontiers in Human Dynamics*, *7*, 1608911. Advance online publication. DOI: 10.3389/fhumd.2025.1608911

Alem.AI. (2025). AILA digital influencer profile. Instagram. https://www.instagram.com/reel/DPGjxKfDCgt/

Aljemely, Y. (2024, October). Challenges and best practices in training teachers to utilize AI: A systematic review. [). Frontiers Media SA.]. *Frontiers in Education*, *9*, 1470853. DOI: 10.3389/feduc.2024.1470853

Al-kfairy, M., Mustafa, D., Kshetri, N., Insiew, M., & Alfandi, O. (2024). Ethical challenges and solutions of generative AI: An interdisciplinary perspective. *Informatics (MDPI)*, *11*(3), 58. DOI: 10.3390/informatics11030058

Allen, L. K., & Kendeou, P. (2023). ED-AI lit: An interdisciplinary framework for AI literacy in education. *Policy Insights from the Behavioral and Brain Sciences*. Advance online publication. DOI: 10.1177/23727322231220339

Almakaty, S. S. (2025). Emerging trends in communication and media education in the digital age: A global analysis and comparative study. *Preprints*. DOI: 10.20944/preprints202410.1022.v2

Almatrafi, O., Johri, A., & Lee, H. (2024). A systematic review of AI literacy conceptualization, constructs, and implementation and assessment efforts (2019–2023). *Computers and Education Open*, *6*, 100173. DOI: 10.1016/j.caeo.2024.100173

Almeida, P. (2021, September). Chamber of Deputies, Santos, C., University of Brasília, Farias, J., & University of Brasília. (2021). Artificial Intelligence Regulation: A framework for governance. *Ethics and Information Technology*, *23*(3), 505–525. Advance online publication. DOI: 10.1007/s10676-021-09593-z

Almubarak, A., Alhalabi, W., Albidewi, I., & Alharbi, E. (2025). An AI-powered framework for assessing teacher performance in classroom interactions: A deep learning approach. *Frontiers in Artificial Intelligence*, *8*, 1553051. DOI: 10.3389/frai.2025.1553051 PMID: 40969168

Alshater, M. M. (2022). Exploring the role of artificial intelligence in enhancing academic performance: A case study of ChatGPT. *Available at SSRN* 4312358. DOI: 10.2139/ssrn.4312358

Amaral, A., Jones, G. A., & Karseth, B. (2002). Governing higher education: Comparing national perspectives. In *Governing Higher Education: National perspectives on institutional Governance* (pp. 279–298). Springer Netherlands. DOI: 10.1007/978-94-015-9946-7_14

Analyti, E., Charitou, R., Pesmatzoglou, E., Stavrogiannopoulou, M., Schoina, I., Travlou, C., & Mitroyanni, E. (2024). Virtual reality in education: Transforming learning through immersive technology. *Technium Education and Humanities*, *10*(October), 1–11. DOI: 10.47577/teh.v10i.11766

Anderson, B. (1991). *Imagined communities: Reflections on the origin and spread of nationalism*. Verso.

Angus, D. L. (2001). Professionalism and the Public Good: A Brief History of Teacher Certification.

Aquino, C. J., & Salvador, R. (2024). Exploring the Interrelated Roles of Text, Author, and Reader in Identity Formation through Literature. *Journal of Interdisciplinary Perspectives*, *2*(3). Advance online publication. DOI: 10.69569/jip.2024.0042

Aravantinos, S., Lavidas, K., Voulgari, I., Papadakis, S., Karalis, T., & Komis, V. (2024). Educational approaches with AI in primary school settings: A systematic review of the literature available in Scopus. *Education Sciences*, *14*(7), 744. DOI: 10.3390/educsci14070744

Armoni, M., Meerbaum-Salant, O., & Ben-Ari, M. (2015). From Scratch to "real" programming. *ACM Transactions on Computing Education*, *14*(4), 25. Advance online publication. DOI: 10.1145/2677087

Asharari, T. M. H. (2023). An analytical study of the social studies course at the secondary education stage (course system): The joint program in the Kingdom of Saudi Arabia in promoting awareness of national identity in line with Vision 2030. *Information Sciences Letters*, *12*(2), 757–773. DOI: 10.18576/isl/120218

August, D., & Shanahan, T. (2010). Response to a review and update on developing literacy in second-language learners: Report of the national literacy panel on language minority children and youth. *Journal of Literacy Research*, *42*(3), 341–348. DOI: 10.1080/1086296X.2010.503745

Ayyoob, A., & Sajeev, A. (2024b). Diversity, Equity, and Inclusion: Employees Perspectives on Sustainable Business Practices. *Routledge EBooks*, 348–367. DOI: 10.4324/9781003487180-27

Ayyoob, A., & Sajeev, A. (2024c). Navigating Sustainability: Assessing the Imperative of ESG Considerations in Achieving SDGs. *ESG Frameworks for Sustainable Business Practices*, 53–84. DOI: 10.4018/979-8-3693-3880-3.ch003

Ayyoob, A., & Sajeev, A. (2024d). Role of Social Entrepreneurship in Sustainable Development. *Advances in Business Strategy and Competitive Advantage Book Series*, 193–224. DOI: 10.4018/979-8-3693-4338-8.ch008

Ayyoob, A., & Sajeev, A. (2025). Resilient and Sustainable Organizations. IGI Global EBooks, 35–58. DOI: 10.4018/979-8-3373-0608-7.ch003

Ayyoob, A., & Sajeev, A. (2024a). Corporate Sustainability: The Role of Consumer Skepticism, Transparency, and Marketing in Greenwashing Practices. *Corporate Governance Insight*, *6*(2), 51–68. DOI: 10.58426/cgi.v6.i2.2024.51-68

Aziz, M. A., Azizullah, A., & Baloch, S. (2024). Emerging trends and issues in English language teaching: A bibliometric analysis. *Journal of Asian Development Studies*, *13*(1), 1004–1016. DOI: 10.62345/jads.2024.13.1.83

Bailin, S., & Siegel, H. (2003). Critical thinking. *The Blackwell guide to the philosophy of education*, 181-193.

Baker, T., & Smith, L. (with Anissa, N.). (2019). Educ-AI-tion rebooted? Exploring the future of artificial intelligence in schools and colleges. Nesta.

Baldrich, K., Pérez-García, C., & Santamarina Sancho, M. (2025). Artificial intelligence in academic literacy: Empirical evidence on reading and writing practices in higher education. In *Frontiers in Education* (Vol. 10, p. 1701238). Frontiers., DOI: 10.3389/feduc.2025.1701238

Ballantyne, K. G., Sanderman, A. R., & Levy, J. (2008). *Educating English Language Learners: Building Teacher Capacity. Roundtable Report*. National Clearinghouse for English Language Acquisition & Language Instruction Educational Programs.

Bandura, A., & Wessels, S. (1997). *Self-efficacy*. Cambridge University Press.

Banerjee, R. (2024, August). Education 4.0: Use of AI tools in classroom. In *ARTIFICIAL INTELLIGENCE IN EDUCATION* (p. 108).

Banik, B. G., & Gullapelly, A. (2025). AI-Powered gamification and interactive learning tools for enhancing student engagement. In *Driving Quality Education Through AI and Data Science* (pp. 283–310). IGI Global Scientific Publishing. DOI: 10.4018/979-8-3693-8292-9.ch013

Bansal, G., Wu, T., Zhou, J., & Kim, J. (2024). Beyond chatbots: Large language models as educational agents. *Cognitive Computation*. Advance online publication. DOI: 10.1007/s12559-024-10235-1

Barrett, M. (2018). Young people's civic and political engagement and global citizenship. *UN Chronicle*, *54*(4), 44–46. DOI: 10.18356/11734699-en

Barve, S., Mao, A., Shi, J. M., Juneja, P., & Saha, K. (2025). Can we debias social stereotypes in AI-generated images? Examining text-to-image outputs and user perceptions. *arXiv preprint arXiv:2505.20692*. https://doi.org//arXiv.2505.20692DOI: 10.48550

Batini, F., & Toti, G. (2024). Shared reading aloud to enhance language and literacy. *Education 3-13, 52*(7), 946-962.

Beard, A. (2020, March 19). Can computers ever replace the classroom? *The Guardian*. https://www.theguardian.com/technology/2020/mar/19/can-computers-ever-replace-the-classroom

Bećirović, S., Polz, E., & Tinkel, I. (2025). Exploring students' AI literacy and its effects on their AI output quality, self-efficacy, and academic performance. *Smart Learning Environments*, *12*(1), 29. DOI: 10.1186/s40561-025-00384-3

Belland, B. R., Walker, A. E., Kim, N. J., & Lefler, M. (2017). Synthesizing results from empirical research on computer-based scaffolding. *Review of Educational Research*, *87*(2), 309–344. DOI: 10.3102/0034654316670999

Bewersdorff, A., Zhai, X., Roberts, J., & Nerdel, C. (2023). Myths, mis- and preconceptions of artificial intelligence: A review of the literature. *Computers and Education: Artificial Intelligence*, *4*, 100143. Advance online publication. DOI: 10.1016/j.caeai.2023.100143

Biesta, G. (2010). *Good education in an age of measurement: Ethics, politics, democracy*. Paradigm.

Bircan, M. A., Şeref, İ., & Nacaroğlu, O. (2025). The effect of STEM themed story writing training with artificial intelligence tools on the digital literacy and 21st century skills of preservice teachers. *Education and Information Technologies*, *30*(15), 1–20. DOI: 10.1007/s10639-025-13625-2

Blokhin, I. N. (2016). Understanding in the system of mass communication effects. In S. G. Korkonosenko (Ed.), The age of information: Media in the modern world. St. Petersburg readings: Proceedings of the 55th International Forum (April 21-22, 2016). Higher School of Journalism and Mass Communications.

Bolter, J. D., & Grusin, R. (1999). *Remediation: Understanding new media R*. MIT Press.

Bond, M., Khosravi, H., De Laat, M., Bergdahl, N., Negrea, V., Oxley, E., Pham, P., Chong, S. W., & Siemens, G. (2024). A meta systematic review of artificial intelligence in higher education: A call for increased ethics, collaboration, and rigour. *International Journal of Educational Technology in Higher Education*, *21*(1), 4. Advance online publication. DOI: 10.1186/s41239-023-00436-z

Borooah, V. K., & Sabharwal, N. S. (2017). English as a medium of instruction in Indian education: Inequality of access to educational opportunities. *CPRHE research papers, 7*, 1-33.

Boshoff, P., & Fafowora, B. (2025). Digital media literacy in Africa: Towards a research agenda. *African Journalism Studies*, *45*(4), 259–269. DOI: 10.1080/23743670.2025.2478460

Bozkurt, A. (2024). GenAI co-creation, authorship, ownership, academic ethics and integrity in a time of generative AI. *Open Praxis*, *16*(1), 1–10. DOI: 10.55982/openpraxis.16.1.654

Braga Gago, P., Silva, A., & Lucena, C. (2006). Formalizing multi-agent system design using the MaSE methodology. *Journal of Systems Architecture*, *52*(8–9), 501–517. DOI: 10.1016/j.sysarc.2006.02.003

Brata, W. W. W., Padang, R. Y., Suriani, C., Prasetya, E., & Pratiwi, N. (2022). Student's digital literacy based on students' interest in digital technology, internet costs, gender, and learning outcomes. *International Journal of Emerging Technologies in Learning*, *17*(3), 138–151. DOI: 10.3991/ijet.v17i03.27151

Brattland, S. Ø., & Storstad, O. (2025). *2. Kan skolen kompensere for samfunnet? Kunnskapsforskjeller i et flerkulturelt utdanningslandskap. Unge medborgere i en ny tid*. Scandinavian University Press.

Breakstone, J., Smith, M., Ziv, N., & Wineburg, S. (2022). Civic preparation for the digital age: How college students evaluate online sources about social and political issues. *The Journal of Higher Education*, *93*(6), 963–988. DOI: 10.1080/00221546.2022.2082783

Briggs, J., Dearden, J., & Macaro, E. (2018). English medium instruction: Comparing teacher beliefs in secondary and tertiary education. *Studies in Second Language Learning and Teaching*, *8*(3), 673–696. DOI: 10.14746/ssllt.2018.8.3.7

Brinkmann, S., & Kvale, S. (2015). *InterViews: learning the craft of qualitative research interviewing* (3rd ed.). Sage.

Buckingham, D. (2019). Teaching media in a 'post-truth' age: Fake news, media bias and the challenge for media/digital literacy education. *C&E, Cultura y Educación*, *31*(2), 213–231. DOI: 10.1080/11356405.2019.1603814

Buolamwini, J., & Gebru, T. (2018). Gender shades: Intersectional accuracy disparities in commercial gender classification. *Proceedings of the 1st Conference on Fairness, Accountability and Transparency*, 77–91.

Burczyński, T., Kuś, W., Beluch, W., Długosz, A., Poteralski, A., & Szczepanik, M. (2020). *Intelligent computing in optimal design*. Springer. DOI: 10.1007/978-3-030-34161-9

Butler-Kisber, L. (2010). *Qualitative inquiry: Thematic, narrative and arts-informed perspectives*. Sage. Publications., DOI: 10.4135/9781526435408

Butler-Kisber, L. (2018). Poetic inquiry. In *Qualitative inquiry: Thematic, narrative and arts- informed perspectives* (2nd ed., pp. 95–113). Sage Publications., DOI: 10.4135/9781526417978.n7

Bybee, R. W. (2010). Advancing STEM education: A 2020 vision. *Technology and engineering teacher, 70*(1), 30.

Capdeferro, N., & Romero, M. (2012). Are online learners frustrated with collaborative learning? *International Review of Research in Open and Distance Learning*, *13*(2), 26–44. DOI: 10.19173/irrodl.v13i2.1127

Carcamo, B., & Pino, B. (2025). Developing EFL students' multimodal literacy with the use of infographics. *Asian-Pacific Journal of Second and Foreign Language Education*, *10*(1), 16. DOI: 10.1186/s40862-025-00322-3

Cardon, P. W., Fleischmann, C., Aritz, J., Logemann, M., & Heidewald, J. (2023). The challenges and opportunities of AI-assisted writing: Developing AI literacy for the AI age. *Business and Professional Communication Quarterly, 86*(3), 257–295. DOI: 10.1177/23294906231176517

Cassidy, S. (2015). Resilience building in students. *Frontiers in Psychology, 6*, 1781. DOI: 10.3389/fpsyg.2015.01781

Chan, C. K. Y. (2023). A comprehensive AI policy education framework for university teaching and learning. *International Journal of Educational Technology in Higher Education, 20*(1), 38. DOI: 10.1186/s41239-023-00408-3

Chan, C. K. Y., & Hu, W. (2023). Students' voices on generative AI: Perceptions, benefits, and challenges in higher education. *International Journal of Educational Technology in Higher Education, 20*(1), 43. Advance online publication. DOI: 10.1186/s41239-023-00411-8

Chang, S. H. (2025). Research on the construction of a collaborative AI-assisted design model for cultural creativity. *International Journal of Education. Cultura e Scuola, 10*(6), 321–335. DOI: 10.11648/j.ijecs.20251006.12

Chan, H. W. H., & Lo, N. P. K. (2025). A study on human rights impact with the advancement of artificial intelligence. *Journal of Posthumanism, 5*(2), 490. DOI: 10.63332/joph.v5i2.490

Chapple, J. (2015). Teaching in English is not necessarily the teaching of English. *International Education Studies, 8*(3), 1–13. DOI: 10.5539/ies.v8n3p1

Chasubuta, A. R., Ndibalema, P. M., & Loisulie, P. (2024). Technological literacy in using learning management system among students in higher education institutions Tanzania: The case of two selected universities. *Educational Technology Quarterly, 2024*(1), 76–96. DOI: 10.55056/etq.695

Chen, C., & Gong, Y. (2025). The role of AI-assisted learning in academic writing: A mixed-methods study on Chinese as a second language students. *Education Sciences, 15*(2), 141. DOI: 10.3390/educsci15020141

Chen, D., Liu, W., & Liu, X. (2024). What drives college students to use AI for L2 learning? Modeling the roles of self-efficacy, anxiety, and attitude based on an extended technology acceptance model. *Acta Psychologica, 249*, 104442. DOI: 10.1016/j.actpsy.2024.104442

Chen, J. (2026). AI photography and cultural memory: Revisualizing the queer histories of Bugis Street in Singapore through layered gazes. *Humanities & Social Sciences Communications*, *13*(1), 172. Advance online publication. DOI: 10.1057/s41599-025-06473-5

Chen, L., Chen, P., & Lin, Z. (2020). Artificial intelligence in education: A review. *IEEE Access : Practical Innovations, Open Solutions*, *8*, 75264–75278. DOI: 10.1109/ACCESS.2020.2988510

Chen, L., Song, Y., Guo, J., Sun, L., Childs, P., & Yin, Y. (2025). How generative AI supports human in conceptual design. *Design Science*, *11*, e9. DOI: 10.1017/dsj.2025.2

Chen, X. J., Wang, Y., & Li, S. (2024). Challenges of scaling intelligent tutoring systems. *Education and Information Technologies*, *29*, 1–22.

Chi, M. T. H., & Wylie, R. (2014). The ICAP framework. *Educational Psychologist*, *49*(4), 219–243. DOI: 10.1080/00461520.2014.965823

Chiu, T. K. (2021). A holistic approach to the design of AI (AI) education for K-12 schools. *TechTrends*, *65*(5), 796–807. DOI: 10.1007/s11528-021-00637-1

Chiu, T. K. F. (2024). Future research recommendations for transforming higher education with generative AI. *Computers and Education: Artificial Intelligence*, *6*, 100197. DOI: 10.1016/j.caeai.2023.100197

Chiu, T. K. F., Ahmad, Z., Ismailov, M., & Sanusi, I. T. (2024). What are artificial intelligence literacy and competency? A comprehensive framework to support them. *Computers and Education Open*, *6*, 100171. DOI: 10.1016/j.caeo.2024.100171

Chryssolouris, G., Papakostas, N., & Mavrikios, D. (2008). A perspective on manufacturing strategy: Produce more with less. *CIRP Journal of Manufacturing Science and Technology*, *1*(1), 45–52. DOI: 10.1016/j.cirpj.2008.06.008

Code of Administrative Offenses of the Republic of Kazakhstan. (2014, July 5). https://adilet.zan.kz

Code of Ethics of the Journalist of the Republic of Kazakhstan. (2012, October 30). https://online.zakon.kz

Constitution of the Republic of Kazakhstan. (1995, August 30). https://adilet.zan.kz

Cope, B., & Kalantzis, M. (2015). The things you do to know: An introduction to the pedagogy of multiliteracies. In Cope, B., & Kalantzis, M. (Eds.), *A Pedagogy of Multiliteracies: Learning by Design* (pp. 1–36). Palgrave Macmillan. DOI: 10.1057/9781137539724_1

Cope, B., & Kalantzis, M. (2024). A multimodal grammar of artificial intelligence: Measuring the gains and losses in generative AI. *Multimodality & Society*, *4*(1), 6–32. DOI: 10.1177/26349795231221699

Council of Europe. (2018). Reference Framework of Competences for Democratic Culture, Context, concepts and model. (SBN 978-92-871-8573-0). Strasbourg Council of Europe Publishing.

Coyle, D., Hood, P., & Marsh, D. (2010). *CLIL: Content and language integrated learning* (Vol. 9). Cambridge University Press. DOI: 10.1017/9781009024549

Cress, U., & Kimmerle, J. (2023). Generative AI as a catalyst for collaborative knowledge construction. *International Journal of Computer-Supported Collaborative Learning*, *18*(4), 607–614. DOI: 10.1007/s11412-023-09409-w

Criminal Code of the Republic of Kazakhstan. (2014, July 3). https://adilet.zan.kz

Dabis, A., & Csáki, C. (2024). AI and ethics: Investigating the first policy responses of higher education institutions to the challenge of generative AI. *Humanities & Social Sciences Communications*, *11*(1), 1006. Advance online publication. DOI: 10.1057/s41599-024-03526-z

Dai, C. P.. (2024). Adaptive learning systems in AI-supported education. *Educational Psychology Review*, *36*(1), 31. DOI: 10.1007/s10648-024-09855-4

Dearden, J. (2014). English as a medium of instruction–A growing global phenomenon. *British Council*. https://www.britishcouncil.es/sites/default/files/british_council_english_as_a_medium_of_instruction.pdf

Dempere, J., Modugu, K., Hesham, A., & Ramasamy, L. K. (2023). The impact of ChatGPT on higher education. *Frontiers in Education*, *8*, 1206936. Advance online publication. DOI: 10.3389/feduc.2023.1206936

Den Heyer, K., & van Kessel, C. (2015). Evil, agency, and citizenship education. *McGill Journal of Education*, *50*(1), 1–18.

Dignum, V. (2019). *Responsible artificial intelligence: How to develop and use AI in a responsible way*. Springer., DOI: 10.1007/978-3-030-30371-6

Djumanova, S. B. (2025). AI-driven media literacy skills of Uzbek journalists: Key indicators and challenges. Scientific Electronic Journal. *Foreign Languages in Uzbekistan*, *11*(6), 198–215. DOI: 10.36078/1767696698

Docherty, T. (2006). *Aesthetic democracy*. Stanford University Press. DOI: 10.1515/9781503625334

Doiz, A., Lasagabaster, D., & Sierra, J. M. (Eds.). (2012). *English-medium instruction at universities: Global challenges*. Multilingual Matters., https://www.researchgate.net/publication/285573621_English-Medium_Instruction_at_Universities_Global_Challenges DOI: 10.21832/9781847698162

Dorca, F. A., Lima, L. V., Fernandes, M. A., & Lopes, C. R. (2003). Multi-agent tutoring systems for distance education. In *Proceedings of the International Conference on Artificial Intelligence in Education* (pp. 434–435).

Dorias, V. J. (2024). Ecological Themes in Human-Nature Relationships: An Ecocritical Analysis of Bukidnon's Gugud. *International Journal of Language and Literary Studies*, *6*(4), 561–576. DOI: 10.36892/ijlls.v6i4.1960

Drushchak, N., Tyshchenko, V., & Polyakovska, N. (2025, April). Towards Responsible AI in Education: Hybrid Recommendation System for K-12 Students Case Study. In *2025 IEEE/ACM International Workshop on Responsible AI Engineering (RAIE)* (pp. 61-68). IEEE. DOI: 10.1109/RAIE66699.2025.00015

Duranovic, M., Senka, S., & Babic-Gavric, B. (2018). Influence of increased letter spacing and font type on the reading ability of dyslexic children. *Annals of Dyslexia*, *68*(3), 218–228. DOI: 10.1007/s11881-018-0164-z PMID: 30094714

Dyakova, E. G. (2003). Mass political communication in agenda-setting theory: From effect to process. *Political Science (Wellington, N.Z.)*, (3), 42–44.

Ennis, R. H. (2015). Critical thinking: A streamlined conception. I M. Davies & R. Barnett (Eds.), *The Palgrave handbook of critical thinking in higher education* (pp. 31–47). Springer.

Escamilla, K. (2010). Bilingual education programs: Maintenance, transitional, and dual language. *Encyclopedia of Cross-Cultural School Psychology*, 145-149.

Estício, B., Prates, R. O., & Magalhães, M. F. (2015). Supporting pair programming with multi-agent systems. In *Proceedings of the Brazilian Symposium on Software Engineering* (pp. 150–159).

Falkner, R. (2021). *Environmentalism and global international society* (Vol. 156). Cambridge University Press. DOI: 10.1017/9781108966696

Fang, J. W., Chang, C. C., & Hwang, G. J. (2022). Developing computational thinking through intelligent agents. *Journal of Educational Computing Research*, *60*(5), 1301–1324. DOI: 10.1177/07356331211060470

Farahani, M., & Ghasemi, G. (2024). AI and inequality: Challenges and opportunities. *Int. J. Innov. Educ*, *9*, 78–99.

Farrell, T. S. (2020). Professional development through reflective practice for English-medium instruction (EMI) teachers. *International Journal of Bilingual Education and Bilingualism, 23*(3), 277–286. DOI: 10.1080/13670050.2019.1612840

Feng, L., He, L., & Yiganmu, A. (2023). Determinants of students' academic success in English as a medium of instruction (EMI) classes: A systematic review. *Heliyon, 9*(10), e20421. DOI: 10.1016/j.heliyon.2023.e20421 PMID: 37790980

Fenton-Smith, B., Zhou, J., & Galloway, N. (2026). Unpacking the English Medium Instruction (EMI) boom: Exploring student enrolment and driving forces in China and Japan. *Research Papers in Education*, 1–25. DOI: 10.1080/02671522.2026.2633628

Fisher, A. (2011). *Critical thinking: an introduction* (2nd ed.). Cambridge University Press.

Floridi, L., Cowls, J., Beltrametti, M., Chatila, R., Chazerand, P., Dignum, V., Luetge, C., Madelin, R., Pagallo, U., Rossi, F., Schafer, B., Valcke, P., & Vayena, E. (2018). AI4People- An ethical framework for a good AI society: Opportunities, risks, principles, and recommendations. *Minds and Machines, 28*(4), 689–707. DOI: 10.1007/s11023-018-9482-5

Frank, M., Drikakis, D., & Charissis, V. (2020). Machine-learning methods for computational science and engineering. *Computation (Basel, Switzerland), 8*(1), 15. DOI: 10.3390/computation8010015

Freire, P. (2000). *Pedagogy of the oppressed* (30th anniversary ed.). Continuum.

Fullan, M., Quinn, J., & McEachen, J. (2019). *Deep learning: Engage the world change the world.* Corwin Press. DOI: 10.4135/9781506368603

Gaultney, I. B., Sherron, T., & Boden, C. (2022). Political polarization, misinformation, and media literacy. *The Journal of Media Literacy Education, 14*(1), 59–81. DOI: 10.23860/JMLE-2022-14-1-5

Gaur, V., & Sharma, N. K. (2011). A dynamic seller selection model for an agent mediated e-market. *Communications in Computer and Information Science, 191*(Part 2), 284–295. DOI: 10.1007/978-3-642-22714-1_30

Gaur, V., & Soni, A. (2011). Evaluating degree of dependency from domain knowledge using fuzzy inference system. *Communications in Computer and Information Science, 204*, 101–111. DOI: 10.1007/978-3-642-24043-0_11

Gennari, R., Melonio, A., Pellegrino, M. A., & D'Angelo, M. (2023, September). How to playfully teach AI to young learners: a systematic literature review. In *Proceedings of the 15th Biannual Conference of the Italian SIGCHI Chapter* (pp. 1-9). DOI: 10.1145/3605390.3605393

George, A. S. (2023). Preparing students for an AI-driven world: Rethinking curriculum and pedagogy in the age of AI. *Partners Universal Innovative Research Publication, 1*(2), 112–136.

Gilakjani, A. P., & Sabouri, N. B. (2017). Teachers' Beliefs in English Language Teaching and Learning: A Review of the Literature. *English Language Teaching, 10*(4), 78–86. DOI: 10.5539/elt.v10n4p78

Godsk, M., & Møller, K. L. (2024). Engaging students in higher education with educational technology. *Education and Information Technologies*. Advance online publication. DOI: 10.1007/s10639-024-12901-x

Goel, A. K., & Polepeddi, L. (2018). Jill Watson: A virtual teaching assistant for online education. In Dede, C., Richards, J., & Saxberg, B. (Eds.), *Learning Engineering for Online Education* (pp. 120–143). Routledge. DOI: 10.4324/9781351186193-7

Gokhale, A. A. (1995). Collaborative learning enhances critical thinking. *Journal of Technology Education, 7*(1). Advance online publication. https://jte-journal.org/articles/10.21061/jte.v7i1.a.2. DOI: 10.21061/jte.v7i1.a.2

Gonda, M. G. (2014). Role of educational institutions in shaping the future of business and society. *Procedia Economics and Finance, 11*, 635–641. DOI: 10.1016/S2212-5671(14)00229-9

Gonnermann-Müller, J., Haase, J., Fackeldey, K., & Pokutta, S. (2025). FACET: Teacher-centred LLM-based multi-agent systems. *arXiv preprint arXiv:2508.11401.*

González, M., Burguillo, J. C., & Llamas, M. (2012). Case-based reasoning in multi-agent intelligent tutoring systems. *Expert Systems with Applications, 39*(9), 8014–8023.

Graesser, A. C.. (2018). Complex learning environments. *Psychological Science in the Public Interest, 19*(2), 59–92. DOI: 10.1177/1529100618808244

Grivennaya, L. A. (2018). *National identity: Theory and practice.* Publising House of Kozybayev North Kazakhstan University.

Grover, S., & Pea, R. (2018). Computational thinking: A competency whose time has come. In Sentance, S., Barendsen, E., & Schulte, C. (Eds.), *Computer science education: Perspectives on teaching and learning in school* (pp. 19–37). Bloomsbury Academic. DOI: 10.5040/9781350057142.ch-003

Guan, Y., Zhang, C., He, H., Zhang, W., Hu, Z., Bi, T., & Jin, X. (2025). AI literacy predicts computational thinking through multidimensional interactions among Chinese high school students. *Scientific Reports*, *15*(1), 33092. DOI: 10.1038/s41598-025-16712-z

Guess, A. M., Lerner, M., Lyons, B., Montgomery, J. M., Nyhan, B., Reifler, J., & Sircar, N. (2020). A digital media literacy intervention increases discernment between mainstream and false news in the United States and India. *Proceedings of the National Academy of Sciences of the United States of America*, *117*(27), 15536–15545. DOI: 10.1073/pnas.1920498117 PMID: 32571950

Guo, H., & Li, D. (2024). The effect of electronic portfolio-based writing instruction on the second language writing performance and writing self-efficacy of EFL learners: A mixed methods study. *SAGE Open*, *14*(2), 21582440241257697. Advance online publication. DOI: 10.1177/21582440241257697

Gu, X., & Ericson, B. J. (2025, August). Ai literacy in k-12 and higher education in the wake of generative ai: An integrative review. In *Proceedings of the 2025 ACM Conference on International Computing Education Research* V. 1 (pp. 125-140). DOI: 10.1145/3702652.3744217

Hagendorff, T. (2020). The Ethics of AI Ethics: An Evaluation of Guidelines. *Minds and Machines*, *30*(1), 99–120. DOI: 10.1007/s11023-020-09517-8

Hamal, O., El Faddouli, N. E., & Harouni, M. H. A. (2021). Design and implementation of a multi-agent system in education. *World Journal on Educational Technology: Current Issues*, *13*(4), 775–793. DOI: 10.18844/wjet.v13i4.6264

Hare, J. (2024). Enhancing student experience with iterative design. *British Journal of Educational Technology*. Advance online publication. DOI: 10.1111/bjet.13456

Hargreaves, A. (1998). The emotional practice of teaching. *Teaching and Teacher Education*, *14*(8), 835–854. DOI: 10.1016/S0742-051X(98)00025-0

Hattie, J. (2009). *Visible learning: A synthesis of over 800 meta-analyses relating to achievement*. Routledge.

Heffernan, N. T., & Heffernan, C. L. (2014). The assistments ecosystem: Building a platform that brings scientists and teachers together for minimally invasive research on human learning and teaching. *International Journal of Artificial Intelligence in Education, 24*(4), 470–497. DOI: 10.1007/s40593-014-0024-x

Hemraj, S. (2025). AI and the future of creative development: Redefining digital media production. *AI and Ethics*, *5*(5), 1–15. DOI: 10.1007/s43681-025-00765-x

Hernández-Sells, N., Muñoz-Carril, P. C., & González-Sanmamed, M. (2019). Emotion-aware agents in collaborative learning. *Computers & Education*, *138*, 1–12.

Heymann, B. F., & Briedis, M. (2025). Challenging human creativity: An exercise of co-creation with generative artificial intelligence. *Creativity Studies, 18*(2), 570-583.4

Hilb, M. (2020). Toward artificial governance? The role of artificial intelligence in shaping the future of corporate governance. *The Journal of Management and Governance*, *24*(4), 851–870. DOI: 10.1007/s10997-020-09519-9

Hjarvard, S. (2008). *The mediatization of religion: A theory of the media as agents of religious change*. Northern Lights. *Film and Media Studies Yearbook*, *6*(1), 9–26. DOI: 10.1386/nl.6.1.9_1

Hogan, P. C. (2019). Personal Identity and Literature. In *Routledge eBooks*. Informa., DOI: 10.4324/9780429265228

Holmes, N. (2018). Engaging with assessment: Increasing student engagement through continuous assessment. *Active Learning in Higher Education*, *19*(1), 23–34. DOI: 10.1177/1469787417723230

Holmes, T. R. (2023). Narrative Identity through a Constructivist Lens: Introduction. *Journal of Constructivist Psychology*, *1–3*(4), 427–429. Advance online publication. DOI: 10.1080/10720537.2023.2168808

Holmes, W., Bialik, M., & Fadel, C. (2019). *Artificial intelligence in education: Promises and implications for teaching and learning*. Center for Curriculum Redesign.

Honey, M., Pearson, G., & Schweingruber, H. A. (Eds.). (2014). *STEM integration in K-12 education: Status, prospects, and an agenda for research* (Vol. 500). National Academies Press.

Hongli, Z., & Leong, W. Y. (2024). AI solutions for accessible education in underserved communities. *Journal of Innovation and Technology*, 2024. Retrieved from https://iuojs.intimal.edu.my/index.php/joit/article/view/528

Hooda, M., Rana, C., Dahiya, O., Rizwan, A., & Hossain, M. S. (2022). AI for assessment and feedback to enhance student success in higher education. *Mathematical Problems in Engineering, 2022*(1), 5215722.

Hooda, M., Rana, C., Dahiya, O., Rizwan, A., & Hossain, M. S. (2022). Artificial Intelligence for assessment and feedback to enhance student success in higher education. *Mathematical Problems in Engineering, 2022*, 1–19. DOI: 10.1155/2022/5215722

How Kazakhstanis relate to artificial intelligence: trust, irritation and hope. (2025, November 13). *Tribune.kz*. https://tribune.kz/kak-kazahstantsy-otnosyatsya-k-iskusstvennomu-intellektu-doverie-razdrazhenie-i-nadezhdy/

Huang, J., & Tan, M. (2023). The role of ChatGPT in scientific communication: Writing better scientific review articles. *American Journal of Cancer Research, 13*(4), 1148. PMID: 37168339

Huang, S., Long, L., Zhu, Y., & Zhu, J. N. (2026). Human–GenAI collaboration across creative phases: Cognitive mechanisms shaping novelty and usefulness. *International Journal of Information Management, 86*, 102986. DOI: 10.1016/j.ijinfomgt.2025.102986

Hughes, R. (2008). Internationalisation of higher education and language policy: Questions of quality and equity. *Higher Education Management and Policy, 20*(1), 1–18.

Hulekal, R., & As, S. (2025). AI-driven creativity: The role of generative models in event theme and design conceptualization. *Journal of Environmental Management and Tourism, 16*(4), 435–444. DOI: 10.14505/jemt.v16.4(80).07

Hwang, G. J., Sung, H. Y., Hung, C. M., Huang, I., & Tsai, C. C. (2013). Development of a personalized concept map-based learning approach. *Computers & Education, 69*, 121–130. DOI: 10.1016/j.compedu.2013.07.008

Hwang, G. J., Xie, H., Wah, B. W., & Gašević, D. (2020). Vision, challenges, roles and research issues of Artificial Intelligence in Education. *Computers and Education: Artificial Intelligence, 1*, 100001. Advance online publication. DOI: 10.1016/j.caeai.2020.100001

Hwang, Y., & Lee, J. H. (2025). Exploring students' experiences and perceptions of human-AI collaboration in digital content making. *International Journal of Educational Technology in Higher Education, 22*(1), 44. DOI: 10.1186/s41239-025-00542-0

Ignjatović, G. (2024). AI technologies in education: Regulatory frameworks at the international, regional and national level. *Zbornik Radova Pravnog Fakulteta Nis, 63*(103), 235–260. DOI: 10.5937/zrpfn1-55374

Insany, F. D., Nur'ain, S., Utami, W. K., Januar, M. A., & Purwarno, P. (2024). Human-nature Relationship in Riawani Elyta and Shabrina Q. S.'s Novel Rahasia Pelangi: An Ecocritical Approach. [IJEAL]. *International Journal of English and Applied Linguistics*, *4*(1), 28–37. DOI: 10.47709/ijeal.v4i1.3698

Insebayeva, S., & Insebayeva, N. (2021). The power of ambiguity: National symbols, nation-building, and political legitimacy in Kazakhstan. *Europe-Asia Studies*, *74*(4), 660–682. DOI: 10.1080/09668136.2021.1912296

Islam, G., & Greenwood, M. (2024). Generative artificial intelligence as hyper commons: Ethics of authorship and ownership. *Journal of Business Ethics*, *192*(4), 659–663. DOI: 10.1007/s10551-024-05741-9

Islam, M. S., & Stapa, M. B. (2021). Students' low proficiency in spoken English in private universities in Bangladesh: Reasons and remedies. *Language Testing in Asia*, *11*(1), 22. DOI: 10.1186/s40468-021-00139-0

Ismail, A., Aliu, A., Ibrahim, M., & Sulaiman, A. (2024). Preparing teachers of the future in the era of AI. *Journal of AI. MLand Neural Network*, *44*, 31–41.

Ismaili, Y. (2024). AI literacy and adaptive learning in Moroccan education: Advancing critical thinking and personalized learning. *Research on Education and Media*, *16*(2), 20240017. Advance online publication. DOI: 10.2478/rem-2024-0017

Ismanov, A., Kupuyeva, N., Stanalieva, G., Toktogulova, M., & Turdubaeva, E. (2023). *From hate speech to nonviolent communication*. Prevention Media.

Izquierdo-Condoy, J. S., Arias-Intriago, M., Tello-De-la-Torre, A., Busch, F., & Ortiz-Prado, E. (2025). Generative artificial intelligence in medical education: Enhancing critical thinking or undermining cognitive autonomy? *Journal of Medical Internet Research*, *27*, e76340. DOI: 10.2196/76340

Jacques, P. H., Moss, H. K., & Garger, J. (2024). A synthesis of AI in Higher Education: Shaping the future. *Journal of Behavioral and Applied Management*, *24*(2). Advance online publication. DOI: 10.21818/001c.122146

Janks, H. (2010). Language, power and pedagogies. In *N. H. Hornberger & S. L.* McKay.

Janzen, J. (2008). Teaching English language learners in the content areas. *Review of Educational Research*, *78*(4), 1010–1038. DOI: 10.3102/0034654308325580

Jiang, L., Lee, I., & Yu, S. (2024). Conceptualizing multimodal feedback literacy for L2 writing teachers in the digital age. *International Journal of Applied Linguistics*, *34*(3), 987–1003. DOI: 10.1111/ijal.12578

Jiang, Y.-H., Li, R., Zhou, Y., Qi, C., Hu, H., Wei, Y., Jiang, B., & Wu, Y. (2024). AI agent for education: Von Neumann multi-agent system framework. *Proceedings of GCCCE, 2024*, 77–84.

Kabakus, A. K., Bahcekapili, E., & Ayaz, A. (2023). The effect of digital literacy on technology acceptance: An evaluation on administrative staff in higher education. *Journal of Information Science, 51*(4), 512–533. DOI: 10.1177/01655515231160028

Kachru, B. B., Quirk, R., & Widdowson, H. G. (1985). Standards, codification and sociolinguistic realism. *World Englishes. Critical Concepts in Linguistics*, 241-270.

Kalantzis, M., & Cope, B. (2024). Literacy in the time of artificial intelligence. *Reading Research Quarterly*. Advance online publication. DOI: 10.1002/rrq.591

Källkvist, M., & Hult, F. M. (2016). Discursive mechanisms and human agency in language policy formation: Negotiating bilingualism and parallel language use at a Swedish university. *International Journal of Bilingual Education and Bilingualism, 19*(1), 1–17. DOI: 10.1080/13670050.2014.956044

Kalyanpur, M., Boruah, P. B., Molina, S. C., & Shenoy, S. (2022). *The politics of English language education and social inequality: Global pressures, national priorities and schooling in India*. Routledge. DOI: 10.4324/9781003125488

Kang, J., & Yi, Y. (2023). Beyond ChatGPT: Multimodal generative AI for L2 writers. *Journal of Second Language Writing, 62*, 101070. Advance online publication. DOI: 10.1016/j.jslw.2023.101070

Kaplan, R., & Meylani, R. (2025). Dimensions of artificial intelligence literacy: A qualitative synthesis of contemporary research literature. *Journal of Computer and Education Research, 13*(26), 790–825. DOI: 10.18009/jcer.1648380

Kaswan, K. S., Dhatterwal, J. S., & Ojha, R. P. (2024). AI in personalized learning. In *Advances in technological innovations in higher education* (pp. 103–117). CRC Press. DOI: 10.1201/9781003376699-9

Katona, J., & Gyonyoru, K. I. K. (2025). AI-based adaptive programming education for socially disadvantaged students: Bridging the digital divide. *TechTrends, 69*(5), 1–18. DOI: 10.1007/s11528-025-01088-8

Kaur, X., Yadav, Y., & Singh, Z. (2025). A novel approach to streamline requirements engineering for multi-agent systems. In *OASIcs*. ICPEC.

Khalifa, M., & Albadawy, M. (2024). Using artificial intelligence in academic writing and research: An essential productivity tool. *Computer Methods and Programs in Biomedicine Update, 5*, 100145. DOI: 10.1016/j.cmpbup.2024.100145

Khan, W. N. (2024). Ethical challenges of AI in education: Balancing innovation with data privacy. *AI EDIFY Journal*, *1*(1), 1–13.

Khazanchi, R., Khazanchi, P., Warr, M., Mishra, P., Blankenship, R., Jacques, L., & Petit, J. (2025, March). Implications of AI in K-12 and Higher Education. In *Society for Information Technology & Teacher Education International Conference* (pp. 748-751). Association for the Advancement of Computing in Education (AACE).

Kirschner, P. A., Sweller, J., & Clark, R. E. (2006). Why minimal guidance during instruction does not work. *Educational Psychologist*, *41*(2), 75–86. DOI: 10.1207/s15326985ep4102_1

Klieme, E., & Vieluf, S. (2009). Teaching practices, teachers' beliefs and attitudes. *Creating Effektive Teaching and Learning Environments. First Results from TALIS, 2009*, 87–135.

Knight, J. (2005). An internationalization model: responding to new realities and challenges. *Higher Education in Latin America: The International Dimension*, 1-38.

Knight, J. (2016). Transnational education remodeled: Toward a common TNE framework and definitions. *Journal of Studies in International Education*, *20*(1), 34–47. DOI: 10.1177/1028315315602927

Kocak, B., Baessler, B., Bakas, S., Cuocolo, R., Fedorov, A., Maier-Hein, L., Mercaldo, N., Müller, H., Orlhac, F., Pinto dos Santos, D., Stanzione, A., Ugga, L., & Zwanenburg, A. (2023). CheckList for EvaluAtion of Radiomics research (CLEAR): A step-by-step reporting guideline for authors and reviewers endorsed by ESR and EuSoMII. *Insights Into Imaging*, *14*(1), 75. DOI: 10.1186/s13244-023-01415-8 PMID: 37142815

Kong, S. C., Cheung, W. M. Y., & Zhang, G. (2021). Evaluation of an artificial intelligence literacy course for university students with diverse study backgrounds. *Computers and Education: Artificial Intelligence*, *2*, 100026. Advance online publication. DOI: 10.1016/j.caeai.2021.100026

Kress, G. (2003). *Literacy in the new media age*. Routledge.

Kress, G. (2010). *Multimodality: A social semiotic approach to contemporary communication*. Routledge.

Kress, G., & Van Leeuwen, T. (2020). *Reading images: The grammar of visual design*. Routledge. DOI: 10.4324/9781003099857

Kumar, P. (2025). *Language Barriers in Education: Challenges and Opportunities for Marginalized, Rural, and Lower Caste Students in India*. https://www.researchgate.net/publication/388817366_Language_Barriers_in_Education_Challenges_and_Opportunities_for_Marginalized_Rural_and_Lower_Caste_Students_in_India

Kumar, A. (2024). The role of simulation and modeling in AI: A review. *International Journal of Modeling, Simulation and Scientific Computing*, *15*(03), 2430002. DOI: 10.1142/S1793962324300024

Kwemoi, K. C. (2024). The Integration of virtual reality and gamification in education. *Research Output Journal of Biological and Applied Science*, *3*(1), 7–12.

Lam, R., & Ni, Y. (2024). Students' perceptions of multiliteracies development using AI-assisted portfolio assessment. *Pedagogies*, *60*(1), 1–28. Advance online publication. DOI: 10.1080/1554480X.2025.2545212

Lanser, S. S. (2016). Gender and Narrative. *De Gruyter EBooks*, 206–218. DOI: 10.1515/9783110316469.206

Law "On Artificial Intelligence" of the Republic of Kazakhstan. (2025, November 230). https://adilet.zan.kz

Leaton Gray, S., Edsall, D., & Parapadakis, D. (2025). AI-based digital cheating at university, and the case for new ethical pedagogies. *Journal of Academic Ethics*, *23*(4), 1–18. DOI: 10.1007/s10805-025-09642-y

Lee, J.-Y. (2026). Silenced by non-consensual deepfakes? Perceived threat and online self-censorship among female users: Mediating roles of perceived control, belief in a just world, and passive SNS use. *Telematics and Informatics Reports*, *21*, 100279. Advance online publication. DOI: 10.1016/j.teler.2025.100279

Lens. (2025). Retrieved, 2025, from https://www.lens.org/

Létourneau, A., Deslandes Martineau, M., Charland, P., Karran, J. A., Boasen, J., & Léger, P. M. (2025). A systematic review of AI-driven intelligent tutoring systems (ITS) in K-12 education. *npj Science of Learning, 10*(1), 29.

Levido, A. (2024). Media literacy and the concept of 'technologies' in primary school classrooms: Moving beyond technical skills. *Learning, Media and Technology*, *50*(4), 560–572. DOI: 10.1080/17439884.2024.2308609

Liddicoat, A. J. (2003). Internationalisation as a concept in higher education: Perspectives from policy. *Australian Perspectives on Internationalising Education*, 13-26.

Li, J., Yan, Y., & Zeng, X. (2025). Exploring artificial intelligence in inclusive education: A systematic review of empirical studies. *Applied Sciences (Basel, Switzerland)*, *15*(23), 12624. DOI: 10.3390/app152312624

Lim, L. (2015). Critical thinking, social education and the curriculum: foregrounding a social

Lim, T., Gottipati, S., & Cheong, M. (2025). What students really think: Unpacking AI ethics in educational assessments through a triadic framework. *International Journal of Educational Technology in Higher Education*, *22*(1), 56. DOI: 10.1186/s41239-025-00556-8

Lippmann, W. (2004). *Public opinion*. Institute of the Public Opinion Foundation.

Liu, Y., & Wang, H. (2026). Application of deep learning for transformation of Chinese traditional cultural narrative patterns and enhancement of cultural identity empowered by AIGC. *Scientific Reports*, *16*(1), 2505. Advance online publication. DOI: 10.1038/s41598-025-32302-5 PMID: 41444384

Li, X., Gao, Z., & Liao, H. (2024). An empirical investigation of college students' acceptance of translation technologies. *PLoS One*, *19*(2), e0297297. DOI: 10.1371/journal.pone.0297297

Llerena-Izquierdo, J., & Ayala-Carabajo, R. (2025). Ethics of the use of artificial intelligence in academia and research: The most relevant approaches, challenges and topics. *Informatics (MDPI)*, *12*(4), 111. DOI: 10.3390/informatics12040111

Lo, N. P. K. (2024). The confluence of digital literacy and eco-consciousness: Harmonizing digital skills with sustainable practices in education. *Platforms*, *2*(1), 15–32. DOI: 10.3390/platforms2010002

Lo, N., Wong, A., & Chan, S. (2025). The impact of generative AI on essay revisions and student engagement. *Computers and Education Open*, *22*, 100249. DOI: 10.1016/j.caeo.2025.100249

Long, D., & Magerko, B. (2020). What is AI literacy? Competencies and design considerations. *Proceedings of the 2020 CHI Conference on Human Factors in Computing Systems*, 1-16. DOI: 10.1145/3313831.3376727

Longo, M.. (2014). Smart environments and agent-based learning. *Journal of Environmental Protection and Ecology*, *12*(4A), 2225–2235.

Loyola, M., Nelson, J. D., Clifton, G., & Levinson, D. (2023). Narratives in transport research: A thematic and functional analysis. *Transportation Research Interdisciplinary Perspectives*, *17*, 100754. DOI: 10.1016/j.trip.2023.100754

Luckin, R. (2017). Towards AI-based assessment systems. *Nature Human Behaviour*, *1*(3), 1–3. DOI: 10.1038/s41562-016-0028

Luckin, R., Holmes, W., Griffiths, M., & Forcier, L. B. (2018). *Intelligence unleashed: An argument for AI in education*. Pearson.

Lukitasari, M., Murtafiah, W., Ramdiah, S., Hasan, R., & Sukri, A. (2022). Constructing digital literacy instrument and its effect on college students' learning outcomes. *International Journal of Instruction*, *15*(2), 171–188. DOI: 10.29333/iji.2022.15210a

Lynam, S., & Cachia, M. (2018). Students' perceptions of the role of assessments at higher education. *Assessment & Evaluation in Higher Education*, *43*(2), 223–234. DOI: 10.1080/02602938.2017.1329928

Mabini, H., & Gallardo, R. (2024). Digital literacy and critical thinking skills among Grade 5 learners. *International Journal of Innovative Science and Research Technology*, *9*(6), 1589–1597. DOI: 10.38124/ijisrt/IJISRT24JUN413

Macaro, E. (2018). English medium instruction: A research agenda for a worldwide phenomenon. *La didattica delle lingue nel nuovo millennio: Le sfide dell'internazionalizzazione*, 15-20.

Macaro, E. (2022). English Medium Instruction: What do we know so far and what do we still need to find out? *Language Teaching*, *55*(4), 533–546. DOI: 10.1017/S0261444822000052

Mahmoud, S. (2019). Resistance in Postcolonial Literature with Reference to Sahar Khalifeh's Wild Thorns. *International Journal of Language and Literary Studies*, *1*(2), 74–87. DOI: 10.36892/ijlls.v1i2.35

Mahrishi, M., Abbas, A., & Siddiqui, M. K. (2024). *Global Initiatives towards Regulatory Frameworks for Artificial intelligence (AI) in Higher Education*. Digital Government Research and Practice. DOI: 10.1145/3672462

Májovskỳ, M., Černỳ, M., Kasal, M., Komarc, M., & Netuka, D. (2023). Artificial intelligence can generate fraudulent but authentic-looking scientific medical articles: Pandora's box has been opened. *Journal of Medical Internet Research*, *25*(1), e46924. DOI: 10.2196/46924 PMID: 37256685

Manan, S. A., Channa, L. A., & Haidar, S. (2023). *1 Fostering the multilingual agenda in EMI*. English-Medium Instruction Pedagogies in Multilingual Universities in Asia. DOI: 10.4324/9781003173137-3

Manju, D. (2024). Challenges of teaching English language in India: A comprehensive analysis. *International Journal of Emerging Technologies and Innovative Research*, *11*(6), c549–c554.

Mansfield, C. D., Bauer, J. J., Booker, J., Grysman, A., Singer, J., & Fivush, R. (2026). What might we learn about autobiographical narrative processing from artificial intelligence? *Humanities & Social Sciences Communications*, *13*(1), 182. Advance online publication. DOI: 10.1057/s41599-025-06426-y

Mansoor, H. M., Bawazir, A., Alsabri, M. A., Alharbi, A., & Okela, A. H. (2024). Artificial intelligence literacy among university students: A comparative transnational survey. *Frontiers in Communication*, *9*, 1478476. DOI: 10.3389/fcomm.2024.1478476

Mariam, G., Adil, L., & Zakaria, B. (2024). The integration of artificial intelligence (AI) into education systems and its impact on the governance of higher education institutions. *International Journal of Professional Business Review*, *9*(12), e05176. DOI: 10.26668/businessreview/2024.v9i12.5176

Marinovich, A. (2015, March 21). The role of social media in shaping ethnic identity during the political transformations of the Arab Spring. *Electronic Scientific Archive*. https://elar.urfu.ru/bitstream/10995/35366/1/iimvmm_2015_21.pdf

Ma, Y., Zhang, X., Ren, J., Wang, R., Wang, M., & Chen, Y. (2026). Linguistic features of AI mis/disinformation and the detection limits of LLMs. *Nature Communications*, *17*(1), 456. Advance online publication. DOI: 10.1038/s41467-025-67145-1 PMID: 41372163

McGovern, E., Moreira, G., & Luna-Nevarez, C. (2020). An application of virtual reality in education: Can this technology enhance the quality of students' learning experience? *Journal of Education for Business*, *95*(7), 490–496. DOI: 10.1080/08832323.2019.1703096

McSharry, G., & Jones, S. (2000). Role-play in science teaching and learning. *The School Science Review*, *82*, 73–82.

Meirbekov, A., Maslova, I., & Gallyamova, Z. (2022). Digital education tools for critical thinking development. *Thinking Skills and Creativity*, *44*, 101023. Advance online publication. DOI: 10.1016/j.tsc.2022.101023

Meld. St. 34 (2023-2024). En mer praktisk skole [A More Pracitcal School]. Regjerningen [The Government]. Meld. St. 34 (2023–2024) - regjeringen.no

Melo-López, V.-A., Basantes-Andrade, A., Gudiño-Mejía, C.-B., & Hernández-Martínez, E. (2025). The impact of artificial intelligence on inclusive education: A systematic review. *Education Sciences*, *15*(5), 539. DOI: 10.3390/educsci15050539

Meurant, R. C. (2010). EFL/ESL textbook selection in Korea and East Asia-Relevant issues and literature review. In *International Conference on Ubiquitous Computing and Multimedia Applications* (pp. 89-102). Springer Berlin Heidelberg. DOI: 10.1007/978-3-642-13467-8_9

Miao, F., Holmes, W., Huang, R., & Zhang, H. (Eds.). (2021). *AI and education: Guidance for policy-makers*. UNESCO.

Michel-Villarreal, R., Vilalta-Perdomo, E. L., Salinas-Navarro, D. E., Thierry-Aguilera, R., & Gerardou, F. S. (2023). Challenges and opportunities of generative AI for higher education as explained by ChatGPT. *Education Sciences*, *13*(9), 856. Advance online publication. DOI: 10.3390/educsci13090856

Milner, H. (2002). *Civic Literacy: How Informed Citizens Make Democracy Work*. University Press of New England.

Mkrtchyan, N. (2014). The notion of "Kazakhness" behind the symbolic nation-building of Kazakhstan. *SSRN*, *9*(1–2), 16–38. DOI: 10.2139/ssrn.2458368

Moddelmog-Anweiler, E., & Mach, Z. (2022). Religious identities and religious pluralism in Central and Eastern Europe. In *Religion in the public sphere in Central and Eastern Europe* (pp. 13–61).

Mohammad-Roe, S., Paaske, N., Van Hoof, N., & Amitai, A. (2025). Nurturing student engagement: Towards democratic values and attitudes. *Journal of Social Science Education*, *24*(3). Advance online publication. DOI: 10.11576/jsse-7680

Mohrman, K., Ma, W., & Baker, D. (2008). The research university in transition: The emerging global model. *Higher Education Policy*, *21*(1), 5–27. DOI: 10.1057/palgrave.hep.8300175

Moravec, V., Hynek, N., Gavurova, B., & Rigelsky, M. (2024). Who uses it and for what purpose? The role of digital literacy in ChatGPT adoption and utilisation. *Journal of Innovation & Knowledge*, *9*(2), 100602. Advance online publication. DOI: 10.1016/j.jik.2024.100602

Mourtzis, D. (2020). Simulation in the design and operation of manufacturing systems: State of the art and new trends. *International Journal of Production Research*, *58*(7), 1927–1949. DOI: 10.1080/00207543.2019.1636321

Mourtzis, D., Doukas, M., & Bernidaki, D. (2014). Simulation in manufacturing: Review and challenges. *Procedia CIRP*, *25*, 213–229. DOI: 10.1016/j.procir.2014.10.032

Muratbekov, B. (2026, February 12). “Beautiful, but not real“: how AI bloggers are taking over the Internet and why it can be dangerous. TengriNews. https://tengrinews.kz/curious/krasivyie-nenastoyaschie-ii-blogeryi-zahvatyivayut-kaznet-592449/

Mustafa, M., Tlili, A., Lampropoulos, G., Huang, R., Sampson, D. G., & Ifenthaler, D. (2024). A systematic review of literature reviews on artificial intelligence in education (AIED): A roadmap to a future research agenda. *Smart Learning Environments*, *11*(1), 59. Advance online publication. DOI: 10.1186/s40561-024-00350-5

Mustapha, S. S. (2025). Personalized Learning with AI: Adapting Education to Learners’ Needs.

Mustapha, M. J., Lasisi, M. I., & Barabash, V. V. (2024). Are they tools? Anglophone West African countries’ students’ misconception of media literacy and critical thinking for combating misinformation. *The Journal of Media Literacy Education*, *16*(1), 94–103. DOI: 10.23860/JMLE-2024-16-1-7

National Education Policy (NEP). (2020). https://www.education.gov.in/en/nep/about-nep

Ncube, P. D., Dzvapatsva, G. P., Matobobo, C., & Ranga, M. M. (2026). Redefining student assessment in AI-infused learning environments: A systematic review of challenges and strategies for academic integrity. *AI and Ethics*, *6*(1), 68. DOI: 10.1007/s43681-025-00871-w

Neuwirth, R. J. (2024). The global institutional governance of AI: A four-dimensional perspective. In *Int. J. Digit. Law Gov*, *1*(1), 13–153. DOI: 10.1515/ijdlg-2024-0004

Nevokshanova, A. A., & Stefanchikov, I. V. (2019). The role of print media in shaping Uruguayan national identity in the first third of the 20th century. *Litera*, (2), 78–96. DOI: 10.25136/2409-8698.2019.2.29945

Ng, D. T. K., Su, J., Leung, J. K. L., & Chu, S. K. W. (2023). Artificial intelligence (AI) literacy education in secondary schools: A review. *Interactive Learning Environments*. Advance online publication. DOI: 10.1080/10494820.2023.2255228

Nguyen, A., Ngo, H. N., Hong, Y., Dang, B., & Nguyen, B.-P. T. (2022). Ethical principles for artificial intelligence in education. *Education and Information Technologies*, *28*(4), 4221–4241. DOI: 10.1007/s10639-022-11316-w PMID: 36254344

Nguyen, L., & Habók, A. (2023). Tools for assessing teacher digital literacy: A review. *Journal of Computers in Education*, *10*(2), 257–297. DOI: 10.1007/s40692-022-00257-5

Nguyen, T. N. Q., & Nguyen, T. T. (2025). AI literacy in language learning through digital multimodal composing: A systematic review. *VNU Journal of Foreign Studies*, *41*(3), 142–156. DOI: 10.63023/2525-2445/jfs.ulis.5517

Nikolajeva, M., & Scott, C. (2013). *How picturebooks work*. Routledge. DOI: 10.4324/9780203960615

Noble, S. U. (2018). *Algorithms of oppression: How search engines reinforce racism*. NYU Press. DOI: 10.18574/nyu/9781479833641.001.0001

Noelle-Neumann, E. (1996). *The spiral of silence: Public opinion—Our social skin*. Progress-Akademiya; Mir.

Nortio, E., Jasinskaja-Lahti, I., Hämäläinen, M., & Pakkasvirta, J. (2022). Fear of the Russian bear? Negotiating Finnish national identity online. *Nations and Nationalism*, *28*(3), 861–876. DOI: 10.1111/nana.12832

OECD. (2021). AI and the future of skills, Volume 1: Capabilities and assessments. OECD Publishing. DOI: 10.1787/5ee71f34-en

OECD. (2024). The governance of artificial intelligence: Harnessing opportunities and mitigating challenges. In *Research Policy* 53, 104928. DOI: 10.1016/j.respol.2023.104928

Okonkwo, S., & Schmid-Meier, C. (2025, September 17). AI for inclusion?! Challenging the design of educational AI through equity & disability perspectives. AIEOU Inaugural Conference, University of Oxford. *Zenodo*. https://doi.org/DOI: 10.5281/zenodo.17226470

Olszak, I. (2025). Artificial intelligence and the transformation of literacy: Trilingual students' perspectives on AI-supported writing development. *European Journal of Applied Linguistics Studies*, *8*(4). Advance online publication. DOI: 10.46827/ejals.v8i4.664

Østern, A.-L. (2008). Aktiv estetisk respons som utfordring i litteraturundervisning. In A.-L. Østern, A.-L., Otnes, H., & Hestnes, H. (Eds), Esteisk tilnærming til tekstarbeid i språkfagene (Vol 2). Tapir akademisk forlag.

Paaske, N., Mohammad-Roe, S., Smets, W., Amitai, A., Randazzo, N. A., & Huang, L. (2023). Challenges for European teachers when assessing student learning to promote democratic citizenship competences. *Journal of Social Science Education*, *22*(3), 3–22. DOI: 10.11576/jsse-5978

Pan, L., Haq, S., Shi, X., & Nadeem, M. (2024). The impact of digital competence and personal innovativeness on the learning behavior of students: Exploring the moderating role of digitalization in higher education quality. *SAGE Open*, *14*(2), 21582440241265919. Advance online publication. DOI: 10.1177/21582440241265919

Papasarantou, C., Alimisis, D., Geramani, K., & Ioannidis, G. (2002). Introducing Artificial Intelligence in school education: the Edu4AI project. *Proc. of the 17th Edition of the EUTIC–In the Intersection of Art, Science and Technology: Dialogos between Humans and Machines. Corfu, Greece: Department of Audio & Visual Arts, Ionian University*, 272-280.

Paschal, M. J., & Melly, I. K. (2023). Ethical guidelines on the use of AI in education. In *Advances in educational technologies and instructional design book series*, 230–245. DOI: 10.4018/979-8-3693-0205-7.ch013

Pecorari, D., & Malmström, H. (2018). At the crossroads of TESOL and English medium instruction. *TESOL Quarterly*, *52*(3), 497–515. DOI: 10.1002/tesq.470

Pehlivanoglu, D., Zhu, M., Zhen, J., Gagnon-Roberge, A. A., Kern, R. K., Woodard, D., Cahill, B. S., & Ebner, N. C. (2026). Is this real? Susceptibility to deepfakes in machines and humans. *Cognitive Research: Principles and Implications*, *11*(1), 3. Advance online publication. DOI: 10.1186/s41235-025-00700-y PMID: 41501543

Pei, B., Xing, W., & Wang, M. (2021). Academic development of multimodal learning analytics: A bibliometric analysis. *Interactive Learning Environments*, *31*(6), 3543–3561. DOI: 10.1080/10494820.2021.1936075

Pereira, D., Flores, M. A., & Niklasson, L. (2016). Assessment revisited: A review of research in *Assessment and Evaluation in Higher Education. Assessment & Evaluation in Higher Education*, *41*(7), 1008–1032. DOI: 10.1080/02602938.2015.1055233

Photos of Kazakh intelligentsia reinterpreted with the help of AI. (2024, January 31). *TengriNews*. https://tengrinews.kz/curious/foto-kazahskoy-intelligentsii-pereosmyislili-s-pomoschyu-ii-524824/

Pinker, S. (2021). *Enlightenment now: The case for reason, science, humanism, and progress*. Alpina Publisher.

Prambudi, N. L., Putawa, R. A., & Izumi, C. (2024). A quantitative analysis of artificial intelligence's impact on students' mindset and critical thinking in higher education. *International Journal of Informatics and Information Systems*, *7*(4), 168–178. DOI: 10.47738/ijiis.v7i4.222

Prince, M. (2004). Does active learning work? A review of the research. *Journal of Engineering Education*, *93*(3), 223–231. DOI: 10.1002/j.2168-9830.2004.tb00809.x

Punch, P. F., & Aoancea, A. (2014). *Introduction to research methods in education* (2nd ed.). Sage.

Qazi, K. A. (2022). Crossing Borders: Diasporic Identity and Cultural Displacement in Jhumpa Lahiri's The Namesake. *ShodhKosh: Journal of Visual and Performing Arts*, *3*(1). Advance online publication. DOI: 10.29121/shodhkosh.v3.i1.2022.3471

Qian, L., Cao, W., & Chen, L. (2025). Influence of artificial intelligence on higher education reform and talent cultivation in the digital intelligence era. *Scientific Reports*, *15*(1), 6047. DOI: 10.1038/s41598-025-89392-4

Quarteroni, S.. (2025). Refining quality requirements in agent-mediated systems. In *Proceedings of AAMAS 2025.*

Rajbanshi, S. (2025). Recasting methodologies in English language classrooms: Teachers' roles and challenges in the context of NEP 2020. *DLC IMAGE: PRATIBIMBO, 3*(2), 01-06.

Ramamoorthy, S., & Dinesh, A. (2025). *English Medium Instruction (EMI), Challenges, and Coping Strategies: Stances of Dalit Students and Teaches in Institutes of HE in India.* https://www.researchgate.net/publication/394986048_English_Medium_Instruction_EMI_Challenges_and_Coping_Strategies_Stances_of_Dalit_Students_and_Teaches_in_Institutes_of_HE_in_India

Ray, S. T.Dr Shobha Tiwari Ray. (2024). Diasporic Consciousness in Jhumpa Lahiri's Novel "The Namesake.". *Universal Research Reports*, *11*(1), 183–186. DOI: 10.36676/urr.v11.i1.28

Reddy, P., Chaudhary, K., & Hussein, S. (2023). A digital literacy model to narrow the digital literacy skills gap. *Heliyon*, *9*(4), e14878. Advance online publication. DOI: 10.1016/j.heliyon.2023.e14878 PMID: 37025876

Riordan, R., & Griffith, N. (1999). Distributed multi-agent architectures for distance learning. In *Proceedings of CATE 1999.*

Ríos Hernández, I. N., Mateus, J. C., Rivera Rogel, D., & Rosa Ávila Meléndez, L. (2024). Percepciones de estudiantes latinoamericanos sobre el uso de la inteligencia artificial en la educación superior. *Austral Comunicación*, *13*(1), e01302. Advance online publication. DOI: 10.26422/aucom.2024.1301.rio

Rishma, R. D., & Gill, R. (2024). Eco Criticism: Exploring the Interplay between Literature and Environment. *World Journal of English Language*, *14*(4), 563–563. DOI: 10.5430/wjel.v14n4p563

Rızvı, M. (2023). Investigating AI-powered tutoring systems that adapt to individual student needs, providing personalized guidance and assessments. *The Eurasia Proceedings of Educational and Social Sciences*, *31*, 67–73. DOI: 10.55549/epess.1381518

Rodafinos, A., Barkoukis, V., Tzafilkou, K., Ourda, D., Economides, A., & Perifanou, M. (2024). Exploring the impact of digital competence and technology acceptance on academic performance in physical education and sports science students. *Journal of Information Technology Education*, *23*, 19. DOI: 10.28945/5309

Rodríguez, P. A., Duque, N. D., & Ovalle, D. A. (2015). Multi-agent system for knowledge-based recommendation of learning objects. *Advances in Distributed Computing and Artificial Intelligence Journal*, *4*(1), 80–89.

Roe-Mohammad, S., & Tørnby, H. (2023). "I wanted to freeze the moment". Blackout poetry and student agency during the covid lockdown. In *Using innovative literacies to develop leadership and agency: Inspiring transformation and hope*. IGI Global.

Rojas, M. P., & Chiappe, A. (2024). Artificial intelligence and digital ecosystems in education: A review. *Technology. Knowledge and Learning*, *29*(4), 2153–2170. DOI: 10.1007/s10758-024-09732-7

Romero, M. (2025). From consumption to co-creation: A systematic review of six levels of AI-enhanced creative engagement in education. *Multimodal Technologies and Interaction*, *9*(10), 110. DOI: 10.3390/mti9100110

Rudik, I. V., & Onyshchuk, I. Y. (2024). Artificial inteligence tools for developing educational resources: enhancing digital learning experience for teachers and learners.

Ruzmatova, M. (2025, April 4). Qazcontent JSC conducted an experiment on the introduction of AI in media production. *El.kz*. https://el.kz/ru/ao-qazcontent-provelo-eksperiment-po-vnedreniyu-ii-v-mediaproizvodstvo_400018594/?utm

Sachar, S. (2024). Gender Representation in Film and Media. *Gender Representation in Film and Media*, *4*(3), 33–36. DOI: 10.59298/RIJRE/2024/433336

Sah, P. K. (2022). A research agenda for English-medium instruction: Conversations with scholars at the research fronts. *Journal of English-Medium Instruction*, *1*(1), 124–136. DOI: 10.1075/jemi.21022.sah

Sah, P. K., & Li, G. (2018). English medium instruction (EMI) as linguistic capital in Nepal: Promises and realities. *International Multilingual Research Journal, 12*(2), 109–123. DOI: 10.1080/19313152.2017.1401448

Sajja, R., Sermet, Y., Cikmaz, M., Cwiertny, D., & Demir, I. (2024). AI-enabled intelligent assistant for personalized and adaptive learning in higher education. *Information (Basel), 15*(10), 596. DOI: 10.3390/info15100596

Salma, Z., Hijón-Neira, R., & Pizarro, C. (2025). Designing co-creative systems: Five paradoxes in human–AI collaboration. *Information (Basel), 16*(10), 909. DOI: 10.3390/info16100909

Sanzharova, D. (2022, November 12). Karakat Abden proposed imposing a higher tax on Kazakh women who marry foreign nationals. *NewTimes.kz.* https://newtimes.kz/vybory2022/159529-karakat-abden-predlagaet-oblozhit-bolshim-nalogov-kazashek-za-brak-s-inostrancami

Sarkar, S., & Ghosh, A. (2024). *Leveraging artificial intelligence to enhance media literacy and combat misinformation*. SSRN Electronic Journal. DOI: 10.2139/ssrn.4991258

Sarrionandia, B., Peña-Fernández, S., Ángel Pérez-Dasilva, J., & Larrondo-Ureta, A. (2025). Artificial intelligence training in media: Addressing technical and ethical challenges for journalists and media professionals. *Frontiers in Communication, 10*, 1537918. Advance online publication. DOI: 10.3389/fcomm.2025.1537918

Sarvi, J., Munger, F., & Pillay, H. (2015). *Transitions to k–12 education systems: experiences from five case countries*. Asian Development Bank.

Saxena, A. K. (2024). AI in Governance and Policy Making. *International Journal of Science and Research (Raipur, India), 13*(5), 1218–1223. Advance online publication. DOI: 10.21275/SR24519015426

Saxena, P. (2023). The Politics of Power and Resistance in Gurnah's "Afterlives.". *International Journal for Multidisciplinary Research, 5*(2), 1989. Advance online publication. DOI: 10.36948/ijfmr.2023.v05i02.1989

Sayuti, S. A. (2020, August 5). *Literature as a Field of Identity Construction*. Www.atlantis-Press.comAtlantis Press. DOI: 10.2991/assehr.k.200804.061

Schiff, D. (2022). Education for AI, not AI for education: The role of education and ethics in national AI policy strategies. *International Journal of Artificial Intelligence in Education, 32*(3), 527–563. DOI: 10.1007/s40593-021-00270-2

Scholes, L., Rowe, L., Mills, K. A., Gutierrez, A., & Pink, E. (2024). Video gaming and digital competence among elementary school students. *Learning, Media and Technology*, *49*(2), 200–215. DOI: 10.1080/17439884.2022.2156537

Seerat, A. (2025). AI-powered reading support for multilingual learners in higher education: A critical review. *Journal for Social Science Archives Учредители: Ali Institute of Research & Skills Development*, *3*(1), 776–786. DOI: 10.59075/jssa.v3i1.158

Selwyn, N. (2020). *Should robots replace teachers? AI and the future of education*. Polity Press.

Semrl, N., Feigl, S., Taumberger, N., Bracic, T., Fluhr, H., Blockeel, C., & Kollmann, M. (2023). AI language models in human reproduction research: Exploring ChatGPT's potential to assist academic writing. *Human Reproduction (Oxford, England)*, *38*(12), 2281–2288. DOI: 10.1093/humrep/dead207 PMID: 37833847

Seo, K., Tang, J., Roll, I., Fels, S., & Yoon, D. (2021). The impact of artificial intelligence on learner–instructor interaction in online learning. *International Journal of Educational Technology in Higher Education*, *18*(1), 54. DOI: 10.1186/s41239-021-00292-9 PMID: 34778540

Sergeeva, M. G., Tala, M. L., & Zhirnova, A. M. (2025). Impact of digital media literacy on attitude toward generative AI acceptance in higher education. *Frontiers in Education*, *10*, 1563148. Advance online publication. DOI: 10.3389/feduc.2025.1563148

Sesmiarni, Z., Hoque, M. E., Susanto, P., Islam, M. A., & Hendrayati, H. (2024). Adoption of SPACE-learning management system in education era 4.0: An extended technology acceptance model with self-efficacy. *Frontiers in Education*, *9*, 1457188. DOI: 10.3389/feduc.2024.1457188

Setty, R. (2013). Indian education in the 21st century: More than money, manpower, and materials. *Knowledge Cultures*, *1*(03), 65–75.

Shafiee Rad, H. (2025). Reinforcing L2 reading comprehension through artificial intelligence intervention: Refining engagement to foster self-regulated learning. *Smart Learning Environments*, *12*(1), 23. DOI: 10.1186/s40561-025-00377-2

Sharma, M., Kumar, R. N., Sarkar, R., & Majumder, M. S. (2025). Transforming Higher Education for Sustainability: The Role of Digital Leadership in Innovation, Equity, and Resource Management. In *Digital Leadership for Sustainable Higher Education* (pp. 345-364). IGI Global Scientific Publishing.

Sharma, S., & Selwal, A. (2026). Potential of artificial intelligence in deepfake media: From generation to detection mechanisms, state-of-the-art, and challenges. *Computer Science Review*, *60*, 100866. Advance online publication. DOI: 10.1016/j.cosrev.2025.100866

Sheetal, & Kumar, N. (2024). Human Nature Relationships in Ecocritical Context: A Study of Works by J. G. Ballard and Barbara Kingsolver. *International Journal for Research Publication and Seminar, 15*(4), 127–130. DOI: 10.36676/jrps.v15.i4.20

Shetye, S. (2024). An evaluation of Khanmigo, a generative AI tool, as a computer-assisted language learning app. *Studies in Applied Linguistics and TESOL, 24*(1). Advance online publication. DOI: 10.52214/salt.v24i1.12869

Shi, H., Shang, Y., & Chen, S.-S. (2000). A multi-agent system for computer science education. *Proceedings of ITiCSE, 2000*, 1–4. DOI: 10.1145/343048.343051

Shi, L., Ding, A. C., & Choi, I. (2024). Investigating teachers' use of an AI-enabled system and their perceptions of AI integration in science classrooms: A case study. *Education Sciences*, *14*(11), 1187. DOI: 10.3390/educsci14111187

Shyshkin, M. (2024). Narrative as an Interdisciplinary Category: The History of Study. *Fìlologìčnì Traktati*, *16*(2), 133–139. DOI: 10.21272/Ftrk.2024.16(2)-13

Silor, A. C., & Silor, F. S. (2025). Boosting reading comprehension through AI-based learning tools. *International Journal of Learning. Teaching and Education Research*, *24*(9), 61–79. DOI: 10.26803/ijlter.24.9

Silveira, I. F., & Vicari, R. M. (2002). Adaptive multi-agent systems with learning styles. In *Proceedings of AIED 2002*.

Silverman, C. (2015). *Lies, damn lies, and viral content.* Tow Center for Digital Journalism, Columbia University. DOI: 10.7916/D8Q81RHH

Singh, A. (1984). The Indian university grants commission. *Higher Education*, *13*(5), 517–533. DOI: 10.1007/BF00128562

Slade, S., & Prinsloo, P. (2013). Learning analytics: Ethical issues and dilemmas. *The American Behavioral Scientist*, *57*(10), 1510–1529. DOI: 10.1177/0002764213479366

Smagulov, A. (2026, January 8). The blogger who conquered Kaznet turned out to be an AI model. *Kursiv.media.* https://kz.kursiv.media/2026-01-08/assm-zamerzshee-ozero-na-severe-kazakhstana-priznali-idealnym-dlya-kataniya-na-konkakh-2

Smit, U. (2023). English-medium instruction (EMI). *ELT Journal*, *77*(4), 499–503. DOI: 10.1093/elt/ccad018

Somba, S., & Widyaningrum, W. (2024). Visual dictionary for learning vocabulary for young English learners. *Dharmas Education Journal (DE_Journal), 5*(2), 1424-1433.

Spivakovsky, O. V., Omelchuk, S. A., Kobets, V. V., Valko, N. V., & Malchykova, D. S. (2023). Institutional policies on artificial intelligence in university learning, teaching and research. *Information Technologies and Learning Tools, 97*(5), 181–202. DOI: 10.33407/itlt.v97i5.5395

Sriratana, V. (2008). Literature and the Construction of Identity in Alistair MacLeod's No Great Mischief. *Deleted Journal, 1*, 136–151.

Stockwell, P. (2005). *Cognitive Poetics: An Introduction*. Routledge. DOI: 10.4324/9780203995143

Students struggle with online test proctoring systems. (2020, December 17). BYU Daily Universe. https://universe.byu.edu/2020/12/17/students-struggle-with-online-test-proctoring-systems/

Su, J., & Yang, W. (2022). Artificial intelligence in early childhood education: A scoping review. *Computers and Education: Artificial Intelligence, 3*, 100049. Advance online publication. DOI: 10.1016/j.caeai.2022.100049

Sujith, A. V. L. N., Sajja, G. S., Mahalakshmi, V., Nuhmani, S., & Prasanalakshmi, B. (2022). Systematic review of smart health monitoring using deep learning and Artificial intelligence. *Neuroscience Informatics (Online), 2*(3), 100028. DOI: 10.1016/j.neuri.2021.100028

Sun, Y., et al. (2025). Learning processes in multi-agent tutoring systems. *Journal of Educational Technology Research.*

Sun, S., Joy, M., & Griffiths, N. (2005). Learning objects and learning styles in a multi-agent system. *Proceedings of ED-MEDIA, 2005*, 3403–3410.

Suranto, S. (2024). The Analysis of Student's Ability to Identify Parts of Speech. *Global Journal of Social Science and Innovation, 1*(1), 18–26.

Swami, V., Voracek, M., Stieger, S., Tran, U. S., & Furnham, A. (2014). Analytic thinking reduces belief in conspiracy theories. *Cognition, 133*(3), 572–585. DOI: 10.1016/j.cognition.2014.08.006 PMID: 25217762

Taeihagh, A., & the Policy Systems Group. Lee Kuan Yew School of Public Policy, & National University of Singapore. (2021). Governance of artificial intelligence. In *Policy and Society, 40*(2), 137–157. DOI: 10.1080/14494035.2021.1928377

Tarus, J. K., Niu, Z., & Mustafa, G. (2018). Knowledge-based recommendation: A review of ontology-based recommender systems for e-learning. *Artificial Intelligence Review*, *50*(1), 21–48. DOI: 10.1007/s10462-017-9539-5

Timotheou, S., Miliou, O., Dimitriadis, Y., Villagrá Sobrino, S., Giannoutsou, N., Cachia, R., & Ioannou, A. (2023). Impacts of digital technologies on education and factors influencing schools' digital capacity and transformation: A literature review. *Education and Information Technologies*, *28*(6), 6695–6726. DOI: 10.1007/s10639-022-11431-8 PMID: 36465416

Tinmaz, H., Lee, Y. T., Fanea-Ivanovici, M., & Baber, H. (2022). A systematic review on digital literacy. *Smart Learning Environments*, *9*(1), 21. DOI: 10.1186/s40561-022-00204-y

Touretzky, D., Gardner-McCune, C., Breazeal, C., Martin, F., & Seehorn, D. (2019). A year in K–12 AI education. *AI Magazine*, *40*(4), 88–90. DOI: 10.1609/aimag.v40i4.5289

Tsai, Y.-S., Whitelock-Wainwright, A., & Gašević, D. (2020). The privacy paradox and its implications for learning analytics. *Proceedings of the Tenth International Conference on Learning Analytics & Knowledge*, 230–239. DOI: 10.1145/3375462.3375536

Tsao, J., Liang, C. X., Nogues, C., & Wong, A. (2025). Perceptions and integration of generative artificial intelligence in creative practices and industries: A scoping review and conceptual model. *AI & Society*, 1–20. DOI: 10.1007/s00146-025-02667-2

Turner, K. H., Jolls, T., & Hagerman, M. S.. (2025). The importance of digital media literacy. In Christakis, D. A., & Hale, L. (Eds.), *Handbook of children and screens* (pp. 1305–1325). Springer., DOI: 10.1007/978-3-031-69362-5_74

Umar, A. M. A.-T. (2018). The impact of assessment for learning on students' achievement in English for specific purposes: A case study of pre-medical students at Khartoum University: Sudan. *English Language Teaching*, *11*(2), 15–26. DOI: 10.5539/elt.v11n2p15

UNESCO. (2026). (https://www.unesco.org/en)

Urozbaeva, D. (2020). Nation-building in Kazakhstan: The role of national symbols. *Bulletin of the Kazakh-German University*, (2), 32–38.

Utdanningsdirektoratet The Norwegian Directorate for Education and Training (2020). The English Curriculum. Læreplan i engelsk (ENG01-05) | udir.no

Utdanningsdirektoratet, The Norwegian Directorate for Education and Training (2020). Cross-curricular Curriculum. Tverrfaglige temaer | udir.no

Utdanningsdirektoratet, The Norwegian Directorate for Education and Training (2023). *ICCS 2022: Rapport om medborgerskap.*

Vaitovich, O. (2019, August 2). In northern Kazakhstan, the number of applicants wishing to study at local universities has decreased. *Petropavlovsk.News.* https://xn--80aeaj2aesddcjte.news/na-severe-kazakhstana-umenshilos-kolichestvo-zhelayushhikh-uchitsya-v-mestnom-vuze

Valtonen, T., Sointu, E., Kukkonen, J., Kontkanen, S., Lambert, M. C., & Mäkitalo-Siegl, K. (2019). TPACK updated to measure pre-service teachers' twenty-first century skills. *Australasian Journal of Educational Technology, 35*(3), 1–13. DOI: 10.14742/ajet.3518

Varghese, N. V., & Martin, M. (2014). *Governance reforms in higher education: A study of institutional autonomy in Asian countries.* International Institute for Educational Planning.

Velander, J., Taiye, M. A., Otero, N., & Milrad, M. (2024). AI in K-12 Education: Eliciting and reflecting on Swedish teachers' understanding of AI and its implications for teaching & learning. *Education and Information Technologies, 29*(4), 4085–4105. DOI: 10.1007/s10639-023-11990-4

Velilaeva, L. R., & Abdullaeva, N. R. (2020). The concept of "national identity": Theoretical and literary aspects of research. *Universum: Philology and Art Studies, 6*(73), 26–28.

Vieriu, A. M., & Petrea, G. (2025). The Impact of Artificial Intelligence (AI) on students' academic development. *Education Sciences, 15*(3), 343. DOI: 10.3390/educsci15030343

Viswanathan, N., Meacham, S., & Adedoyin, F. F. (2022). Enhancement of online education using a multi-agent approach. *Computers and Education: Artificial Intelligence, 3*, 100057. DOI: 10.1016/j.caeai.2022.100057

Vlachopoulos, D. (2025). Authentic assessment: Bridging higher education and real-world skills through diverse methodologies. In *INTED2025 Proceedings* (pp. 2225-2234). IATED.

VOSviewer. (2026). https://www.vosviewer.com/

Wächter, B., & Maiworm, F. (2014). English-taught programmes in European higher education. *The State of Play In, 15.*

Waham, J. J. (2023). The Exploration of Trauma and Memory in Kazuo Ishiguro's Never Let Me Go and The Remains of the Day. *Journal of Critical Studies in Language and Literature*, *4*(3), 16–21. DOI: 10.46809/jcsll.v4i3.204

Walter, Y. (2024). Embracing the future of Artificial Intelligence in the classroom: The relevance of AI literacy, prompt engineering, and critical thinking in modern education. *International Journal of Educational Technology in Higher Education*, *21*(1), 15. DOI: 10.1186/s41239-024-00448-3

Walter, Y. (2024). Managing the race to the moon: Global policy and governance in Artificial Intelligence regulation—A contemporary overview and an analysis of socioeconomic consequences. *Discover Artificial Intelligence*, *4*(1), 14. Advance online publication. DOI: 10.1007/s44163-024-00109-4

Wang, X., ... (2024). Recursive introspection: Teaching language model agents how to self-improve. In *Advances in Neural Information Processing Systems (NeurIPS 2024)*.

Wang, N., Kim, H., Peng, J., & Wang, J. (2025). Exploring creativity in human–AI co-creation: A comparative study across design experience. *Frontiers of Computer Science*, *7*, 1672735. DOI: 10.3389/fcomp.2025.1672735

Wei, X., Wang, L., Lee, L. K., & Liu, R. (2025). The effects of generative AI on collaborative problem-solving and team creativity performance in digital story creation: An experimental study. *International Journal of Educational Technology in Higher Education*, *22*(1), 23. DOI: 10.1186/s41239-025-00526-0

Welch, A. (2005). From peregrinatio academica to global academic: The internationalisation of the profession. In *The professoriate: Profile of a Profession* (pp. 71–96). Springer Netherlands. DOI: 10.1007/1-4020-3383-4_5

Wilkinson, R. (2013). English-medium instruction at a Dutch university: Challenges and pitfalls. *English-medium Instruction at Universities: Global Challenges*, *324*(10.21832), 9781847698162-005.

Wing, J. M. (2017). Computational thinking's influence on research and education for all. *Italian Journal of Educational Technology*, *25*(2), 7–14.

Yakkala, K. K.Krishna Kashyap Yakkala. (2024). AI-powered assessment tools for E-learning: Enhancing feedback and grading systems. *World Journal of Advanced Engineering Technology and Sciences*, *13*(1), 792–802. DOI: 10.30574/wjaets.2024.13.1.0497

Yang, D., Wu, X., Liu, J., & Zhou, J. (2023). CiteSpace-based global science, technology, engineering, and mathematics education knowledge mapping analysis. *Frontiers in Psychology*, *13*, 1094959. DOI: 10.3389/fpsyg.2022.1094959 PMID: 36704670

Yim, I. H. Y., & Su, J. (2025). AI (AI) learning tools in K-12 education: A scoping review. *Journal of Computers in Education*, *12*(1), 93–131.

Yim, I. H. Y., & Su, J. (2025). Artificial intelligence literacy education in primary schools: A review. *International Journal of Technology and Design Education*, *35*(5), 1–30. DOI: 10.1007/s10798-025-09979-w

Yu, H., & Zhao, L. (2025). LLM-based multi-agent chatbots for vocational education. *International Journal of Educational Technology in Higher Education*, *22*(1).

Zafar, M. B., Ali, H., & Yasin, T. (2025). Reimagining human creativity and learning in the age of generative AI: A multi-method meta-thematic synthesis. *Next Research*, *100802*(4), 100802. Advance online publication. DOI: 10.1016/j.nexres.2025.100802

Zawacki-Richter, O., Marín, V. I., Bond, M., & Gouverneur, F. (2019). Systematic review of research on artificial intelligence applications in higher education—Where are the educators? *International Journal of Educational Technology in Higher Education*, *16*(1), 39. DOI: 10.1186/s41239-019-0171-0

Zhang, J., ... (2024). Multi-agent classroom frameworks with LLM-powered pedagogical roles. In *AIED 2024 Workshop Proceedings*.

Zhang, K., & Aslan, A. B. (2021). AI technologies for education: Recent research & future directions. *Computers and Education: Artificial Intelligence*, *2*, 100025. DOI: 10.1016/j.caeai.2021.100025

Zhang, Y., Kou, X., Song, Z., Fan, Y., Usman, M., & Jagota, V. (2021). Research on logistics management layout optimization and real-time application based on nonlinear programming. *Nonlinear Engineering*, *10*(1), 526–534. https://doi.org/doi:10.1515/nleng-2021-0043. DOI: 10.1515/nleng-2021-0043

Zhou, M., & Peng, S. (2025). The usage of AI in teaching and students' creativity: The mediating role of learning engagement and the moderating role of AI literacy. *Behavioral Sciences (Basel, Switzerland)*, *15*(5), 587. DOI: 10.3390/bs15050587

Zhylkybayeva, D. (2022, February 14). Social media users demanded the revocation of citizenship from Kazakh women who married foreign nationals. *Caravan.kz*. https://www.caravan.kz/news/v-socsetyakh-potrebovali-lishit-grazhdanstva-kazashek-vyshedshikh-zamuzh-za-inostrancev-816312/

Zimmerman, J., & Forlizzi, J. (2017). Speed dating: Providing a menu of possible futures. *She Ji: The Journal of Design, Economics, and Innovation*, *3*(1), 30–50. DOI: 10.1016/j.sheji.2017.08.003

About the Contributors

Jason D. DeHart is a passionate educator, actively engaged in finding what works for connecting readers with literacy practices. DeHart earned his PhD from The University of Tennessee, Knoxville in 2019. He served as a middle grades English teacher for eight years, has worked at the university level at Lee University in Cleveland, Tennessee, as well as at The University of Tennessee, Knoxville and Appalachian State University, and currently works with high school students in Wilkesboro, North Carolina. DeHart's publications include Building Critical Literacy and Empathy with Graphic Novels (NCTE), as well as a number of edited volumes for Routledge and IGI Global. He has written articles and posts for The ALAN Review, English Journal, The Journal of Adolescent & Adult Literacy, Edutopia, Steve Bickmore's YA Wednesday, and Middleweb.

***

Ayyoob A is a Senior Research Scholar in Commerce at the Department of Commerce and Management Studies (DCMS), School of Business Studies, University of Calicut, India. His research interests encompass Corporate Governance, Corporate Sustainability, Diversity, Equity, Inclusion and Belonging (DEIB), and the Sustainable Development Goals (SDGs). He has published numerous research documents in Scopus- and Web of Science–indexed journals and serves as a reviewer for reputed Scopus-indexed journals and edited books. Mr. Ayyoob has presented his research at international conferences abroad and at premier Indian institutions, including IIMs, IITs, IPE, ISOL, and GRFCG. He has facilitated over 40 academic and research workshops, mentors emerging researchers, has served as a judge for management fests, and has chaired academic conferences. His scholarly contributions have been recognized with multiple Best Paper Awards. In addition to academia, he actively engages in consultancy, invited lectures, and sustainability-driven initiatives.

Renalyn Joy Ruiz Alonsabe, MAEd, LPT, is a secondary education scholar-practitioner specializing in English education, adolescent studies, and school-based research innovation. She currently serves as Teacher II and School Research Coordinator at Artemio L. Martin Integrated School, where she leads institutional research initiatives, mentors teacher-researchers, and integrates evidence-based pedagogies in English and Social Sciences instruction. She earned her Bachelor of Secondary Education major in English from Sultan Kudarat State University–Kalamansig Campus in 2013 and passed the Licensure Examination for Teachers in the same year. As an undergraduate, she was a consistent Dean's Lister and a two-time recipient of the Leadership Award (2012–2013) for distinguished service in student governance. She served as Senator of the University Student Government and represented her institution at the 8th National Congress of the Student Council Alliance of the Philippines (SCAP) in Mactan, Cebu City. She completed her Master of Arts in Education major in English at Cotabato State University, where her thesis was recognized with a Certificate of Merit as a nominee for Best Thesis—reflecting her early engagement in rigorous academic inquiry. In 2024, she was awarded the Basic Education Research Fund (BERF 2024) for her phenomenological study, "A Phenomenological Study of High School Students Engaged in Teenage Pregnancy: Basis for School's Intervention Program." The study advances contextualized understandings of adolescent vulnerability and informs the design of responsive, school-based intervention frameworks. For this work, she received the SIGASIG Award (Silver) under the BERF Implementers Excellence Award during the Regional Research Congress in General Santos City. Her research was further recognized at the DepEd SOCCSKSARGEN Regional Research Colloquium (Outstanding Oral Presenter) and the Division Research Congress in Koronadal City (Third Place, Best Oral Presenter – Theme 2: Child Protection). Her scholarly interests include qualitative research methodologies, adolescent lived experiences, child protection policy in basic education, intervention program development, and the institutionalization of research cultures in public schools. Through her work, she contributes to strengthening practitioner-led inquiry and advancing research-informed educational leadership in the Philippine basic education sector.

Susanta Das is a seasoned educator with a proven record of teaching and mentoring diverse students, working at multiple institutions, and providing service to the various initiatives of organizations. He received his Ph.D. and M.A. degrees from Western Michigan University (WMU), USA, and M.Sc. degree from Banaras Hindu University (BHU), India all in Physics. He continued his research as a Marie-Curie post-doctoral fellow at Stockholm University Stockholm, Sweden on beam diagnostics for the DESIREE (Double ElectroStatic Ion Ring ExpEriment) in the project DITANET (Diagnostic Techniques for particle Accelerators – a Marie-

Curie initial training NETwork), at the Indian Institute of Science Education and Research-Kolkata, India on high-pressure physics as a Project Scientist-B, and at the University of Electro-Communications, Tokyo, Japan on ion-surface interactions as a Post-doctoral fellow. Throughout his career, Dr. Das worked and collaborated with many researchers, Ph.D., master, and visiting students from different countries. He further visited many countries to discuss research and an international conference participant (UK, Italy, Germany, Greece, Belgium, Bulgaria, Romania, Brazil etc.). He co-authored several research articles in WoS/Scopus indexed international journals, conference proceedings, and scholarly book chapters published by renowned international publishing houses. Beyond his research endeavors, Dr. Das has a storied history of service to academic and administrative committees, exhibiting his commitment to the growth and development of educational institutions. His experience includes tenure at Central University South Bihar, Sri Sri University, and P.K. University before assuming his current role at Ajeenkya DY Patil University. He received the Marie-Curie post-doctoral fellowship in Sweden, Science Academies' Summer Research Fellowship in India, Gwen Frostic Doctoral Fellowship, Department Graduate Research and Creative Scholar Award by WMU, and Leo R. Parpart Doctoral Fellowship by Dept. of Physics, WMU, among many others, throughout his academic journey. At present, Dr. Das continues to delve into cutting-edge fields, with a keen interest in nanotechnology, quantum computing, and data science. His multifaceted contributions, spanning teaching, research, and administrative leadership, showcase a dedicated professional who is instrumental in advancing the vision and mission of the institutions he serves.

Pooja Dehankar is working in Department of Artificial Intelligence and Data Science, School of Engineering, Ajeenkya DY Patil School of Engineering, Pune. She has completed BE in Computer Engineering from Priyadarshini College of Engineering, Nagpur and ME in Information Technology from Sinhgad College of Engineering, Pune. She has done Post Graduate Diploma in Advance Computing. She is currently pursuing Ph.D. from Symbiosis International Deemed University, Pune. She has 17 years of experience in academics. Her area of interest are Artificial Intelligence, Cyber Security and Data Mining. She has published papers in Scopus Journals. She actively participates in workshops, faculty development programs, short term training programs, conferences and webinars.

Pooja Dehankar is working in the department of Artificial Intelligence and Data Science,Ajeenkya DY Patil School of Engineering, Savitribai Phule Pune University, Pune. She has completed BE in Computer Engineering from Priyadarshini College of Engineering, Nagpur and ME in Information Technology from Sinhgad College of Engineering, Pune. She has done Post Graduate Diploma in Advance Computing,Pune. She has 16 years of experience in academics. Her area of interest are Artificial Intelligence, Cyber Security and Data Mining. She has published papers in Scopus Journals. She has also published book chapters in IGI-Global,Notion Press, BlueRoseONE. She actively participates in workshops, faculty development programs, short term training programs, conferences and webinars.

Vibha Gaur holds a Ph.D. from the University of Delhi. With over 30 years of teaching experience in computer science, she has taught a wide range of undergraduate and postgraduate courses. Her research specializes in Requirement Engineering, Software Development Models, Multi-agent Systems, and computational intelligence using Fuzzy Logic and Cognitive Maps. She has published more than 40 papers in international conferences and journals.

Deepak Gupta is a distinguished academician with over 20 years of teaching experience and expertise in Computer Science and Engineering. He holds a Ph.D. in Computer Engineering and has an extensive research portfolio, including many international journal papers, multiple conference proceedings, and several books. His research interests span machine learning, artificial intelligence, and data mining. Currently, Dr. Gupta serves as an Associate Professor and Head of Department of CSE (Emerging Branches) at ITM Gwalior, MP, India. He has also contributed significantly to the field through patents and copyrights and actively engages as a reviewer, conference chair and editor.

Hamna K is working as an ABPM (Assistant Branch Postmaster) with India Post. She holds a Master's degree in English Literature from the University of Calicut, India. A highly dedicated and academically inclined individual, she has a strong interest in literary studies and interdisciplinary research. Her research contributions include publications in peer-reviewed journals, and she has actively participated in national and international conferences, where she has presented several research papers. Her academic pursuits reflect a commitment to scholarly excellence, critical inquiry, and knowledge dissemination. Ms. Hamna K is an aspiring researcher and academic, with a keen interest in advancing research in literature and related fields.

Ramesh Kumar is currently working as an Assistant Professor of Law & Research Coordinator of School, R&D, School of Law, LFBA, Lovely Professional University, Phagwara, Kapurthala, Punjab-144411, India. He acts also as a Human Rights Activist. His focus on research in respect of International Human Rights Law, Education, Juristic, Biology, Forensic and Medical Sciences, Education and Law. He possesses B.A., LL.B. (1st University Topper), LL.M. (International Human Rights Law), UGC-NET (Law, UGC- Accredited- MP-SET (Law) MPPSC,

DCA, PGDIM, Ph.D. (Law)-International Human Rights Law, Jiwaji University (A State Government University), Gwalior, (Mp), India. He is the member of various National/International Research Institutions.

Kritikka Kunte is an undergraduate student pursuing a Bachelor of Technology degree in Artificial Intelligence and Data Science at the School of Engineering, Ajeenkya D Y Patil University, Pune, Maharashtra, India. With a strong academic orientation toward data-driven problem solving, she has developed a focused interest in the domains of data analytics and data science, supported by both theoretical foundations and applied project experience. Throughout her academic journey, Kritikka has cultivated proficiency in core programming and analytical competencies, including Python, SQL, and Java, along with essential data science methodologies such as data preprocessing, exploratory data analysis (EDA), and machine learning techniques. She is proficient in industry-relevant tools and platforms, including Advanced Microsoft Excel, Matplotlib, Tableau, and Power BI, to derive insights from complex datasets and present them in a structured and interpretable manner. Her practical exposure includes the successful completion of projects such as Ocean Salinity Analysis, which involved analyzing environmental datasets to identify patterns and trends, and Speech Recognition and Translation, where she explored applied machine learning concepts in natural language processing. These projects reflect her ability to translate conceptual knowledge into functional, real-world solutions. Kritikka has further strengthened her technical profile through professional certifications, including the AWS re/Start Graduate credential from Amazon Web Services, a certification in Software Development, and Python training certified by Google. Her engagement in competitive and collaborative academic environments is demonstrated by her participation in the Smart India Hackathon (SIH) and by securing Second Runner-Up in an inter-collegiate Tableau competition, highlighting her analytical aptitude and visualization skills. With a growing interest in advanced transportation systems and data-centric engineering solutions, Kritikka brings a multidisciplinary perspective to the GHC Hyperloop Project Competition hosted at IIT Madras. She aspires to contribute meaningfully to innovative, technology-driven initiatives that integrate artificial intelligence, data science, and sustainable engineering to address complex global challenges.

Amera C. Malaco is a faculty member at the College of Teacher Education, Sultan Kudarat State University, Philippines. Her research focuses on education, environmental conservation, and stewardship. She advocates for transformative and localized learning approaches that foster biodiversity awareness and sustainable practices, contributing to the advancement of quality education in the ASEAN region.

Rohan Rajoriya awarded Bachelor's degree in Information Technology and a Master's degree in Computer Science and Engineering from RGPV (Rajiv Gandhi Proudyogiki Vishawavidyalaya) Bhopal. He is currently employed as Lecturer (Selection Grade) in Department of Information Technology at Kalaniketan Polytechnic College, Jabalpur, Madhya Pradesh (Government Autonomous Institute). He is having 3 years of software industrial experience and 16 years of teaching experience and has multiple publications to his credit. Artificial Intelligence, Machine Learning, IIoT, Cyber Security and other related issues are among his research interests. He published 20+ research papers in leading international journals. He is currently member of the "Board of Studies" for Computer Science Engineering/Information Technology/Computer Hardware and Maintenance in Rajiv Gandhi Proudyogiki Vishwavidyalaya Bhopal (DiplomaWing).

Shuchita Mudgil awarded Bachelors of Technology in Information Technology from Anna University Guindy Chennai and Master's degree in Computer Science and Engineering from RGPV(Rajiv Gandhi Proudyogiki Vishawavidyalaya) Bhopal. She is currently employed as Lecturer (Selection Grade) in Department of Information Technology at Kalaniketan Polytechnic College, Jabalpur, Madhya Pradesh (Government Autonomous Institute). She is having 19 years of teaching experience and has multiple publications to her credit. Artificial Intelligence, Machine Learning, Cloud Computing, IoT and other related issues are among her research interests. She is reviewer board member in IJISET, IJIRT, IJRAR and editor in IIP proceedings conference. She published 20+ research papers in leading international journals. She is currently member of the "Board of Studies" for Computer Science Engineering/ Information Technology/Computer Hardware and Maintenance in Rajiv Gandhi Proudyogiki Vishwavidyalaya Bhopal (DiplomaWing).

Guljahon Ozodova is a faculty member in the Department of Philology at Urgench State Pedagogical Institute, Urgench, Uzbekistan. She is engaged in teaching and academic activities in linguistics, language studies, and literary education. Her academic interests include language pedagogy, textual analysis, and the development of students' communication and critical reading skills. She is committed to learner-centered instruction and the effective integration of linguistic theory with classroom practice. Guljahon Ozodova actively contributes to academic and methodological initiatives aimed at strengthening philological education and promoting quality teaching and research in higher education.

Krutika Patre, is an aspiring programmer and technology enthusiast, currently pursuing Engineering in Artificial Intelligence and Data Science. With a passion for learning, she is building experience in a variety of programming languages and technologies, including C, C++, Python, Data Structures (DS), HTML, CSS, and JavaScript, DBMS (My SQL). After learning this programming language, she has created interest in Full Stack Development. She had also attended an Arduino-Based Automation course at Dolphin Labs to improve my software knowledge. There, she learned how to work with sensors, microcontrollers, and circuit design. She has written review paper on Sustainable engineering on build environment. She is doing researching and learning many topics related to AI, Policy and governance and related to my interest. She has taken part in hackathons, workshops, and tech events to explore many fields. She is also working with a group on Hyperloop. Being part of this project has really helped her grow, especially in areas like teamwork, innovation, and systems thinking.

Divyang Raval is a distinguished Lecturer in Electrical Engineering Department currently working in the GTU - Institute of Technology & Research (Mevad, Mehsana, Gujarat). he has experience in higher education. Serving as the Lecturer in computer engineering department & Electrical Engineering Department, in Silver Oak University Ahmedabad, Shree Swaminarayan Polytechnic Gandhinagar. Mr. Divyang academic credentials are robust, including Diploma, B.E. and M.E. (Electrical Power Systems). He has contributed in the Various Research paper & Patents in Field of IoT, Solar Systems & AI / ML and Develop many Projects in IoT (Internet of Things) using various AI / ML Techniques.

Shiva Saini holds an M.C.A. and an M.Tech. in Computer Science from Kurukshetra University, Haryana. She has been working as an Assistant Professor at Acharya Narendra Dev College for over nine years. Her research interests include multi-agent systems, educational technology, and AI-driven learning frameworks

Fahad A. Salendab is a scholar and leader in the field of higher education, holding a Ph.D. in Educational Administration and a Master of Arts in English Language Teaching. As a Licensed Professional Teacher and Associate Professor, he has dedicated his career to advancing the quality of education through research, teaching, and leadership. A multi-awarded faculty member, Dr. Salendab is recognized for his outstanding contributions to education, research, and institutional development. He is a registered Writer, Author, and Editor of the National Book Development Board (NBDB) and serves as an editor for IGI Global Scientific Publishing, contributing to the dissemination of high-quality academic scholarship. He has published various books, book chapters, and research articles, reflecting his sustained engagement in scholarly writing and knowledge production. Several of his scholarly articles are also registered with the Intellectual Property Office of the Philippines (IPOPHL), highlighting his commitment to intellectual and academic innovation. His commitment to research is further demonstrated through his role as a Regular Member of the DOST–National Research Council of the Philippines, where he collaborates on initiatives addressing critical issues in education and development. He also serves as an editorial board member for various national and international research journals, supporting the advancement of scholarly publishing and peer-reviewed academic discourse. As an active participant in accreditation processes, Dr. Salendab ensures the continuous improvement of academic programs, demonstrating his strong commitment to quality assurance and institutional growth.

Sunil Sankathala is pursuing B. Tech. in Computer Science and Engineering at Ajeenkya D Y Patil University, with a diverse range of interests that bridge technology, sustainability, and innovation. His academic focus lies in computer science fundamentals like programming, data structures, algorithms, and software development. He actively supplements this with hands-on experience in web development and robotics. Beyond the core curriculum, He has a strong research inclination in emerging and impactful fields. His current research interests include Artificial Intelligence in Healthcare, bioplastics, nano bioplastics, e-waste management, and solid waste management—areas where he believes technology can make a meaningful difference in solving real-world problems. He has been publishing research articles and book chapters in reputed national and international journals and books. He is also part of an ambitious Hyperloop project, which involves interdisciplinary collaboration and cutting-edge engineering aimed at revolutionizing transportation. Working on this project has enhanced his skills in teamwork, innovation, and systems thinking. In the tech domain, he has developed proficiency in web development using technologies such as HTML, CSS, JavaScript, and React. His interests in robotics further reflect building smart, responsive systems that interact with the physical world. Throughout his course, he has helped strengthen problem-solving and collaborative skills. He is proficient in languages such as Python, C, C++, MySQL, Ubuntu, Machine Learning and familiar with frameworks and tools like React, Git. He actively participates in hackathons, coding competitions, and tech events to challenge himself and learn from peers. He is also a quick learner and highly adaptable, with an eagerness to stay updated with the latest trends in the tech world. He aspires to become a skilled software engineer and contribute to building innovative solutions that have a positive impact on society. The long-term goal is to work in a dynamic environment where knowledge, grow professionally, and make meaningful contributions to the field of technology. Driven by a spirit of exploration and sustainability, he aims to contribute to technological solutions that address both human and environmental needs. The long-term goal is to become a versatile engineer and researcher, working at the intersection of computer science, environmental innovation, and human well-being.

Janisha Sharma is an undergraduate student pursuing B.Sc. (Hons.) Computer Science with Research at the University of Delhi. Her academic interests lie in Artificial Intelligence, Machine Learning, and the application of intelligent systems in education. Her research work particularly focuses on Multi-Agent Systems in Education, exploring the use of AI-driven collaborative frameworks to enhance learning experiences and educational technologies. She is passionate about interdisciplinary research that combines computer science with real-world social and educational impact.

Nurullaeva Shakhlo Uktamovna is a faculty member in the Department of Primary Education at Karshi State University, Karshi, Uzbekistan. She is engaged in teaching and academic activities focused on primary education pedagogy, curriculum development, and learner-centered instructional practices. Her academic interests include innovative teaching methods, classroom management, learner assessment, and inclusive education in primary schools. She is committed to strengthening foundational literacy and numeracy skills through effective pedagogical approaches. Nurullaeva Shakhlo Uktamovna actively contributes to academic and institutional initiatives aimed at enhancing the quality of primary teacher education.

Aryan Vasa is a passionate and self-driven Bachelor of Technology (B.Tech.) student specializing in Computer Science Engineering at Ajeenkya DY Patil University, Pune. Currently in his third year, Aryan is committed to building a solid foundation in core technical domains, including web development, data science, and artificial intelligence. With an inquisitive mindset and a strong eagerness to explore diverse fields, he strives to balance his academic journey with hands-on learning and project development. Originally from Jamnagar, Gujarat, and having completed his schooling in Rajkot under the ICSE board, Aryan has always been drawn toward technology, logic, and creativity. He is actively engaged in learning full-stack development while also keeping a close eye on the evolving job market, particularly the shift toward AI and generative technologies. His academic curiosity extends to research in advanced topics such as Generative AI and Digital Synthetic Outputs, for which he is currently writing a comprehensive review article. Aryan has also been a dedicated athlete, having played basketball for over ten years. This experience has helped him develop teamwork, discipline, and a growth mindset. In addition, he enjoys writing analytical and review-based content, merging his technical knowledge with strong communication skills. Committed to personal growth, Aryan maintains a balanced lifestyle that includes regular workouts, general fitness, and a focus on healthy eating. While continuously learning, he aims to contribute meaningfully to India's tech innovation landscape and become a versatile engineer capable of solving real-world problems through thoughtful design and smart solutions. Whether developing web applications, studying emerging technologies, or sharing knowledge through articles and mentorship, Aryan Vasa stands out as a motivated learner and a future-ready technologist.

Raj Kumar Verma, is acting as a Faculty in Law, Government Shrimant Madhavrao Scindia (SMS) PG College, Shivpuri, Jiwaji University, Gwalior, Madhya Pradesh, India His recent focus on Education, Criminal Law and International Human Rights Law Research.

Rohit Kumar Verma, is working as a Human Rights Activist, Gwalior, Madhya Pradesh His recent focus on Education, International Human Rights Law, Education, Juristic, Biology, Forensic Science and Law as to the implementation of laws by way of Enforcement system.

Index

Symbols

A

B

C

D

E

F

G

H

I

www.ingramcontent.com/pod-product-compliance
Lightning Source LLC
LaVergne TN
LVHW081531300926
849161LV00006B/1383
* 9 7 9 8 2 6 0 0 2 1 6 3 7 *